Praise for
The Liberation of Method

"Through constructive conversations with a diversity of voices—ignored, neglected, and minoritized within biblical studies—Janzen helps his readers hoist antennae to heed the strong ethical component inherent in their readings. He calls for an ethical turn in biblical studies and a cultural turn to justice and emancipation, arguing that 'liberation and not method' should be the goal. This contribution is bold and refreshing, and is deserving of recognition and appreciation. It is a superb resource for those interested in biblical methodology, the academy, and issues of justice."

—Monica Jyotsna Melanchthon, academic dean and associate professor of Hebrew Bible/Old Testament, Pilgrim Theological College, University of Divinity, Australia

"This accessible, erudite, engaging, and often movingly honest book deserves a guaranteed place on university reading lists. It is a model of empathetic listening, understanding, and response. Those who have experienced marginalization, including self-marginalization in order to feel accepted, are given the center ground. Had this book been available when I was starting out as a biblical scholar, it would have made a profound difference to my well-being within academia. I couldn't recommend it more highly."

—Deryn Guest, honorary senior lecturer, University of Birmingham, and author of YHWH *and Israel in the Book of Judges: An Objects-Relations Analysis* (Cambridge University Press, 2018)

"Traditionally, the majority of biblical scholars have used primarily historical-critical methods that focus on the past. Janzen offers an extensive and detailed analysis of the African American, Asian American, Latino/Latina, and queer biblical scholars who are using a range of other approaches to address the present. Janzen argues convincingly that explorations of biblical texts should incorporate these new methods and insights. His conclusion is one that we should all reach: if the discipline does not consider this newer work, it is not just failing to expand its historical-critical methodologies; it is being unethical."

—Cheryl B. Anderson, professor of Old Testament,
Garrett-Evangelical Theological Seminary, Evanston, IL,
and author of *Ancient Laws and Contemporary Controversies: The Need for Inclusive Biblical Interpretation*
(Oxford University Press, 2009)

The Liberation of Method

The Liberation of Method

The Ethics of Emancipatory Biblical Interpretation

David Janzen

FORTRESS PRESS
MINNEAPOLIS

THE LIBERATION OF METHOD
The Ethics of Emancipatory Biblical Interpretation

Unless otherwise noted, the author considers all Scripture translations to be his own.

Cover image: Ekely/iStock
Cover design: Brice Hemmer

Print ISBN: 978-1-5064-7458-8
eBook ISBN: 978-1-5064-7459-5

For Patricia

and for my parents,

who helped lay the foundations for this work

Contents

1

Introduction

The Ethics of Emancipatory Biblical Interpretation

Liberation and Method: The Basic Question

Scholars and students of biblical studies typically do not reflect very much on the question as to how we should go about deciding what a given biblical text might mean. When it comes to making such decisions, we do what we were taught and what we see our teachers and colleagues doing all the time as they read biblical texts and investigate their contexts, and so we come to do our interpretive work by habit. There is nothing particularly odd about this, and scientific fields, for example, operate the same way, as scientists also tend not to put much thought into why they work in the ways they do or how to justify the assumptions that underlie their research.[1] No academic field has good reason to change its basic practices, after all, unless its members come to believe that they have been mistaken about some of their important assumptions. This can happen from time to time, however, which is why, for example, chemistry students are no longer taught Aristotle's four elements of matter but instead the periodic table. That particular change was the result of chemists of the eighteenth and nineteenth centuries arriving at a consensus that their field had wrongly conceived of the building blocks of the material world and a developing belief that chemistry would have to investigate things differently as it replaced earlier assumptions about the way the world is with newer ones. One could make the argument that a somewhat similar large-scale shift in regard to the basic assumptions that underlie the work that biblical scholars do has taken root in our field over the last half century. The change in our discipline has not been as

1. Thomas S. Kuhn, *The Structure of Scientific Revolutions*, 2nd ed. (Chicago: University of Chicago Press, 1970), 43–46.

sweeping as that of the chemical revolution—which, admittedly, took place over a far longer period of time[2]—but newer ways of reading texts have appeared in biblical studies, something due in large part to the entrance of marginalized scholars into the academic field, people who sometimes see the world in rather different ways than their more socioeconomically privileged peers.

Depending on one's perspective, however, the mainstream of biblical studies has changed very little over the last two centuries. Although marginalized readers, especially women, scholars from the Two-Thirds World, people of color, and members of the LGBTQ community, have introduced to the discipline new approaches to biblical interpretation, these have not displaced more traditional ways academics read biblical texts, but largely remain on the field's margins, as their practitioners generally do. I argue in this book, however, that these marginalized readings brought into the field by marginalized readers provide biblical studies with an ethically necessary way of reorienting what more privileged scholars like me have been doing. Since the beginnings of the modern academic study of the Bible in the late eighteenth and early nineteenth centuries, mainstream biblical studies has been dominated by the historical critical method, something that some scholars who reflect on how academics should read the Bible still claim is a necessary part of valid interpretation. My less privileged colleagues have convinced me, however, that what should take priority in the field's work is not historical investigation into the biblical texts but the ethical imperative to provide liberative readings for the many millions of people who find themselves fighting against oppression and who see the Bible as a key resource in their emancipatory struggles. Following their guidance, I will argue that while the ethical imperative of liberation and the historical critical method need not be in conflict, liberation and not method should take priority when academics interpret texts. The mainstream of the field should reorient itself to the leadership of its marginalized members reading for liberation and so rethink its goals for interpretation. In the following chapters, I provide one way to justify why the field should follow the guidance of the members it has minoritized and privilege liberation over method.

2. For a brief survey of the study of the chemical revolution, see Matthew Daniel Eddy, Seymour H. Mauskopf, and William R. Newman, "An Introduction to *Chemical Knowledge in the Early Modern World*," *Osiris* 29 (2014): 1–15.

Insofar as we can speak of mainstream academic biblical interpretation, we refer in large part to the many scholars who pursue a whole range of ways of analyzing biblical texts and their contexts that are often given the collective moniker of the historical critical method. The wide array of interpretive interests that could be categorized as such are all focused on answering historical questions about the biblical texts and their ancient environments. The Society of Biblical Literature, the largest organization of biblical scholars in the world, notes in the report of its 2019 survey of its members that more of them selected historical criticism as describing the way in which they approach their research than any other category they could choose from.[3] The fact that so many biblical scholars focus on historical questions as they try to understand biblical texts seems to make intuitive sense, given that the texts are thousands of years old and that their authors lived in cultures that no longer exist. There are many different kinds of historical questions about the texts and their contexts that the academic field pursues. For example, under the assumption that we will have a better sense of what the biblical authors were trying to say if we can know more about the ancient cultures in which they lived and that formed their views of things, some studies attempt to determine the dates of particular biblical writings and investigate the religious, social, political, and/or economic contexts in which they were produced. Other historical studies look for ways in which ancient editors might have added to and altered earlier versions of the texts so that we are able to distinguish the different parts of a particular work written by different people and do not confuse the message of an ancient author with ones inserted later by such editors or redactors. Others examine the different manuscripts that provide us with the oldest testimonies to the wordings of texts, trying to determine which ones most closely reflect what a biblical author actually wrote. Some focus on linguistic issues, examining the meanings of words, phrases, and sentences in biblical Hebrew and New Testament Greek, languages that have not been spoken in millennia. Depending on the particular interests of a scholar, a single academic work might choose to do one or two or all of these things, or even pursue different paths of historical investigation. Scholars who justify their use of historical approaches to understanding biblical texts sometimes

3. "2019 SBL Membership Data," Society of Biblical Literature, accessed March 24, 2021, p. 7, https://tinyurl.com/25cyfa6p. Sixty-seven percent of Society of Biblical Literature members completed the survey (p. 2).

say it provides us with the original sense of a writing, the author's intended sense, the literal sense, or the plain sense.[4]

At the root of the historical critical method is the notion that the biblical texts were written so long ago, in languages and cultures that are in many ways foreign to us, that we will not understand what their authors intended to say, nor how the texts would have been understood by their ancient readers, without historical investigation. The many kinds of such investigations make some scholars uncomfortable with using the word *method* to describe their totality. If by *method* we mean "a systematic, orderly series of steps a scholar follows in order to analyze a text from a particular vantage point," something that allows us "to identify and articulate the interpretation or meaning of a text,"[5] then there really is not such a thing as a historical critical method, because there is no single set of steps that biblical scholars follow in the many kinds of historical investigations they pursue. James Barr says that the different sorts of historical work biblical scholars do amount to "a group of theories that formalize valuable intuitions" rather than a method;[6] A. K. M. Adam refers to this collection of different kinds of historical investigations as "an array of interpretive moves" and prefers to call it "technical biblical interpretation."[7] The term *historical critical method* is still used quite frequently in the field, however, and so I will use it here to encompass academic investigations that attempt to answer the sort of historical questions that biblical scholars tend to ask. Sometimes those questions have little or no direct bearing on determining the meaning of a specific biblical text but are devised instead to better understand issues of historical and cultural context that help us make sense of the worlds that would have formed and influenced biblical authors.

Contemporary biblical scholarship certainly does much more than ask historical questions, but some scholars invested in conducting historical research, and even some whose focus is elsewhere, argue that the historical critical method is an indispensable part of what academic biblical studies does, since it will not

4. For a discussion and examples of such claims, see David R. Law, *The Historical-Critical Method: A Guide for the Perplexed* (London: T&T Clark, 2012), 14–20.
5. Mark K. George, "Postmodern Literary Criticism: The Impossibility of Method," in *Method Matters: Essays on the Interpretation of the Hebrew Bible in Honor of David L. Petersen*, ed. Joel M. LeMon and Kent Harold Richards, RBS 56 (Atlanta: Society of Biblical Literature, 2009), 459.
6. James Barr, *History and Ideology in the Old Testament: Biblical Studies at the End of a Millennium* (Oxford: Oxford University Press, 2000), 47.
7. A. K. M. Adam, *Faithful Interpretation: Reading the Bible in a Postmodern World* (Minneapolis: Fortress, 2006), 1.

otherwise be possible to understand what the ancient authors were trying to say. Whatever else it is biblical scholars want to do, says Barr, "genuine biblical criticism" must involve historical work.[8] The Bible "is intelligible only in terms of its historical context," claims Van Austin Harvey,[9] and John Barton writes that historical criticism—or biblical criticism, as he prefers to call it—is nonnegotiable in any academic study of the Bible, since texts cannot be properly understood without knowledge of their cultural and linguistic contexts.[10] In this way of looking at things, if we fail to do historical investigation of the texts and their contexts, then we will let our own biases, religious and otherwise, determine what the texts mean. Without historical study of the texts, writes Leo Perdue, "there is no objective or attainable knowledge and every view is capable of acceptance or rejection."[11] There is no objectivity without the historical method, in other words, and in its absence we will make the texts say whatever we want them to say, without any way to judge the validity of our interpretations. It is historical criticism that provides us with the literal sense of the text, as Markus Bockmuehl puts it, and that is why, he says, it should remain a "core element" of the field.[12] The continuing dominance of historical criticism as scholars read the Bible tells us that this is still the case, and it certainly seems to dominate as well in the ways that biblical studies is taught at both the undergraduate and graduate levels.[13]

Not all scholars are so certain that the historical critical method is the necessary aspect of biblical interpretation that establishes an objective basis for meaning, however. It is precisely because of claims that the method provides an objective meaning for the biblical texts that Fernando Segovia describes it as "remarkably

8. Barr, *History and Ideology*, 45.
9. Van Austin Harvey, *The Historian and the Believer: The Morality of Historical Knowledge and Christian Belief* (Urbana: University of Illinois Press, 1996), 5.
10. John Barton, *The Nature of Biblical Criticism* (Louisville, KY: Westminster John Knox, 2007), 86, 101–2.
11. Leo G. Perdue, *Reconstructing Old Testament Theology: After the Collapse of History*, OBT (Minneapolis: Fortress, 2005), 341.
12. Markus Bockmuehl, *Seeing the Word: Refocusing New Testament Study*, STI (Grand Rapids, MI: Baker Academic, 2006), 46.
13. Dale Martin's study of the pedagogy of biblical studies at ten seminaries and divinity schools in the United States concluded that most students are taught historical critical and often no other interpretive approaches (*Pedagogy of the Bible: An Analysis and Proposal* [Louisville, KY: Westminster John Knox, 2008], 1–28). Susanne Scholz's study of biblical studies curricula in liberal arts colleges in the United States concluded that pedagogy was largely grounded in historical criticism (*The Bible as Political Artifact: On the Feminist Study of the Hebrew Bible* [Minneapolis: Fortress, 2017], 11–17), and her study of biblical studies textbooks used for undergraduate courses found them also to privilege historical questions (pp. 18–21).

inbred and thoroughly hegemonic,"[14] the product of privileged scholars who see their work as definitively establishing meaning. Like Segovia, Justin Ukpong argues that those sorts of claims exclude the work of interpreters who are uninterested in historical questions, particularly the work of scholars who belong to groups who have been marginalized in Western society and in the field of biblical studies. Arguments for the necessity of historical study, he writes, "promote the ideology of dominance" of the West,[15] reflecting the insistence of Western scholars that the Bible must be studied in the ways that they have traditionally claimed produce objective meaning. Some marginalized scholars maintain that arguments for the necessity of historical criticism are unconvincing and that the notion that the true meaning of the texts can only be accessed through such work is "a dangerous ideological and political assertion," as Mary Ann Tolbert puts it,[16] and "ideologically suspect," as Musa Dube says.[17] In her experience, writes Makhosazana Nzimande, Western biblical scholars whose work is rooted in historical criticism simply "assume epistemological dominance" rather than even trying to justify why they are generally uninterested in nonhistorical studies of the Bible and in collaborating with scholars outside of the field's mainstream.[18] Brian Blount echoed this view in his 2018 presidential address to the Society of Biblical Literature, stating that those with interpretive power in biblical studies have generally been scholars whose work is historically focused and that the tendency of this mainstream is to marginalize those who are interested in pursuing other ways of reading the texts.[19] So the historical critical mainstream of the field has become an obstacle to the study of the Bible in Africa, writes David Adamo,[20] and a "straight-jacket" from

14. Fernando F. Segovia, "'And They Began to Speak in Other Tongues': Competing Modes of Discourse in Contemporary Biblical Criticism," in *Reading from This Place*, ed. Fernando F. Segovia and Mary Ann Tolbert (Minneapolis: Fortress, 1995), 1:13.
15. Justin S. Ukpong, "New Testament Hermeneutics in Africa: Challenges and Possibilities," Neot 35 (2001): 151.
16. Mary Ann Tolbert, "When Resistance Becomes Oppression: Mark 13:9–27 and the Poetics of Location," in Segovia and Tolbert, *Reading from This Place*, 2:341.
17. Musa W. Dube, "Toward a Post-colonial Feminist Interpretation of the Bible," in *Reading the Bible as Women: Perspectives from Africa, Asia, and Latin America*, ed. Katherine Doob Sakenfeld and Sharon H. Ringe, SemeiaSt 78 (Atlanta: Society of Biblical Literature, 1997), 23.
18. Makhosazana K. Nzimande, "Being 'Apart' and 'Together' at the Same Time? A Response to Hans de Wit," in *African and European Readers of the Bible in Dialogue: In Quest of a Shared Meaning*, ed. Hans de Wit and Gerald O. West, SRA 32 (Leiden: Brill, 2008), 31–35 (quotation from p. 34).
19. Brian K. Blount, "The Souls of Black Folk and the Potential for Meaning," JBL 138 (2019): 8–9.
20. David Tuesday Adamo, "Decolonizing the Psalter in Africa," in *Postcolonial Perspectives in African Biblical Interpretations*, ed. Musa W. Dube, Andrew M. Mbuvi, and Dora Mbuwayesango, GPBS 13 (Atlanta: Society of Biblical Literature, 2012), 299.

which Asian biblical interpretation had to free itself, says George Soares-Prabhu.[21] In the end, there is nothing necessary about the historical critical method when it comes to reading and using biblical texts, argues Vincent Wimbush, and because the mainstream of the discipline has been shaped by Western academic institutions that use historical study to validate their own existence, it is "essentially an elitist and socio-politically conservative phenomenon and practice."[22]

Criticisms of the historical critical mainstream of biblical studies often appear in writings that argue the field should have a liberative rather than historical focus. Liberative or emancipatory studies of the Bible aim to challenge cultural, religious, social, economic, and political injustice in order to produce interpretations that can be of use to marginalized readers who see the Bible as a resource in confronting such oppression. For those who have traditionally been pushed to the margins by Western culture—in particular, women, people of color, the vast majority of the population of the Two-Thirds World, and the LGBTQ community—the effects of oppression are very real and experienced on a daily basis. Biblical scholars who call such communities home often bring the experiences, needs, and questions of those groups to their academic work. They can argue, as Elisabeth Schüssler Fiorenza and Fernando Segovia do, that the field should reorient itself so that it focuses on challenging injustice in the academy, in religious institutions, and in broader society.[23] This is precisely the goal of South Asian feminist readings of the Bible, says Monica Melanchthon;[24] of African American interpretation, writes Mitzi Smith;[25] and of Korean postcolonial feminist biblical analysis, says Seong Hee Kim.[26]

21. George M. Soares-Prabhu, "Two Mission Commands: An Interpretation of Matthew 28:16–20 in Light of a Buddhist Text," *BibInt* 2 (1994): 264.
22. Vincent Wimbush, "In Search of a Usable Past: Reorienting Biblical Studies," in *Toward a New Heaven and a New Earth: Essays in Honor of Elisabeth Schüssler Fiorenza*, ed. Fernando F. Segovia (Maryknoll, NY: Orbis, 2003), 179–81, quotation from p. 181.
23. Elisabeth Schüssler Fiorenza, *Democratizing Biblical Studies: Toward an Emancipatory Educational Space* (Louisville, KY: Westminster John Knox, 2009), 4–5; Fernando F. Segovia, "Cultural Criticism: Expanding the Scope of Biblical Criticism," in *The Future of the Biblical Past: Envisioning Biblical Studies in a Global Key*, ed. Roland Boer and Fernando F. Segovia, SemeiaSt 66 (Atlanta: Society of Biblical Literature, 2012), 334–36.
24. Monica Jyotsna Melanchthon, "Engaging Women's Experience in the Struggle for Justice, Dignity, and Humanity: Hebrew Bible Readings by South Asian Women," in *Feminist Interpretation of the Hebrew Bible in Retrospect*, ed. Susanne Scholz, RRBS 5, 8–9 (Sheffield, UK: Sheffield Phoenix, 2013–16), 2:63.
25. Mitzi J. Smith, *Insights from African American Interpretation* (Minneapolis: Fortress, 2017), 16–18.
26. Seong Hee Kim, "Our (Neither) Mother and (Nor) Father in Heaven: A Postcolonial Reading of the Lord's Prayer," in *Korean Feminists in Conversation with the Bible, Church and Society*, ed. Kyung Sook Lee and Kyung Mi Park, BMW 24 (Sheffield, UK: Sheffield Phoenix, 2011), 69–70.

Scholars such as these use the resources available to them as professionals in the field of biblical studies to fight the many different kinds of oppression their communities face. While the specifics of oppression can vary widely from context to context, they do share in common the experience of being treated as less than fully human, as lacking the basic intelligence or ability to speak coherently on their own behalf and to act as agents to effectively better their own lives. So, for example, James Cone writes that the ideological basis of the North Atlantic slave trade was the belief on the part of whites that those of African descent were nonhumans, a belief that still manifests itself today.[27] Raquel St. Clair echoes this sentiment and emphasizes the dehumanization of Black women in particular.[28] The same can be said for the poor in Latin America, write Gustavo Gutiérrez and Elsa Tamez; those in power who control the economic lives of the poor betray little interest in whether they live or die, let alone in what they think or want, and so in essence treat them as nonpersons.[29] Nancy Cardoso Pereira emphasizes that this is particularly true of women in Latin America, who have often been treated as "non-women."[30] The experience of being regarded as less important and of less competence than a human adult has been a constant experience of more privileged white women as well, and those of European descent since the dawn of first-wave feminism in the nineteenth century have had to argue that they are fully human and entitled to the same rights as men.[31] Slavery is one result of dehumanization but others include the dismissal of the needs, concerns, and interests of marginalized communities, as groups with more socioeconomic privilege work with biases that are sometimes unconscious but always rooted in notions that the ways the less privileged go about doing things are not as good or important as their own. Dehumanization can manifest itself in the belief that the lower socioeconomic status of the marginalized is not an issue that the more powerful need to address,

27. James H. Cone, A *Black Theology of Liberation*, rev. ed. (Maryknoll, NY: Orbis, 1986), 12–15.
28. Raquel St. Clair, *Call and Consequences: A Womanist Reading of Mark* (Minneapolis: Fortress, 2008), 6.
29. Gustavo Gutiérrez, *The Power of the Poor in History*, trans. Robert B. Barr (Maryknoll, NY: Orbis, 1983), 90–92; Elsa Tamez, *The Amnesty of Grace: Justification by Faith from a Latin American Perspective*, trans. Sharon H. Ringe (Nashville, TN: Abingdon, 1993), 37–43.
30. Nancy Cardoso Pereira, "Changing Seasons: About the Bible and Other Sacred Texts in Latin America," in *Feminist Interpretation of the Bible and the Hermeneutics of Liberation*, ed. Silvia Schroer and Sophia Bietenhard, JSOTSup 374 (Sheffield, UK: Sheffield Academic, 2003), 53.
31. Esther Fuchs, "Reclaiming the Hebrew Bible for Women: The Neoliberal Turn in Contemporary Feminist Scholarship," *JFSR* 24 (2008): 45–46.

that the questions and interests of the marginalized are unsophisticated and of little concern, and that they would be better off allowing those at the social center to lead and guide them to the right ways of doing things.

It would be unfair to suggest that biblical scholars committed to the priority of the historical critical method do not believe that the ethical imperative to fight dehumanization is important, but it is fair to say that some of them argue it cannot be the first concern of the field. If one believes that the biblical texts cannot be understood apart from historical work that aims to make sense of them in their ancient contexts, then questions about their relevance for liberation from dehumanization can only be discussed secondarily, after questions about historical meaning have been handled. One well-known explanation and defense of this position was articulated by Krister Stendahl in the middle of the twentieth century. He argued that the primary task of academic biblical studies is to determine what the biblical texts meant when they were first written. A text may well have a different meaning for modern readers, Stendahl maintains, but this is the sort of thing that theologians and pastors (or, we could add, people with emancipatory ideals) are interested in. When biblical scholars are overly concerned with describing the current meaning of a text for their contemporaries, says Stendahl, they lose "enthusiasm" and "respect" for describing what it meant for the biblical author.[32] Using the historical critical method, scholars aim at discovering "what these words meant when uttered or written by the prophet, the priest, the evangelist, or the apostle," and we can check our conclusions in regard to that authorial meaning against "the material itself."[33] The historical method, he says, "yields the original in its own terms, limiting the interpretation to what it meant in its own setting."[34] So for Stendahl, students and scholars of the Bible must first commit ourselves to respect for authorial intention, and we can compare our conclusions in this regard to "the material itself." We could, if we wished, go on to a second step of finding ways to read these texts in light of our contemporary concerns, but that is work that must be judged by the results of the primary historical goal of biblical scholarship. For Stendahl, "theological renewal and creativity has as one of its

32. Krister Stendahl, "Biblical Theology: A Program," in *Meaning: The Bible as Document and as Guide* (Philadelphia: Fortress, 1984), 20–21. This is a reprint of the original version of this essay, published in 1962 in *The Interpreter's Dictionary of the Bible.*
33. Stendahl, 22.
34. Stendahl, 29.

components a strong exposure to the 'original' beyond the presuppositions and inherited frame of thought of our immediate predecessors in the theological task."[35] To put his point another way, historical criticism provides us with the "original" text, and this becomes the criterion we can use to judge contemporary liberative applications of it, or any other uses to which we want to put it, thus ensuring that our presuppositions and biases do not lead us to a meaning completely unrelated to what the text meant in its original ancient setting. Stendahl thus effectively sees a ditch that isolates the primary work of biblical scholars, which establishes what the text meant, from any secondary attempts to use the text to address contemporary issues, the validity of which must be judged by historical conclusions.

Stendahl did not create this ditch between historical method, understood to be the priority of biblical scholars, and contemporary application, liberative or otherwise, that must be judged by the textual meaning established through historical criticism, but he did do a good job of articulating a belief held to one degree or another by many in the field. Method, writes Stephen Moore, "has long been the *sine qua non* of biblical studies as an academic discipline. Methodology is what is meant to keep our discourse on the Bible from being subjective, personal, private, pietistic, pastoral, devotional, or homiletical. Methodology, in short, is what maintains the partition between sermon and scholarship."[36] For many scholars committed to historical criticism, one simply cannot begin academic study of the Bible with the needs and experiences and questions of the oppressed rather than with historical questions, because then there would be nothing to check subjective readings of biblical texts. Stendahl is hardly the only biblical scholar to claim that historical criticism is necessary to establish an "original" text that can judge the validity of attempts to apply it to contemporary concerns, something that entails the priority of historical questions and research. James Barr, for example, writes that an important point of the historical study of the Bible is that it can be used to critique meanings of the texts that people currently hold.[37] John Barton and Leo Perdue argue that one cannot use biblical texts to support liberative goals before one has established through historical method what these texts actually mean, or

35. Stendahl, 41.
36. Stephen D. Moore, "A Modest Manifesto for New Testament Literary Criticism: How to Interface with a Literary Studies Field That Is Post-literary, Post-theoretical, and Post-methodological," *BibInt* 15 (2007): 23.
37. Barr, *History and Ideology*, 47–48.

else one's interpretation will be governed by one's own biases, not the objective meaning of the texts.[38] When one believes that texts have stable meanings, then one generally also believes that it is irresponsible to displace that meaning with one's own, since in that case one fails to "allow the voice of the text to be heard."[39] We have to balance our desire to use the biblical texts for liberative purposes with "the ethics of accountability for the historical past of the text," writes Hans de Wit, or else "one is quickly doomed to hear just the echo of one's own voice."[40] Stendahl's ditch does not prevent anyone from using the Bible to meet contemporary needs, but it does demand that biblical scholars privilege the work of the historical critical method over liberation, since the former provides us with an original text that becomes a standard to judge the validity of attempts to use it for liberative goals. Biblical scholars have to do their own work on their side of the ditch; if this does not take priority, then attempts to use the Bible in a fight against dehumanization will end up being only misuse that reflects our own biases, not the texts' objective meanings.

Given the dominance of the historical critical method in biblical studies, it would appear that this view of things is still a pervasive one in the field. It has marginalized and kept in the minority readings that privilege liberative goals; dominated by an "elite social group," writes Monica Melanchthon, mainstream biblical criticism often does not see the analysis done by these minoritized scholars as actual scholarship.[41] It might surprise many middle-class scholars to hear themselves described as part of an elite, although the Western middle class is part of an economic elite from the perspective of those who live in the Two-Thirds World,[42] and the field of biblical studies is still dominated by a demographic elite—75 percent of those who responded to the 2019 survey of the Society of Biblical Literature's membership identified themselves as male, and 85 percent of respondents were

38. Perdue, *Reconstructing Old Testament Theology*, 341–42; Barton, *Nature of Biblical Criticism*, 48–49.
39. Law, *Historical-Critical Method*, 235–36.
40. Hans de Wit, "Exegesis and Contextuality: Happy Marriage, Divorce or Living (Apart) Together?," in Wit and West, *African and European Readers of the Bible*, 24–25.
41. Monica Jyotsna Melanchthon, "Unleashing the Power Within: The Bible and the Dalits," in Boer and Segovia, *Future of the Biblical Past*, 50.
42. According to the World Bank, the average per capita income in 2018 in the United States was US$62,795, and $36,750 in the European Union. In India, where Melanchthon is from, it was $2,010. Even in countries the World Bank classified as upper middle income, it was $9,212, while in those designated as least developed by the United Nations it was $1,058, making a middle-class salary in North America or Western Europe seem elite indeed. "GDP per Capita," World Bank, accessed June 22, 2020, https://data.worldbank.org/indicator/NY.GDP.PCAP.CD.

of European descent.[43] Neither gender identification, wealth, nor race necessarily determines how one will decide to read biblical texts, but it stands to reason that those with less direct experience of oppression will fail to feel or notice its effects in comparison with those who have less socioeconomic privilege. For those who find themselves in dominant and elite demographic categories, it will be easier to discount the liberative needs of minoritized communities and the questions that many biblical scholars rooted in those groups want to answer. Without remotely the same sorts of experiences of or exposure to forces of oppression, it is less difficult to affirm the field's traditional focus on the texts as ancient artifacts that may not have any message that is terribly relevant for those struggling for liberation in the contemporary world. For more privileged scholars, it becomes more difficult to see why one would want to begin interpretations of biblical texts not with historical critical concerns but with those of African women, as Dora Mbuwayesango does,[44] or with questions that ask about oppression rather than historical context, as Musa Dube does,[45] or with the goal of meeting the needs of Latino/a readers, as Latino/a biblical scholars often do.[46] If one believes that textual meaning is inextricably linked to what an ancient author was trying to say or that it cannot be accessed without constant study of the ancient languages and contexts of the texts' original readers, then one must privilege historical method over liberation. This is not a belief that necessarily rejects academic readings of biblical texts done with the oppressed in mind, but it is to assert the validity of Stendahl's ditch, which maintains that the main historical job of biblical scholars must take primacy over any other kind of research they might want to do and that emancipatory readings of texts are secondary to and judged by historical critical conclusions.

However, from the perspective of many marginalized scholars who prioritize the liberative needs of groups fighting oppression, the sort of worldview manifested in Stendahl's ditch is simply one more aspect of dehumanization, an institutional claim that the traditional approaches of an academy dominated by white males must be given priority and must be used to judge the validity of nonhistorical readings,

43. "2019 SBL Membership Data," 8, 10.
44. Dora Rudo Mbuwayesango, "Feminist Biblical Studies in Africa," in *Feminist Biblical Studies in the Twentieth Century: Scholarship and Movement*, ed. Elisabeth Schüssler Fiorenza, SBLBW 9.1 (Atlanta: Society of Biblical Literature, 2014), 74–77.
45. Musa W. Dube, *Postcolonial Feminist Interpretation of the Bible* (St. Louis, MO: Chalice, 2000), 97.
46. Francisco Lozada Jr., *Toward a Latino/a Biblical Interpretation*, RBS (Atlanta: Society of Biblical Literature, 2017), 11–12.

and this is why they can refer to it as an obstacle to the study of the Bible among minoritized groups. If one argues that answering historical critical questions is the necessary first step in interpretation, then only those privileged with the resources to embark on academic study can ultimately function as judges of interpretation, and the less privileged can only be followers when it comes to reading biblical texts, dependent on the verdicts elite scholars pass upon their readings. The question we are faced with, then, is whether liberation or method should take precedence in biblical studies, and if this is an ethical question, as I will argue, it is also one that asks about the relation between meaning and texts.

Ethical Texts: A Hermeneutical Solution

The focus of this study, then, is a hermeneutical one, since it makes an argument as to how we should go about interpreting texts. In the debate between liberation and method, I side with those who have abandoned the sort of worldview Stendahl and others have articulated, one that insists on the primacy of historical criticism in biblical studies. I side with those who read for liberation in part because, as I argue in chapters 2 and 3, there is no necessary connection between historical contexts, meaning, and texts, ancient or otherwise. Another key reason why I side with liberative scholars in this matter is ethical in nature, a matter chapter 4 pursues. If we need not adhere to historical method to understand biblical texts, then we should follow moral commitments that we hold and choose an ethical standard to judge whether or not we have produced good or bad interpretations, and marginalized scholars pursuing emancipatory readings have long been discussing the field's ethical need to fight dehumanization in the work we do. One assumption that I make in this argument is that it is an ethical good to fight oppression whenever we can reasonably do so, which is why we can follow the principles for ethical liberative interpretation set out by marginalized scholars, the focus of chapter 5. These scholars have concretized these principles in thousands of examples of textual interpretation, and chapter 6 surveys some of these. Chapters 7 and 8 use these principles and models to provide academic liberative readings of, respectively, an entire biblical book and a single passage, to show what it might look like for a privileged scholar such as myself to follow the lead in interpretation of my less privileged colleagues, having been convinced by their arguments of the ethical necessity to read for emancipation. And while the book as a whole is focused on why individual scholars should aim to follow the liberative agenda set in the margins of the discipline, the concluding chapter notes that there are larger systemic problems in biblical studies that will have to be addressed if this emancipatory project is to become widespread in the field.

One might hold to the ethical belief that we should fight oppression because this is an important part of one's religious beliefs, but this agenda for reading the Bible is one atheists can pursue as well. The best version of liberal democracy, at least as envisioned by John Rawls, is organized by the idea that society is a fair system of cooperation between free and equal individuals,[47] something radically opposed to dehumanization. But, writes Rawls, the stability of such organization depends on the fair treatment of these equal individuals such that there is equality of opportunity, especially in regard to education and employment; an equitable distribution of income and wealth; and availability of health care, for there is no real protection of democratic liberties without these things. The concepts of freedom and equality are of no benefit to those who are condemned by sociopolitical forces to live in fear of their physical safety or in desperate poverty and without reliable access to health care, and societies that refuse to confront problems like these are clearly not dedicated to the view that a fair system of cooperation should exist for all of its members or that all of them should be treated equally.[48] One need not be religious to believe that we should fight oppression, in other words.[49] If, however, one is not persuaded on religious or philosophical grounds that we have an ethical duty to do what we can to promote fair and equal societies, ones that recognize and treat everyone as fully human, regardless of their gender identification, race, sexual orientation, class, disability, or religious beliefs, and that this entails basic standards of equality in other realms of life, then one might not find this book's overall argument terribly compelling, since it assumes rather than justifies this ethical imperative.

My experience leads me to believe, however, that many of us who were or are being educated in the mainstream of the discipline of biblical studies already hold

47. John Rawls, *Political Liberalism*, rev. ed. (New York: Columbia University Press, 1996), 9.
48. Rawls, lvii–lix.
49. Rawls, in fact, believed that religious beliefs have virtually no place in the discussions of the public good within liberal democracies (*Political Liberalism*, 49–50), but for a rebuttal to this idea see Jeffrey Stout, *Democracy and Tradition*, NFB (Princeton, NJ: Princeton University Press, 2004), 63–85.

beliefs like these, and this is an important reason why I think many of us can be persuaded by our less privileged peers to follow their lead in creating a field driven by emancipatory goals. But it is because so many of us have been grounded in an education that prioritizes historical work that we might find it more difficult to free ourselves from beliefs like those reflected in Stendahl's ditch concerning the necessity and primacy of historical work over liberative goals. For this reason, chapters 2 and 3 are devoted to a discussion of the relation between texts and meaning. In these chapters, I will rely in particular on the arguments of pragmatists, particularly the thought of Richard Rorty[50] and of others who discuss hermeneutical issues as pragmatists like him tend to. One of the important reasons why I find a pragmatist approach so helpful for the liberative agenda I believe biblical studies should follow is the insistence of this school of philosophy that its work make a practical difference in the world. Pragmatism abandons traditional philosophical questions except insofar as they can be judged to make a positive difference in people's lives, writes Hilary Putnam,[51] and Rorty says that the point of philosophy is to create "cultural change" in order to "find better ways of helping us overcome the past in order to create a better future."[52] Philosophers, writes Philip Kitcher,

50. Any philosophical school will manifest a range of beliefs among its members, some of them incompatible, and have intramural arguments, and this is true of pragmatism as well. Not all pragmatists agree with all aspects of Rorty's neopragmatism, and what is sometimes called new pragmatism is to some degree a reaction against some important aspects of his thought (see, e.g., Alan Malachowski, *The New Pragmatism* [Durham, UK: Acumen, 2010]). Some argue he moved too far away from key principles of the nineteenth- and early-twentieth-century founders of the movement, but while Richard Bernstein can call Rorty's brand of pragmatism "idiosyncratic" (*The Pragmatic Turn* [Cambridge: Polity, 2010], 127), Jeffrey Stout could also refer to him only a few years before Rorty's death as "the most important contemporary pragmatist" (*Democracy and Tradition*, 64). For those who are aware of the differing opinions in regard to Rorty's thought among pragmatists, chapters 2 and 3 will provide some reasons why I am largely in agreement with his view of things, particularly in regard to hermeneutical issues. I will rarely make mention of those disputes, however, and then only in the notes, since for the purposes of this book, when I refer to pragmatism I am referring to a Rortyan version of it.

For my hermeneutical purposes, I have cast a fairly wide net over the concept of pragmatism and include the work of figures who, like Rorty, consistently apply the label of pragmatist to their writings, as well as to others such as Wilfrid Sellars who are more suspicious of the term yet whose research appeals to the same sorts of principles commonly adopted by pragmatists (for the case of the pragmatist tendencies in Sellars's writings, see Robert B. Brandom, *From Empiricism to Expressivism: Brandom Reads Sellars* [Cambridge, MA: Harvard University Press, 2014], 5–7). This includes the writings of figures outside of the field of philosophy, most notably Stanley Fish, whose hermeneutical insights from a background in literary criticism have much in common with a Rortyan view of the world and of texts.

51. Hilary Putnam, "What Makes Pragmatism So Different?," in *Pragmatism as a Way of Life: The Lasting Legacy of William James and John Dewey*, ed. David Macarthur (Cambridge, MA: Harvard University Press, 2017), 36–54.

52. Richard Rorty, *Philosophy as Cultural Politics: Philosophical Papers*, vol. 4 (Cambridge: Cambridge University Press, 2007), 169.

need to consider "what, if anything, makes their intended contributions worth having," which is precisely the ethical question I urge students and scholars of biblical studies to ponder about our work. Some philosophical research does have positive effects, Kitcher writes, such as that which investigates problems posed by global poverty or examines the conditions of modern democracy, but he maintains that "unless one can show that the more abstract questions do contribute to the solution of problems of more general concern, . . . they should be seen as preludes to philosophy rather than the substance of it."[53] If one substitutes "historical investigations" for "the more abstract questions" and "biblical studies" for "philosophy," then we have a fair statement of our discipline's problem as I understand it: the field's central historical concerns should at most play a supporting role in liberative investigations that are still generally pursued only at its margins.

Chapters 2 and 3 will point to another key reason why I find pragmatism, and particularly Rorty's brand of it, so helpful in regard to my hermeneutical concerns, for there I argue that biblical scholars have been unable to provide good justifications for why historical questions must be part of academic interpretations of the Bible. A basic position of Rorty and like-minded thinkers is that the world is not knowable to us until humans make it that way through the ideas and speech and concepts about it that we create. This means that the world, insofar as we can ever discuss and make sense of it, is something created through the worldview or sets of beliefs provided by the social groups we belong to. *The world* in this sense includes texts, so in this way of looking at things, there is no textual meaning that exists outside of interpretation, our thinking about and discussion of texts, since texts, like everything else, can only make sense to us once we interpret them. Meaning is no more inherent to texts than it is to any other set of objects in the world, and we can only judge the validity of interpretations by appealing to other interpretations or to beliefs we already hold. Our worldviews limit the interpretations we are willing to accept, so we are predisposed by our communities' belief systems to read texts in particular ways and arrive at particular conclusions in regard to their meanings. In this understanding, textual meaning is created by readers' interpretations and nothing else, and so there is no necessary connection between historical context, texts, and meaning. As a result, historical work is not a necessary part of academic

53. Philip Kitcher, *Preludes to Pragmatism: Toward a Reconstruction of Philosophy* (Oxford: Oxford University Press, 2012), 220–21.

biblical interpretation (although it certainly can be an optional part), and as the marginalized scholars whose work I discuss in chapter 4 argue, claims to the contrary have led the field to largely ignore liberative needs, interests, and interpretations, and to silence those scholars who want to pursue emancipatory goals.

In making the claim in chapters 2 and 3 that readers and their communities are responsible for determining textual meaning, I by no means want to discount the views of those who see the Bible as inspired scripture. The project I have in mind is something determined by ethical rather than religious commitment, although for many students and scholars of biblical studies it will be their religious beliefs that predispose them to fight oppression. But for readers who understand the Bible as scripture, I would simply make the point that divine omniscience is a quality that humans lack, and just because the divine mind can be aware of particular truths does not necessarily mean that humans can be. My argument throughout the book is focused on what humans can know, since my concern is with the field of biblical studies, an academic discipline that, like all other academic disciplines, is subject to the limitations of human imagination and methods when it comes to organizing knowledge. This is not an objection to the belief in the divine inspiration of biblical literature, it is merely an awareness of the limitations of humans as we try to make sense of it. So I am concerned by the ways people might construe arguments like that advanced by Anthony Thiselton, for example, who says that if the meaning of a text is something that interpretive communities and their readers produce, then there is nothing for the Christian church to fall back on to judge its own doctrine.[54] This is part of his argument that religious doctrine could not be reliable unless there is some aspect of meaning to scripture that humans do not produce, and my concern with this sort of objection to understanding the meaning of biblical texts as a human production is that it might lead some to settle on a particular reading of a text, one promoted by the more socioeconomically privileged readers who tend to wield interpretive power, and then to divinize it, taking a limited human understanding to be the equivalent of omniscient divine intention that no one should ever challenge.[55] The pragmatist

54. Anthony Thiselton, *Thiselton on Hermeneutics: Collected Works with New Essays* (Grand Rapids, MI: William B. Eerdmans, 2006), 514.
55. The notion of fallibilism is also an important aspect of pragmatism, as we will see in chapter 3. While we may not have any reason to doubt any of the beliefs we currently hold, it is possible that we could find future reasons to change any one or set of them. This understanding of fallibilism should be called corrigibilism, says Isaac Levi (*Pragmatism and Inquiry: Selected Essays* [Oxford: Oxford University Press, 2008], 4–5), since it reflects the notion that one's beliefs are always open to correction.

understanding of texts and meaning that I aim to justify in the following chapters does not exclude readers of faith but can open a door for all readers to a more ethical standard of interpretation.

The way Rorty and others look at the world frees us from the strictures of Stendahl's ditch and its demand that the work of historical critics be used as the objective criterion to judge any sort of liberative reading, and it frees us to look to marginalized colleagues in the field who urge us to use our work as students and scholars to honor the ethical commitment we have to fighting oppression whenever that is reasonably possible. From the pragmatist point of view that Rorty holds, what a particular group believes to be a true or objective or necessary way to interpret is so simply because this is what the set of beliefs that make up that group's worldview dictates. As a result, dialogue is important for pragmatists, since we need to challenge the web of beliefs we have to see if it is as coherent as we assume it is, and the best way to do this is to dialogue with groups whose worldviews are somewhat different from ours. In the field of biblical studies, chapter 4 argues, marginalized scholars have done a good job of explaining to the discipline's mainstream why much of the work we do fails to live up to our own ethical standards, and these explanations will leave some of us wondering how to better align our professional activities with beliefs about the evils of dehumanization that we already hold.

Readers familiar with the study of hermeneutics might wonder why I have decided to ground my general understanding of interpretation and its approach to dialogue in the work of pragmatism rather than that of Hans-Georg Gadamer, especially since the title of this book clearly reflects that of Gadamer's *Truth and Method*, arguably the best-known work about hermeneutics produced in the twentieth century. There is actually much that Gadamer's hermeneutical approach has in common with the pragmatist understanding of texts that I am following, including his claim that our communities provide us with language that shapes the way we see the world and understand texts.[56] This means, says Gadamer, that we can only

56. The world is not knowable to us except insofar as we construe it in language with which our worldview provides us, says Gadamer (see *Truth and Method*, 2nd ed., trans. Joel Weisenheimer and Donald G. Marshall [New York: Continuum, 1995], 438–56), and this means that we can make no truth claim about the way things are without fitting it into the web of beliefs that already exists in our worldview (Hans-Georg Gadamer, "What Is Truth?," trans. Brice W. Wachterhauser, in *Hermeneutics and Truth*, ed. Brice W. Wachterhauser, NUSPEP [Evanston, IL: Northwestern University Press, 1994], 42). Arguments like these, writes Fred Dallmayr, sound very much like those advanced by pragmatists like John Dewey ("Hermeneutics and Inter-cultural Dialogue," in *Gadamer's Hermeneutics and the Art of Conversation*, ed. Andrzej Wierciński, ISHP 2 [Berlin: Lit Verlag, 2011], 70–71).

encounter textual meaning in the way our tradition has already created it, with the result that we are unable to interpret any work outside of the prejudices or prejudgments with which our tradition provides us when we read.[57] Our interpretive work is based in our "historically effected consciousness," as Gadamer puts it, by which he seems to mean that our view of the world and the texts in it have been shaped by the ways in which our tradition has continually interpreted and reinterpreted these texts, while our prejudices, rooted in this tradition, guide us as we interpret the texts yet again and subtly alter the tradition that has formed us.[58] Dialogue is central to this process, Gadamer writes, although he often refers to dialogue as something that is done with a text that our tradition has caused to speak, since it is tradition that first provides us with textual meaning and with appropriate ways of reading.[59] That is not all dialogue means for him, however, and he also writes of allowing others to challenge the interpretations of tradition in conversation.[60]

Gadamer's understanding of dialogue does not seem satisfactory to all of his interlocutors, and this is sometimes related to their unease with his concept of tradition. Since my own attempt to prioritize liberation in the interpretation of biblical texts is based in part in pragmatism, which does have some points of contact with Gadamer's understanding of interpretation, then these are critiques that I will have to take very seriously. Gadamer actually does very little to define what he means by tradition, but his reference to being shaped by "the Greco-Christian tradition"[61] can sound narrow and exclusive from a twenty-first-century perspective. From an Asian American point of view, says the biblical scholar Sze-kar Wan, Gadamer's understanding of tradition is far too monolithic and simplistic, since Asian

57. See, for example, Gadamer, *Truth and Method*, 254–64.
58. Gadamer, *Truth and Method*, 300–307. There is not, to be fair, complete agreement as to what Gadamer means in the discussion on these pages—see, for example, Hans Robert Jauss, *Question and Answer: Forms of Dialogic Understanding*, trans. Michael Hays, THL 68 [Minneapolis: University of Minnesota Press, 1989], 204–5—but for interpretations like mine, see John D. Caputo, *Radical Hermeneutics: Repetition, Deconstruction, and the Hermeneutic Project*, SPEP (Bloomington: Indiana University Press, 1987), 108–12; and Georgia Warnke, *Gadamer: Hermeneutics, Tradition and Reason* (Stanford, CA: Stanford University Press, 1987), 79–80.
59. For example, Gadamer, *Truth and Method*, 369–79.
60. For example, Hans-Georg Gadamer, "Reply to Jacques Derrida," trans. Diane P. Michelfelder and Richard E. Palmer, in *Dialogue and Deconstruction: The Gadamer-Derrida Encounter*, ed. Diane P. Michelfelder and Richard E. Palmer, SSCCP (Albany: State University of New York Press, 1989), 52–54. For the centrality of dialogue with others in Gadamer's hermeneutic, see Georgia Warnke, "Hermeneutics, Ethics, and Politics," in *The Cambridge Companion to Gadamer*, ed. Robert J. Dostal (Cambridge: Cambridge University Press, 2002), 79–101.
61. Hans-Georg Gadamer, "On the Problem of Self-Understanding," in *Philosophical Hermeneutics*, trans. and ed. David E. Lange (Berkeley: University of California Press, 1976), 46.

Americans live in a multiplicity of traditions that can provide them with many and even contradictory ways of interpreting texts.[62] Whatever else Gadamer might mean when he talks about tradition, writes Terry Eagleton, he can clearly see only one, a tradition in which "'art' means chiefly the classical monuments of high German tradition," and so, says Eagleton, what Gadamer appears to mean by tradition is really just a set of views shared by "a club of the like-minded,"[63] a club that would exclude readers who find their interpretive homes in other traditions. The texts Gadamer had in mind when writing *Truth and Method* were important to that high German or elite Western tradition, for when cultures value certain texts very highly, says Barbara Herrnstein Smith, they will repress aspects of them they find alienating, and these texts will then be understood within those cultures as reflecting the ideologies of the established elite.[64] This means, however, that others outside of Gadamer's elite club and, for that matter, outside of the elite club of mainstream biblical studies can experience the texts valued by such elites very differently. For women and other marginalized groups, writes Veronica Vasterling, "the binding force of tradition becomes a repressive force," and the use of the word *truth* when we refer to our interpretations can end up being only a "more respectable name for power" that supports the goals of a socioeconomic elite and justifies or ignores the subjugation of the less privileged.[65] In later chapters of this book, in fact, we will find examples of marginalized scholars who refer to certain interpretations of biblical texts that have been used to justify the oppression of their communities.

Gadamer never really reflects on the problem of how to deal with the possibility that one's tradition may be used to oppress others and repress their interpretations.[66] His concept of hermeneutics is based in the notion that we can reform our tradition as we interpret, but he never clearly explains how that is possible, given the power

62. Sze-kar Wan, "Betwixt and Between: Toward a Hermeneutics of Hyphenation," in *Ways of Being, Ways of Reading: Asian American Biblical Interpretation*, ed. Mary F. Foskett and Jeffrey Kah-Jin Kuan (St. Louis, MO: Chalice, 2006), 144–46.
63. Terry Eagleton, *Literary Theory: An Introduction* (Minneapolis: University of Minnesota Press, 1983), 73.
64. Barbara Herrnstein Smith, *Contingencies of Value: Alternative Perspectives for Critical Theory* (Cambridge, MA: Harvard University Press, 1988), 49–52.
65. Veronica Vasterling, "Postmodern Hermeneutics? Toward a Critical Hermeneutics," in *Feminist Interpretations of Hans-Georg Gadamer*, ed. Lorraine Code, RC (University Park: Pennsylvania State University Press, 2003), 168.
66. See, for example, Richard J. Bernstein, *Beyond Objectivity and Relativism: Science, Hermeneutics, and Practice* (Philadelphia: University of Pennsylvania Press, 1983), 155–56; and Caputo, *Radical Hermeneutics*, 310n7.

he believes tradition has to shape our worldview, which may be why on occasion he refers to interpretation as a "miracle."[67] Gadamer may believe that our interpretive work will allow us to identify some of our tradition's prejudices or prejudgments about a text as false,[68] but he never explains how we will be able to critique the tradition that informs the way we understand texts in the first place.[69] So if, like Gadamer and the pragmatists, I believe that any understanding of texts is inevitably shaped by the worldview that one's community provides, then I will need to clearly explain how I believe anyone could ever change their view as to how to read biblical texts and how they could be able to test their interpretive presuppositions to see if they are oppressive or not. While Gadamer believes that dialogue with others will save us from the false prejudices of our tradition, sometimes dialogue will not cause us to change at all. We may not be able to accept the judgment of someone who has experienced our tradition very differently than we have, someone who reads a particular text not as reflecting a culture's or religion's highest ideals but as justifying the subjugation of their community and so as dehumanizing. If I am going to argue that the mainstream of the field of biblical studies must dialogue with communities and scholars who have experienced the interpretive tradition of the field as oppressive and as marginalizing them and their readings, then I will need to show how this dialogue can function and why I believe it can lead to change.

My larger arguments in this regard in the following chapters are founded in pragmatist concepts of the text and of the self. Stanley Fish maintains that, once we have accepted the notion held by some pragmatists and others that the meaning of texts or anything else is established through the worldviews our communities provide us, "the fact of a particular thing being socially constructed is not a fact you can do anything with,"[70] but I do not believe he is entirely correct about this. If pragmatists like Fish can convince us that it is not authors but readers and their

67. For example, Gadamer, *Truth and Method*, 163, 292; and Hans-Georg Gadamer, "The Problem of Historical Consciousness," trans. Jeff L. Close, in *Interpretive Social Science: A Reader*, ed. Paul Rabinow and William M. Sullivan (Berkeley: University of California Press, 1979), 147.
68. Gadamer, *Truth and Method*, 295–96.
69. Richard J. Bernstein, "From Hermeneutics to Praxis," in *Hermeneutics and Praxis*, ed. Robert Hollinger (Notre Dame, IN: University of Notre Dame Press, 1985), 285–87; Tom Rockmore, "Gadamer's Hermeneutics and the Overcoming of Epistemology," in *The Specter of Relativism: Truth, Dialogue, and* Phronesis *in Philosophical Hermeneutics*, ed. Lawrence K. Schmidt, NUSPEP (Evanston, IL: Northwestern University Press, 1995), 66–67.
70. Stanley Fish, *Professional Correctness: Literary Studies and Political Change* (Oxford: Clarendon, 1995), ix.

communities who determine textual meaning,[71] then students and scholars of biblical studies who used to believe in the validity of something like Stendahl's ditch and thought that they had to privilege historical work can instead follow the paths of interpretation blazed by marginalized scholars dedicated to liberation, prioritizing ethical goals of emancipation over historical ones. This understanding of how change is possible is not rooted in a Gadamerian view of the self, one established by a monolithic force Gadamer calls tradition, but in a pragmatist concept of the self as constructed through its simultaneous membership in multiple communities, producing in each person a whole web of beliefs that are generally but not entirely consistent with each other.[72] When we have enough in common with other groups, we may be able to hear them when they point to a lack of consistency in that web, and so we may be convinced to change one or some of our beliefs, causing us to reweave the web to some degree. Indeed, writes Rorty, the whole point of thinkers is to help their communities reweave their beliefs when dialogue leads them to notice gaps and inconsistencies,[73] since the goal of inquiry is to arrive at a more consistent worldview that one can more logically justify to oneself and others.[74] If many or even most mainstream scholars already believe that it is an ethical good to fight oppression whenever this is reasonably possible, then such a belief will uneasily coexist with others provided to them by the academic field about the necessity to prioritize historical work. Yet since the discipline has been unable to provide good reasons why historical criticism should be a necessary part of academic biblical studies, as chapters 2 and 3 argue, those ethical beliefs can take priority in shaping what we do once we pay attention to the arguments of marginalized scholars that chapter 4 discusses, ones that critique the discipline's general understanding of the historical critical method. Mainstream scholars convinced by arguments like these might then be willing to alter what we do in our professional work and

71. For some of Fish's arguments in this regard, see *Is There a Text in This Class? The Authority of Interpretive Communities* (Cambridge, MA: Harvard University Press, 1980), 303–55.
72. See, for example, Willard Van Orman Quine, *From a Logical Point of View: Nine Logico-Philosophical Essays*, 2nd ed. (Cambridge, MA: Harvard University Press, 1980), 42–43; Richard Shustermann, "The Gadamer-Derrida Encounter: A Pragmatist Perspective," in Michelfelder and Palmer, *Dialogue and Deconstruction*, 219; and Richard Rorty, *Objectivity, Relativism, and Truth: Philosophical Papers*, vol. 1 (Cambridge: Cambridge University Press, 1991), 93.
73. Richard Rorty, *Essays on Heidegger and Others: Philosophical Papers*, vol. 2 (Cambridge: Cambridge University Press, 1991), 17–18.
74. Rorty, *Objectivity, Relativism, and Truth*, 100–101.

prioritize the goals and examples of liberative readings our marginalized colleagues have provided us, the focus of chapters 5 and 6.

So while I find Gadamer's understandings of tradition, self, and change through dialogue to ultimately be unconvincing, his view of a world constructed through language has enough in common with the sort of pragmatism I am drawing on that I am aware that merely appealing to a pragmatist understanding of texts is not a hermeneutical panacea. Some pragmatists have expressed concern that their school of philosophy has overvalued Western tradition and has not dealt comprehensively enough with the failures of liberal democracies to live up to their ideals and treat all of their citizens as fully human by providing them with the resources and support they need to thrive as equal members of open societies.[75] Unless we can also enter into a dialogue with those who can appeal to our ethical beliefs and ask how that might make us want to change some of the aspects of how we think of biblical scholarship, we cannot expect our discipline to change.

A better field of biblical studies, one that uses the ethic of liberation as a criterion to judge its output rather than standards based in historically focused work, is one that will have to turn for its leadership to scholars and communities currently marginalized by the field. They have experienced oppression in ways that those of us with more socioeconomic privilege have not, they have long been involved in the struggle against it, and they are already aware of the sorts of reading strategies that do and do not work for their different communities. The dominance of the mainstream of the field, however, often results in "a hermeneutics of authority and control," says Sharon Ringe,[76] and this is why marginalized scholars like Makhosazana Nzimande and Musa Dube have often experienced a general lack of interest from the larger discipline in regard to their interpretive questions and approaches that read for liberation.[77] More privileged scholars are not in the position

75. See, for example, the critiques of Richard Rorty in this regard by Cornell West (*The American Evasion of Philosophy: A Genealogy of Pragmatism* [Madison: University of Wisconsin Press, 1989], 206–10) and Jeffrey Stout (*Ethics after Babel: The Languages of Morals and Their Discontents* [Boston: Beacon, 1988], 229–32). Rorty's own view of the ideal open society is much like Rawls's, a liberal democracy with a robust social safety net—for an interesting discussion of this, see his *Philosophy and Social Hope* (London: Penguin, 1999), 243–51—but the concern on the parts of other pragmatists is that his promotion of this ideal lacks specificity as to how to achieve it.

76. Sharon H. Ringe, "Asian Readings of the Bible: A North American Feminist Response," *BibInt* 2 (1994): 374.

77. Nzimande, "Being 'Apart' and 'Together,'" 31–32; Musa W. Dube, "Border Crossing in Diasporic Academic Space," in *The Bible, Centres and Margins: Dialogues between Postcolonial African and British Biblical Scholars*, ed. Musa W. Dube and Johanna Stiebert (London: T&T Clark, 2018), 8–10.

to provide others with liberation, as Ada Isasi-Díaz argues,[78] for that simply assumes the minoritized do not have the intelligence or ability to lead an emancipatory fight, and that the more privileged must impose their solutions on problems faced by the oppressed, an attitude that only dehumanizes them and contributes to the problem of oppression. More privileged scholars like me also need liberation from worldviews that have allowed us to benefit from the oppression of others without considering the cost, or by rationalizing it away, as R. S. Sugirtharajah notes,[79] and so in the chapters that follow I look to the principles and models of liberative analysis my minoritized colleagues in biblical studies have provided in order to justify to other students and scholars in the field why we should prioritize the liberative goals and follow principles and examples of interpretation that come from what is currently the margins of the field.

There is no one set way to do this. As a model, we could turn to Elisabeth Schüssler Fiorenza's concept of the *ekklēsia*, a term that she uses when discussing biblical studies' future not in the sense of "church," which is how students of New Testament Greek have encountered it, but as reflecting the broader sense of the Greek word as a public assembly, and her ideal vision of the *ekklēsia* is a forum that regards everyone as equally human, providing space for all voices, especially marginalized ones, to interpret biblical writings from the perspectives of their experiences.[80] Cheryl Anderson promotes a similar ideal in her picture of an inclusive and ethical field of discourse for biblical studies, although her vision is of a specifically Christian community, and so she combines the ideals of participatory democracy with the prophetic tradition that she sees as continuing within liberal Christianity.[81] Not everyone is as certain as Schüssler Fiorenza that her *ekklēsia* is as truly inclusive of the marginalized as she believes it to be—Musa Dube, for example, argues that it devalues non-Christian traditions that she sees as key to an ethical interpretation of the Bible in Southern Africa[82]—but it should be the job of

78. Ada María Isasi-Díaz, *Mujerista Theology: A Theology for the Twenty-First Century* (Maryknoll, NY: Orbis, 1996), 1.
79. R. S. Sugirtharajah, "A Postcolonial Exploration of Collusion and Construction in Biblical Interpretation," in *The Postcolonial Bible*, ed. R. S. Sugirtharajah, BC 1 (Sheffield, UK: Sheffield Academic, 1998), 94.
80. Elisabeth Schüssler Fiorenza, *The Power of the Word: Scripture and the Rhetoric of Empire* (Minneapolis: Fortress, 2007), 70–82.
81. Cheryl B. Anderson, *Ancient Laws and Contemporary Controversies: The Need for Inclusive Biblical Interpretation* (Oxford: Oxford University Press, 2009), 165–70.
82. Dube, *Postcolonial Feminist Interpretation*, 27–31.

the field to make our space of discourse not one that merely includes marginalized voices but one that looks to them for guidance. To structure the discipline in ways such that voices arguing for liberation are excluded and silenced is to fail to see those speakers as fully human,[83] to manifest a belief that they are unable to speak intelligently for themselves, or to assume that what they do say does not have any bearing on "real" biblical scholarship and so has nothing to contribute to the field. Since readers create texts, as I will argue, we need to create the best ones we can,[84] where *best* is determined by the ethical criterion of liberation, but this will not be possible until more privileged scholars look to more marginalized ones for leadership. They have spent decades in the discipline arguing for the need to do ethical emancipatory interpretation and provided thousands of examples as to how to go about such work; in the end, this book is an acknowledgment that they have made their point persuasively and an encouragement to their more privileged fellows to recognize this fact and turn to them for leadership.

We/They: Unity and Difference

I am a white, male, middle-class scholar who received a fine education in biblical studies, with particular emphasis on historical critical issues. And while I and others in my privileged social location have become convinced of the need for biblical studies to be driven by emancipatory goals articulated by our peers in the field who are fighting for their communities' liberation,[85] I am aware that the unearned social privileges we enjoy make our experiences of life very different from those of people with fewer such benefits. I am not poor, and my experiences of oppression are not remotely as personal or as constant as theirs. Minoritized scholars are sometimes suspicious when they see more privileged colleagues use the word *we* in their interpretations of texts, writes Jione Havea, immediately wary of the fact

83. See, for example, Jean-Pierre Ruiz, *Readings from the Edges: The Bible and People on the Move*, SLC (Maryknoll, NY: Orbis, 2011), 5–8.
84. This follows the thought of Vincent L. Wimbush, *Scripturalectics: The Management of Meaning* (Oxford: Oxford University Press, 2017), 144–46.
85. See also, for example, Gerald O. West, *Biblical Hermeneutics of Liberation: Modes of Reading the Bible in the South African Context*, 2nd ed., BibLib (Maryknoll, NY: Orbis, 1995); Daniel Patte, *Ethics of Biblical Interpretation: A Reevaluation* (Louisville, KY: Westminster John Knox, 1995); and Mark G. Brett, *Decolonizing God: The Bible in the Tides of Empire*, BMW 16 (Sheffield, UK: Sheffield Phoenix, 2008).

that the assertion of solidarity in the pronoun inevitably excludes someone.[86] It is not possible for me to interact with scholars from less privileged contexts than my own and not be aware that I am part of a *we* that excludes them and that my experiences of the world may lead me to conclusions about biblical texts that hardly seem self-evident to them. There is no clear border where *we* ends and *they* begins, however, and as Althea Spencer Miller argues, it is not possible to impose a clear-cut binary distinction as we try to determine who is more and less privileged. Jamaican women, she writes, may not be minorities in Jamaica, but they are in the field of biblical studies, and while women of European descent are less privileged than men of the same background, they also have benefited from the victimization of others in a way that women of color generally have not. Her point, of course, is that the same person can be both more and less central and privileged, depending on the context in which they find themselves.[87] Some students and scholars reading this book will immediately recognize that, like me, they inhabit positions of greater socioeconomic privilege than the vast majority of the planet's population, but for others the case will be more complicated. Shanell Smith, for example, writes that her approach to reading biblical texts reflects both her minoritized status and her status as a scholar, which provides her with greater socioeconomic privilege than most other African American women have, and so, she says, she is both victimized by and benefits from repressive social forces.[88]

Anyone with enough educational background to interact with key concepts of academic biblical hermeneutics will already be privileged to some degree, and there will always be others less privileged to whom we must turn for hermeneutical guidance. I am hoping that all readers will find this book enlightening, then, but part of its message to more privileged readers is that we will have little to contribute to emancipatory dialogue before we do quite a bit of listening. The hope is that there is a larger *we* that can be forged in the field based on liberative rather than historical assumptions and goals, although it would not be a group that could ignore

86. Jione Havea, "Wet Bible: Stor(y)ing Jonah with Sia Figiel," in *Sea of Readings: The Bible in the South Pacific*, ed. Jione Havea, SemeiaSt 90 (Atlanta: Society of Biblical Literature, 2018), 47.
87. Althea Spencer Miller, "Feminist Pedagogies: Implications of a Liberative Praxis," in *Feminist New Testament Studies: Global and Future Perspectives*, ed. Kathleen O'Brien Wicker, Althea Spencer Miller, and Musa W. Dube, RCC (New York: Palgrave Macmillan, 2005), 28; and see also Kwok Pui-lan, *Postcolonial Imagination and Feminist Theology* (London: SCM, 2005), 17–18.
88. Shannel T. Smith, *The Woman Babylon and the Marks of Empire: Reading Revelation with a Postcolonial Womanist Hermeneutics of Ambiveilence* (Minneapolis: Fortress, 2014), 11–12.

the many differences between different interpreters from different cultures and socioeconomic strata, the many *theys*, in other words. The existence of a broader group within biblical studies interpreting with liberative goals in mind would not erase differences between the more and less privileged, nor between different marginalized groups struggling against dehumanization, each of which encounters oppression in different forms and cultural contexts, and each of which must therefore find its own strategies for combating it. More privileged scholars like me will not be able to provide them with liberative interpretations and approaches, although hopefully our role as dialogue partners will both provide less privileged groups with useful resources and help more privileged readers enable our communities to see the need to liberate ourselves from worldviews that prevent us from noticing how we participate in oppression and how we might act against it in our own contexts.

Yet even if the larger field changes in the ways that I hope it will, one could always argue that this is unlikely to make much of a difference in the larger world, since there is only so much influence scholarly work done in a discipline in the humanities can have. This is true, although simply to maintain that something is difficult or likely to have little positive effect is not an ethical argument for giving up on liberative struggles. The same limited influence exists for the field of philosophy but, writes Rorty, that should not stop philosophers from promoting tolerance and an open democratic society, because that sort of work "is just one more nudge in the right direction—the sort of modest little contribution to social progress to which a somewhat peripheral academic discipline may aspire."[89] We could apply the same sentiment to biblical studies, but because many of us teach students who will go on to be leaders in churches, synagogues, and other religious organizations, students for whom the study of the Bible is of some importance, it is possible that a field widely devoted to liberative readings could have even a bit more influence than philosophy as we urge our students to follow the lead of marginalized scholars who prioritize and promote liberative readings and urge them to ask those who will look to them for religious guidance to do likewise.

In an attempt to create this *we*, this field with a broader commitment to prioritizing liberation in biblical interpretation, it will not always be easy for those

89. Richard Rorty, *Truth and Progress: Philosophical Papers*, vol. 3 (Cambridge: Cambridge University Press, 1998), 58.

trained to assume that historical method must take priority over anything else to join this group. It will seem odd to say, as some pragmatists do, that good interpretation is whatever serves our purposes[90] rather than something necessarily grounded in historical work, and that rational objectivity amounts to adhering to what one's group believes[91] since we can only justify our interpretations and the reasoning through which we reach them by appealing to other interpretations and beliefs our communities find credible, not to some sort of text-in-itself that exists outside of the meanings humans have created.[92] If we want to forge such a group that includes many people who are part of mainstream biblical scholarship or who are being educated in it, but who currently do not see any way out of prioritizing historical work or how to argue that liberative goals and the concerns of the marginalized should take precedence over this and need not be judged by it, then it will be important for them to see that they need not do any historical work to understand the biblical texts. That, then, is the goal of chapters 2 and 3, after which I will argue in chapters 4 through 6 that if there is an ethical *we* to be forged in the field, it is one that should be based in the leadership of minoritized scholars fighting for liberation.

90. Jeffrey Stout, "What Is the Meaning of a Text?," NLH 14 (1982): 1–12; Rorty, *Objectivity, Relativism, and Truth*, 89.
91. Richard Rorty, *Philosophy and the Mirror of Nature* (Princeton, NJ: Princeton University Press, 1980), 361.
92. Fish, Is *There a Text in This Class?*, 342; Richard Rorty, *Consequences of Pragmatism (Essays: 1972–1980)* (Minneapolis: University of Minnesota Press, 1982), 154.

2

The Meaningful Text

The Historical Critical Method and the Speaking Text

As I set off to show that biblical scholarship should privilege the concerns of marginalized communities in its work, I need to establish that the field should be driven by ethical concerns rather than by methodological ones. I begin that discussion in this chapter by arguing that there is no reason why academics must do historical research in order to understand what biblical texts say, which is an argument that, for readers who accept it, can make it easier to privilege our ethical commitments to liberation in our research and teaching. I aim to show here that texts that can have meaning for us, things we can make sense of and discuss, are the creations of readers. It is a claim that many in the discipline will find counterintuitive, and to explain the idea I devote this chapter to a distinction between what I will call the physical text—the marks that readers physically see on the page—and the meaningful text. The meaningful text is a product of reading, of the interpretation and analysis that any reader must undertake when working with any text, and so the meaningful text is the production of the reader, the end result of interpretation. Readers complete the creation of the meaningful text when they believe they have arrived at understanding, when they conclude that interpretive work has provided them with meaning. This work relies on the physical text for evidence, but only when the meaningful text is created is there something that readers can understand and discuss; only then is there something other readers can disagree with on the basis of different meaningful texts they have created. And if the text in the sense of something that can have meaning for us is our creation, then there is no necessary connection between authorial intention or ancient historical context and the meanings readers create. Readers could always decide they want to investigate the question of what an author was trying to say in a particular passage, but I will argue over the course of the following chapters that this decision should be driven in all cases by an ethical commitment to addressing liberative issues raised by the marginalized.

If we think of the phrase *meaningful text* as being synonymous with the word *interpretation*, then perhaps this idea is not terribly difficult to understand, for we have all had the experience of arriving at an interpretation of a series of dots and lines that makes up a physical text only to find it is fairly different from interpretations that others have created. Academic readers disagree as to the meanings of texts all the time, and anyone familiar with sectarian disputes in Christianity and Judaism is aware that the same can be said about the ways different religious groups argue over how to understand particular passages. My argument here is that there is nothing inherent to the physical text itself that limits our interpretations, for as a set of dots and lines on a page, the physical text cannot limit or do anything else at all, and if we decide to take these marks as evidence of some sort of meaning, then we are the ones who are responsible for producing that meaning. This distinction between a physical and meaningful text is my own terminology and not a common way that biblical scholars have of talking about texts, but it is a heuristic device that is a more helpful way of understanding the relation of meaning and texts than the concept of the speaking text employed by some scholars committed to historical criticism, who describe the text as having a voice, as I will discuss in this section of the chapter. From their standpoint, it is the job of biblical scholars to listen to the voice of the text, something that is best done with the historical critical method. So when Krister Stendahl distinguished between the primary historical focus of biblical scholars and the work of others to apply the texts to contemporary issues, the point of this separation was, as chapter 1 discusses, to allow academics to produce "the original in its own terms," what a biblical text "meant when uttered or written by the prophet, the priest, the evangelist or the apostle."[1]

And while many mainstream biblical scholars committed to the necessity and priority of historical study might not agree with Stendahl that there is a distinction between what the texts meant to their authors and what they now mean to their readers,[2] they sometimes do write about biblical texts as acting like people, just as

1. Stendahl, "Biblical Theology," 11–44 (quotations from pp. 29 and 22, respectively).
2. For example, as part of an argument for the necessity of historical criticism, John Barton writes that "the texts mean what they mean, what they have always meant" (*Nature of Biblical Criticism*, 102).

Stendahl does when he refers to "the original in its own terms." *Terms*, of course, are things that people have and communicate through speech and other means. Like Stendahl, David Law, for example, writes about the need to "treat the text on its own terms," and the terms the text sets down demand that it be investigated with the historical critical method. It is in this way, Law says, that we will "allow the voice of the text itself to be heard."[3] Paul Joyce writes that "texts make some claim upon the reader," and Roy Harrisville also says there is "a claim made by the biblical text."[4] Discussing texts as if they were persons who could speak and have terms and make claims thus assumes that, like people, they have certain rights, as A. K. M. Adam notes.[5] As chapter 1 mentions, Hans de Wit writes of the ethical need to be accountable to the historical context of the text,[6] a sentiment echoed by F. W. Dobbs-Allsopp, who says that "respect for the other morally compels us to strive for a just estimation of the past on its own terms,"[7] and by Larry Hurtado, who says that deference to the ancient authors is the ethical basis of a historical critical approach that aims "to respect the text as it is."[8] When thinking of texts as speaking, we think of them as people, in which case it would logically follow that we would have ethical obligations to them as we do to actual humans and so need to take their speech seriously.

Sometimes arguments for the necessity of historical criticism combine the sense of the text as having personhood in some way with vaguer ontological terms, such as when Stendahl writes about "the material itself" to which historical critics pay

3. Law, *Historical-Critical Method*, 235–36.
4. See Paul Joyce, "First among Equals? The Historical-Critical Approach in the Marketplace of Methods," in *Creating the Boundaries: Essays in Biblical Interpretation in Honour of Michael D. Goulder*, ed. Stanley E. Porter, Paul Joyce, and David E. Orton, BIS 8 (Leiden: Brill, 1994), 23; and Roy A. Harrisville, *Pandora's Box Opened: An Examination and Defense of Historical-Critical Method and Its Master Practitioners* (Grand Rapids, MI: Eerdmans, 2014), 173. Although both Joyce and Harrisville make these statements in the context of discussing the necessity of historical interpretation, they understand the claims that the texts make differently. Joyce writes that historical criticism grounds the texts in their historical contexts and that this provides texts with ethical claims that rule out reading the Hebrew Bible / Old Testament in light of New Testament texts ("First among Equals?," 23–24). Harrisville, on the other hand, argues that the historical meaning of biblical texts cannot be separated from the ways in which those texts were later received, and so it is not illegitimate to read texts from the Hebrew Bible / Old Testament in the ways in which New Testament writers understood them (*Pandora's Box Opened*, 167–68), since the claim he believes biblical texts make is to a Christian message.
5. Adam, *Faithful Interpretation*, 58.
6. de Wit, "Exegesis and Contextuality," 24–25.
7. F. W. Dobbs-Allsopp, "Rethinking Historical Criticism," *BibInt* 7 (1999): 268.
8. Larry W. Hurtado, "New Testament Studies at the Turn of the Millennium: Questions for the Discipline," SJT 52 (1999): 174–76, quotation from p. 176.

attention in their interpretation,[9] or when James Barr says that historical study "turns to the Bible in itself."[10] It is possible that claims like these are related to the idea that the biblical texts, as links between us readers and their authors, exist individually of and prior to those of us who are interpreting them. Harrisville writes that "the observation is irritatingly obvious that the text has a temporal priority. However attractive the notion that the interpreter gives life to the text, the text is there, it exists ahead of, prior to, the interpreter. If it were not already there, there would be nothing to interpret."[11] Because of this priority, he writes, "the interpreter is not in control."[12] Dobbs-Allsopp makes a similar point when he refers to the text as "a reality independent of the critic." Historical facts are things that interpreters must use their imaginations to make sense of, he writes, "but a substantiality there is. Stars and mountains do exist, and they are not simply figments of our interpretive imaginations."[13] His point is that texts, like stars and mountains, exist independently of and prior to observers, so interpreters have to deal with what is there and not simply replace it with whatever they would like to see.

It is not difficult to connect this understanding of the text as "a reality independent of the critic" and as having "temporal priority" to the concept of the speaking text, at least once we have decided that the biblical texts are the medium through which their ancient authors communicate. When scholars refer to the texts as speaking and as having terms, they are obviously using metaphors, since texts cannot literally speak or do anything else; on one level, they are simply a series of dots and lines on a page. But if we decide to see them as a way to hear the speech of their authors, then we can see why scholars might metaphorically refer to them as speaking, and why they might then insist we should devote our resources to learning as much as we can about the historical and linguistic contexts of those ancient authors. Yet the concept of a text speaking on behalf of its author, and so the metaphor of the speaking text, will be misleading if one believes it can function as an argument for the necessity of techniques associated with the historical critical method to interpret biblical texts. This is because one can inadvertently understand such metaphors to mean that the text itself can guide us toward its

9. Stendahl, "Biblical Theology," 21–22.
10. Barr, *History and Ideology*, 49.
11. Harrisville, *Pandora's Box Opened*, 165.
12. Harrisville, 167.
13. Dobbs-Allsopp, "Rethinking Historical Criticism," 265.

already existing meaning, something Harrisville certainly implies when he writes that the text must become "the interpreter's interpreter."[14] Language like this suggests the text is a person who really can speak and have terms and is not merely a stand-in for one. And if we say that the text must guide and limit our work as we attempt to determine its meaning, that we must "respect the text as it is," then we are thinking of it as a person who could interrupt and correct our interpretations of its words and sentences.

But texts cannot literally interrupt and correct us, and to refer to them as speaking or limiting or as having terms is to suggest that we have already basically determined what a given text means before we even start our investigation. A text can take no action; it cannot literally guide or limit us, unless we have already taken action on its behalf, specifying the limits of what it can mean, and that, of course, is our action, not the text's. We clearly could not rely on something meaningless to guide us and compare to our interpretation, because if something has no meaning, then we obviously cannot understand it and cannot use it to do anything. We embark on exegesis to determine what the text means, yet if we say we are guided in this work by "the text as it is" we simply seem to insist that we have already determined the meaning of the text and that we will make it say what we have already predetermined it should say. To use metaphors that refer to the text as something that can speak like a person and answer the different questions we put to it really only hides the fact that interpreters and not authors determine its meaning, as some biblical scholars have pointed out, a matter that the next section of the chapter will pursue in more depth. Mary Ann Tolbert, for example, writes that historical criticism is better suited than other forms of interpretation to hiding the fact that the interpreter is creating meaning,[15] and Dale Martin refers to the belief that the texts speak and provide us with their meanings, even when such meanings might be used to support oppression, as "the sin of Christian textual foundationalism."[16] The belief in a speaking text, writes Vincent Wimbush, was used by Europeans to justify their project of colonization, and it was an important part of their construction of a world in which they believed those of European descent

14. Harrisville, *Pandora's Box Opened*, 162.
15. Tolbert, "When Resistance Becomes Oppression," 2:343–44.
16. Dale B. Martin, *Sex and the Single Savior: Gender and Sexuality in Biblical Interpretation* (Louisville, KY: Westminster John Knox, 2006), 1–3.

should control the planet and hold people they deemed to be of lesser status and sophistication as slaves.[17] To say that we must listen to what the text in itself says is to use a metaphor that can hide the fact that we have already spoken for it, and then claim we are powerless to control the authority of this speech, no matter how ethically questionable it might be.

Perhaps the easiest way to deal with this problem is simply to say that metaphors that describe the text as speaking or otherwise acting or having the status as a person are not very helpful ones to use. One could abandon such metaphors and still argue, as J. J. M. Roberts does, that the Bible is not readable unless we can translate the ancient languages in which it was written and have some awareness of the literary conventions the authors followed, something that demands the historical study of languages no longer spoken and of literary genres used in cultures that no longer exist. Many biblical stories allude to places and figures of which we would know nothing had historians not put serious effort into the study of ancient Palestine, the Near East, and the Eastern Mediterranean and their languages and cultures, and so the more historical work we can do to decipher such things, the more we will know about what an author was trying to say, Roberts argues.[18] But while the ancient origins of the texts make it appear self-evident that it is not possible to arrive at meaning without doing historical work that would allow us, metaphorically speaking, to listen to the voice of the text, that is simply untrue. Many people, including scholars, come to conclusions about what biblical texts mean without any sort of historical investigation. Mercy Oduyoye, for example, writes that Africans can feel an affinity with and locate themselves in the Bible's cultures and social structures. They feel as if they have experienced the same sort of history the Bible narrates: the takeover of their land by others; ethnic strife and tribalism; rules governing what one eats; the connection between religion and all other aspects of life; and so on.[19] Sam Tshela echoes this point, at least in regard to the Basotho, who, he says, simply do not see an important historical difference

17. See, for example, Vincent L. Wimbush, *White Men's Magic: Scripturalization as Slavery* (Oxford: Oxford University Press, 2012), 52–54, 60–66.
18. J. J. M. Roberts, "Historical-Critical Method, Theology, and Contemporary Exegesis," in *Biblical Theology: Problems and Perspectives in Honor of J. Christiaan Becker*, ed. Steven J. Kraftchick, Charles D. Myers Jr., and Ben C. Ollenberger (Nashville, TN: Abingdon, 1995), 131–41.
19. Mercy Amba Oduyoye, "Biblical Interpretation and the Social Location of the Interpreter: African Women's Reading of the Bible," in Segovia and Tolbert, *Reading from This Place*, 2:35–36.

between themselves and the biblical stories.[20] African slaves in the United States identified with the enslaved Israelites of the exodus story, writes Allen Callahan,[21] and, says Raquel St. Clair, African American women feel a deep connection to the imagery of the cross and Jesus as a cosufferer who can understand their experience as being treated as less than human, and these interpreters use no techniques of historical criticism to arrive at their understandings of biblical stories and conclusions about their importance.[22] Dalit Christians in India find a "natural affinity" with the experiences of marginalized communities in biblical texts, writes Kondasingu Jesurathnam,[23] and queer biblical scholars can look to forge relations and identifications with biblical figures, making connections across time, says Joseph Marchal.[24] These attitudes toward biblical texts fly in the face of the notion that the cultural distance between modern and ancient societies is unbridgeable without historical work. Madipoane Masenya describes the many similarities she sees between the proverbs of ancient Israel and those of the Sotho and the similarities between the two cultures this illuminates;[25] Gregory Cuéllar points to the overlap in themes, purpose, and imagery between Isaiah 40–55 and the *corridos* or songs that arose out of the Mexican immigrant experience in the United States;[26] Mmpula Lefe discusses the ways in which her experience as a Motswana woman allows her to grasp the social location of the story of 2 Kings 5:1–19;[27] R. S. Wafula refers to the similarities in the political relationships between empire and the colonized in

20. Sam Tshela, "Uncelebrated Readers of the Bible: The Illustrative Case of Early Basotho Christians," in Dube, Mbuvi, and Mbuwayesango, *Postcolonial Perspectives*, 110.
21. Allen Dwight Callahan, *The Talking Book: African Americans and the Bible* (New Haven, CT: Yale University Press, 2006), 86.
22. St. Clair, *Call and Consequences*, 4–6. St. Clair, however, argues that it would be more helpful for African American women to identify with Jesus's healing and his assistance toward the poor (p. 20).
23. Kondasingu Jesurathnam, *Dalit Liberative Hermeneutics: Indian Christian Dalit Interpretation of Psalm 22* (Delhi: ISPCK, 2010), xvi.
24. Joseph A. Marchal, "How Soon Is (This Apocalypse) Now? Queer Velocities after a Corinthian Already and a Pauline Not Yet," in *Sexual Disorientations: Queer Temporalities, Affects, Theologies*, ed. Kent L. Brintall, Joseph A. Marchal, and Stephen D. Moore, TTC (New York: Fordham University Press, 2018), 47.
25. Madipoane Masenya (ngwana' Mphahlele), "Wisdom and Wisdom Converge: Selected Old Testament and Northern Sotho Proverbs," in *Interpreting the Old Testament in Africa: Papers from the International Symposium on Africa and the Old Testament in Nairobi, October 1999*, ed. Mary Getui, Knut Holter, and Victor Zinkuratire, BTA 2 (New York: Peter Lang, 2001), 133–46.
26. Gregory Lee Cuéllar, *Voices of Marginality: Exile and Return in Second Isaiah 40–55 and the Mexican Immigrant Experience*, AUS 7/271 (New York: Peter Lang, 2008), 82–95, 105–34.
27. Mmpula Lefe, "Reading the Bible amidst the HIV and AIDS Pandemic in Botswana," in Wit and West, *African and European Readers of the Bible*, 289–96.

postexilic Israel and postcolonial Kenya;[28] and this list could go on and on. Its point, however, is that the claim that important aspects of biblical meaning are impossible to reach without historical criticism is not universally shared.

One could always conclude that these scholars and communities should not be so sure that they understand the biblical texts as well as they claim to and that historical work has to be done to see if what they believe about the texts is actually true. Such a conclusion would, of course, position those who practice the historical critical method as the final arbiters of meaning and is based in the assumption that what really matters about the texts is what they meant to their ancient audiences and authors. Since, however, it is interpreters who create meaning by producing interpretations, it might seem that aiming to discover what an ancient author was trying to say is up to individual interpreters and what they deem to be the best and necessary ways to approach texts. Unless one believes there is some sort of meaning inherent to the physical text, the assertion that the only valid meaning a text can have is the one an author intended for it is just that, an assertion, given that readers with no training in historical criticism appear to make sense of biblical texts all the time. One could make the argument that they are not making the right sense of the texts, but that would be an argument, not a claim made by inanimate marks on a page. But while interpreters uninterested in determining authorial intention might not see any need to do historical work, it would be fair to say that they are relying on historical work done by others if, for example, they were to use dictionaries of biblical Hebrew and New Testament Greek to look up words, or if they rely on translations scholars have produced. To use the historical work of others is not, however, the same thing as doing historical work oneself, and the mere use of a biblical Hebrew lexicon in interpretation does not make a reader a historian any more than using an English dictionary to look up a word I do not know in an English-language text makes me a lexicographer. So while I am not arguing that no aspects of historical study produced by the modern field are useful, I am arguing that one can create a valid academic interpretation of a biblical text without doing any historical work at all. As I explain in the following chapters, I have no wish to maintain that historical criticism should not be a part of biblical studies, I simply believe the method should be peripheral and not central to the field.

28. R. S. Wafula, *Biblical Representations of Moab: A Kenyan Postcolonial Reading*, BTA 19 (New York: Peter Lang, 2014), 17–19, 26–30.

The metaphor of the speaking text understands the text to be the way authors communicate, and while authors do communicate through texts, we are under no particular obligation to aim to have our interpretations correspond to what authors were trying to say, unless we belong to a community of interpreters that says we must do so when in particular contexts. This, at least, is the argument that I will pursue in the rest of this and the following chapter. In the next section of this chapter, I intend to show that it helps to distinguish between a physical and meaningful text as we consider the relation between text and meaning. To see only "the text" can make us miss the fact that, while the author may have been responsible for the marks on the page, the physical text that exists before we begin our interpretive work, the interpreter is the one responsible for recognizing those marks as evidence and producing a meaningful text that creates understanding. There is nothing wrong with referring to what a text says or does or urges or demands, so long as we are clear that this is the meaningful text we have produced in interpretation. And once we no longer assume that meaning must be connected to authorial intention or historical context, then we can see historical critical work is not necessary, although we are perfectly free to use its techniques if we wish to. The ideal of method need not stand in the way of the ideal of liberation, as later chapters argue, and method should be determined by the liberative goals readers have.

The Meaningful Text: The Example of the Story of Jephthah's Daughter

The claim that the text is something that readers create may not seem self-evident—Harrisville, we recall, stated that it is "irritatingly obvious" that the text precedes the reader and so that it claims priority and control over the interpreter, and Dobbs-Allsopp referred to the physical presence of the text, like the stars and mountains, as something that preexists interpreters and that they must deal with. And they appear to raise good points: How can we interpret if there is not already a text that is there, something we encounter on the page in front of us that we must sit down and look at and interpret, and if that is the case, how could the text be the reader's creation? My argument about the text as the production of the interpreter acknowledges the fact that there obviously is a physical text that preexists interpreters and that we obviously can use the word *text* to refer to the lines and dots that we see printed on the page (or carved into stone or pressed into clay), something I am calling the physical text. But I also refer to the meaningful text, a text that we can understand and make truth claims about, something that we can associate with meaning.[29] Meaning is the production of someone's work of interpretation, and it is that work, which uses the physical text as evidence, that produces the meaningful text. We are aware of the physical text as light reflects off of it and strikes our corneas, but that is not a terribly interesting sense of the word *text*. When we talk about texts, we are generally interested in what they mean, what their significance is, and when someone cannot decipher the writing system or language in which a text is written, then they will admit, if they are honest, that they cannot read or interpret it. If someone who knows biblical Hebrew, for example, were to look at a biblical text written in that language with someone who had no training in Hebrew, both would be looking at the same physical text, but it would not be possible for the non-Hebrew reader to create a meaningful text on the basis of the marks on the page. Both can see the physical text, in other words, but only one is able to use it as evidence in the creation of a meaningful text. If a number of interpreters who can read biblical Hebrew disagree as to the meaning, then they will have produced multiple meaningful texts on the basis of the evidence of a single physical text. They need not literally write them down; I am thinking of a meaningful text as the end result of interpretation, what one has when, after reading and analysis, one says, "I understand."

This distinction between a physical and meaningful text might seem counterintuitive, since in our normal experience the difference between the two does not really seem to matter. We have all had the experience of reading the same work independently of other people, only to discover that we agree as to what it says. Having this sort of experience over and over makes it appear as if meaning is simply present in the physical text, waiting for readers to come and properly interpret it. Moreover, we have all had the experience of learning things or being changed in some other way by reading, and if we are the ones who create the text and its meaning, it might seem difficult to explain how we could learn or otherwise change ourselves through our own process of the creation of the

29. In formulating this distinction between physical and meaningful text, I am relying in part on arguments that Richard Rorty makes in *Objectivity, Relativism, and Truth*, 78–92.

text,[30] so this too suggests that meaning must be directly related in some way to the physical text.

Perhaps the only thing in our general experience that might even suggest that readers are entirely responsible for the creation of meaningful texts is when two or more people or groups differ radically in regard to the meaning of the same writing. Anyone with experience working in the field of biblical studies has encountered many cases like this, and it is perhaps easiest to illustrate the distinction between the physical and meaningful text by using one such example of disagreements among interpreters, since concrete examples make theoretical ideas easier to grasp. I turn, then, to six different interpretations of the story of Jephthah's daughter in Judges 11:29–40, just one of the literally thousands of biblical passages where we can find important discrepancies among scholarly readings but also one in which the interpreters have no disagreements in regard to the marks on the page, what I am calling the physical text. In these verses, Jephthah is the head of the Israelite forces fighting the Ammonites, and he vows to God that, should God give him victory, he will sacrifice whatever (*'ăšer*) comes out of his house to meet him on his return. The ambiguity of the Hebrew word *'ăšer* does not rule out the sacrifice of a human being—that is, we could translate the word as "whoever" rather than "whatever," because *'ăšer* can be used in both senses—and since it is his daughter who comes out of his house to meet him as she celebrates his victory, he sacrifices her in order to fulfill his vow, an act with which she seems to be in agreement. "Do to me as it went out from your mouth," she says to her father in an apparent reference to the vow he spoke, asking only for permission to go to the mountains with her companions to mourn before the sacrifice (Judg 11:36).

The story of Jephthah's daughter is one that I have written about before, and in my analysis of it—in the interpretation or meaningful text that I created, I could say—I related it to the larger literary context in which the story appears, that of the so-called Deuteronomistic History, or Dtr for short. Dtr is generally understood to consist of the books of Deuteronomy, Joshua, Judges, Samuel, and Kings, and while not all scholars of the Hebrew Bible / Old Testament believe that these

30. For objections like these to the notion that the meaning of the text is entirely the reader's creation, see, for example, Kevin J. Vanhoozer, *Is There a Meaning in This Text? The Bible, the Reader and the Morality of Literary Knowledge* (Leicester: Apollos, 1998), 169–71; and Thiselton, *Thiselton on Hermeneutics*, 514.

were all composed by the same author (or, scholars more frequently believe, by the same author with some later redactional or editorial insertions), many if not most do. I drew on this larger context of the story to argue that Jephthah's sacrifice of his daughter and her acquiescence to the act violate the law in Deuteronomy 12, a chapter within Dtr that prohibits child sacrifice to the God of Israel. The apparent belief of Jephthah and his daughter that God approves of the sacrifice, an assumption that neither the narrator nor God supports in this story, shows how neither of them is aware of the law code that begins in Deuteronomy 12 and runs for many chapters, a law code that, Moses repeatedly insists in Deuteronomy, Israel must adhere to if they wish to remain and prosper in the land (e.g., Deut 4:1–40; 6:1–25; 8:1–20). So the story of Jephthah's sacrifice of his daughter is, I argued, a critique on the part of Dtr's author (often called the Deuteronomist) of Israel's moral failure to learn and keep the law, something that is a constant theme of Dtr, particularly in the book of Judges, in which Israel repetitively violates divine law by worshipping foreign gods and is repetitively punished by their God for these violations. Jephthah would have avoided the murder by sacrificial ritual of his only child had either of them been aware that Israel's God explicitly forbade such a sacrifice in the law code contained in Dtr, just as Israel as a whole would have avoided its defeats in battle and removal from the promised land to Babylon that we read about in the book of Kings, at the end of Dtr, had they remained faithful to the law.[31] While my attempt to establish authorial intention in regard to the story consists largely of a close reading of the text, it still involves historical work when I assume that I can read the bulk of Deuteronomy through Kings as the composition of the same author, one who wrote after Israel had been destroyed and the people taken into exile in Babylon and who composed this work in Babylonian exile in order to explain why it occurred. For the purposes of my argument, the historical context of the writing is key, since it privileges authorial intention and assumes the intention behind the story of Jephthah's daughter can only be fully understood once we have some sense of the historical events the author was trying to explain.

I have hardly been the only one who has attempted to establish what the author of this story meant by it. Thomas Römer does so also, although he creates a very different interpretation or meaningful text in this regard than I do, even though

31. David Janzen, "Why the Deuteronomist Told the Story about the Sacrifice of Jephthah's Daughter," JSOT 29 (2005): 339–57.

we have no disagreements in regard to the physical text, the dots and lines that make up the Hebrew words and sentences in the passage. Because the human sacrifice in this narrative violates the prohibition against such an act in Dtr's law code, Römer writes, it is hard to believe that the Deuteronomist wrote the story of Jephthah's daughter. So he sees it as a much later insertion into the text by an editor or redactor, one who was aware of Euripides's version of the ancient Greek story of the sacrifice of Iphigenia by her father. God does not react to Jephthah's horrific sacrifice, just as the divine world in the story of Iphigenia is silent. For Römer, the story is not a good example of an important Deuteronomistic theme, as I claim, but a critique of one, specifically of the notion that God will intervene to save the innocent and punish the wicked. This is not a story that could have been added to Dtr until the Hellenistic period, writes Römer, since its author was obviously someone who knew Greek literature.[32] So Römer and I are both interested in what the author has to say, but we have identified two different authors located at two different points in history, one of whom writes the story in the historical context of the Babylonian exile to emphasize an important theme of Dtr and one of whom writes the story centuries later than that in order to critique an important emphasis of Dtr.

Peggy Day has also used historical criticism to read Judges 11:29–40, and like Römer she draws connections with the story of Iphigenia, but she also sees a parallel with the Greek story of Kore or Persephone, whose descent to and return from the underworld have been linked to rites of passage of ancient Greek females from childhood to a state of fertility. Day's point in drawing this parallel is not to establish a dating for the story in the Hellenistic period but to show how it, like the story of Kore, functioned as an explanation for an annual life-cycle ritual. Day believes such a ritual existed in ancient Israel to mark females' transition to maturity, since the conclusion of the story of Jephthah's daughter says that female Israelites commemorate her every year, repeating the act of mourning that she undertook in the story with her companions before her sacrifice. Day argues that by grounding this annual festival in the story of Jephthah's daughter, the author signals that, as young females transition into the social world of adults, they have to put the well-being of others before their own, just as Jephthah's daughter does

32. Thomas Römer, "Why Would the Deuteronomists Tell about the Sacrifice of Jephthah's Daughter?," JSOT 23 (1998): 27–38.

when she is willing to die so her father can fulfill his vow.[33] Day clearly does historical work here, most particularly in reconstructing the existence of an ancient Israelite ritual and in explaining the author's decision to create a story that links that ritual to a patriarchal worldview. In her interpretation—in the meaningful text she creates, that is—her emphasis is not really on how the story reflects the author's larger interests throughout Dtr but on how it provides meaning for a ritual that Day believes existed when the author was writing.

Esther Fuchs's interpretation of the story is not historically focused, and she instead reads the story of Jephthah's daughter alongside narratives of other women in Judges, some of whom, like the anonymous daughter, are victims of male violence, and some of whom stand up to male characters in the stories. The ideal daughter in Judges, she writes, is just like Jephthah's, virginal and innocent, doing her duty to her father by submitting to his wishes and to the nation by lauding his victory over Israel's enemies. The story, she writes, manages to portray Jephthah as a sympathetic character despite his sacrificial murder of his daughter, and Fuchs's interest lies not in trying to reconstruct some kind of authorial intent behind the story but in asking what impression it leaves in regard to the social place of women in the minds of readers.[34] Unlike my reading, for example, Fuchs's does not see the historical context of the story's author as key to understanding its meaning. The meaning she arrives at is not terribly different from the one Day presents—for both, the story points to the necessity of women to submit to the claims a patriarchal society makes on them—although authorial intention is not Fuchs's stated concern.

Juliana Claassens, in her reading of the story, specifically foregrounds the interests of contemporary women in Malawi, and she concludes that the story has a very different meaning from that advanced by Fuchs or Day. The story is in fact one about resistance to a patriarchal order, she writes; the annual ritual of mourning enacted by the women of Israel for Jephthah's daughter, which the end of the story reports, becomes a language of resistance that protests dominant and oppressive power structures. In Claassens's reading, the point of the annual ritual

33. Peggy L. Day, "From the Child Is Born the Woman: The Story of Jephthah's Daughter," in *Gender and Difference in Ancient Israel*, ed. Peggy Day (Minneapolis: Fortress, 1989), 58–74.
34. Esther Fuchs, *Feminist Theory and the Bible: Interrogating the Sources*, FSSTS (Lanham, MD: Lexington, 2016), 71–94.

is not to praise the daughter's obedience but to give voice and agency to women who believe that social structures that demand women's submission unto death to a patriarchal order are radically unjust. Claassens relates this to the resistance displayed by women in Malawi who use menstruation taboos to protect themselves from sexual contact with partners who could infect them with HIV: like the women of Israel in Judges 11, they use ritual and the protection it provides to protest the death sentence to which their society would condemn them.[35] So Claassens's interpretation or meaningful text is specifically focused on how the story can be encountered by a contemporary marginalized group, regardless of the specifics of authorial intention.

The same might be said of Valerie Cooper's interpretation of the story, and her meaningful text specifically foregrounds her experience as an African American woman, doubly marginalized by race and gender, just as Jephthah's daughter was doubly marginalized by her gender and social location. (Judg 11:2 tells us that Jephthah was the son of a prostitute, disinherited by his brothers and so able to live only on the margins of Israelite society.) Black women suffer for the men they love, writes Cooper, just as the daughter of the story suffers for her father, and they often find themselves in the situation of choosing between what will hurt them and what will hurt their men, just as Jephthah's daughter must choose between her own death and having her father fail to fulfill a vow made to God, a failure the daughter believed would result in his punishment at the hands of the divine world. In some cases, Cooper writes, all that is left for African American women is mourning, as is the case for the daughter who leaves with her female companions to mourn before returning for the sacrifice.[36] In the meaningful text she creates, Cooper emphasizes not authorial intention but the manner in which the story resonates with the experiences of a particular group of contemporary women.

So here are six different readings that refer to the same physical text, Judges 11:29–40. There are not any disagreements among us as to the dots and lines on

35. L. Juliana M. Claassens, *Claiming Her Dignity: Female Resistance in the Old Testament* (Collegeville, MN: Liturgical, 2016), 71–84.
36. Valerie C. Cooper, "Some Place to Cry: Jephthah's Daughter and the Double Dilemma of Black Women in America," in *Pregnant Passion: Gender, Sex, and Violence in the Bible*, ed. Cheryl A. Kirk-Duggan, SemeiaSt 44 (Atlanta: Society of Biblical Literature, 2003), 181–91.

the page, which is to say that there are no disagreements as to the physical text.[37] This agreement among us contrasts, however, with the noticeable disagreements as to the meaning of the story. Römer and I focus on authorial intention but draw opposite conclusions in regard to meaning, in part because we do not agree as to who the author was. Day is also interested in the question of authorial intention and uses techniques associated with historical criticism, although her interest is not in reading the story in relation to Dtr as a whole as mine was; like Römer, she finds more fruitful points of contact with ancient Greek literature rather than within the larger context of Dtr, although these connections serve different purposes for the two of them. The interpretation at which Fuchs arrives (or the meaningful text she creates in her interpretation) is like Day's—an ethical message that urges women to submit themselves to what a patriarchal society understands to be a higher moral good—yet she gets to her conclusion without doing historical work. That is also true of Claassens's approach, although her understanding of the moral significance of the story is largely the opposite of the one Fuchs and Day see, since Claassens concludes Judges 11:29–40 is about an ethic of resistance to oppressive social structures, not a story that urges accommodation to them. And Cooper, like Claassens, is interested in how the story reflects the experiences of a particular group of women of African descent, but for her the emphasis lies on mourning, not resistance. Cooper's scholarly work in general focuses on religion, race, and society, not biblical studies, and her analysis of the story of Jephthah's daughter does not exercise any of the techniques associated with the historical critical method.

Why is there such variety among these interpretations when none of us has any serious disagreements with the others about the wording of the text? The answer is not that some of us used historical criticism and focused on authorial intention while others did not, because those of us whose work aimed to get at the author's intentions came up with different and incompatible meanings. Authors can, of course, aim to communicate more than one message in a text, but that fact is not enough to explain this particular interpretive variety, since one of us concluded

37. This is not to say that there are no textual critical issues at all in Judges 11:29–40—it would seem that the Old Greek had a slightly different text than the Masoretic Text in 11:31, 35, and 36—but all of the interpreters in question read with the Masoretic Text throughout. For those readers not familiar with textual criticism or terms like *Old Greek* and *Masoretic Text*, some discussion of these issues appears in chapter 8.

the story emphasizes an important theme of Dtr and another that it contradicts a key theme of Dtr. This example leads us to an important point, although it is one that anyone with a modicum of experience in the field of biblical studies already knows: when different scholars aim to reach historical conclusions, including ones about authorial intention, they can disagree rather drastically. We can even see from our comparison of interpretations that readers are responsible for the creation of the authors, as well as their intentions, for I created an author called "the Deuteronomist," and Römer created one called "the redactor," and these creations were based on our readings of the text and of Deuteronomy through Kings as a whole.[38] But once I completed my analysis of Judges 11:29–40, I believed that I had arrived at the meaning that my author intended to convey. This meaning was my creation, since it was the result of my interpretation, but I believed that, if I could have a conversation with the author I thought was responsible for the story, they would agree with me. But it is, of course, only through this act of creation of meaning that I could have a text that I could discuss and make truth claims about. It was, in fact, only through my analysis of the books of Deuteronomy through Kings that I could have an author I could discuss and make truth claims about, since after analyzing those books, I came to the conclusion that they have so much in common that most of the material in them was composed by the same person. And in regard to Judges 11:29–40, it was not until I completed my interpretation, until I created meaning through my analysis, that I had anything that I could talk about in regard to the meaning of the text, although before that time I could have

38. It is because I see a basic unity of thought governing most of the material from Deuteronomy through Kings that, like other scholars, I come to the conclusion that one author is responsible for the bulk of that material and, following scholarly tradition, I call that author "the Deuteronomist." My interpretation, which creates a meaningful text, is predicated upon and reinforces my beliefs about authorship. Römer creates a different meaningful text, one where there is not as much unity of thought, and where passages like Judges 11:30–31 and 34–40 contradict important themes that run through those books. In the modern world—and not just in biblical studies—appeals to an author have given readers a handy way to make sense of texts, as Roland Barthes and Michel Foucault pointed out. Those familiar with biblical studies will be aware of many ways in which scholars do this; by referring to "the Deuteronomist" or to "Paul," for example, we justify readings we carry out. We feel that we can use Deuteronomy to help us make sense of Judges, and Galatians to help us make sense of Romans. But we are only able to create these authors and their beliefs and writing habits by creating the meaningful texts we believe they wrote, because, we have concluded, such texts exhibit unity of thought. In Römer's meaningful text of the Deuteronomistic History, "the Deuteronomist" is not responsible for Judges 11:30–31, 34–40, just as for New Testament scholarship in general "Paul" is not the author of 1 Timothy. See Roland Barthes, "The Death of the Author," in *Image Music Text*, trans. Stephen Heath (New York: Hill & Wang, 1977), 142–48; and Michel Foucault, "What Is an Author?," in *Language, Counter-Memory, Practice: Selected Texts and Interviews*, trans. Donald F. Bouchard and Sherry Simon (Ithaca, NY: Cornell University Press, 1977), 113–38.

talked about the meaning that others had created. My awareness of those other interpretations shaped the meaning I produced, in fact, an idea I shall return to in the next chapter.[39]

This exercise hopefully clarifies why I see it as useful to distinguish between the physical and meaningful texts. A meaningful text, whether or not it is actually written down, is my creation of meaning, whereas the physical text is not.[40] Yet when we talk about texts, we are normally involved in discussions about what they mean, and those conversations cannot take place until we have created the meaning through our analysis. On the basis of the comparison of the readings of the story of Jephthah's daughter, it does not seem that mere knowledge of the vocabulary and grammar of the text we are interpreting necessarily guarantees anything about the interpretation or meaning that a reader will create, even the meaning created by readers interested in authorial intention. We could say that a physical text is something that authors produce as they write marks on a page, and certainly this text precedes interpreters. But there is no meaning inherently associated with those dots and lines; interpreters have to decide that those marks are a particular kind of evidence and then use that evidence to create meaning, and only once they have done this, only once they have a meaningful text, are they in a position to make assertions about the meaning of a passage and have discussions about it. Two readers who both have a good knowledge of the vocabulary and grammar of a biblical language and who both work with the goal of searching for authorial intention can still arrive at very

39. Most readers of biblical texts are members of religious communities in which the Bible is understood to be authoritative in some sense, and many such readers will feel that quite a number of biblical texts are familiar even before they read them for the first time, since they are immersed in groups that have told and retold biblical stories. Hans Robert Jauss borrows from the thought of Gadamer in distinguishing between understanding as the meaning readers expect to find based on the traditions in which they are rooted, and interpretation as the work that their own readings actually accomplish (*Toward an Aesthetic of Reception*, trans. Timothy Bahti, THL 2 [Minneapolis: University of Minnesota Press, 1982], 139–46). Since interpreters have been formed by their communities and their traditions of understanding the texts, understanding in this sense will always shape interpretation.

40. Although, as those who have done work in textual criticism are aware, this latter claim is somewhat simplistic. This is an issue that will come up in chapter 8 in regard to a specific example of the interpretation of a text, but I can note briefly here that textual critics deal with ancient (or at least very old) textual witnesses to the same passage that disagree with each other, and they try to resolve such discrepancies. Insofar as they do such work, their conclusions as to what a biblical author originally wrote in Hebrew or Greek produce a physical text. When we take textual criticism into account, that is, then the physical text, at least within the discipline of biblical studies, is also a scholarly construction.

different interpretations—or can produce very different meaningful texts—when looking at the same series of dots and lines. Readers do indeed take the physical text to be evidence when they read, but evidence and meaning constructed on the basis of that evidence are two different things. A gun can be presented in a courtroom as evidence of a crime, but what the gun means, how it functions as evidence, what its significance is in regard to the case being decided by the court, will depend on the narrative that an attorney is able to establish in regard to it. A meaningful text is, in essence, a narrative established in regard to a physical text; letters and words and sentences on a page have no meaning until someone speaks for them, provides a narrative that makes sense of them as evidence. The narrative could appear as a translation, a commentary, a sermon, a civil rights rally, a series of thoughts one has, an academic monograph, or something else. In a courtroom, the prosecuting and defense attorneys will discuss the same pieces of evidence but will often construct very different narratives around them, and as we have seen, different biblical scholars can do the same thing when dealing with the same physical text. The evidence in both cases has no meaning until it becomes part of someone's narrative, and different interpreters can construct very different narratives for the same piece of physical evidence. The physical evidence itself, however, whether a biblical text in a scholarly argument or a gun in a courtroom, cannot do or mean anything at all until narratives are created around it, and even at that point it is really those who create the narratives who are responsible for what the evidence means or does.

There is one aspect of the comparison of the different interpretations of Judges 11:29–40 that might seem to undermine the distinction between physical and meaningful texts that I am trying to draw: there was broad agreement among the interpreters as to the series of events in the story, and this is why I felt that it was uncontroversial to summarize them at the beginning of this exercise. None of us disagreed in major ways in this regard, none of us thought Judges 11:29–40 is a narrative about a circus, or a romance, or invaders from Mars. How could we be in such agreement if the text itself were not guiding us to the same conclusions? One way to answer this question is to follow something like Wolfgang Iser's explanation of interpretation, one received favorably by some biblical scholars. All texts have gaps, writes Iser, because no text can describe the world or characters the author creates in an infinitely complete manner. A gap or blank is "a vacancy in the overall system of the text," and readers have to fill these in themselves.[41] This is a continuous task for them as they make their way through a given text, and as they do so they constantly reformulate their overall conception of what the text means. Each segment of the text means something only in relation to its other sections, but it is readers who have to fill in the gaps between the sections and organize them in relation to each other, and so they are, in effect, responsible for the creation of structure and meaning as they interact with the text.[42] For Iser, a text is present prior to the reader, as Harrisville and Dobbs-Allsopp argue, but Iser says the text limits the meanings readers can come up with because they are only filling in blanks. The text "allows a spectrum of actualizations," as he puts it; texts "initiate 'performances' of meaning rather than actually formulating meaning themselves."[43] Authors' ideal readers would be exactly like themselves and would fill in the gaps in their texts just as they would,[44] but real readers cannot just give up their own beliefs and inhabit someone else's, and so different readers will actualize meaning in different ways.[45] Texts can guide interpretation for Iser, but meaning is ultimately the product that readers create through their interactions with the text.[46]

So perhaps Iser's approach allows us to make sense of both the similarities and the variety among the interpreters of the story of Jephthah's daughter that we saw in the example. We could conclude that the similarities among the readings reflect meaning present in the text and that the differences reflect the gap-filling each interpreter embarked on. And certainly some biblical scholars see something like Iser's understanding of the relation between author, text, readers, and meaning as a useful way of explaining why different readers can legitimately arrive at different meanings while still preserving the text itself as something that exercises some sort of power or authority that limits the conclusions readers can come to. Anthony Thiselton, for example, refers to Iser's conclusions about texts and meanings and says that readers concretize potential already present in the text,[47] while Daniel Patte also sounds like Iser in claiming that texts do not have meanings but

41. Wolfgang Iser, *The Act of Reading: A Theory of Aesthetic Response* (London: Routledge & Kegan Paul, 1978), 180–83.
42. Iser, 183–85, 195–98.
43. Quotations from Iser, 24, 26–27.
44. Iser, 28–29.
45. Iser, 36–38.
46. Iser, 9–10.
47. Thiselton, *Thiselton on Hermeneutics*, 490–92.

"potentialities of meaning" that can be actualized, something that can control interpretation even as different readers organize it into different meanings.[48] Brian Blount does not rely on Iser, although his view of the connection between text, interpreter, and meaning sounds much like Iser's approach as he argues that aspects of the text such as its grammar should influence interpretation, but that meaning also relies on the belief system of the interpreter. The result, he writes, is that a text cannot mean just anything, but the same sentence can have different meanings for different interpreters,[49] a sentiment echoed by Justin Ukpong.[50]

In the end, however, Iser's approach does not work to support the argument that there is some sort of meaning associated with physical marks on a page that somehow exists independently of the work of interpreters. Interpreters will always have to do the work of looking at the dots and lines and deciding what kind of evidence they provide as they work to create meaning. Simply because a group of readers might agree in regard to some aspects of the meaning of a given work, such as the way that the six interpreters in our example agreed as to the series of events in the story of Judges 11:29–40, does not mean that a text "allows a spectrum of actualizations" or that texts "initiate 'performances' of meaning," as Iser puts it. The physical text, as we know, is not a person and cannot "allow" or "initiate" anything. By granting the text personhood, something that can initiate and perform, Iser simply returns us to the concept of a speaking text, a metaphor based on the premise that inanimate objects are animate.[51] But by distinguishing between the physical text, an inanimate object that humans can decide to see as evidence, and the meaningful text, the narrative they create based on how they have decided to understand that evidence, we are able to affirm both that a text preexists interpreters and that interpreters create the text, because we are thinking of two different things. If this still leaves unresolved the mystery as to how we six interpreters of the passage ended up in agreement in regard to the series of events in the story of Jephthah's daughter even while disagreeing in regard to other aspects of the passage, a fuller explanation will

48. Patte, *Ethics of Biblical Interpretation*, 93–99.
49. Brian Blount, *Cultural Interpretation: Reorienting New Testament Criticism* (Minneapolis: Fortress, 1995), 7–16, 27–28.
50. Ukpong, "New Testament Hermeneutics in Africa," 156–57.
51. Stanley Fish provides a much fuller discussion of the kind of critique of Iser I have in mind in *Doing What Comes Naturally: Change, Rhetoric, and the Practice of Theory in Literary and Legal Studies*, PCI (Durham, NC: Duke University Press, 1989), 68–86.

have to wait until the next chapter, although a short version of it is that we were all taught how to read in very similar ways, which means that we will often look at the same textual evidence and, more often than not, agree as to the way in which we should make sense of it. This agreement, however, is not the result of anything an inanimate object does but of our work, which will be influenced by things such as our education, and when aspects of our education coincide with those of other interpreters, we should not be surprised when some aspects of our interpretations are similar as well.

Conclusion: The Reader as Author

I am making a distinction between physical and meaningful texts because I am suspicious of scholarly arguments that claim the text we see on the page demands that we privilege historical work and the search for authorial intention. The text acquires personhood in these arguments, a "voice" and "terms" that it cannot literally have, and the metaphor of the speaking text sometimes only hides the fact that interpreters speak for it. The text acquires some sort of vague ontological status—"the text in itself"—and according to some who view texts in these ways, all of these things apparently mean that biblical scholars must focus on authorial intention, since texts are able to limit the conclusions at which good interpreters can arrive. Whatever others might like to do with the texts, whatever concerns they may wish to bring to them, can only be done after biblical scholars have completed their historical work. This, at any rate, is the view of interpretation based on what I have been calling Stendahl's ditch, which stands between the primary historical work of biblical scholars and any other kind of interpretation someone might want to do and which insists that the validity of the latter is judged to at least some degree by the former.

One of the reasons I am suspicious of claims like this is precisely because they rely so heavily on metaphors for the personhood of texts, and these claims, minoritized scholars argue, keep liberative readings on the margins of the field, as we will see in chapter 4. Texts are not literally people, though, so why should interpretation have "respect for the text as it is"? Realizing that this claim is based on a metaphor, how should we literally interpret it? To say that it means we must privilege authorial intention only begs the question as to why interpretive work must focus on that, since interpreters are the ones responsible for creating meaning. Perhaps having respect for the text means that we should revere it so highly that we do no more than repeat it exactly as we see it on the page, dot for dot, line for line, and word for word. In the context of interpretation, however, this would be a ridiculous and useless exercise, because we would not see it as helpful for arriving at interpretation or meaning. If we want meaning, then we have to use the physical text as evidence as we work to create an interpretation that provides us with meaning, something we construct, and only at that point do we have a text that we can discuss or defend or ridicule. This is as true if the physical text is in English as it is if it is in biblical Hebrew or New Testament Greek. So, for example, we could have children who are native English speakers memorize the famous soliloquy from act 3 of *Hamlet*—the one that begins with "To be or not to be"—but we might also be unconvinced that they knew what it meant even after they had memorized it and could repeat it word for word (an exercise that demonstrates a certain kind of respect for the text). Can they explain the clause "'Tis a consummation devoutly to be wished," or "When he himself might his quietus make," or "Who would fardels bear?" If not, then we would know that they had not understood these clauses, even though they could repeat perfectly the words we see on the page. It would not be until they could tell us what these clauses meant, and what the soliloquy as a whole means, not until they could put these things *in their own words*, that we would be satisfied in regard to their interpretation. In establishing whether their interpretations, their words and sentences that explain the meaning of the soliloquy, are correct, we would not turn to the physical text that we are trying to make sense of. To say that "Who would fardels bear?" means "Who would fardels bear?" does not provide us with interpretation or meaning. Rather, in order to establish that the children really know what the soliloquy means, we would have to compare their interpretations with our own, judge their words about the text by ours. We would, in short, be comparing two creations of meaning, two interpretations or meaningful texts, and we would not be comparing a meaningful text to a physical text, because that does not help us establish meaning. Meaning will have to be our production, our own words, with the result that the original text—one that we can understand and that can be meaningful to us, at any rate—is our creation, because we can only make sense of words and sentences by explaining them with other words and sentences. It is the interpretation, and the meaning we create through it, that becomes the original text for us.[52] The more interpreters have in common, the more likely it is that they will come to similar conclusions about how to make sense of a text, as chapter 3 discusses, but if their belief systems diverge in important ways, we would expect the meaningful texts they create would also.

So if I want to show that the question "Who would fardels bear?" means, in the context of Hamlet's soliloquy, "The burden of sin and sorrow in this life isn't worth enduring," I cannot demonstrate this by returning to the line in the play. All that would accomplish is the repetition of the question, "Who would fardels bear?," the meaning of which I am trying to establish, and no one would understand this move as evidence that supports my explanation. To advance an interpretation, I can only use other words and sentences to make an argument for this. So the fact that a physical text preexisted all six of us interpreters of Judges 11:29–40 does not in and of itself enforce a universal limit on what that passage can mean, since the physical text is not meaningful, not something that can be understood before interpreters make it understandable, although readers will see it as a piece of evidence in the narrative that they construct, a narrative that is the reader's own interpretation and that thus is the meaning the reader creates. Only after interpreters have created meaning can they use their meaningful texts to critique different readings of the same story, which is to say different meaningful texts. Insofar as we can talk about texts that make sense to us as readers, meaning originates with interpreters, not authors (although authors are, of course, in the position of interpreting their own work), and so there is nothing about the physical texts authors create that necessitates the pursuit of authorial intention as we create meaningful texts. Interpreters are, in essence, the authors of meaningful texts. We could decide that we want to discover what an author meant as they composed a particular text—in most of the reading we do, we simply assume that the author would agree with our meaning—but there is no necessary connection between authorial intention and the meaning of the text. Whatever claims supporters of historical criticism might make, they cannot truthfully say that they turn to the text or have respect for it

52. This is Jacques Derrida's point in "Différance," trans. Alan Bass, in *A Derrida Reader: Between the Blinds*, ed. Peggy Kamuf (New York: Columbia University Press, 1991), 61–66. Derrida notes as well that our explanations of and commentaries on a text seem to have their basis in an original text where we see a reality or "a full presence" that lies beyond our discussions of it, but he points out that this original only exists in and through our discussions of it; see his "Structure, Sign and Play in the Discourse of the Human Sciences," in *Writing and Difference*, trans. Alan Bass (London: Routledge, 2001), 352–56.

while others do not, because there is no text they can read until they and/or the group of interpreters with whom they broadly agree create one, which puts them in the same position as everyone else.

It certainly is true that most readers of the Bible work with texts others have translated into their native languages, and the translation of languages that no one has spoken for thousands of years is in itself historical work, as Roberts pointed out. This does not mean, however, that they are under any obligation to carry out historical work themselves. The mere decision on the part of a scholar not to use historical critical techniques when analyzing a text does not mean that the analysis should not be considered as work done within the field of biblical studies. One could look at Cooper's reading of the story of Jephthah's daughter as a narrative that resonates with the experience of African American women and conclude that, as a scholar who focuses on religion, race, and society, Cooper is simply operating on her own side of Stendahl's ditch, relying on the historical work of biblical scholars that had to be done first. But since the text is always the reader's creation, then there is not much point in making the distinction Stendahl and others do between what the author thought the text meant and how contemporary readers might want to apply it. There is nothing inherently wrong with trying to determine what an author might have thought in regard to the meaning of their text, but since the meaningful text is the creation of the reader and not the author, it is not clear why it is necessary to do this. We cannot determine if one person has done a better job of interpretation than another until we know what a good job looks like, but as I will argue in the next chapter, there is nothing that can help us determine this except for agreement among interpreters. We can only decide that what Cooper is doing in her interpretation of the story of Jephthah's daughter is qualitatively different than what "real" biblical scholars do if we have drawn very clear boundaries around the field that exclude her sort of reading. As we saw, though, there are some notable similarities between her approach and the approach of Claassens, who is a biblical scholar. Given that Cooper's interpretation of the story of Jephthah's daughter has some similarities with one created by a biblical scholar, and given that it appears in a collection of essays written and edited by biblical scholars and published by the Society of Biblical Literature, it is not really clear that what she did in her interpretation cannot be considered as scholarly biblical criticism. Even more importantly, though, I will argue in the following chapters, it is ethically problematic to exclude the concerns of marginalized communities from the field of biblical studies. It is precisely those concerns that should guide the work that biblical scholars do.

To sum up my argument in this chapter, we could say that there is no "text in itself," if by that we refer to textual meaning that somehow exists independently of any interpretive work, because interpreters are responsible for the creation of meaning as they read. Texts speak and do things like exhort or condemn or limit only insofar as we have created them and produced interpretations based on the ways we have chosen to make sense of the evidence of the physical text. This heuristic device of distinguishing between physical and meaningful texts is my own, but as chapter 1 mentions, this is a view of texts largely in accord with the way pragmatists like Rorty and other like-minded thinkers understand them. The notion that there is no text in itself that can ground our interpretations, no original text except for the ones we create, is perhaps more frequently associated with Jacques Derrida,[53] but his understanding of texts has been embraced by some pragmatists.[54] For pragmatists, there is no such thing as an uninterpreted text that we can use to judge the validity of interpretations because we cannot use something without meaning, something we therefore do not understand, as a basis to judge anything. Only interpretation creates meaning, and so we can only judge interpretations through other interpretations,[55] and this is true whether we are talking about texts or anything else. We will not be able to understand anything until we have ideas and concepts and language about it that make sense to us, which is to say that fit well in the belief systems we already hold. So, as the next chapter argues, our interpretations, whether of texts or anything else, are things that must fit into our worldview, which is a human creation.[56]

While some might be tempted to call this view of things postmodern, that term is used so broadly[57] as to be unhelpful, and the principles attributed to postmodern hermeneutical approaches by biblical scholars are often ones that I disagree with.

53. For example, Derrida, "Structure, Sign and Play."
54. For example, Rorty, *Consequences of Pragmatism*, 90–109; and Fish, *Doing What Comes Naturally*, 37–67.
55. See, for example, Fish, *Is There a Text in This Class?*, 342.
56. See, for example, William James, *Pragmatism: A New Name for Some Old Ways of Thinking* (London: Longmans, Green, 1910), 6–8, 57–58; and Donald Davidson, *Inquiries into Truth and Interpretation*, 2nd ed. (Oxford: Clarendon, 2001), 183–98.
57. For some of the many definitions given to the word, see the Bible and Culture Collective, *The Postmodern Bible* (New Haven, CT: Yale University Press, 1995), 8–12.

For example, Larry Hurtado writes that postmodernism sees "each interpretation [as] equally valid in principle,"[58] and J. de Waal Dryden says that from a postmodern point of view, "the text is an active force that advances toward the reader with its own agendas."[59] Neither description applies to my view of texts and meaning, so it would be more precise to refer to it as pragmatist and antirepresentationalist, since I work with the pragmatist understanding that our interpretations do not represent meaning that preexists interpretive work, since that is not possible.[60] The ways we interpret or produce meaning must fit with the basic worldviews we have, as chapter 3 discusses, and these worldviews or belief systems provide us with the language and concepts we need to understand the world in the first place. The world and texts outside of human interpretive activity are neither true nor false because they can mean nothing at all to us and are not understandable by us until we use our worldviews to make sense of them,[61] and we will be guided in that activity by the beliefs we hold about the best ways to interpret, beliefs provided to us by the communities we belong to.

So while the physical text might preexist us, it is only a set of marks on a page, for interpreters are the ones who put in the effort to create a meaningful text, and chapter 3 continues the discussion of how our communities provide us with belief systems in regard to interpretation. Because there is no "material in itself" or "text in itself"—things understood as existing prior to any human interpretation—by which we can judge our interpretive methods, and because our interpretation produces the text insofar as we use that word to refer to something meaningful rather than to uninterpreted marks on a page, we have nothing to judge our hermeneutical approaches and the conclusions they produce except other approaches and conclusions and the beliefs that ground them.[62] So there is no reason why we would have to use the historical critical readings of the story of Jephthah's daughter to judge the validity of an interpretation like Cooper's, which is interested in how it reflects the experience of African American women. It is not even clear how we

58. Hurtado, "New Testament Studies," 172.
59. J. de Waal Dryden, *A Hermeneutic of Wisdom: Recovering the Formative Agency of Scripture* (Grand Rapids, MI: Baker Academic, 2018), 6.
60. For one of Richard Rorty's explanations of antirepresentationalism, see *Objectivity, Relativism, and Truth*, 1–17.
61. Stout, *Ethics after Babel*, 54.
62. For example, Richard Rorty, *Contingency, Irony, and Solidarity* (Cambridge: Cambridge University Press, 1989), 51–52; and Fish, *Doing What Comes Naturally*, 51–52, 55–56.

would use those historical interpretations to assess Cooper's work, given that the ones I discussed were contradictory. To argue that, for example, Römer's historical interpretation is correct and that all other readings of the story of Jephthah's daughter should not be in contradiction with it would be itself an argument and an interpretation, not the speech of the physical text that could tell us Römer's interpretation is better or more true than Cooper's or anyone else's. And since readers are responsible for creating meaning, the assertion that students and scholars of biblical studies must first do proper historical work on one side of Stendahl's ditch before venturing to the other to interpret for their contemporary contexts is an argument as well, not something an uninterpreted text demands of us.

I will turn in the next chapter to consider how the communities we belong to influence the decisions we make about using the physical text as evidence for the meaningful texts we create, and how they establish goals of interpretation, goals that themselves influence how we decide to interpret and use the physical text as evidence. We will recognize some goals as better than others, and might, for example, see the goal of providing textual resources to Malawian women threatened by infection with HIV because of a patriarchal social structure that obliges women to have sex with their partners when they demand it as better than a search for authorial intention. As chapter 4 discusses, however, any goals we decide to pursue in interpretation should be based on ethical decisions we make. Since the historical critical method is not something that all interpreters need to use all the time, we can at that point begin to discuss why the ethic of liberative interpretation should guide the work biblical scholars do, and why this ethical decision should take priority over any methodological choice we decide on.

3

Community, Evidence, and Hermeneutical Change

Evidence, Worldview, and Objectivity

In chapter 2, I referred to the physical text as evidence for the meaning interpreters create—the meaningful text, as I called that creation—but in this chapter, I begin to move to the significance of this for the liberative project for biblical studies that has been modeled in the work of marginalized scholars in the discipline. On the one hand, we could say that the knowledge that there is no necessary reason for academics to do historical work in interpretation frees us to prioritize ethical concerns in research and teaching as more privileged scholars start to learn to read for emancipation. On the other hand, once we have become habituated to doing things in a particular way, such as consistently asking historical questions in our work, it becomes harder to change. This first part of the chapter explains some of the difficulties involved in changing deeply ingrained habits that we academics have: believing, like everyone else, that our worldviews, provided by the communities in which we claim membership, are largely correct, we see the work we do now as objective and as providing good understandings of texts and their contexts. Our belief systems determine how we interpret evidence, and so appeals to evidence by those trying to convince us to change our habits often do not work, because people whose worldviews are rooted in communities and belief systems different from our own will often understand "the facts" of evidence in ways that are incompatible with our own interpretations. Despite this view of community, worldview, and evidence, which follows Rorty's pragmatist thought, all of us know that people change over time, and in the second section of the chapter, I point out that important change can happen when we feel forced to rethink some of our beliefs. What minoritized biblical scholars reading for liberation are often asking their more privileged peers to do is to honor ethical beliefs that we already hold about the evils of oppression and to regularly look to these in our professional work. This change does not prevent us from using interpretive approaches in which we have already developed expertise, as the following chapters explain, it simply makes ethical criteria the first ones we draw on to judge the quality of our conclusions. To that extent, the change many of us need to make to read for liberation is quite small but can have significant effects. It is because so little change is required in our belief systems for this to happen, and because this change better aligns our ethical commitments and our professional work once we realize that historical research is an optional and not a necessary part of what we do as scholars, that I have hope biblical studies can become a more ethical field.

Because the communities to which we belong ground our ways of seeing the world, they exercise enormous influence over how we read. For most readers of the Bible, their religious communities have provided them with meaningful texts of many biblical passages before they even undertake their own interpretations, and their own acts of reading might do little more than confirm their agreement with the meanings their communities have come up with. When it comes to the interpretation of texts, however, communities do much more than provide their members with meanings of individual passages, for they also give them examples and guidelines and norms that govern their interpretative work, things that function to limit the conclusions that community members can come to as they read. This is why we will hardly be surprised when different members of the same community often produce meaningful texts that are largely in agreement with each other. For any group, including religious and scholarly ones, there are certain parameters for proper interpretation, certain limits on what can be understood as evidence and how that evidence can be interpreted, and certain logical moves that are acceptable in interpretation. When community members are faced with the sensory data of the dots and lines that make up the physical text, there are only so many ways that it will be possible for them to use that data as evidence in their production of meaning, for interpretation will be limited by the community's worldviews and concerns.

Our normal ways of reading, then, are so deeply grounded in our belief systems that determine how we see the world that they can sometimes seem like the only legitimate ways to go about the work of interpretation. When this is true for academics, they will on occasion describe their community's preferred modes of interpretation as objective, and the issue of objectivity is one raised from time to time in hermeneutical discussions in biblical studies, often by those particularly invested in the historical critical method. John Barton writes that historical criticism aims for "reasonable objectivity," and he defines this as "a refusal to simply read one's own ideas into the text or to have no sense of detachment from it."[1] Objectivity as Barton seems to mean it is a concept that developed in the scientific fields of the nineteenth century, as their practitioners became concerned that they themselves might be standing in the way of arriving at the truth, that their backgrounds and interests and beliefs would mold the interpretation of data in improper ways. The whole point of scientific objectivity is to negate subjectivity, the influence of the subject on the conclusions in regard to the object that they are studying.[2] Biblical scholar James Barr writes that objectivity in its ideal sense is the same thing as a method that could eliminate "all ideology, bias, and presupposition."[3] Arguments for historical criticism as ensuring objectivity in biblical studies have been concerned in particular with a need to exclude readers' religious biases from influencing their interpretive work,[4] but for those who believe historical criticism is a necessary way to interpret biblical texts, any contemporary concern unrelated to the search for the biblical texts' original meanings and ancient contexts violates the scholarly demand to be objective. That is why Barton urges detachment from the text under examination and hopes that interpreters will not simply replace the text with their ideas, and why Leo Perdue says that without historical criticism there can be "no objective or attainable knowledge" of the texts' meanings.[5]

For some biblical scholars, an appeal to objectivity reflects a particular way of understanding the role of the physical text in the discipline's interpretive endeavors. F. W. Dobbs-Allsopp, we might recall from the previous chapter, writes that texts are "a reality independent of the critic," and like natural objects of the sort scientists study, such as stars and mountains, there is a substantiality that exists,

1. Barton, *Nature of Biblical Criticism*, 49.
2. Lorraine Daston and Peter Galison, *Objectivity* (New York: Zone, 2007), 34–37.
3. Barr, *History and Ideology*, 71.
4. See, for example, Harvey, *Historian and the Believer*, 43–48; and John J. Collins, *The Bible after Babel: Historical Criticism in a Postmodern Age* (Grand Rapids, MI: William B. Eerdmans, 2005), 5.
5. Perdue, *Reconstructing Old Testament Theology*, 341.

which means that, like such objects, texts "are not simply figments of our interpretive imaginations."[6] When saying that there is a text that preexists interpreters, Dobbs-Allsopp is referring to what I am calling the physical text, a collection of dots and lines. Even if there were no human interpreters today who could read ancient Hebrew, Aramaic, and Greek, the biblical texts written in those languages would still be there, existing in the physical world (assuming the paperlike substances on which they were copied in the ancient world had survived the ravages of time, at least), just as the stars and mountains would exist in the physical world even if hominids had never evolved to say interesting things about them. The physical text is an "extra-linguistic reality," as Roy Harrisville puts it,[7] present in the world that exists outside of our speech or language about it, and so it is part of the evidence that we draw on to create meaningful texts, just as things in the natural world are things scientists draw on to say meaningful things about nature, and they are not things we can simply ignore as we do interpretive work to explain them.

For some pragmatists, there is also a similarity between the study of texts and the study of the physical world, insofar as both scientists and interpreters of texts create narratives about things they have decided to recognize as evidence. Physical texts, like stars and mountains, would continue to exist if all humans disappeared tomorrow, but this is not some sort of argument that explains how physical texts or the stars could have meaning apart from the interpretive work humans do. I drew a distinction between physical and meaningful texts in chapter 2 specifically in order to clarify this point: the physical text may preexist interpreters, but it has no meaning in and of itself; the physical text is simply evidence interpreters use to create meaningful texts. It is the meaningful text, not the physical one, that has meaning, and the meaningful text is the reader's production. However, we will only think to come up with particular meanings and particular arguments on the basis of the worldviews or sets of beliefs we already hold, and members of different communities hold somewhat different worldviews. For example, I will not read Genesis 1–2 as a literal account of the beginnings of the universe since I do not belong to a community with a belief system that would permit that sort of reading, but a creationist does belong to such a group and so understands those chapters differently than I do. One important reason why the creationist and I will produce

6. Dobbs-Allsopp, "Rethinking Historical Criticism," 265.
7. Harrisville, *Pandora's Box Opened*, 154.

different interpretations of these chapters is because there are some very basic differences in the things we believe about biblical literature, and if these beliefs are central and core to our hermeneutical understandings, then it will be unlikely that either of us will convince the other of the correctness of our reading. In that case, it will not help if I lay out the evidence that I believe demonstrates why one should not take these chapters to be literal descriptions of the origins of the cosmos, such as the contradictions I see between Genesis 1:1–2:4a and 2:4b–25, which lead me to conclude that these are two different creation accounts composed by two different people. Someone deeply committed to a belief in the literal accuracy of the Bible will not see my interpretation of the text as evidence for contradiction, just as they will not accept that the conclusions of modern scientific fields in regard to the origins of the universe invalidate their literal understanding of these chapters.[8]

Worldview shapes how we decide to interpret our sense perceptions and make decisions as to what is or is not evidence for a particular investigation, and the interpretations we produce will almost always support the belief system that has created them in the first place, whether it was created in the field of biblical studies or in the natural sciences.[9] To illuminate the point with an example, we can return to the interpretations of the story of Jephthah's daughter in Judges 11:29–40, which chapter 2 discusses. Thomas Römer's reading of that passage, we might remember, differs from my own in important part because his view of the composition of the Deuteronomistic History (Dtr) is different from mine. He sees this writing that runs from Deuteronomy to Kings as a work produced by means of a fair amount of later insertions added by editing or redaction,[10] and so it is perhaps not overly surprising that he uses the concept of redaction to explain the origin of the bulk of Judges 11:29–40.[11] One important piece of evidence Römer presents in

8. For just one of the many extensive creationist defenses of the literal accuracy and coherence of Gen 1–2, see Don Batten et al., *The Creation Answers Book* (Eight Mile Plains, Australia: Creation Ministries, 2006).
9. Mary Hesse makes this point in regard to scientific knowledge in *Revolutions and Reconstructions in the Philosophy of Science*, HSP (Brighton, UK: Harvester, 1980), 173–74.
10. See Thomas Römer, *The So-Called Deuteronomistic History: A Sociological, Historical and Literary Introduction* (London: T&T Clark, 2007).
11. Römer, "Why Would the Deuteronomists Tell?," 28–30. Römer certainly is not alone in arriving at this conclusion; see also, for example, Sebastian Grätz, "Jiftach und seine Tochter," in *Geschichte Israels und deuteronomistische Geschichtsdenken: Festschrift zum 70. Geburtstag von Winfried Thiel*, ed. Peter Mommer and Andreas Scherer, AOAT 380 (Münster, Germany: Ugarit, 2010), 122; and Lauren A. S. Monroe, "Disembodied Women: Sacrificial Language and the Deaths of Bat-Jephthah, Cozbi, and the Bethlehemite Concubine," CBQ 75 (2013): 37–38.

his argument that most of the passage was not an original part of Dtr but was added later by a redactor is the appearance of the clause *ʿābar bĕnê ʿammôn*, "he crossed over to the Ammonites," at the very end of 11:29, as Jephthah moves to confront the Ammonites in battle, and the appearance of a similar clause at the very beginning of 11:32, where we see *wayyaʿăbōr yiptāḥ ʾel bĕnê ʿammôn*, "Jephthah crossed over to the Ammonites." Sandwiched between these two phrases is 11:30–31, the verses that contain the fateful vow Jephthah makes that will result in his eventual sacrifice of his daughter in 11:34–40. Römer's theory is that the redactor came across an earlier version of Dtr that already included 11:29 and 11:32–33, the verses that recount Jephthah's defeat of the Ammonites. The redactor added the story of the vow in 11:30–31, but upon doing so had to remind readers at the beginning of 11:32 that Jephthah was on the way to fight the Ammonites, which explains the near repetition of the phrase from 11:29, already present in the earlier version of Dtr, at the beginning of 11:32, the redactor's transition back to the already existing story. And since 11:34–40, the story of the sacrifice, is obviously related to the vow of 11:30–31, Römer sees 11:34–40 as part of the redactional insertion also. As further evidence for this story as redactional, Römer argues that the narrative of the sacrifice criticizes the Deuteronomistic belief that God saves the innocent and punishes the wicked, and thus that the narrative of the vow and sacrifice hardly appears to be a story that would have been present in the original version of Dtr.

When it comes to the study of Dtr, I am much more reticent than Römer to see redactional insertions, and I will often disagree with others who claim to find material in Dtr that they see as redactional, arguing at many points that what they think is a later addition was actually composed by the Deuteronomist, and that they have failed to take account of the ways in which putatively redactional material actually makes perfect sense when we assume only one author was involved.[12] Unsurprisingly, then, I can find a way to argue that the verses that Römer attributes to the redactor were composed by the Deuteronomist themself. I can explain the near repetition of the phrase Römer identifies as evidence for redaction as something that makes sense from the hand of a single original author: Jephthah was on his way to fight the Ammonites, as 11:29 tells us, but made his vow during the journey, as we see in 11:30–31, and so the author believed it made sense to remind readers

12. For example, David Janzen, *The Necessary King: A Postcolonial Reading of the Deuteronomistic Portrait of the Monarchy*, HBM 57 (Sheffield, UK: Sheffield Phoenix, 2013), 25–43.

in 11:32 that the battle was about to begin, since that sets off the chain of events that leads to the sacrifice. Moreover, the two similar phrases in 11:29 and 32 both use the Hebrew verb *'ābar*, "to cross over," a word that appears so frequently in the larger story devoted to Jephthah (11:17, 19, 20, 29 [three times], 32; 12:1 [two times], 3, 5) that it is really the thematic verb of his narrative, as Michaela Bauks points out.[13] Since his story is one focused to an important extent on which peoples belong on which pieces of land, and the problems involved in "crossing over" into the lands of others, we can hardly be surprised when we find multiple references to Jephthah crossing over into battle against the Ammonites, a people who, he claims, have illegitimately crossed over into Israelite territory (11:12–28). In other words, just because we see more than one reference to Jephthah crossing over to the Ammonites does not mean that we should take it as evidence for redaction, since the idea of crossing over and the verb that expresses it are obviously key to his larger story. And as I discussed in chapter 2, I believe the story of the vow and sacrifice reflect an important theme of Dtr, Israel's failure to know and keep the law, the work's ultimate explanation of the many invasions experienced by the people as a whole and the suffering that results. Jephthah and his daughter exhibit no awareness of the law in Deuteronomy that forbids child sacrifice, and so they—and most particularly the daughter, of course—suffer for it, a microcosm of the larger story of the destruction of Israel for its lawlessness that works its way through Dtr as a whole and culminates in the destruction of Jerusalem at its conclusion. The result, then, is that I do not recognize as evidence for redaction either of the two things that Römer presents as such and as supporting his interpretation.

So although the two of us encountered the same dots and lines in the physical text—we were faced with the same sensory data, in other words—one of us turned some of those dots and lines into evidence for redaction and the other one did not, and an important reason why this is so involves our different beliefs in regard to the amount of redactional work we can find in Dtr. Someone who wanted to resolve this disagreement could suggest that we both reexamine the more general assumptions that we make about the redaction of the books we believe make up Dtr. Yet this reexamination is unlikely to help, because the only way to do this is to appeal to many more passages like this one where Römer sees redaction and I do

13. Michaela Bauks, *Jephtas Tochter: Traditions-, religions- und rezeptionsgeschichtliche Studien zu Richter* 11, 29–40, FAT 71 (Tübingen, Germany: Mohr Siebeck, 2010), 12–13.

not, and our different beliefs about this will simply predispose us to find ways to explain those individual passages such that they fit well with beliefs that we already hold: in most of those cases I will find ways to argue that it is perfectly possible to see the Deuteronomist as the author, whereas Römer will maintain that his readings of the passages as redactional make sense. We will not resolve whose basic core beliefs about interpretation are correct by returning to the evidence of the physical text because our general beliefs about how to make sense of that evidence will inform the ways in which we interpret the marks we see there in the first place.

Once we see that there can be no bias-free appeals to the sensory data of the physical text to resolve interpretive disputes, since our worldviews and all the biases that accompany them are what determine how we turn sensations of the physical text into evidence, then we can see that it is not possible to learn any new piece of knowledge without having a whole set of beliefs that allows one to make sense of it. The notion that there could be "nonverbal episodes of awareness," knowledge that does not presuppose a set of beliefs and presuppositions about the world, is what Wilfrid Sellars calls the Myth of the Given, for nothing in the uninterpreted physical world, not even a physical text, has an inherent meaning, something that is just given.[14] Our worldviews, on the other hand, are given to us by our communities, writes Richard Rorty, and they construct a world for us that allows us to make sense of perceptions and understand a particular piece of sensory data to be evidence for a particular argument.[15] This world is what everyone in our community knows to be true, what goes without saying, and for those who lived in ancient Greece, it just went without saying that the Homeric gods exist, just as for our communities it goes without saying that the physical world does. The world as we see it is constructed for us by the belief systems we hold,[16] and they allow us to deal with and explain the things we encounter.

So in the interpretation I created of the story of Jephthah's daughter, I could not have arrived at my conclusions as to its meaning and significance without a whole set of beliefs as to how to turn the marks on the page into Hebrew words and sentences and how to translate those sentences into English. I also held a whole set

14. Wilfrid Sellars, *Empiricism and the Philosophy of Mind* (Cambridge, MA: Harvard University Press, 1997), 68–79 (quotation from p. 73).
15. Rorty, *Consequences of Pragmatism*, 5, 14.
16. Quine, *From a Logical Point of View*, 44.

of beliefs about the compositional history of the books of Deuteronomy through Kings, about the viability of many earlier scholarly studies of the story, about the norms and standards of good scholarly research and writing in my discipline, about the grammar of the English language, and many other sets of beliefs as well. All of them had to be in place before I could make sense of the dots and lines on the page and come up with the interpretation or meaningful text of Judges 11:29–40 that I did. To say there is no interpretation of biblical texts or anything else outside of the worldviews with which our communities provide us, sets of beliefs that allow us to make sense of our perceptions of things like physical texts, is really an extension of the point chapter 2 makes, that there is nothing we can know about sensory perceptions until we use our words and concepts to understand them. As a result, the biases and presuppositions and interests that are part of readers' belief systems are just necessary aspects of how we make sense of texts. Some readers believe that academic readings of the Bible must never be influenced by the religious proclivities of the readers, and others that all biblical texts have been inspired by God and so are literally accurate. "The world does not speak," as Rorty puts it. "Only we do,"[17] and when we want to speak truly about things in the world, then we will have to interpret our sensory perceptions of it through beliefs we have accepted as true.

Things that exist outside of humans' mental processes, like the uninterpreted physical text of Judges 11:29–40, can cause us to have linguistic reactions and produce concepts through our speech about them, at least insofar as our worldviews limit the kinds of things we can do with that physical text. In my case, my training and experience as a biblical scholar compel me to deal with that passage in certain ways, but the physical text of the verses does not justify the meaning I created, because only the beliefs I hold about Hebrew grammar, proper academic arguments, the validity of studies of Dtr, and so on do that. Those are the beliefs I appeal to in order to argue that I have come up with a good interpretation of the passage, and so those beliefs, shaped by the communities of which I am a member, justify what I should do with the evidence of the physical text. Those beliefs I use to interpret thus justify the new beliefs I will hold after I have completed my work of interpretation, such as ones about the meaning and significance of the passage,

17. Rorty, *Contingency, Irony, and Solidarity*, 6.

or the overall message of Dtr, or why I should stop agreeing with interpretations of the passage I used to think were correct. Rorty's pithy way of putting this is that "what counts as an accurate report of experience is a matter of what a community will let you get away with,"[18] which is to say that the worldview with which your community has provided you gives you the range of proper ways of conceiving of particular pieces of sensory data, something that corresponds to the range of explanations of that data the community is willing to accept.

A number of things follow from the fact that we cannot make sense of our perceptions of physical texts apart from the worldviews we hold. One of these is that it is best not to think of objectivity as a method or anything else that eliminates biases and presuppositions but rather as the standards and norms that our group uses to interpret, things that fit well with the beliefs (or biases and presuppositions) the group understands to be true.[19] Objective research is not bias-free; it just conforms to a certain set of ideologies and biases a community agrees are true. So the claim that there can be no objective knowledge of the Bible without historical critical work is the reflection of a belief held by many (although certainly not all) biblical scholars about necessary aspects of interpretation and is nothing more or less than this. Something else that follows from the notion that our interpretations of texts depend on and conform to our worldviews is that the stricter a group's norms and standards for interpretation are, the more agreement in interpretation among its members we will expect to see. Biblical studies, like other disciplines in

18. Rorty, *Philosophy as Cultural Politics*, 11. Donald Davidson refers to this idea as salience: how we decide to understand sensory data, something that is done in language, is based on what our community decides is salient, with the result that community members will use the same sorts of sentences to respond to the same sorts of sensory stimuli (*Truth, Language, and History: Philosophical Essays*, vol. 5 [Oxford: Oxford University Press, 2005], 61).
19. James, *Pragmatism*, 6–8; Fish, *Doing What Comes Naturally*, 436–38; Rorty, *Truth and Progress*, 60. One of the key points of difference between Rorty's neopragmatism and the thought of the new pragmatists turns on this issue of objectivity as the consensus of the group, since new pragmatists often want a more robust understanding of objectivity than Rorty provides, something closer to Cheryl Misak's statement that objectivity means distinguishing between thinking you are right and being right (*Truth, Politics, Morality: Pragmatism and Deliberation* [London: Routledge, 2000], 77). But simply to argue, as Steven Levine does, that our interaction with the world often results in instinctual reactions to stimuli (*Pragmatism, Objectivity, and Experience* [Cambridge: Cambridge University Press, 2019], 228–29) does not help in this regard, because the only way to know if we are right or wrong about a belief we hold is to engage in inquiry, something articulated in language formed by belief, not in nonlinguistic instinct. We could say with Robert Brandom that we create representations of the world and confer on them a normative structure that we see as authoritative and objective, but that is perfectly compatible with Rorty's view of objectivity, as Brandom acknowledges (*Perspectives on Pragmatism: Classical, Recent, and Contemporary* [Cambridge, MA: Harvard University Press, 2011], 111–15).

the humanities, has room for many different ways to interpret texts, even if we can refer to historical critical approaches as dominant in our field. The natural sciences, writes Thomas Kuhn, have imposed much stricter systems of interpretation than other academic fields have and, unlike ones in the humanities, do not expose their students to arguments about competing approaches to interpretation.[20] This does not make the sciences more objective than the humanities; it just more sharply limits the sets of beliefs practitioners of those disciplines can appeal to in making sense of the evidence they are trying to interpret.

However, one aspect of biblical studies in which the field imposes fairly strict standards and norms for interpretation is in the area of linguistics, and no matter where they study, students of biblical Hebrew and New Testament Greek are taught very similar standards and norms as to how to deal with the evidence of the physical text when they go about the work of translation. Despite the fact that the six interpretations of Judges 11:29–40 discussed in chapter 2 have many differences, all the interpreters agreed about the basic series of events of the story, and this is because we have very similar beliefs in regard to thc grammar and vocabulary of biblical Hebrew. Those of us who have been taught biblical Hebrew know perfectly well that when we come across עָבַר בְּנֵי עַמּוֹן, a series of dots and lines in the physical text of Judges 11:29, we can transliterate it as something like *ʿābar bĕnê ʿammôn*, and translate it in this context as something like "he crossed over to the Ammonites." This interpretive work with the physical text does not in and of itself determine how we should use this translation in making sense of the rest of the story of Jephthah's daughter—we will have other beliefs that will tell us how to do that—but those of us who have completed introductory courses in biblical Hebrew will, in this particular context, arrive at roughly the same translation for this series of three Hebrew words because we hold very similar beliefs in regard to things like the parsing of Hebrew verbs and how possession can be expressed in that language, and these beliefs restrict the ways we can make sense of those dots and lines. I would know that someone who can look at that particular physical text and come up with a translation somewhat like the one I did has translated correctly, not by comparing their translation to the dots and lines but by comparing it to beliefs and explanations

20. Kuhn, *Structure of Scientific Revolutions*, 160–66.

concerning the grammar and vocabulary of biblical Hebrew that are universally shared in the discipline.

One final point that follows from the fact that we rely on our beliefs to turn perception into evidence we can make sense of is that there is no way to test those sets of beliefs except by comparing them to other sets. For example, one could argue that the discipline that studies biblical Hebrew has good and rational reasons for the rules and guidelines and norms it has developed to make sense of texts in the language, and that is quite true. But the only way we can demonstrate that those rules and norms are good and rational ones is by using our own speech to justify them. We will have to compare our beliefs about Hebrew grammar and vocabulary to other beliefs we have because we think that they, like the ones we are trying to justify, are true, as we will hardly accept an argument predicated on beliefs we think are false. We recognize our beliefs about biblical Hebrew or New Testament Greek to be true because they fit together with other parts of our worldviews, since we can only test ideas by comparing them with other ideas, not to evidence that exists in the world uninterpreted by any worldview. Because we work with beliefs we think are true and justify them with others that we also think are true, we never have any reason to believe we are in massive error about the way the world is,[21] and if other people with different worldviews conclude we are wrong about some parts of our general outlook on things, we will likely think the same about them.

Community and Hermeneutical Change

One of the points I aimed to make in the preceding discussion on how our interpretive habits are formed by our worldviews provided to us by the communities to which we belong was to explain why it might be very difficult to get anyone to change their minds about how they go about making sense of texts. It is a key issue for a book written in the hopes of convincing more students and scholars in biblical studies to privilege the work done by their marginalized peers, a goal that seems to founder on the same problem of Gadamer's view of tradition. As chapter 1 mentions, Gadamer's understanding of tradition has enough in common with the pragmatist picture of the world I am following that I need to take critiques of his views in this

21. Davidson, *Inquiries into Truth*, 200–201.

regard very seriously. Like pragmatists, Gadamer believes our worldviews shape us and the ways we read and understand texts, and he too rejects the notion that texts speak for themselves. They appear to do so, Gadamer says, because our interpretive tradition has already imbued them with meaning before we approach them and interpret them somewhat differently. Yet if tradition shapes us and the ways we understand texts to the degree that it seems as if they have voices, how could we ever hope to read them differently? It is a deeply held tenet of pragmatism that we never have any need to justify beliefs we are entirely certain are true; Charles Peirce, the founder of the movement, pointed out that the whole reason one takes up an investigation is to move from a state of doubt about something to a state of belief, so we have no need to question things we are certain are true. We direct our inquiry instead only at matters about which we are in doubt.[22] And if we say with pragmatists and others that deeply held beliefs anchor the ways we can read texts, something that might sound like Gadamer's description of tradition, then why would we expect anyone to change their hermeneutical beliefs, given that no one has any reason to suspect they are gravely mistaken about what the world is like and how they should read? Since we have all experienced change, however, even in our understandings as to how to make sense of texts, perhaps the pragmatist account of interpretation I have been following is flawed in some way, but I want to show in this final part of the chapter that it actually provides hope that we might be able to construct a more ethical version of the field of biblical studies than currently exists.

To make this point, and to sharpen one of the problems the first section of the chapter has raised regarding the possibility of change, I will begin by developing an idea I mentioned there, the notion that we inherit the belief systems we hold about interpretation and everything else from the communities we belong to. We would expect someone who grows up in a particular religious group to end up reading biblical texts in accordance with that group's presuppositions, standards, and norms, and rejecting interpretations that do not fit well with that belief system. If one chooses to become an academic biblical scholar, it will be unsurprising if, having been exposed to years of teaching and models of scholarship from the mainstream of the field, one ends up reading biblical texts in ways that conform to the

22. Charles S. Peirce, *The Essential Peirce: Selected Philosophical Writings*, ed. Nathan Houser and Christian Kloesel (Bloomington: Indiana University Press, 1992–98), 1:115.

worldview of a field shaped by cultural and religious forces such as the Renaissance, the Protestant Reformation, the Enlightenment, and the development of German universities in the nineteenth century.[23] The evolution of the discipline over time in reaction against and in concert with various religious, political, economic, and cultural forces results in a community of members who believe there are certain limits to what is acceptable in the academic study of the Bible. Michel Foucault rightly noted that each field of study will have general agreement on such issues as accepted pedagogies, admissible objects of interpretation, approved techniques to interpret them, and agreement to propositions considered to be true and that these function as subtle ways of guarding the boundaries of a discipline. These sorts of things separate the kinds of readings a field accepts from ones it does not and define who is and who is not acting properly as a professional in the discipline or, to put that another way, playing the field's language game or participating in its discourse. An academic field will simply not recognize an interpretation of something to be true unless it is spoken as part of a discourse that is already recognized as producing truth.[24] The result, then, is that biblical scholars produce interpretations and evidence for them by using the methods and techniques they have been taught and that have become part of the habitual ways they go about their work.[25]

And it is because our communities provide us with these beliefs and habits that we most certainly cannot come up with just any evidence or produce just any text that we would like. The community imposes standards on us, as Stanley Fish observes, and will not validate interpretations that do not live up to those standards.[26] As a mainstream biblical scholar, I cannot work with the belief that the Bible is everywhere literally accurate and use that belief to create evidence in the formation of a meaningful text because the field's worldview, shaped by history in the ways it has been, does not permit me to act on a belief like that in my professional interpretive

23. For studies of factors that shaped the modern field of biblical studies, and historical criticism in particular, see Jonathan Sheehan, *The Enlightenment Bible: Translation, Scholarship, Culture* (Princeton, NJ: Princeton University Press, 2005); Thomas A. Howard, *Protestant Theology and the Making of the Modern German University* (Oxford: Oxford University Press, 2006); and Michael C. Legaspi, *The Death of Scripture and the Rise of Biblical Studies*, OSHT (Oxford: Oxford University Press, 2010).
24. Michel Foucault, "The Discourse on Language," trans. Rupert Swyer, in *The Order of Things* (New York: Pantheon, 1971), 215–37.
25. For a longer discussion of the text as interpretation shaped by community, and on the role of habit in this shaping, see Fish, *Is There a Text in This Class?*, 147–73.
26. Fish, *Doing What Comes Naturally*, 321–22.

work. And because what we are willing to accept as evidence and fact is shaped by our belief systems, facts for people in one community may well not be facts for people in another, and so different communities cannot resolve their interpretive differences by appealing to "the facts."[27] When it comes to creating meaning for biblical texts, this might seem obvious when we compare, for example, the belief system of a biblical scholar who is devoted to historical critical work and that of a Christian fundamentalist, for it is not a fact for the biblical scholar that the Bible is literally true, just as it is not a fact for the fundamentalist that Moses did not write the Pentateuch or that Paul did not write 1 Timothy.

As a result, we will generally discount and ignore the readings of texts produced by those who have fairly different interpretive beliefs than our own, and some biblical scholars will do so by making the claim that academic interpretations not produced with at least some historical critical work are simply wrong. The alternative to this strict acknowledgment of the historical critical method alone as objective, they argue, leaves us at a hopeless relativist impasse when trying to determine what texts mean. If we abandon the sort of worldview embodied by Stendahl's ditch, in which historical critical work must be done first and then used to judge other interpretations, this argument goes, then we will be left with no way to judge interpretation at all, since the interpretations and interpretive norms and standards of all groups will be considered to be equal.[28] Barbara Herrnstein Smith uses the term Egalitarian Fallacy in reference to the claim that if one method used to establish meanings of texts is not accepted by readers as the only way in which they can be read—is not accepted as universally valid, to put this another way—then all judgments in regard to textual meaning are equally valid. If we were to follow the reasoning of the Egalitarian Fallacy, then we would believe that if we cannot agree on a single basic method or approach to biblical interpretation, we would have to throw up our hands and conclude that anybody could use any method they desired in their readings, and thus that we would have no basis to judge the validity or truth of any meaning that any reader wanted to advance. This logic does not work, though, Smith writes, because if someone objects that there simply is no universally valid method—that, for example, it is not necessary

27. Fish, 53–54.
28. For example, Bockmuehl, *Seeing the Word*, 50–55; Perdue, *Reconstructing Old Testament Theology*, 341–42; and Law, *Historical-Critical Method*, 236–37.

to use historical criticism to arrive at the meaning of a biblical text—that does not put the one who objects in the position of having to accept the results of all interpretive methods.[29] On a practical level, we need not worry about the relativism of the Egalitarian Fallacy because the worldview of our social group shapes and limits what we can see as legitimate interpretation, and one can never be in the position of seeing all interpretations as valid because one can never be without a belief system that makes particular ways of looking at texts seem authoritative and others seem wrong.[30]

Yet even though we generally have no reason to doubt the ways in which we go about interpreting texts and no reason to question why we ignore readings that radically differ from those our community normally produces, we do change our beliefs about meaning all the time. We can, for example, change and add to our beliefs about what a text means by encountering new information from the text itself as we read further and further into it. If it is a text in biblical Hebrew, then my beliefs about ancient Hebrew grammar and vocabulary provide me with a program or rules to make sense of the marks on the page, something Isaac Levi calls routine decision-making.[31] As I read further into the passage, the new information I gather can, because of the beliefs I hold about how to make sense of ancient Hebrew and about many other things, make me change my beliefs as to what the text is about, whether or not I agree with its message, how much it is like a different text I was comparing it to when I began to read, and so on. We can also change our beliefs about a text because we change. New experiences, for example, can cause us to look for different things when we read, to ask new questions of texts we had previously read, or to be suspicious of a message we had happily accepted during an earlier reading. I could develop a deeper understanding of Hebrew before I return to reread a text or spend time with refugees on the border between Mexico and the United States. And someone could cause me to change my mind as to what a writing means or what its main emphases are or whether it is good or bad because they bring me new information I feel compelled to accept or because they show me that I have overlooked beliefs I already hold that I should bring to bear on the interpretation of a given passage.

29. Smith, *Contingencies of Value*, 98–101.
30. Fish, *Is There a Text in This Class?*, 319–21.
31. Levi, *Pragmatism and Inquiry*, 21.

It is in particular this last cause of change—dialogue—that I will focus on in the following chapters, for minoritized biblical scholars at the margins of the field have been showing the rest of the discipline that we have often overlooked ethical beliefs we have as we go about our professional work, and that if we were to stop doing that, we would produce better interpretations. We have let one set of values and habits, those associated with the mainstream of biblical studies and its concern with historical issues, overshadow important ethical beliefs we hold about the evils of dehumanization and the need to combat it. The reason why pragmatism, and particularly its understanding of the self, gives me hope that biblical studies can become a more ethical field is because its picture of the self is of one that belongs to different groups at the same time and that pull us in somewhat different directions, leaving us with worldviews that are not entirely consistent.[32] These groups include ones into which we are born, and one could recognize one's family as a community, or one's country, or the group of people who are native speakers of one's dialect, or those who belong to what one considers as one's race. Part of community involves having things in common, but perhaps more often we think of it as having shared sympathy with others, as when we forge communities of close friends. We choose to join such groups, just as we can choose to join groups because we largely share their belief systems and goals, as would be the case when one becomes part of an academic guild, a religious organization, a political party, an underground terrorist cell, a book club, and so on. We belong to some communities by filiation and others by affiliation, and we can use our choices in affiliation to resist the claims of the groups we were born into, as Edward Said notes,[33] but all of them will have some effect on how we see the world. The belief systems of the ones in which we currently claim membership cannot stand in massive contradiction with each other, since an individual would find it impossible to belong to such different groups at

32. As Marjorie Miller puts it, one has identity when one functions as a member of a community, but we should really refer to the *identities* each one of us has, since we are simultaneously members of different communities ("Pragmatism and Feminism," in *The Cambridge Companion to Pragmatism*, ed. Alan Malachowski [Cambridge: Cambridge University Press, 2012], 234). These different communities will not always have entirely compatible goals when it comes to inquiry, and Isaac Levi argues that this sort of value pluralism in pragmatist thought can be traced back to Peirce, who recognized that the pursuit of one particular goal of inquiry would be done at the expense of others (*Pragmatism and Inquiry*, 39).
33. Edward Said, *The World, the Text, and the Critic* (Cambridge, MA: Harvard University Press, 1983), 24–25.

the same time,[34] but there will be minor variations among them or else we would not consider them to be different.

The pragmatist view of the self is one made up of a web of beliefs, one that will need to be rewoven from time to time when we encounter evidence that challenges some of them or when we notice inconsistencies among them,[35] the result both of belonging to different communities with somewhat different belief systems and of dialogue with others who will be more apt to notice such inconsistencies among beliefs than the person who holds them. To take a simple example of what such a reweaving of beliefs might look like, we could think of a case of individuals who claim both family and place of employment as two of the important groups they belong to. They may see their careers as helpful and as doing a lot of good for the world, and their work community may be founded on an ethical commitment that prizes the ways in which it benefits others, and as part of this value system, the work community asks its members to devote more time to their jobs. But it is not hard to imagine how, for some people who find themselves in this scenario, this ethical system might clash with those of their families, communities that evaluate one's use of time somewhat differently. In our hypothetical case, we can see that the partners and children of the individuals in question might accuse them of not meeting the family's desired moral goods, things in conflict at this point with those of their work community.

The problem the individuals in our example run into is not a choice between good and evil, for they see their work as beneficial, but they also value their families and believe that it is important to spend time with them. They are being asked instead to choose between good and good, since two ethical systems of two communities to which they belong are incompatible at this point. Sidney Hook refers to a conflict like this as "the tragic sense of life"; it is supposed to be simple to choose between good and evil, but a choice between two goods will be a much

34. As Donald Davidson points out, it would not even be possible to disagree with another person or group without knowing quite a bit about their beliefs, but since we cannot understand others without assuming that we agree as to many things—such as the meanings of words and basic concepts—disagreement is not possible unless the beliefs of the two parties agree in most respects (*Inquiries into Truth*, 196–97). That being said, we frequently tend to focus on our disagreements with the belief systems of others rather than the many points where our worldviews overlap.
35. See, for example, James, *Pragmatism*, 57–61; Rorty, *Objectivity, Relativism, and Truth*, 93–94; and Rorty, *Philosophy and Social Hope*, 77–78.

more difficult ethical matter.[36] Nonetheless, writes Isaiah Berlin, the essence of human life is having to deal with colliding sets of values, and it is not possible to imagine a life in which this does not happen,[37] because none of us belongs to only one community. Once we recognize there is a conflict between somewhat incompatible beliefs we hold, we will simply have to reorganize them in the way that most easily fits with the other ones we have. It is possible that some of the individuals in our example will disagree with the evidence their families bring to them and will argue there is no conflict between the demands of work and family, and that they have been living up to the ethical responsibilities they have in regard to both groups. This would suggest they disagree with some of the specific beliefs their family members have as to just what their familial obligations are. Some of them, on the other hand, may agree that they have overlooked their familial duties, and the inconsistency in their beliefs will, when brought to light, cause them to prioritize their commitments to their families.

It will never be possible to doubt everything we believe because, as the first section of the chapter argues, we need beliefs we would never think of doubting to make sense of the world in the first place, and there can be no interpretation of texts and no ability to doubt without them.[38] But if someone convinces us that our web of beliefs is not as consistent as we thought it was, we will, if trying to be as consistent and coherent as possible, change some of them. We will aim to alter as few as possible, however, because once we have corrected the flaw that has been pointed out, we will otherwise feel our worldview does a good job of explaining the way things are.[39] And for many students and scholars of biblical studies, only minor reweaving in their hermeneutical beliefs will be required to privilege ethical goals in interpretation and to be open to the leadership of marginalized scholars in this regard. If we already believe we should fight dehumanization and oppression when we can reasonably do so, then we hold the basic conviction that stands at the heart of emancipatory interpretations of the Bible. We will still be able to

36. Sidney Hook, "Pragmatism and the Tragic Sense of Life," *Proceedings and Addresses of the American Philosophical Association* 33 (1959–60): 5–26.
37. Isaiah Berlin, "The Pursuit of the Ideal," in *The Crooked Timber of Humanity: Chapters in the History of Ideas*, ed. Henry Hardy (Princeton, NJ: Princeton University Press, 1990), 13–14.
38. Fish, *Is There a Text in This Class?*, 360–61. As Peirce pointed out, we delve into inquiry because we doubt a particular belief, but investigations can only proceed by beginning with beliefs we know to be true (*Essential Peirce*, 1:109–23).
39. James, *Pragmatism*, 58–60.

use the interpretive techniques, including historical ones, in which we have been trained and developed expertise, as the following chapter argues, and so we need not abandon our beliefs that these approaches to texts are good for interpretation. Scholars reading for liberation, as we will see in chapter 4, are simply asking us to honor our ethical beliefs and use our training and experience in service of emancipatory goals. Freed of Stendahl's ditch, for many of us, this shift involves little change, although one would expect that there will be important effects of that alteration.

Biblical studies, like any other academic discipline, controls its discourse—limits what amount to proper academic work in the field, in other words—as its gatekeepers in academic departments and editorial boards and professional societies recognize some kinds of activities as valid and refuse to recognize others. Yet the boundaries of acceptable interpretation in this and every other academic discipline are being redrawn all the time,[40] even if only very slowly, and biblical studies is flexible enough that minoritized scholars prioritizing liberative goals were able to force their way into the field, even if generally only to its margins. More privileged scholars like me, however, have often ignored the ethical worldview we share in common with those whose work the field has placed in the minority. The following chapters will argue that once we start paying attention to the ethical arguments our minoritized peers have been making, we may well be convinced to follow their leadership and privilege emancipatory goals in our professional work. They are appealing to ethical beliefs we already hold, and since the discipline has been unable to provide cogent arguments for why we should privilege historical critical method in academic biblical interpretation, there is an inconsistency in the belief systems of those of us who recognize this yet do not address the ethical issues in our research and teaching to which our marginalized colleagues are pointing us.

When we act by our community's standards, the result is that we tend to act out of habit without worrying about justifying what we do, since these actions seem best fitted to the way the world is. I produce the kind of academic work I do because I think it is the right way to go about dealing with biblical texts and their contexts and because I see other people doing those things as well. Rational behavior is, in the end, group behavior, the actions we undertake based in our

40. Fish, *Is There a Text in This Class?*, 343–45.

community's belief system that provides us with a picture of the way the world really is.[41] We generally do not notice or think about the idea that the world, insofar as we can understand it and make meaning of it, is the production of our community's worldview. Sometimes when people in a field try to justify the ways in which they produce knowledge, they will refer to what Jean-François Lyotard calls a metanarrative, an appeal beyond discourse and belief to something that allegedly exists outside of human thought in the world-in-itself and that is believed to provide a guarantee of the truth and legitimacy for what the field does.[42] In biblical studies, this kind of justification often refers to a speaking text that exists independently of interpretation and that has a "voice" and "terms." I have been arguing in this and the previous chapter that there is no world or text that can be meaningful to us until the worldviews we hold, given to us by the communities we belong to, provide us with beliefs to make sense of them. This reflects Lyotard's observation that groups create narratives or stories about the way the world is, and these narratives maintain that the best ways to go about making sense of the world are those sanctioned by the group.[43] Some of us in the field of biblical studies who practice historical criticism, for example, can tell ourselves that we have found the way to discover the true meanings of the biblical texts because we allow the voice of the text to be heard and can check our results by comparing them to the text itself. Whatever else anyone might want to do with these texts, our narrative says, they will have to pay attention to the results of our historical work, or else their conclusions will not produce true meaning.

Historical criticism is not all there is to the academic study of the Bible, even though, as I discussed in the first chapter, it is still the dominant method of interpretation. Even interpreters who are largely interested in other approaches to biblical texts have been trained in its various aspects and often use them in their readings of texts. Yet we have marginalized colleagues who, while they can speak that language of the mainstream field, have also found more ethical goals to drive their work. If we all have a duty to test the coherence of our belief systems, then more privileged scholars like me, whose unearned socioeconomic privilege has

41. Rorty, *Objectivity, Relativism, and Truth*, 197–202.
42. Jean-François Lyotard, *The Postmodern Condition: A Report on Knowledge*, trans. Geoff Bennington and Brian Massumi, THL 10 (Minneapolis: University of Minnesota Press, 1984), xxiv–xxv.
43. Lyotard, *Postmodern Condition*, 18–23.

allowed us to benefit from the dehumanization of others, have a particular need to test our worldviews and ask if there are ways to become better, more ethical scholars. We decide upon interpretations and interpretive practices based on the goals we have, which is why pragmatists say that good interpretations are ones that serve our purposes and help us meet our goals.[44] The goals we decide to pursue matter because some of them are better than others. We can only make the judgment as to what is hermeneutically better or worse based on beliefs we hold, but we should aim to have as coherent a set as we can when we make such decisions. If we can acknowledge that historical criticism is not a necessary part of academic biblical interpretation, then our privileging of it suddenly appears to sit in uneasy tension with ethical beliefs we already have. It makes some sense, then, to believe that dialogue with less privileged peers whose work is dedicated to liberation will provide helpful ways to test our presuppositions about our professional work, and it is to such dialogue that I now turn.

44. Stout, "What Is the Meaning of a Text?," 1–12; Rorty, *Objectivity, Relativism, and Truth*, 89.

4

The Need for Change in Biblical Studies

Ethical Problems with the Historical Critical Method

As important as dialogue with others is when we want to test the coherence of our beliefs, we can hardly expect that it will always lead to change. Entering into conversation with others with somewhat different views will often just result in a renewed sense of the correctness of one's own worldview, something that will affirm why we think others are wrong. As an example of this, we can turn to a multiyear project that had groups of nonscholarly readers from different cultures and countries analyze biblical texts, each group exchanging the report of their interpretive work with that of another from a different culture who had read the same passage.[1] The goal was to see how readers might be transformed through such a beginning to intercultural dialogue on biblical interpretation, and the organizers of the project argued that this did lead some of the groups to reflect on their own cultures and to view their dialogue partners differently, but that this simply did not happen all of the time.[2] In one case, for example, a group of readers from Sokhanya in South Africa was partnered with a group from Zaandam in the Netherlands. Both produced interpretations of John 4, but neither altered its understanding of the text in light of the other's reading, and the group from Sokhanya found the analysis

1. For much more extensive introductions to and explanations of the project, see Hans de Wit, "Through the Eyes of Another: Objectives and Backgrounds," in *Through the Eyes of Another: Intercultural Reading of the Bible*, ed. Hans de Wit et al. (Elkhart, IN: Institute of Mennonite Studies, 2004), 3–53; and Hans de Wit and Janet Dyk, "Introduction," in *Bible and Transformation: The Promise of Intercultural Bible Reading*, ed. Hans de Wit and Janet Dyk, SemeiaSt 81 (Atlanta: Society of Biblical Literature, 2015), 1–16.
2. Hans de Wit and Janet Dyk, "Concluding Reflections," in Wit and Dyk, *Bible and Transformation*, 450–57.

of their Dutch counterparts "unacceptable" and "unbecoming."[3] Anyone who has participated in dialogue about biblical texts with others whose worldviews incline them to read those texts differently will have encountered situations like this; as in the intercultural reading experiment, sometimes communities' understandings of how to read the Bible will simply be too different to allow for much of a conversation, as Eric Anum noted in regard to the project.[4]

Dialogue that results in a person or group changing their mind will have to be conducted on topics on which the two parties already share quite a bit in common. If worldview is composed of a more or less coherent set of beliefs we hold about the way things are, and we assume our beliefs are true, we will want to change as few of them as possible when confronted with evidence we feel compelled to accept but that obviously contradicts some assumptions we have. That is to say, as chapter 3 discusses, in situations like these we will always try to minimize the reweaving of our webs of beliefs, for we need our beliefs to make sense of the world and we generally think they are largely correct. Yet since at least some more privileged students and scholars of biblical studies already share the ethical beliefs their marginalized colleagues rely on when trying to convince us to prioritize liberative readings of the Bible, there is a greater possibility that we will be able to acknowledge the inconsistencies in our worldviews that they point to and rearrange our beliefs as to what we should do in our professional work as teachers and researchers. As this chapter discusses, minoritized scholars reading for liberation are generally not asking us to stop doing historical criticism but to stop insisting that it is a necessary part of valid academic interpretation and that it is free of bias. Chapters 2 and 3 pointed out that the field has not provided good reasons to privilege historical investigation as a necessary part of valid biblical scholarship and that if many scholars continue to act as if it had, that is due to the habits we have developed through being members of the mainstream community of the discipline. In this chapter I will look at some of the criticisms marginalized scholars have leveled against these interpretive habits that, they point out, have blinded some of us to the fact that historical criticism is based

3. Danie van Zyl, "The Eyes of the Other as Porthole and Mirror: The Communication between Sokhanya and Zaandam," in Wit et al., *Through the Eyes of Another*, 204–7.
4. Eric Anum, "Unresolved Tension and the Way Forward," in Wit et al., *Through the Eyes of Another*, 176–78.

on ideological presuppositions that lock up the real significance of the biblical texts in the past rather than making them available as a resource for liberative struggle. Moreover, they argue, our insistence that the field prioritize historical study has not prevented well-meaning scholars from producing unethical results that reflect our memberships in powerful but racist, sexist, and homophobic cultures that have affected our worldviews. In fact, insisting on the legitimacy of something like Stendahl's ditch that largely confines biblical studies to historical work and that sees no other interpretations as valid if they do not recognize the priority of such study has kept readings for liberation at the margins of the field. As a result, some marginalized scholars maintain, they themselves sometimes feel compelled to erase key aspects of their identities when they wish to succeed in the field, and so demands to privilege historical criticism as a necessary part of all academic interpretive work have acted to suppress liberative readings meant to benefit groups fighting oppression.

What scholars who have been kept at the margins of the discipline ask of their more privileged colleagues, then, is that we become part of a liberative solution to the problem of dehumanization by honoring the ethical beliefs that we already hold. We can privilege liberative goals in interpretation by aligning our professional work with our belief that we should fight oppression whenever that is reasonably possible, but this does not demand the abandonment of the techniques in which we have been trained and have expertise, including historical critical ones, as chapters 5 and 6 demonstrate. The result, then, is that following the lead of our minoritized peers will not demand a vast change in what we already believe are good ways to go about interpretation. More privileged students and scholars will not be able to read exactly as our marginalized colleagues do, but this will not prevent us from producing work that we recognize as scholarly, as chapters 7 and 8 demonstrate. As a result, we will be able to operate with more coherent worldviews, ones that can incorporate our ethical beliefs into our professional work as we urge our own socioeconomically privileged communities to seriously consider how we have been complicit in oppression and how we can act against it, while also aiming to produce academic work useful to our minoritized colleagues as they and their communities fight their dehumanization.

This means, as those colleagues tell us, that we will have to give up on the notion of the historical critical method as a neutral and bias-free approach to biblical texts and their ancient contexts. There can be no interpretation or knowledge of any sort without the belief systems and their biases and presuppositions about the way the world is, as chapter 3 argues, although this runs counter to the way many people in the discipline understand historical criticism. When John Van Seters, for example, writes that historical critics developing a history of Israel in the Iron Age are not involved in a theological or ideological project,[5] he assumes that such historical work, when done properly, is ideologically neutral, reflecting no bias at all, and designed neither to benefit nor to harm any particular group. The fact of the matter, however, is that a decision to ignore politics or contemporary ideological struggles is still a political and ideological decision: "Every philosophical colloquium necessarily has a political significance,"[6] and a decision to produce nonideological work in the sense that Van Seters understands the idea is not an apolitical one. It is to choose not to contribute to a struggle against oppression and to say that our hands are tied by methodological imperatives, because the only thing good biblical scholars should want to do is to work on their side of Stendahl's ditch and arrive at true answers to historical questions. Our hands, however, are not tied by method, as I discussed in chapters 2 and 3, and to do nothing in the face of oppression and suffering is to choose to accept their presence. As Tikva Frymer-Kensky puts it, "There is no value-neutrality with regard to oppression: if one does not consciously address a problem, one becomes part of the problem."[7] There are millions of people for whom the Bible is an important resource in the face of the oppression they endure, and what biblical scholarship does and does not do in light of this suffering matters, even if the impact of our work might be small. If we manage never to produce work that someone could conceivably use to fight for liberation, including work aimed to alert the more privileged to their ethical duties to be allies in this fight, then we have chosen the side of oppression.

The case is not that historical critics operate with a covert oppressive agenda of which they are aware but deliberately hiding from their readers and students. My point simply has to do with blind spots. As members of a field, we are taught

5. John Van Seters, "A Response to G. Aichele, P. Miscall and R. Walsh, 'An Elephant in the Room: Historical-Critical and Postmodern Interpretations of the Bible,'" *JHS* 9 (2009): art. 26 (pp. 4–5).
6. Jacques Derrida, "The Ends of Man," in *Margins of Philosophy*, trans. Alan Bass (Chicago: University of Chicago Press, 1982), 109.
7. Tikva Frymer-Kensky, *Studies in the Bible and Feminist Criticism* (Philadelphia: Jewish Publication Society, 2006), 162.

how to act by it, and through our research and watching what our peers do we develop habits, ones that, in the field of biblical studies, normally privilege historical critical work. Habits, as chapter 3 discusses, can blind us to contradictions among our beliefs, especially when there is little in our own experiences that pushes us to confront those contradictions. Biblical studies is an overwhelmingly white and male discipline, as chapter 1 mentions, and so it is largely populated by those who come from the more privileged sections of society that generally have no cultural or economic reason to question a status quo that has done reasonably well by them. The case is not that no males of European descent have ever experienced oppression, and there are many intelligent and well-educated biblical scholars, including some white males, toiling in part-time and non-tenure-track positions with little job security and limited benefits.[8] However, the communities we come from will limit the sorts of interests we will have and questions we will think to ask about the biblical texts, and if the groups with which we most closely identify have no recent experience of oppression, and if they have often prospered due in part to the oppression of others that we fail to see, it will be much harder for us to question what we habitually do and to see issues of social justice as matters we should address in our professional work.

So "the historical-critical method is perhaps the most suitable praxis for white, male, middle-class academics," writes Kwok Pui-lan, "because they alone can afford to be 'impartial,' which literally means 'non-committed.' Oppressed women and men of all colors find that the historical-critical method alone cannot help them to deal with the burning questions they face."[9] In apartheid-era South Africa, says Madipoane Masenya, academic biblical studies was largely taught by white men who benefited from the political status quo and who focused on the biblical texts as ancient documents without relevance for contemporary political conflicts, although their African students did not have the luxury of studying the Bible

8. In the Society of Biblical Literature's 2019 survey of its membership, of the 3,848 respondents who reported on their status as faculty (this number excludes those who stated they were retired or unemployed), 1,692 (44 percent) indicated they did not hold tenured or tenure-track positions. Of those individuals, 1,247 (about 74 percent) identified as males, roughly equal to the percentage of male membership of the Society of Biblical Literature as a whole. These figures were not further subdivided by race, however. "2019 SBL Membership Data," 5.
9. Kwok Pui-lan, "Racism and Ethnocentrism in Feminist Biblical Interpretation," in *Discovering the Bible in the Non-biblical World* (Maryknoll, NY: Orbis, 1995), 86.

as something detached from their everyday struggles.[10] If European and North American biblical theology has almost nothing to say about oppression, writes Elsa Tamez, we should not be surprised, because its practitioners generally have no real experience of the level of oppression and suffering experienced by so many of the world's poor;[11] it simply does not occur to many of us that this might be an important problem to address, and the result is that the field's mainstream aligns itself with structures of dominance that have no interest in addressing issues of oppression as it marginalizes those who struggle for justice.[12] When this happens, says Vincent Wimbush, biblical scholars become apologists for Western regimes of power,[13] because in our professional work we act as if this oppression, rooted in the power exercised by Western institutions, does not exist and as if nothing needs to be done about it. And when mainstream biblical studies fails to address issues of oppression and liberation that are at the center of interest to those on the margins of society and of the field, writes Cheryl Anderson, it does so because it has adopted as a norm the perspective of white males, who as a group are largely unaffected by the suffering the marginalized experience and thus who often do not notice it, and so the needs and interests of those outside of that mainstream remain unimportant.[14]

Nor is a broader ignorance about such issues a defense for refusing to address oppression in our professional work, for that lack of knowledge reflects a kind of innocence that Eduardo Mendieta calls "epistemic privilege" and describes as "a luxury of a power position. Only a certain type of subject, in a certain location can afford not to know, or can derive substantive benefits from not knowing, or from being in the orchestrated position of being able to claim 'plausible deniability.'"[15] Modern biblical studies has traditionally rooted its "plausible deniability" in an

10. Madipoane Masenya (ngwan'a Mphahlele), "A Wooden Spoon from the Pot: She Speaks," in *Women and the Society of Biblical Literature*, ed. Nicole L. Tilford, BSNA 29 (Atlanta: Society of Biblical Literature, 2019), 213–15.
11. Elsa Tamez, *Bible of the Oppressed*, trans. Matthew J. O'Connell (Maryknoll, NY: Orbis, 1982), 4.
12. See Spencer Miller, "Feminist Pedagogies," 21.
13. Wimbush, *Scripturalectics*, 12–14.
14. Cheryl B. Anderson, "Biblical Interpretation as Violence: Genesis 19 and Judges 19 in the Context of HIV and AIDS," in La Violencia *and the Hebrew Bible: The Politics and Histories of Biblical Hermeneutics on the American Continent*, ed. Susanne Scholz and Pablo R. Andiñach, SemeiaSt 82 (Atlanta: Society of Biblical Literature, 2016), 126–27.
15. Eduardo Mendieta, "The Ethics of (Not) Knowing: Take Care of Ethics and Knowledge Will Come of Its Own Accord," in *Decolonizing Epistemologies: Latina/o Theology and Philosophy*, ed. Ada María Isasi-Díaz and Eduardo Mendieta, TTC (New York: Fordham University Press, 2012), 60.

assertion that its main focus must be on the contexts of authors who have been dead for many centuries, an approach that distances biblical texts from contemporary concerns.[16] The assertion of the worldview manifested in Stendahl's ditch is that the main goal of biblical scholars is to ask historical questions, and since scholars need only do that, there is no necessity to interact with the work of interpreters who have nonhistorical interests, and as a result scholars can feel as if they have no need to learn about the issues the less privileged understand to be of burning concern. But when the mainstream field sequesters biblical texts from these concerns, writes Susanne Scholz, it is complicit in the violence and oppression it fails to address.[17] The field's "terms of membership" require an apolitical stance, Wimbush points out, and so it simply provides validation for the elitist academic and religious institutions that have shaped it, because the members of the field have agreed to put themselves in a position where they cannot challenge this elitism and its dangerous effects.[18] However, he writes, the experiences of African Americans "should always dramatically challenge biblical scholars to ask whether biblical scholarship focused merely upon historiography or literary-rhetorical artfulness can ever be considered benign."[19] How one decides to produce an interpretation or meaningful text will reflect the questions one might decide to ask and the goals one has in the act of interpretation, and this will depend on the communities one belongs to and the sorts of experiences members of those communities tend to have, but more privileged biblical scholars are perfectly able to dialogue with the work of minoritized scholars and get some sense of their experiences and concerns. It is possible that a white male reading the story of Jephthah's daughter in Judges 11 might never think to ask how female readers, ancient or modern, could encounter this narrative as one promoting female submission to patriarchal social structures, a submission that could result in their deaths, yet chapter 2 points out that some female scholars have identified this as the key aspect of the story. White male scholars might never think to ask how women of color could see Judges 11 as

16. See, for example, Uriah Y. Kim, *Identity and Loyalty in the David Story: A Postcolonial Reading*, HBM 22 (Sheffield, UK: Sheffield Phoenix, 2008), 20; and Scholz, *Bible as Political Artifact*, 70.
17. Susanne Scholz, "How to Read the Bible in the Belly of the Beast: About the Politics of Biblical Hermeneutics within the United States," in Scholz and Andiñach, La Violencia *and the Hebrew Bible*, 137–40.
18. Wimbush, "In Search of a Usable Past," 179–80.
19. Vincent L. Wimbush, "Introduction: Reading Darkness, Reading Scriptures," in *African Americans and the Bible: Sacred Texts and Social Textures*, ed. Vincent L. Wimbush (Eugene, OR: Wipf & Stock, 2000), 14.

a protest against such structures, or as a model for the mourning they are forced to undergo because of the marginalized positions they occupy in society, but dialogue with minoritized colleagues can open our eyes to just these sorts of readings and the needs and concerns that lie behind them. It is possible that a white male might never think of the story of Hagar in Genesis 16 as one that is about the rape of an African slave by a patriarch of Israel, nor ask what it says about the experiences of enslaved women and their descendants, but as Delores Williams observes, African American women have thought quite a bit about this.[20] Their communities and their experiences simply lead them to different questions about the text and provide them with different goals to pursue in their interpretations, and that is precisely the reason why, if we want to act upon our ethical beliefs as students and scholars of biblical studies, it is important to interact with scholars who emerge from these communities and whose work is driven by ethical concerns grounded in their communities' struggles for liberation.

Historical critics sometimes refer to the standard of objectivity to justify what they do, and the modern understanding of objectivity, as chapter 3 discusses, developed in the nineteenth century out of the fear that the observer's biases would stand in the way of a true evaluation of data, but we have seen that there cannot be any evaluation of data at all, and so no truth, without the belief systems that create those biases. All objectivity can really refer to, then, is an agreement among a group of interpreters as to how to go about their work.[21] Historical criticism can seem to be an important and necessary thing to do when we assume that we are faced with texts produced in cultures remote from our contemporary ones and their concerns, but this assumption has the effect of shutting up the true meaning of the Bible in the past, as Severino Croatto argues,[22] and is also one that is ignorant of the reality of millions of people who see no such ditch between themselves and the biblical texts. To argue that we cannot understand the texts if we do not do historical work is itself a presupposition, something rooted in a particular belief system about valid interpretation. As chapter 2 mentions, most readers of the Bible,

20. Delores S. Williams, "Hagar in African American Biblical Appropriation," in *Hagar, Sarah, and Their Children: Jewish, Christian, and Muslim Perspectives*, ed. Phyllis Trible and Letty M. Russell (Louisville, KY: Westminster John Knox, 2006), 172–73.
21. Rorty, *Philosophy and the Mirror of Nature*, 335.
22. J. Severino Croatto, *Biblical Hermeneutics: Toward a Theory of Reading as the Production of Meaning*, trans. Robert R. Barr (Maryknoll, NY: Orbis, 1987), 8–9.

including some who are scholars, regularly create meaning through their interpretations of biblical texts without relying on any of the techniques of historical criticism. One could certainly argue that these readings would not be possible without scholarly work that used techniques associated with the historical critical method to create lexicons and translations, but my point is simply that to rely on earlier historical work is not the same thing as doing such work oneself as one goes about interpretation. My arguments in the previous two chapters were meant to establish the idea that no good reasons have been offered to demand that all research must include some historical evaluation if we are to recognize it as valid biblical criticism, let alone insist that the results of historical criticism be the arbiter of nonhistorical readings because it alone can create an "original" text. Claims to the contrary are grounded in a particular cultural perspective, one that is not shared by many of those from the margins of the discipline, as the examples in this regard in chapter 2 demonstrate.[23]

The historical critical method is objective only in the sense that much of the field turns to its techniques in its professional work, not because it is free of bias and presupposition, as chapter 3 points out, since no mode of interpretation ever could be. However, when more privileged scholars do our work in the belief that we interpret without ideology, pursuing historical questions in research that harms no one, we not only fail to notice the tacit support that we lend to oppressive status quos, but we also often do not see how the conclusions at which we arrive sometimes explicitly violate important aspects of ethical beliefs we have. Shawn Kelley makes this point when he argues that racism permeates modern thought and so permeates mainstream biblical studies, a field created by the modern world. For example, key aspects of the work of Rudolf Bultmann, arguably the most influential New Testament scholar of the twentieth century, relied on the thought of Martin Heidegger, whose philosophical writings drove groundbreaking developments in his own discipline. As important a philosopher as Heidegger was, however, he was also a member of the Nazi party and supported its racist and anti-Semitic agenda. When Bultmann contrasted the freedom and authenticity of Pauline Christianity with a Judaism that he portrayed as inauthentic and legalistic, argues Kelley, he

23. See also Fernando F. Segovia, "Toward a Hermeneutics of the Diaspora: A Hermeneutics of Otherness and Engagement," in Segovia and Tolbert, *Reading from This Place*, 1:70–71.

was adopting key aspects of this racism.[24] Or, to take another example of a scholar's historical work reflecting racist beliefs, R. S. Sugirtharajah discusses the ways in which Joachim Jeremias's influential study of Jesus's parables portrayed the population of Palestine as an exotic but unsophisticated and lazy Oriental people, reflecting standard nineteenth- and twentieth-century European attitudes toward the East, attitudes the continent's powers used to justify their appropriation of other peoples' land and labor in colonization.[25]

My point here is not that historical criticism is inherently anti-Semitic and racist, or that it cannot be practiced without arriving at racist conclusions, but that our use of it will be affected by other beliefs we hold that have been provided to us by communities of which we are members. There is nothing about the techniques associated with the method that can guarantee that it will not reflect those communities' racist or sexist or homophobic notions, and this is why well-intentioned mainstream biblical scholars can be influenced by such beliefs and arrive at racist, sexist, and/or homophobic interpretations of biblical texts. It matters, then, that we choose ethical goals before we embark upon any kind of study, and that we listen to scholars from communities that have been negatively impacted by sexism, racism, colonization, and homophobia. The work done by means of historical criticism or any other kind of reading we choose to undertake will reflect political and ideological goals that derive from the various communities and cultures to which scholars belong, even when they are not aware that this is the case. Certainly, the work of influential nineteenth- and twentieth-century figures in Old Testament theology, which was strongly influenced by historical criticism, was permeated by anti-Semitism. Jon Levenson notes that even though such scholars were experts in the study of the Old Testament, they could write as if Judaism did not exist, or as if it could exist only as a religion incomplete without Christianity. Julius Wellhausen, one of the most important figures of nineteenth- and early-twentieth-century biblical scholarship, portrayed Judaism as Bultmann did, cut off from religious vitality. He wrote "at a time of swelling Jew-hatred," says Levenson, and never challenged the anti-Semitism of his age, although he died in Germany only a generation

24. Shawn Kelley, *Racializing Jesus: Race, Ideology and the Formation of Modern Biblical Scholarship*, BibLim (London: Routledge, 2002), 129–64.
25. R. S. Sugirtharajah, *Asian Biblical Hermeneutics and Postcolonialism: Contesting the Interpretations*, BibLit (Maryknoll, NY: Orbis, 1998), 102–4.

before the Holocaust. It is no wonder, then, that at the beginning of the twentieth century, Solomon Schlechter, a scholar of Judaica, argued that anti-Semitism was central to the worldviews of those who practiced historical criticism.[26]

The historical study of the Bible sometimes still reflects this kind of anti-Semitism. When it comes to the part of the field that studies the Hebrew Bible, Levenson writes, it often is a study of the Christian Old Testament;[27] even New Testament scholars tend to know the biblical Hebrew of the Old Testament rather than the Mishnaic Hebrew of postbiblical Judaism, although the latter would be far more relevant for their work.[28] Many scholars still follow the distinction between a preexilic ancient Israelite religion and a postexilic Judaism popularized and promoted by Wellhausen. For Wellhausen, Judaism began only after the Babylonian exile, and he described it as inferior to the authentic spirit of preexilic ancient Israelite religion. It was that earlier, better, and non-Jewish religion that Jesus revived, Wellhausen wrote, as early Christianity shook itself free from the stultifying Judaism of Jesus's contemporaries. Wellhausen was influenced by a general drive in nineteenth-century German scholarship to distinguish Protestantism's religious roots from Judaism, writes James Pasto, part of a program that could provide the emerging German state with a religious identity that did not exacerbate the divide between Catholics and Protestants.[29] As Kelley points out, scholars continued to contrast the freedom of the message of the historical Jesus with the religion overseen by his Jewish contemporaries, who are often portrayed by New Testament scholars as unable to think and act authentically, shackled by their culture.[30] This sort of scholarly creation of the historical Jesus and of the meaningful texts of the New Testament unconsciously reflects the thought not just of Bultmann and Wellhausen but of nineteenth- and twentieth-century political movements that were overtly anti-Semitic. Working by habit, we pick up the habits of our teachers and

26. Jon D. Levenson, *The Hebrew Bible, the Old Testament, and Historical Criticism: Jews and Christians in Biblical Studies* (Louisville, KY: Westminster John Knox, 1993), 42.
27. Joseph Blenkinsopp writes that, particularly in the subfield of Old Testament theology, the Old Testament was seen as a work that is fulfilled in the salvation history of Christ, and so practitioners tended to ignore the significance of writings that led to important developments in postbiblical Judaism. See his "Old Testament Theology and the Jewish Christian Connection," JSOT 28 (1985): 6–11.
28. Levenson, *Hebrew Bible, the Old Testament, and Historical Criticism*, 85–86.
29. James Pasto, "When the End Is the Beginning? Or When the Biblical Past Is the Political Present: Some Thoughts on Ancient Israel, 'Post-exilic Judaism,' and the Politics of Biblical Scholarship," SJOT 12 (1998): 157–202.
30. Kelley, *Racializing Jesus*, 165–210.

peers, even when they are not always virtuous ones, and even an event as horrific as the Holocaust can fail to cure us of them. Martin Noth, for example, decided to conclude his history of ancient Israel with the story of the failed Jewish rebellion against Roman power in the early second century CE, an event that followed soon after the completion of the New Testament writings. He referred to the rebellion as "the ghastly epilogue of Israel's history," which, as Levenson notes, seems like an odd phrase to use, not only because Jews continued to live in Palestine for centuries after this, but also because Noth, a German scholar, wrote this less than a decade after the Holocaust.[31] One can read Noth here as suggesting that Judaism came to an end once the New Testament was completed, the real goal of Judaism's existence, allowing him to ignore the Holocaust altogether.

Racism enters the field because those of us who work in it do not exist in some kind of cultural vacuum but belong to other communities with other beliefs, and in general we work to make sure our overall sets of beliefs fit together, just as everyone else does. We cannot be surprised, although we should be saddened, that we find anti-Semitic work produced by scholars who live in cultures influenced by anti-Semitism. Nor is it surprising that, for example, twentieth-century British scholars used historical criticism to reflect the racism inherent to European colonialism when composing biblical commentaries for Indian churches. While the authors of the Indian Church Commentaries may have been interested in arriving at authorial intention, they also described superstition, laziness, and mendacity as aspects of Indian society, notes R. S. Sugirtharajah. They maintained that pre-British culture in India was barbarous and superstitious, and claimed that colonialism and Christianity were of great benefit to the subcontinent.[32] The Christian Students' Library, a series of textbooks produced in the middle of the twentieth century for Indian seminary students, used historical criticism to contrast an objective Christianity with a mythical Hinduism.[33] Historical criticism developed and was embraced by the Western academy at the same time as the West's colonizing drive of imperial expansion was reaching its height, as Uriah Kim observes, and so we cannot be shocked—although, again, we should be saddened—that it adopted aspects of the

31. Levenson, *Hebrew Bible, the Old Testament, and Historical Criticism*, 86–87.
32. Sugirtharajah, *Asian Biblical Hermeneutics*, 54–85.
33. R. S. Sugirtharajah, "Biblical Studies in India: From Imperialistic Scholarship to Postcolonial Interpretation," in *Teaching the Bible: The Discourses and Politics of Biblical Pedagogy*, ed. Fernando F. Segovia and Mary Ann Tolbert (Maryknoll, NY: Orbis, 1998), 286–92.

broader thought and interests of colonialism that pervaded the cultures of those of European descent.[34] The West justified its control of much of the rest of the planet through the belief that others would benefit from Western rule, a belief that accompanied the Enlightenment's certainty that the ways the West went about doing things and thinking about the world were universally valid, the ways that every human being should think and act. This belief too became part of historical criticism, writes Kwok Pui-lan. We have already come across arguments by biblical scholars in chapter 2 to the effect that historical criticism is the indispensable (or universal) method necessary for arriving at the meaning of biblical texts, a narrative based in what Lyotard would call a metanarrative about "the text in itself." And once the field was able to establish this narrative as fact, it was free to ignore other ways of reading the Bible, such as ones that did not begin with a commitment to looking at it as a collection of writings from an ancient and distant world, or ones that did not always insist on historical work and that did not always arise out of the academy.[35] The belief that historical criticism was the universally valid method of reading meant that non-European methods of interpretation could then be considered to be inferior, argues Abraham Smith, a belief that relied on and supported an ideological basis for racism.[36]

It is not only marginalized scholars who have made arguments like these, but marginalized scholars primarily have been the ones pointing out that the mainstream of the discipline silently supports different forms of the racism—not to mention the sexism and homophobia—of the larger cultures to which its members belong. These sorts of things become difficult to overlook once we pay attention to the arguments of minoritized scholars who can show us how the field's claims about the objectivity and ideological neutrality of the historical method also have the result of dismissing their interpretive work. Those who, like Van Seters, understand their historical research to be nonideological tend to use the term *ideology* pejoratively, as something that refers to beliefs that are inappropriate to engage when doing biblical research, since they will cause one to perceive of and portray texts and their contexts inaccurately. Mitzi Smith writes that this sort

34. Kim, *Identity and Loyalty*, 15–20.
35. Kwok, *Postcolonial Imagination*, 79–80.
36. Abraham Smith, "Taking *Spaces* Seriously: The Politics of Space and the Future of Western Biblical Studies," in *Transforming Graduate Biblical Education: Ethos and Discipline*, ed. Elisabeth Schüssler Fiorenza and Kent Harold Richards, GPBS 10 (Atlanta: Society of Biblical Literature, 2010), 73–83.

of characterization of liberative approaches to texts has been used to marginalize readings, such as some produced by African American scholars, that do not prioritize historical criticism.[37] We know, however, that no knowledge is possible without our preexisting sets of beliefs, and so we can also use the word *ideology* in a rather different way, as a term equivalent to *belief system* or *worldview*. The question as to whether a certain belief or set of them might consistently lead to false conclusions and interpretations can only be decided by appealing to other beliefs, as chapters 2 and 3 discuss, since it is not possible to vouch for them by comparing them to an extralinguistic world like "the text in itself." In this broader understanding of ideology, we can hardly claim that historical criticism is not ideological, since that is not true of any method.

One damaging result of the claim that historical work alone is objective and value neutral, argues Monica Melanchthon, is the concomitant belief that other approaches to biblical texts, in particular ones committed to the interests of oppressed groups, should not be considered as real biblical scholarship because they do not use appropriate methods.[38] If the choice to use the interpretation of biblical texts to fight for liberation is not seen as objective by mainstream scholarship, then it is obviously understood to be subjective, and so of far less value than the rigorous historical techniques that predominate in the Western academy.[39] It is thus a simple matter for mainstream biblical studies, through its assumptions in regard to the universality of the historical method, to devalue and ignore readings that aim to address economic, political, social, and religious oppression, writes Kwok,[40] even when most Jews and Christians look to biblical literature as a resource to make sense of current rather than ancient concerns.[41] Politically oriented study of the Bible, especially when done by scholars from the Two-Thirds World, says Musa Dube, is then often dismissed by the field as "some form of academic tourism," when it is not ignored entirely, which is how her own work has sometimes been treated.[42]

37. Smith, *Insights from African American Interpretation*, 14–16.
38. Melanchthon, "Unleashing the Power Within," 49.
39. Mary Ann Tolbert, "Defining the Problem: The Bible and Feminist Hermeneutics," in *The Bible and Feminist Hermeneutics*, ed. Mary Ann Tolbert, SemeiaSt 28 (Chico, CA: Scholars, 1983), 117–18.
40. Kwok, *Postcolonial Imagination*, 79–80.
41. Tolbert, "When Resistance Becomes Oppression," 2:345.
42. Musa W. Dube, "Rahab Is Hanging Out a Red Ribbon: One African Woman's Perspective on the Future of New Testament Scholarship," in Wicker, Spencer Miller, and Dube, *Feminist New Testament Studies*, 177–202 (quotation from p. 193).

The result, then, is that minoritized scholars can be placed in the position of conforming to a mode of scholarship developed by and for fairly privileged white males and their communities and be taught to ignore the issues that they might see to be important for themselves and their communities, all in the name of teaching "real" biblical scholarship that we believe to be the only kind that can get to the truth of the texts. So when historical criticism is promoted as the universal method for interpretation, female scholars who wish to succeed in academia feel pressure to do just the same things as the male gatekeepers in the field do, writes Heather McKay, but in doing so become complicit in the discipline's discourse that ignores the concerns and oppression of women and so provides tacit support for this very oppression.[43] Maria Dixon has written about the ways in which she feels torn between the largely white mainstream of biblical studies, with its demands for apolitical scholarship, and her feelings of responsibility to the Black community to address issues of social justice and diversity.[44] Minoritized scholars are faced with the choice of becoming academics recognized as important and productive members of the discipline, bracketing out their communities' concerns, or to be figures relegated to the margins in an academic ghetto, as Sze-kar Wan puts it,[45] a point echoed by Timothy Sandoval.[46] As a result, scholars from the Two-Thirds World who train in the North can lose the ability to "speak in their own tongue, to ask their own questions," writes Dube.[47]

When mainstream biblical criticism only tolerates but does not truly engage liberative approaches, we are involved in the marginalization of the communities for whom those approaches have been created. Deryn Guest, for example, writes that the most important problem that a lesbian-identified approach to biblical texts must deal with is lesbians' invisibility,[48] and so points directly to the marginalization of

43. Heather A. McKay, "On the Future of Feminist Biblical Criticism," in *A Feminist Companion to Reading the Bible: Approaches, Methods and Strategies*, ed. Athalya Brenner and Carole Fontaine (Sheffield, UK: Sheffield Academic, 1997), 81–82.
44. Maria Dixon, "The Exiled Native: The Paradox of the Black Scholar," in *God Loves Diversity and Justice: Progressive Scholars Speak about Faith, Politics, and the World*, ed. Susanne Scholz (Lanham, MD: Lexington, 2013), 141–55.
45. Wan, "Betwixt and Between," 142–44.
46. Timothy J. Sandoval, "How Did You Get to Be a Latino Biblical Scholar? Scholarly Identity and Biblical Scholarship," in *Latino/a Biblical Hermeneutics: Problematics, Objectives, Strategies*, ed. Francisco Lozada Jr. and Fernando F. Segovia, SemeiaSt 68 (Atlanta: Society of Biblical Literature, 2014), 289–90.
47. Dube, "Border Crossing," 10–11.
48. Deryn Guest, *When Deborah Met Jael: Lesbian Biblical Hermeneutics* (London: SCM, 2005), 111.

lesbians in society and of their readings of texts in the field of biblical studies. If we insist historical criticism is a universally valid method, the necessary way to arrive at the meaning of biblical texts, then we have to put ourselves in the position of insisting that the discipline cannot prioritize the needs and interests and burning concerns of the marginalized because we have a duty to focus on the original meanings of the texts, a view that fails to notice that interpreters create those original meanings. In this scenario, if the marginalized wish to participate in biblical studies, then they must erase their identities as members of minoritized communities as much as possible when they act as professionals in the field and abandon whatever interests and concerns and questions they might have as lesbians or Latinas or African Americans—become invisible as lesbians, Latinas, and African Americans, in other words, at least insofar as they do their scholarly work. Those identities, we would be implying, are what hold individuals back from doing the true work that rational and objective humans should do if they want to understand what the biblical texts mean. As we know from chapters 2 and 3, however, historical criticism is not a universal method, and we can see that claiming that it is only further contributes to marginalization, something that, I would hope, violates the ethical beliefs of the readers of this book. The historical critical method cannot save us from adopting assumptions that are sexist or racist or homophobic, so if we wish to continue to use it and not violate important ethical beliefs we hold, then we have to use it with ethical goals in mind. The ethics of liberation, rather than method, will have to be the basic principle that grounds our work, and our readings will have to be guided by an emancipatory ethic that resists dehumanization, something that takes priority over methodological choices.

The Primacy of Liberative Dialogue

Thanks to this first round of dialogue with the works of marginalized scholars, we can see that there is such a thing as an ethically unhealthy level of commitment to the historical critical method, a level one reaches when one insists that the academic or "real" study of biblical literature must involve historical work of some kind, or that this work is bias-free, or that it must be used to judge nonhistorically focused biblical interpretation—all assumptions of a worldview reflected in what I have been calling Stendahl's ditch. Assuming that we hold ethical beliefs that predispose us to avoid giving silent support to oppressive regimes of power, to avoid unintentionally arriving at conclusions that violate important ethical beliefs we hold, and to avoid preventing marginalized scholars from pursuing interpretations driven by the liberative needs of their communities, then we cannot ask that the discipline prioritize historical questions. This is not the same thing as demanding that biblical studies never take up historical questions again, but it is a request that students and scholars not use the norms and conclusions of historical study as the ultimate criteria to judge academic biblical interpretation. Assuming that we are ethically committed to supporting struggles against dehumanization and oppression whenever this is reasonably possible, and assuming also that we do not wish to be moral hypocrites, it makes sense that we use this ethical standard as the primary arbiter through which we determine whether or not we have produced good scholarly work.

Insofar as we can conceive of academics as professional thinkers, Richard Rorty writes, they serve their communities by asking where their webs of beliefs need reweaving, probing for gaps and inconsistencies in worldviews,[49] and this is an important service that marginalized scholars reading for liberation have provided biblical studies. For many more privileged scholars, as I mentioned at the beginning of this chapter, this reweaving of our beliefs that allows us to prioritize liberation rather than method in our professional work is possible because we already share some of the same ethical concerns about dehumanization and oppression with our less privileged colleagues. The arguments in chapters 2 and 3 that point out that interpreters and their reading communities create the original texts also make it easier for us to accept this rearrangement of priorities as we go about our work, for they help us see historical criticism as an option rather than a necessity, and scholars reading for liberation do use techniques associated with the method, as we will see in the next chapter. Nothing in the arguments I surveyed in this chapter suggests a need to abandon interpretive approaches that we already use with regularity, they simply point out that we have an ethical responsibility to aim to use them for liberative ends. Given that there are millions of people who see the Bible as authoritative in some fashion and who are not treated as free and equal individuals, but instead are oppressed because of their race, gender identification, poverty, class, sexual orientation, religious beliefs, and/or disability, and so

49. Rorty, *Essays on Heidegger and Others*, 17–18.

given that it matters to them whether biblical literature could be understood as something that can be used to combat oppression and provide them with hope, it matters why we decide to use historical criticism or any other method of reading biblical texts and what we hope to gain from the work we set out to do. Any interpretive method could be used for liberative ends, and certainly historical criticism was used to critique aspects of oppressive religious and social status quos in the late-nineteenth and twentieth centuries.[50] The current problem with the field of biblical studies, writes R. S. Sugirtharajah, is not the techniques of historical criticism themselves but the fact that "they have been in the hands of people whose social bias has placed a limitation on their use." Historical criticism was used to liberate the Western middle class, says Sugirtharajah, but it has often been deployed with the opposite effect in regard to women, people of color, and those in non-Western societies, who were taught by the mainstream of biblical studies that their own traditions could not be used to interpret the Bible properly.[51] Yet despite the fact that Sugirtharajah sees historical critical techniques as "developed by the bourgeois class to maintain its class interests," he also believes that they still can be used in liberative ways.[52]

So if we are able to rearrange our beliefs about the work we do as students and scholars of biblical studies, we can continue to use historical criticism and the other techniques in which we have experience and training. To argue that we should prioritize liberation in our work is not, when thinking about this in regard to the historical critical method, a zero-sum game but rather a matter of how to direct our work and judge its quality. Minoritized scholars have been arguing

50. See, for example, Vincent L. Wimbush, "Biblical Historical Study as Liberation: Toward an Afro-Christian Hermeneutic," JRT 42 (1985–86): 14–17; and Scholz, *Bible as Political Artifact*, 72–74. Scholz argues as well that, at the height of the Nazi era, Gerhard von Rad insisted on an "objective" approach to biblical studies as an implicit rejection of Nazi hermeneutics and propaganda ("How to Read the Bible in the Belly," 140–44; *Bible as Political Artifact*, 126–34). While I am not sure that I believe Scholz's argument that this established the norm of "objective" study of the Bible in the field—that approach was solidified in the nineteenth century, a point she makes as well (*Bible as Political Artifact*, 137)—her conclusion that von Rad's historical work, in its context, could be read as a rejection of the overt racism endemic to Nazism certainly has merit. Von Rad's overall legacy in regard to anti-Semitism, however, is more complicated than this, as Jon Levenson discusses in *The Hebrew Bible, the Old Testament, and Historical Criticism*, 33–61.

51. R. S. Sugirtharajah, "Critics, Tools, and the Global Arena," in *Reading the Bible in the Global Village: Helsinki*, ed. Heikki Räisänen et al. (Atlanta: Society of Biblical Literature, 2000), 52–53.

52. R. S. Sugirtharajah, "Introduction," in *Voices from the Margin: Interpreting the Bible in the Third World*, ed. R. S. Sugirtharajah (London: SPCK, 1991), 4.

for the necessity to set ethical goals for interpretation for quite some time,[53] but insofar as we feel ethically compelled to accept those goals, it would follow that we also have to accept the leadership and guidance of marginalized scholars in this endeavor. As the previous section of the chapter mentions, and as chapter 5 will discuss in greater depth, marginalized communities have had different experiences of oppression and liberation than more privileged ones, and this has led them to read the biblical text with somewhat different questions and expectations. They have the immediate experiences of the negative effects of oppression, they stand in need of liberation, they alone can speak knowledgeably as to what sorts of reading strategies will and will not be helpful in specific struggles for liberation, and so ultimately they must set the agenda. As a model for a more ethical field, then, we might think of Elisabeth Schüssler Fiorenza's depiction of the *ekklēsia* or open public space I mentioned in chapter 1, where everyone is understood to be equally human, where there is equal space for all voices, especially marginalized ones, and where everyone has the ability to interpret experiences and texts from their own perspectives. She sees this as something that must develop from the grassroots,[54] and if we wish to think of the grassroots as representing the perspectives and needs of the marginalized, then that is where biblical studies needs to turn. So Schüssler Fiorenza, for example, states that one way in which we can properly evaluate our work is by asking whether our approaches and results promote the well-being of women at the bottom of the sociopolitical ladder.[55] We will not know what their needs are in this regard, however, unless we know a fair bit about their world and experiences, and as a result we who fill the more privileged positions in the field must begin by listening to those who have intimate knowledge of the experiences and struggles of individuals in socioeconomic locations like this.

The need to begin interpretation with the experiences of the oppressed is a consistent theme in liberative readings, for only the oppressed know their own

53. For example, Tolbert, "When Resistance Becomes Oppression," 2:345–46; Nicole M. Simopoulos, "Who Was Hagar? Mistress, Divorcee, Exile, or Exploited Worker: An Analysis of Contemporary Grassroots Readings of Genesis 16 by Caucasian, Latina, and Black South African Women," in *Reading Other-Wise: Socially Engaged Biblical Scholars Reading with Their Local Communities*, ed. Gerald O. West, SemeiaSt 62 (Atlanta: Society of Biblical Literature, 2007), 71; and L. Juliana Claassens, "An Abigail Optic: Agency, Resistance, and Discernment in 1 Samuel 25," in *Feminist Frameworks and the Bible: Power, Ambiguity, and Intersectionality*, ed. L. Juliana Claassens and Carolyn J. Sharp, LHBOTS 630 (London: Bloomsbury, 2017), 31.

54. Schüssler Fiorenza, *Democratizing Biblical Studies*, 4–7.

55. Schüssler Fiorenza, *Power of the Word*, 66.

cultures and their own contexts of oppression well enough to know how best to confront oppression there. To believe that we know more about their lives than they do and so to ignore their speech and see them as incapable of fighting oppression is to strip them of agency and dehumanize them. This is why, as chapter 5 discusses, liberative readings must begin with the experiences of the marginalized and why those of us who are in more privileged social positions will have to follow the agendas they set, ones that begin with experiences that we do not share, with the result that it is not possible for us to speak first in a liberative dialogue. But this commitment to acknowledging the true humanity of others by truly listening to and considering their arguments does not oblige me to consider the arguments of those whose approaches to interpretation violate important ethical values I hold, and so I do not feel as if I have to consider the arguments of biblical interpretation that proceed from, for example, overtly racist groups. Approaches like those are based in belief systems so inimical to my own that I do not see how I would be able to seriously consider, let alone accept, them; they would run up against so many of my other beliefs that there would be no way I could undertake a program of reweaving to accommodate them.[56] All I can do is reject them, but this is not the case when it comes to interpretive strategies that are in accord with my own ethical beliefs in regard to treating others as fully human and working to reduce suffering and oppression in the world.

The result is, then, that the voices behind these liberative approaches are the ones that are most likely to demonstrate to me how I have been avoiding the disjuncture between my own ethical worldview and my professional commitments. There is a reason why, for example, Native American feminist theologies interrogate the contradictions in claims concerning the centrality of equality and democracy in the United States, a nation founded on slavery and genocide,[57] and a reason why many people of European descent who live there fail to even notice these contradictions: they are simply more apparent to the communities who have been harmed by them than to the ones whose privilege is in part a result of them. Once alerted to the

56. Rorty argues that people who participate in different language games certainly can communicate with each other, but they will be unable to resolve disagreements if they cannot resolve the more basic disjuncture between the beliefs that underlie the two language games; see Rorty, *Philosophy and Social Hope*, 62.
57. Andrea Smith, "Dismantling the Master's House with the Master's Tools: Native Feminist Liberation Theologies," in *Hope Abundant: Third World and Indigenous Women's Theology*, ed. Kwok Pui-lan (Maryknoll, NY: Orbis, 2010), 79–81.

contradictions in the beliefs we hold, contradictions that we can now see have made us complicit in shaping the field of biblical studies in an ethically problematic way, we will assumedly want to listen to the experiences of the marginalized to understand their goals and solutions. Those of us who hold more privileged positions will, over time, have things that we can contribute from our scholarly resources; we too come from societies and religious traditions with liberative ideals, even if our communities often fail to live up to them. We will not be able to speak for the marginalized or tell them what sorts of interpretive strategies they should pursue or what kinds of meaningful texts to create or provide for their liberation, and we will not always understand them perfectly, with the result that there will be times when dialogue is not always successful. We will be able to use their work to speak to our own academic and religious communities and suggest ways for them to change, and as we become more aware of the experiences of the marginalized and their needs and worldviews, we can put our resources at their service, from which they can pick and choose as they see fit. None of this will be possible without a dialogue where more privileged students and scholars of biblical studies begin by listening, however, and we move now to listen to some of the basic goals and approaches marginalized scholars have and use in the liberative interpretation of the Bible.

5

Listening, Part 1

Basic Goals and Approaches

Introduction: The Ethical Imperative to Listen

If we wish to make concern for the consequences of oppression and the ethical imperative of liberation formative for biblical studies, then it stands to reason that those of us who inhabit more privileged positions in the world and the field begin by listening to those who suffer the effects of oppression most directly, whose communities have the greatest need of liberation, and who have been working to achieve it long before others of us saw any necessity to contribute to this struggle. To fail to listen to their needs and agendas and to fail to follow their lead is to disavow the liberative project altogether, I argue in the first part of this chapter, before I move in the second section to survey basic liberative goals and approaches to reading by biblical scholars from marginalized communities. As chapter 1 mentions, dehumanization, as the common denominator of different forms of oppression, is the failure to see other groups of people as competent enough to be considered as truly human and able to make good decisions as "real" humans do. To avoid this, those of us from more privileged communities who wish to contribute to the liberative cause with the resources we can bring as biblical scholars cannot read the texts on behalf of the oppressed, for that is simply to repeat the dehumanization of oppression through the assumption that the marginalized are not competent to do so themselves. In the final part of the chapter, I will begin to address the question of what kind of role socioeconomically privileged scholars can take in this dialogue in which their marginalized peers speak first and set the interpretive agenda.

More privileged scholars who want to be in solidarity with those struggling for liberation have an ethical duty to begin by listening to what their minoritized colleagues are saying. In important part, this is because, as Ada Isasi-Díaz puts it in introducing *mujerista* discourse as liberative work that begins from the perspectives and experiences of Latinas in the United States, "liberation is not something one person can give another but . . . is a process in which the oppressed are protagonists, participants in creating a different reality from the present oppressive one."[1] The more privileged certainly cannot assume that we know how to provide for the liberation of the minoritized, an assumption that falls into the trap of promoting dehumanization, reflecting a dangerous elitism. We do not know enough about oppression and liberation to speak first in this dialogue, for we do not have remotely the same knowledge of minoritized communities and cultures and the situations in which they find themselves, and so we could not know what forms of resistance might work best for them. In her discussion of the *mujerista* struggle for liberation, Isasi-Díaz writes that non-Latinas can be in solidarity with this struggle but that this solidarity consists of ethical behavior or praxis that responds to Latinas' own speech and actions that further their liberation.[2] When it comes to the place of biblical interpretation meant to support those emancipatory goals, says Lily Fetalsana-Apura, "the context of the text is the text's co-text," by which she means that the context of liberative struggles against oppression from which the marginalized read is the text they should use to make sense of biblical literature.[3] In this way of looking at things, privileged biblical scholars do not have the context to read in place of the minoritized, although, having begun with a great deal of listening to what our marginalized peers are saying, we can bring to our own more privileged academic and religious communities what we have learned from them, and we can aim to produce work that might be of use to marginalized communities in their liberative struggles. In all cases, however, we can only begin by listening to the marginalized and by following their lead in interpretation, looking to them for guidance as to how to best do our own work as we enter into dialogue with them.

1. Isasi-Díaz, *Mujerista Theology*, 1.
2. Isasi-Díaz, 86–91.
3. Lily Fetalsana-Apura, *A Filipino Resistance Reading of Joshua 1:1–9*, IVBS 9 (Atlanta: Society of Biblical Literature, 2019), 160.

In the next section of the chapter, then, I continue the dialogue with marginalized biblical scholars by listening to their basic liberative goals and approaches to biblical texts. These scholars themselves emphasize that their communities' experiences of oppression and struggles for liberation must be the place where their work begins. In African biblical hermeneutics, writes Justin Ukpong, it is the poor who have "epistemological privilege" and who use their experiences to make sense of the Bible in ways they find to be liberative.[4] Gregory Cuéllar writes from a very different context than that of Ukpong—that of the Mexican diaspora in the United States—but makes a similar point when arguing that if we do not begin with the experiences of the marginalized, then we simply re-create a colonized Other.[5] He uses language from postcolonial theory here, a manner of reading texts that asks what effects colonization and its aftermaths have had on the literatures produced by the cultures affected by them. In describing the experience of a Black man living in a European colony, Frantz Fanon referred to the identity of the colonized as being created by the colonizers in order for the latter to construct their own identity.[6] The Self of the colonizers can then be distinguished from the Other of the colonized, who are "absolute evil" and "the negation of values,"[7] those who are uncivilized and unethical and uneducated and who do not have the capacity to rule themselves wisely. Even in the postcolonial period, colonial thought shapes the worldviews of the privileged and marginalized alike, as it does when biblical scholars insist that the real way to read biblical texts is that developed by Europeans. Those of us who belong to the dominant socioeconomic cultures in the postcolonial world must be wary that we do not simply assume, as Fanon's colonizers did, that the more privileged know better, or that the oppressed are victims unable to fend for themselves, which is just to reproduce the colonial mindset in which those of European descent need to care for and rule over those who appear to the colonizers and their postcolonial successors to be childlike by nature. And the case is no different if we aim to speak to more privileged communities about the problem of

4. Justin Ukpong, "Intercultural Hermeneutics: An African Approach to Biblical Interpretation," in *The Bible in a World Context: An Experiment in Contextual Hermeneutics*, ed. Walter Dietrich and Ulrich Luz (Grand Rapids, MI: William B. Eerdmans, 2002), 21–22.
5. Cuéllar, *Voices of Marginality*, 11–15.
6. See, for example, Frantz Fanon, *The Wretched of the Earth*, trans. Constance Farrington (New York: Grove, 1963), 36; and Frantz Fanon, *Black Skin, White Masks*, trans. Charles Lam Markmann (New York: Grove, 1967), 110.
7. Fanon, *Wretched of the Earth*, 41.

oppression; they cannot take responsibility for the liberation of the marginalized without dehumanizing them—which would mean they would not be contributing to liberation at all—and so if they wish to be in solidarity with liberative struggle, then they too must follow the directions of interpretation set by the marginalized and so begin to see how they can emancipate themselves from their postcolonial mindsets. The notion that liberative readings must begin with the experiences of those struggling against oppression makes perfect sense when one's goal is to learn from and be in solidarity with the fight of the marginalized to liberate themselves from it: liberation begins with their speech and the exercise of their agency, and only they fully know what it is to be oppressed, just as only the exercise of their agency can result in liberation.

If we are to commit ourselves to work guided by a liberative ethic, then we need to listen to the voices that speak from their experiences of oppression and struggles for liberation, so that our interpretations can be of some use to that fight. So womanist scholars, for example, who read texts from the perspectives of African American women, emphasize that the experiences of those women are where they begin in their interpretations;[8] since marginalized scholars reading for liberation aim to provide resources to support particular communities in emancipatory struggles, then they must begin with the needs, experiences, and questions that arise from those contexts. And this is also why scholars reading the Bible with Dalit communities in India privilege Dalit experience in their interpretations aimed at liberation,[9] just as Asian women scholars privilege the struggles of Asian women in theirs;[10] African women scholars, the experiences of African women in theirs;[11] queer, lesbian, and gay scholars, queer, lesbian, and gay experiences in theirs;[12] and

8. For example, Cheryl A. Kirk-Duggan, "Slingshots, Ships, and Personal Psychosis: Murder, Sexual Intrigue, and Power in the Lives of David and Othello," in Duggan, *Pregnant Passion*, 39; and Stephanie Buckhanon Crowder, *When Momma Speaks: The Bible and Motherhood from a Womanist Perspective* (Louisville, KY: Westminster John Knox, 2016), 33–36.
9. For example, C. I. David Joy, *Mark and Its Subalterns: A Hermeneutical Paradigm for a Postcolonial Context*, BW (London: Equinox, 2008), 52–54; and Monica Jyotsna Melanchthon, "Dalit Women and the Bible: Hermeneutical and Methodological Reflections," in Pui-lan, *Hope Abundant*, 110–11.
10. For example, Kwok, *Postcolonial Imagination*, 40–41; and Monica Jyotsna Melanchthon, "Toward Mapping Feminist Biblical Interpretations in Asia," in Fiorenza, *Feminist Biblical Studies*, 116–17.
11. For example, Makhosazana K. Nzimande, "Reconfiguring Jezebel: A Postcolonial *Imbokodo* Reading of the Story of Naboth's Vineyard," in Wit and West, *African and European Readers of the Bible*, 223–34; and Mbuwayesango, "Feminist Biblical Studies in Africa," 71–72.
12. For example, Mona West, "Reading the Bible as Queer Americans: Social Location and the Hebrew Scriptures," *ThSex* 10 (1999): 234–35; Guest, *When Deborah Met Jael*, 157–64; and Ken Stone, *Practicing Safer Texts: Food, Sex and Bible in Queer Perspective*, QTS (London: T&T Clark, 2005), 15–16.

so on. If these are the sorts of experiences where liberative readings begin, then more privileged scholars, whose experiences of the world have been very different, will not be able to contribute to liberation with our own work without first listening to the goals and approaches of communities like these and their biblical scholars. If there is an ethical imperative that commits us to being on the side of liberation, there is also an ethical imperative that we begin by listening.

Our starting point in the next section of the chapter, then, will be listening to the basic goals and approaches to reading of marginalized scholars committed to liberation, but to remind ourselves of conclusions reached in the previous chapters, we need not worry that these perspectives are subjective in the sense that they will allow readers to arrive at whatever meanings they want. We could take as an example Mitzi Smith's comment that womanist scholars see Black women and women of color in general as the creators of true epistemologies.[13] What she means by this is that approaches to the biblical texts that develop out of the backgrounds and experiences of women of color will provide them with true interpretations, where *true* has the sense of "best suited to the liberative struggle of women of color." But this does not somehow demand that we must argue that Black women, or readers in solidarity with them, can advance just any argument about the meanings of texts. Our interpretations are always constrained by the communities we come from, as I argue in chapter 3; there are only so many kinds of approaches one's reading communities will permit, and our worldviews, formed by these cultures, have provided us with belief systems that allow us to accept only a particular range of meanings. If we believe that the liberation of women of color from dehumanizing forces is a pressing issue because of the commitments that our ethical beliefs place upon us, then the best readings that we can perform are ones that we believe will contribute to that liberation, but this does not imply that we can advance arguments that we do not believe to be true, or at least not if we want to be intellectually honest. For example, if I truly believe that the Deuteronomist wrote the story of Jephthah's daughter to warn of the destruction of Israel that results from failing to know and do Torah, then I cannot in good faith argue that the author did not have this meaning in mind. I also know, however, that I do not

13. Mitzi Smith, "'This Little Light of Mine': The Womanist Biblical Scholar as Prophetess, Iconoclast, and Activist," in *I Found God in Me: A Womanist Biblical Hermeneutics Reader*, ed. Mitzi J. Smith (Eugene, OR: Cascade, 2015), 114.

have to talk about authorial intention at all if I have other goals for my interpretation. The question What are the criteria of a good interpretation? begs another: What are our goals for interpretation in the first place? Good interpretive work is, as pragmatists put it, work that serves our purposes, which means that it does a good job of answering the questions we have. Another way to put that is to say it meets our criteria of what makes a good reading, and these criteria are rooted in the goals for interpretation with which we start out.

In the case of the story of Jephthah's daughter, one's interpretive goal might be that of Cooper's, which is to ask how African American women encounter the story, and it is difficult to imagine how someone without a great deal of awareness of the experiences of Black women in the United States would be competent enough to read the passage with that goal. It might be that of Claassens's, which is to ask how Malawian women threatened with HIV infection might be able to encounter the story as liberative. In either case, I am able to see the interpretations or meaningful texts that Cooper and Claassens create as true without having to violate any of my beliefs about the date and composition of the Deuteronomistic History and the role of Judges 11:29–40 in it, precisely because these beliefs are not, given Cooper's and Claassens's interpretive goals, terribly relevant. By beginning with ethical goals, we are not in the position of accepting any interpretation as true, the erroneous conclusion of the Egalitarian Fallacy that chapter 3 discusses. Our communities' interests, guidelines, and norms in regard to interpretation will form and limit our readings in ways that will seem natural, what most obviously corresponds to "the text in itself," although this natural or normal sense of how to interpret can be thrown into question if one joins or enters into dialogue with another community that approaches interpretation with somewhat different interests and expectations.

Dialogue is important, as chapter 3 argues, because it allows us to test our worldviews and see if our beliefs hold together as well as we think they do, or at least it will when we engage the thought of those with rather different worldviews than our own. Chapter 4 shows that scholars from marginalized cultures have made a strong case that the assumptions and claims from the discipline's mainstream about the necessity of the historical critical method have led many of us to ignore our ethical beliefs in our professional work. Because their home communities allowed them to bring different goals and assumptions to the field, they have often experienced a clash of reading cultures as they entered the discipline, and so they were able to notice, long before the notion became more broadly accepted in biblical studies, that everyone's scholarship is shaped by some set of communal interests. What can seem obvious to minoritized scholars often is not to those of us rooted in the dominant cultures out of which the field developed, which is yet another key reason why real dialogue about a more ethical future for the discipline must begin with minoritized speech.

Marginalized scholars were able to see before the rest of the field that privileging the historical critical method is a way of privileging the interests of dominant groups because their own communities were disadvantaged in the decision to equate historical work with objectivity. It was only when the marginalized began to speak in biblical studies, or at least only when some of their more privileged peers began to listen to them, that some within the field's mainstream became aware that what they had simply assumed to be value neutral—their belief that true biblical studies could largely be equated with historical work, the objectivity of which was protected by Stendahl's ditch—really was not, says Tikva Frymer-Kensky.[14] The notion that the experiences and liberative actions of the oppressed provide the basis for academic work was widespread in liberation theology from Latin America long before the idea took hold in the field of biblical studies (or parts of it, at any rate), and it was the awareness that emancipatory action precedes academic reflection that led Gustavo Gutiérrez to write that the work of scholars can only "limp after" the liberative struggle of the poor.[15] Writing from a similar context, Severino Croatto argues that "exegesis is eisegesis, and anybody who claims to be doing only the former is, wittingly or unwittingly, engaged in ideological subterfuge."[16] Exegesis, the "leading out" of meaning from the text, is simply another way the field of biblical studies has of referring to "objectivity," which, as I discussed in the previous chapters, is just a way of talking about what the field normally does, although many see it as grounded in a metanarrative about a speaking text that has some sort of meaning inherent in it that needs to be led out by scholars who listen carefully to what it says. The field has traditionally understood

14. Frymer-Kensky, *Studies in the Bible and Feminist Criticism*, 159.
15. Gustavo Gutiérrez, *A Theology of Liberation: History, Politics, and Salvation*, rev. ed., trans. Caridad Inda and John Eagleson (London: SCM, 1988), 11.
16. J. Severino Croatto, *Exodus: A Hermeneutics of Freedom*, trans. Salvator Attanasio (Maryknoll, NY: Orbis, 1981), 2.

eisegesis as a "leading in" of meaning and something that scholars must avoid, since it amounts to a subjective importing of meaning that ignores what the text is saying. But what liberation theologians like Croatto understood, before biblical scholars in any number were able to acknowledge it, is that our communities and experiences shape our interpretations, and that to refuse to acknowledge this is to hide, even from oneself, the political stance to interpretation one has already adopted. Using terms like *exegesis* and *eisegesis* allows the field to guard the limits of its discourse and permit historical investigations while stifling liberative ones, arguing that objective exegesis is the only way to hear what the text has to say. This is just the sort of way communities act in order to hide their exercise of power, as Foucault observed, something chapter 3 briefly discusses. But long before Foucault, the eighteenth-century slave and abolitionist activist Olaudah Equiano recognized that the way Europeans viewed the Bible as a speaking text, something that justified European dominance and African slavery, managed to obscure the fact that this "plain sense" of scripture was simply a European creation.[17]

As I mentioned in chapter 2, Mary Ann Tolbert has argued that scholarly work based in historical criticism makes it easy to hide the fact that interpreters create meaning,[18] and that is particularly the case for those of us whose education in biblical studies is rooted in the historical method and whose backgrounds are in the cultures that created the modern field. Historical criticism seems objective to us, but Isasi-Díaz points out that objectivity is simply the subjectivity of the privileged;[19] those with interpretive power set the rules of the debate, so what appears to them as the natural and normal way to read becomes the only correct way to do so. Because Isasi-Díaz is right about the nature of objectivity, and because this means we need not begin our work by privileging historical method, we are free to do our academic work guided in the first instance by ethical considerations, work that necessarily begins with listening to the emancipatory goals and interpretive approaches of those struggling for liberation.

17. Wimbush, *White Men's Magic*, 178.
18. Tolbert, "When Resistance Becomes Oppression," 2:343–44.
19. Isasi-Díaz, *Mujerista Theology*, 76–77.

Listening: Basic Goals and Approaches

Because a good interpretation is one that does a good job of meeting the interpretive needs we have, our listening of necessity begins with some of the most basic goals marginalized communities and the biblical scholars who call those groups home aim to achieve in order to meet their liberative needs and with the approaches to the texts they use to achieve them. The variety among these communities and the experiences of their members is vast, but insofar as they struggle for liberation, we do see some overlap as biblical scholars from these groups discuss general goals for interpretation and approaches to the biblical texts and their ancient and contemporary contexts. Liberative scholars located in different marginalized communities sometimes emphasize how their work differs from that of other scholars who also have an emancipatory focus; Black feminist and womanist scholars, for example, whose research aims to address the situations of African American women, have argued that feminist biblical scholars of European descent have often failed to appreciate the roles that race and class play in the subjugation of women of color.[20] Nonetheless, the fact that both groups look for ways to fight oppression based at least in part in sexism tells us they have something in common, even though womanist and Black feminist thought pays attention to the effects of multiple sources of oppression in ways white feminism sometimes has not. And, in fact, biblical scholars writing for liberation within one minoritized community will sometimes comment on the overlap between their work and that of scholars from others. Randall Bailey, for example, says that so little Black biblical scholarship was available when he was a graduate student that he read feminist biblical interpretation to develop liberative approaches to the texts that would fit his context as an African American scholar and that he "became convinced of the interrelationships of liberation movements."[21] Justo González says that it was his encounter with liberation theology and feminist theology that led him to develop

20. For example, Renita J. Weems, "Re-reading for Liberation: African American Women and the Bible," in Schroer and Bietenhard, *Feminist Interpretation of the Bible*, 23–24; Nyasha Junior, *An Introduction to Womanist Biblical Interpretation* (Louisville, KY: Westminster John Knox, 2015), xix; and Crowder, *When Momma Speaks*, 21.
21. Randall C. Bailey, "My Journey into Afrocentric Biblical Interpretation," in *The Africana Bible: Reading Israel's Scriptures from Africa and the African Diaspora*, ed. Randall C. Bailey (Minneapolis: Fortress, 2010), 20.

his liberative approach from a Hispanic context.[22] Gay and lesbian readers have adopted some of the same strategies when dealing with biblical texts they identify as oppressive as female and Black interpreters, writes Deryn Guest,[23] and Caryn Tamber-Rosenau writes that queer biblical criticism builds on feminist criticism.[24] Lynne St. Clair Darden argues that womanist and postcolonial biblical criticism have quite a bit in common in regard to their interpretive goals and the ways their practitioners reach them,[25] and Jeremy Punt says the same about postcolonial and queer interpretation, noting that both investigate marginality, exclusion, and the ways in which institutions construct identity.[26] And insofar as one of the goals of queer readings of the Bible is to discover how interpretation has been used to support claims that particular kinds of sexuality are abnormal, writes Joseph Marchal, it was preceded in this regard by womanist interpretation, which demonstrates how the dominant culture and its reflection in biblical scholarship associate bodies of color with deviant sexuality.[27]

So if we should not assume that all emancipatory approaches to reading biblical texts share precisely the same aims and interpretive strategies, we also need not assume they have nothing in common. We will explore some specific examples of liberative readings in the next chapter, and begin here with more general observations. The best place to begin in this regard is with what is perhaps the most general and obvious point of connection between many of these readings, the stated desire to have scholarship contribute to some sort of struggle for liberation. So Elisabeth Schüssler Fiorenza, writing from a feminist perspective, says that biblical studies must aim to create the *ekklēsia* she describes, an open democratic space that has the goal of allowing all voices to be heard and of furthering the

22. Justo L. González, *Santa Biblia: The Bible through Hispanic Eyes* (Nashville, TN: Abingdon, 1996), 26–27.
23. Guest, *When Deborah Met Jael*, 247–56.
24. Caryn Tamber-Rosenau, *Women in Drag: Gender and Performance in the Hebrew Bible and Early Jewish Literature*, BI 16 (Piscataway, NJ: Gorgias, 2018), 15–18.
25. Lynne St. Clair Darden, "A Womanist-Postcolonial Reading of the Samaritan Woman at the Well and Mary Magdalene at the Tomb," in Smith, *I Found God in Me*, 184–90.
26. Jeremy Punt, "Queer Theory, Postcolonial Theory, and Biblical Interpretation: A Preliminary Exploration of Some Intersections," in *Bible Trouble: Queer Reading at the Boundaries of Biblical Scholarship*, ed. Teresa J. Hornsby and Ken Stone, SemeiaSt 67 (Atlanta: Society of Biblical Literature, 2011), 329.
27. Joseph A. Marchal, "On the Verge of an Introduction," in *Bodies on the Verge: Queering Pauline Epistles*, ed. Joseph A. Marchal, SemeiaSt 93 (Atlanta: Society of Biblical Literature, 2019), 21–23.

well-being of all.[28] The goal of biblical interpretation in this discourse, she writes, should be "emancipatory praxis,"[29] or liberative action, to put that another way, and this demands concern for injustice and the marginalization of women but also for other forms and manifestations of domination such as racism, poverty, and colonialism, since these "are inflected by gender and themselves inflect gender."[30] This is a recognition that women who are victims of racism, poverty, and colonialism tend to suffer more and in different ways than men do who are also subject to these evils and that these things contribute to the lower socioeconomic status in which poor women and women of color, especially in postcolonial contexts, find themselves. So if we are to search for a criterion by which we can evaluate biblical interpretations, she writes, then it must be by asking whether they promote the well-being of women at the bottom of the sociopolitical ladder, those most in need of liberation.[31]

And this notion that liberative biblical interpretation has the end of addressing dehumanization manifested through the silencing of marginalized voices and the refusal to promote their liberative aims is widespread as a stated objective among biblical scholars with emancipatory goals. Justin Ukpong writes that African biblical studies attempts to create "a holistic empowerment of the personhood, lives and cultures of all sectors of African peoples for the realization of their full humanity and for their becoming subjects rather than objects of their situation," and so to "make the voiceless and the marginalized more fully human."[32] Womanist and Black feminist biblical scholarship endeavor to help women around the globe struggle against oppression, says Gay Byron,[33] and do so by condemning imperialism, colonialism, racism, sexism, and heterosexism that oppress and dehumanize, says Wilda Gafney.[34] What Madipoane Masenya calls *bosadi* biblical hermeneutics, interpretation that focuses on "the unique experiences of an African South African woman, with a commitment to her liberation," is the use of interpretation to

28. Elisabeth Schüssler Fiorenza, *Rhetoric and Ethic: The Politics of Biblical Studies* (Minneapolis: Fortress, 1999), 10–11; Schüssler Fiorenza, *Power of the Word*, 70–82.
29. Elisabeth Schüssler Fiorenza, *Bread Not Stone: The Challenge of Feminist Biblical Interpretation* (Boston: Beacon, 1995), 63.
30. Schüssler Fiorenza, *Power of the Word*, 13.
31. Schüssler Fiorenza, 66.
32. Ukpong, "New Testament Hermeneutics in Africa," 159.
33. Gay L. Byron, "The Challenge of 'Blackness' for Rearticulating the Meaning of Global Feminist New Testament Interpretation," in Wicker, Spencer Miller, and Dube, *Feminist New Testament Studies*, 96.
34. Wilda C. M. Gafney, "A Black Feminist Approach to Biblical Studies," *Enc* 67 (2006): 392.

confront and defeat sexism, racism, classism, the stigmatization of those living with HIV/AIDS, and xenophobia.[35] A basic goal of biblical interpretation within the Caribbean context is to study how interpretations allow for resistance to oppression and support social transformation, writes Oral Thomas;[36] a lesbian-identified hermeneutic aims to change the way biblical texts are used in enforcing oppression, writes Deryn Guest;[37] a Dalit hermeneutic is liberative and praxis oriented, emphasizing concern for the marginalized, writes Jeeva Kumar Ravela.[38] I could continue to add examples, but hopefully these suffice to demonstrate that a basic criterion of a good liberative reading is that it aims for liberative transformation in the contemporary world, something that could function as a response in a struggle against oppression and dehumanization in their many manifestations.

So if emancipation is the basic goal that drives liberative readings, what approaches have marginalized scholars taken in their professional work to achieve it? The use of the historical critical method is not a criterion of a good liberative reading, since liberation rather than method drives the agenda, although for some scholars focused on emancipatory readings, historical work is key to their approach.[39] For example, at the center of Schüssler Fiorenza's interpretive work is a historical reconstruction of the Christian communities that existed before the New Testament texts were written; women were not marginal in these groups, she argues, but the New Testament authors marginalized them.[40] At the core of Jesus's teaching was the reconstitution of a new Israel, she writes, an egalitarian community that included women, prostitutes, the poor, and all the marginalized as fully enfranchised members.[41] His movement was rooted in a vision of God as Sophia, the Greek work for wisdom, and Jesus's followers saw him as Sophia-God's

35. Madipoane Masenya (ngwan'a Mphahlele), "Stuck between the Waiting Room and the Reconfigured Levirate Entity? Reading Ruth in Marriage-Obsessed African Contexts," in Claassens and Sharp, *Feminist Frameworks and the Bible*, 166.
36. Oral A. W. Thomas, *Biblical Resistance Hermeneutics within a Caribbean Context*, BW (London: Equinox, 2010), 5–6.
37. Guest, *When Deborah Met Jael*, 109–10.
38. Jeeva Kumar Ravela, *Struggle for Land Rights in 1 Kings 21: A Dalit Hermeneutic Perspective* (Delhi: ISPCK, 2012), 98–99.
39. Of course, whenever an interpreter does some sort of historical reading, we will decide whether that historical work is good or bad based on our experience in regard to different aspects of the historical critical method. My point here is that we should not use those criteria to judge the effectiveness of liberative readings *qua* liberative readings.
40. Elisabeth Schüssler Fiorenza, *In Memory of Her: A Feminist Theological Reconstruction of Christian Origins*, 2nd ed. (London: SCM, 1994), xx.
41. Schüssler Fiorenza, 118–30.

prophet and child and saw her—Wisdom is consistently personified in the Bible as a woman—as desiring a discipleship of equals.[42] These ideas are only partially visible in the New Testament writings themselves, Schüssler Fiorenza argues, because their authors obscured much of the radical egalitarian message of the original Jesus movement, and so her approach demands historical work that can reconstruct that earlier community, since she sees its tradition of *ekklēsia* as an open public space that treats everyone as fully human as authoritative for Christian life and ethics.[43]

Gale Yee's approach to biblical texts through ideological criticism is a somewhat different project than Schüssler Fiorenza's, since Yee focuses on modes of economic production that resulted in sexist and racist ideologies that were part of the cultures that formed the biblical texts,[44] an approach that obviously demands historical work to discover the economic and social structures of ancient communities.[45] Historical work, and particularly that based on archaeological findings, is central to Carol Meyers's argument that ancient Israel was not a patriarchy, even though the biblical texts can make it seem as if it was. We can conclude on the basis of archaeological evidence that household tasks were divided up by gender in early Israel, she writes, and that there was a near parity of labor among men and women, meaning that their lives were complementary and interdependent.[46] This does not mean there was gender equality in that period, she warns, since males' cultural authority favored them in inheritance and allowed them to control female sexuality, but ancient Israel was a heterarchy, a term that refers to a variety of hierarchies in the same society that contain competing power structures, and not simply patriarchal ones.[47] Historical work is central as well to Teresa Okure's analysis of New Testament passages about divorce in their first-century context, something that demands an examination of Jewish customs of that time, allowing her to argue that by forbidding a practice that only men could initiate, Jesus wanted to restore what he understood to be a divinely intended equality between men and

42. Schüssler Fiorenza, 130–40.
43. Schüssler Fiorenza, *Power of the Word*, 101–9.
44. Gale A. Yee, *Poor Banished Children of Eve: Woman as Evil in the Hebrew Bible* (Minneapolis: Fortress, 2003), 4–5.
45. See, for example, Yee, *Poor Banished Children of Eve*, 29–58.
46. Carol Meyers, *Discovering Eve: Ancient Israelite Women in Context* (Oxford: Oxford University Press, 1988), 168–73.
47. Carol Meyers, "Was Ancient Israel a Patriarchal Society?," JBL 133 (2014): 8–27.

women.[48] Historical work, or at least the branch of it called redaction criticism, is key to Irmtraud Fischer's argument that the original version of the story of Hagar in Genesis 16 did not legitimate oppression since, she writes, God's command to Hagar in 16:9 to return to slavery under Sarai, her owner, was a later addition by a redactor or editor, not part of an earlier version of the story.[49] Through her examination of the public roles of women in ancient Roman society, Susan Hylen concludes that women did speak in public in particular situations, although their speech was considered to be of less importance than men's. So in a passage like 1 Corinthians 14:34, which commands women to be silent in the church, first-century readers would have understood it as an affirmation of a cultural norm, but because 1 Corinthians 11 assumes women pray and prophesy during worship, the command of 14:34 would not have been seen by Christians in a Greco-Roman setting as an absolute principle.[50]

Again, I could continue to add examples, but the point is that there are clearly cases where minoritized scholars find the tools of historical criticism to be central to a liberative project. There are some who pursue liberative readings who argue that historical method is necessary in all interpretive work for the same reasons that some in the mainstream of the field of biblical studies do, and who insist that the use of its techniques is nonnegotiable because we must listen to "the voice of the text"[51] and allow the text "to speak for itself and not merely mirror the ideas of the interpreters."[52] Other marginalized scholars have argued that without historical criticism, we cannot understand the meanings of the narratives we want to read,[53] or that its use is necessary to avoid ideological readings that skew the text's meaning,[54] or that we need to use it to avoid making the text say anything we want.[55] All of these claims rely, in the end, on the idea of a text with

48. Teresa Okure, "Reading from This Place: Some Problems and Prospects," in Segovia and Tolbert, *Reading from This Place*, 2:60–64.
49. Irmtraud Fischer, *Women Who Wrestled with God: Biblical Stories of Israel's Beginnings*, trans. Linda M. Maloney (Collegeville, MN: Liturgical, 2005), 18–19.
50. Susan E. Hylen, *Women in the New Testament World*, EBS (Oxford: Oxford University Press, 2019), 131–59.
51. Adele Reinhartz, "Feminist Criticism and Biblical Studies on the Verge of the Twenty-First Century," in Brenner and Fontaine, *Feminist Companion to Reading the Bible*, 34.
52. Schüssler Fiorenza, *Bread Not Stone*, 131.
53. Johanna Stiebert, *Fathers and Daughters in the Hebrew Bible* (Oxford: Oxford University Press, 2013), 12.
54. Carlos Mesters, *Defenseless Flower: A New Reading of the Bible*, trans. Francis McDonagh (Maryknoll, NY: Orbis, 1989), 119–20.
55. Blount, *Cultural Interpretation*, 7.

personhood that can speak even before interpreters act to provide meaning for the marks on the page. As I argued in chapter 2, however, this is not a terribly good way to conceive of texts, which are not people and cannot literally speak, and so there is no necessary connection between the ancient context, the text, and its meaning, or, as I put it, between the ancient context and the meaningful text, which is created by readers. The fact that we can find scholars focused on liberation making these sorts of arguments, which sound as if they come from the mainstream of the field, simply shows the influence of that mainstream and its ability to present historical criticism as natural and necessary when it comes to scholarly readings.

Some liberative scholars, however, are skeptical of the historical critical method and can question the very idea that it is a useful tool to achieve emancipatory goals. Their discomfort with this suite of approaches stems from the sorts of arguments I surveyed in the last chapter that critique claims from the mainstream of biblical studies for its necessity or universality. Its influence in a field that often portrays it as a necessary part of scholarly work has led to a devaluing of other methods, even among some scholars devoted to fighting oppression, and so David Adamo refers to a "colonization of biblical studies" in Africa by Western scholars who insist the Bible be interpreted there as it is in the Western academy, undermining other methods such as African cultural readings.[56] Others, such as Kwok Pui-lan, have made similar comments in regard to the way this central method of the field dismisses the concerns of marginalized communities as irrelevant[57] and devalues some of the approaches those communities have developed to fight for liberation, such as nonacademic readings from marginalized groups.[58] Some see historical criticism as so clearly aligned with the mainstream of the field that has no interest in liberative concerns that they are wary of its use by those who try to fight oppression. Esther Fuchs, for example, critiques Schüssler Fiorenza's historical search for a gynocentric Christian community that existed earlier than the patriarchal texts of the New Testament as research that relies on an androcentric method that ignores the final forms of the biblical texts as we currently have

56. Adamo, "Decolonizing the Psalter in Africa," 299–301.
57. Kwok Pui-lan, "Jesus / the Native: Biblical Studies from a Postcolonial Perspective," in Segovia and Tolbert, 73–74.
58. Kwok, *Postcolonial Imagination*, 79–80.

them. The latter, after all, are the texts that contemporary religious communities actually use, sometimes for oppressive ends, and by focusing on historical issues of which the vast majority of Christians have no awareness, Fuchs argues, Schüssler Fiorenza simply avoids dealing with contemporary interpretations of biblical texts that legitimate oppression. Fuchs insists historical critical readings simply repeat, articulate, and justify the sexism inherent in the ancient cultures that produced them, or at least they do when scholars insist that their only job is to understand what biblical writers were trying to say, something that does not involve ethical evaluations of those messages.[59]

Since liberation and not method should drive biblical studies, I cannot agree with Schüssler Fiorenza when she writes that scholars "must" use historical criticism, even though she also argues that its use has to be accompanied by an analysis of the networks of power its techniques reflect.[60] These networks of power include the ones Kwok critiques when she refers to the marginalization of nonacademic readings that are the result of the claims for the necessity of historical criticism, and those criticized by Sarojini Nadar when she writes that the historical critical mainstream of the field has made the Bible inaccessible to communities of faith such as her own in South Africa.[61] The very claim that historical criticism is necessary because that is the sort of study the text demands is an exclusivist one embedded in the networks of power exercised by the privileged Western academic mainstream. So if scholars are going to continue to use the method in liberative settings, then they should be clear that it is subservient to liberative goals and that their use of it does not view marginalized readings, historical or otherwise, as an optional part of what the field does. One can certainly use aspects of the historical critical method without believing in its universal validity, the claim that it must be used in any valid academic interpretation, and it is precisely because scholars working toward liberation have been able to use it in ethical ways that the participants at

59. For example, Esther Fuchs, *Sexual Politics in the Biblical Narrative: Reading the Hebrew Bible as a Woman*, JSOTSup 310 (Sheffield, UK: Sheffield Academic, 2000), 19–23; and Esther Fuchs, "Biblical Feminisms: Knowledge, Theory and Politics in the Study of Women in the Bible," *BibInt* 16 (2008): 208–9.
60. Schüssler Fiorenza, *Democratizing Biblical Studies*, 56–57.
61. Sarojini Nadar, "A South African Indian Womanist Reading of the Character of Ruth," in *Other Ways of Reading: African Women and the Bible*, ed. Musa W. Dube (Atlanta: Society of Biblical Literature, 2001), 160.

an early twenty-first-century conference of feminist biblical scholars reached the consensus that it can be useful for liberation.[62]

And because emancipatory work begins with liberative goals and not a commitment to a particular method, many scholars from different marginalized communities point out that no single method predominates in the work of biblical scholars from their particular group. Since there are so many different communities struggling for liberation in so many different contexts, there cannot be any method privileged in and of itself, argues Yak-Hwee Tan, for the social location of readers and interpreters and the challenges they face set the parameters for these methodological decisions in any given case.[63] Whatever method we use has to be one that works, writes Claudia Camp,[64] but that will depend on the goals we have, as Dora Mbuwayesango points out;[65] only once we know where we are trying to go can we choose a road to get there. And the variety of interpreters and their experiences, situations of oppression, and strategies of liberation and biblical readings to support them means that, even within groups that one might think of as a single community, such as feminist scholars from Latin America, or feminist scholars from India, or the community of womanist biblical interpreters, there is no one methodological approach that predominates.[66] Methodological choices have to "limp after" (to use Gutiérrez's language) the needs and decisions that emerge from marginalized communities that want to use biblical texts as a liberative resource.

One important need of some marginalized readers is to find ways to deal with oppressive texts, something that we could call a suspicious approach to interpretation. Since I have been arguing that readers create meaning, an oppressive text is one that a community feels unable to interpret as anything except supportive

62. Silvia Schroer, "'We Will Know Each Other by Our Fruits': Feminist Exegesis and the Hermeneutics of Liberation," in Schroer and Bietenhard, *Feminist Interpretation of the Bible*, 6.
63. Yak-Hwee Tan, "The Question of Social Location and Postcolonial Feminist Hermeneutics of Liberation," in Schroer and Bietenhard, *Feminist Interpretation of the Bible*, 173–74.
64. Claudia V. Camp, *Wisdom and the Feminine in the Book of Proverbs*, BLS 11 (Sheffield, UK: Almond Press, 1985), 11.
65. Dora Mbuwayesango and Susanne Scholz, "Dialogical Beginnings: A Conversation on the Future of Feminist Biblical Studies," JFSR 25 (2009): 96–97.
66. See, for example, Elsa Tamez, "Feminist Biblical Studies in Latin America and the Caribbean," in Schüssler Fiorenza, *Feminist Biblical Studies*, 50–51 on the lack of a dominant method used by Latin American feminist biblical scholars; see also, for example, Melanchthon, "Engaging Women's Experience," 2:64, in regard to the same point for South Asian feminist readings; and see, for example, Junior, *Introduction to Womanist Biblical Interpretation*, 113, who makes the same point in regard to womanist interpreters.

of the unethical domination of others. Given the limitations of interpretation communities place on readers' ability to make sense of the physical text, we cannot simply wish such meaning away. A suspicious approach to interpretation in the context of such a creation of textual meaning is one that identifies a text as dangerous and draws attention to and warns of its oppressive aspects, precisely the sort of ethical evaluation that the discipline's mainstream avoids. Some feminist biblical scholars, for example, argue that all biblical texts were produced by androcentric cultures, which means that it is important to read with suspicion and to expose dangerous patriarchal texts that support the marginalization of women.[67] It is essential simply to highlight texts that can be used to legitimate violence against women, writes Nancy Bowen, for only then can we see where and how to mount a resistance against them, particularly in regard to the way in which they are put to oppressive uses. These texts are part of the cultural heritage of the places where Judaism and Christianity have spread, so we need to reveal the sexism, violence, and patriarchy they promote and disavow them.[68] When engaged in interpretation, says Alice Bach, it is important not to be the ideal readers of the texts their narrators seem to desire, agreeing with them at all points in regard to their presuppositions about the way the world is, who women are, and how they should behave,[69] and so she refers to a reading strategy in which she is suspicious of and argues with biblical narrators to expose the patriarchal agendas of the authors who created those voices.[70] We can see a suspicious approach rather like this in Fuchs's strategy to read the text through what she describes as a deconstructivist approach and as a hermeneutics of resistance in regard to the traditional meanings scholars and religious communities

67. See, for example, Mary Ann Tolbert, "Protestant Feminists and the Bible: On the Horns of a Dilemma," in *The Pleasure of Her Text: Biblical and Historical Texts*, ed. Alice Bach (Philadelphia: Trinity Press, 1990), 18; Phyllis Trible, "Five Loaves and Two Fishes: Feminist Hermeneutics and Biblical Theology," in *The Promise and Practice of Biblical Theology*, ed. John Reumann (Minneapolis: Fortress, 1991), 62–63; and J. Cheryl Exum, *Fragmented Women: Feminist (Sub)versions of Biblical Narratives*, JSOTSup 163 (Sheffield, UK: JSOT, 1993), 11–12.
68. Nancy R. Bowen, "Women, Violence, and the Bible," in *Engaging the Bible in a Gendered World: An Introduction to Feminist Biblical Interpretation in Honor of Katherine Doob Sakenfeld*, ed. Linda Day and Carolyn Pressler (Louisville, KY: Westminster John Knox, 2006), 186–99.
69. Alice Bach, "Signs of the Flesh: Observations on Characterization in the Bible," in *Women in the Hebrew Bible: A Reader*, ed. Alice Bach (New York: Routledge, 1999), 352.
70. Alice Bach, *Women, Seduction, and Betrayal in Biblical Narrative* (Cambridge: Cambridge University Press, 1997), 14–15.

have assigned to the texts,[71] an approach that can expose the ways female characters have been constructed within them.[72]

One way in which oppressive aspects of a text can be revealed is through a focus on marginalized characters, such as females or foreigners or figures of low social status, especially ones who play only minor roles in a narrative. These are the characters assigned to "nothingness" in the texts, as Judith McKinlay puts it,[73] by authors who were generally elite males. This sort of interpretation is very different from mainstream ones, since it is not interested in the characters and ideas to which interpreters have normally paid attention but focuses instead on the characters traditional academic and religious interpretations have chosen to marginalize and apparently see as of little importance. Such readings result in the creation of different meaningful texts where our interpretations find oppression or liberative aspects that are absent from the ones we have come to see as obvious. Tikva Frymer-Kensky, for example, found it helpful to focus her interpretive lens on women who are secondary characters in the narratives in which they appear, as she was interested in the social structures of the communities from which the biblical texts emerged and the variety of roles women played in them, some of which were more prominent than traditional readings of the text might suggest.[74] Juliana Claassens, on the other hand, has focused on stories of female characters in the texts with the aim of remembering their resistance against oppression—as an example, we need only think of her reading of the story of Jephthah's daughter, discussed in chapter 2—the sorts of acts frequently downplayed by male memory and something that can point contemporary women toward liberative acts of resistance in their own contexts.[75] Fuchs has concentrated much of her interpretive work on studying the portrayal of women in the Hebrew Bible more generally, looking for larger patterns in the ways they are depicted, arguing that even in stories where women are protagonists, such as those of Ruth and Esther, they are positively portrayed because they submit to patriarchal social structures; a good woman in biblical

71. Esther Fuchs, "A Feminist Hermeneutics of Resistance: A Jewish Response to Interpretive Hegemony," in Scholz, *Feminist Interpretation of the Hebrew Bible*, 2:153–54.
72. Esther Fuchs, "Sexual Biblical Politics as an Interventionist Interrogation: The Israelite and Foreign Woman in Feminist Literary Approaches," in Scholz, *Feminist Interpretation of the Hebrew Bible in Retrospect*, 3:36–37.
73. Judith E. McKinlay, *Reframing Her: Biblical Women in Postcolonial Focus*, BMW 1 (Sheffield, UK: Sheffield Phoenix, 2004), 94–95.
74. For example, Frymer-Kensky, *Studies in the Bible and Feminist Criticism*, 163–66.
75. Claassens, *Claiming Her Dignity*, 139–52.

texts, that is, is one who inhabits only the social space and roles permitted to her by patriarchal culture so that she can act in ways that benefit men.[76]

For others, it is important to provide a voice to characters who have been marginalized in the texts and so to retell their stories in liberative ways. Wilda Gafney, for example, uses what she describes as the "sanctified imagination" of the African American Christian tradition as well as rabbinic biblical interpretation to construct what she refers to as womanist midrash, through which she can reread and retell stories of minor female biblical characters, creating meaningful texts in which they can speak and act in emancipatory ways and contexts.[77] The idea that a scholar could decide to retell a character's story might seem to fall precisely into the trap of creating whatever meaning for the text we like, since by using the term *midrash*, Gafney signals that she is doing more than simply trying to locate authorial intention. For example, her meaningful text of Numbers 12 produces a story in which God strikes Miriam with leprosy but then immediately expresses regret for this act.[78] This makes her interpretation of the narrative unique among scholarly readings, as far as I am aware, since it alone presents divine repentance as part of the meaningful text of the passage. When Gafney refers to womanist midrash as retelling, I understand her to mean that she clearly recognizes that her interpretations or meaningful texts do not entirely correspond to what she believes an author might have intended to say in a given passage but that limiting her work to that historical question would not be sufficient for her goals, which look to the experiences of Black women and the communities of which they are a part as her authoritative norm for interpretation.[79]

Mainstream scholars retell or rewrite biblical texts as well, but they do so with different goals than liberative scholars like Gafney. For example, when Joel Baden reads the narrative of David in the book of Samuel, he discusses a number of the stories that refer to the deaths and assassinations of David's rivals for the throne of Israel, stories that explicitly absolve David of any involvement in that violence. Yet these passages, Baden argues, were written to enhance the picture of David, since the "real" or historical David of Baden's work was almost certainly behind

76. See, for example, Fuchs, *Feminist Theory*, 37–41.
77. Wilda C. Gafney, *Womanist Midrash: A Reintroduction to the Women of the Torah and the Throne* (Louisville, KY: Westminster John Knox, 2017), 2–3.
78. Gafney, 133–35.
79. Gafney, 3–4.

some of the killings that smoothed his path to the kingship.[80] In constructing a picture of the historical David, Baden has rewritten the story of Samuel; like Gafney, he recognizes a distinction between authorial intention and truth, but he and Gafney define truth in this context differently. One important reason why this is so is because they have different goals for interpretation: Baden wants to create a picture of what he understands to be the true historical David and not the version of him in Samuel, and Gafney aims to construct a text that Black women could find useful for their liberative struggles, which includes a true (or at least truer) picture of God who does not countenance (or at least repents of) unjust punishment. Gafney is not the only liberative biblical scholar creating what she refers to as the retelling of biblical stories, and we can note as well that Schüssler Fiorenza refers to a need for feminist scholars to retell biblical narratives from a feminist perspective;[81] that Musa Dube says that African women should retell biblical stories, and even create new characters for them, to meet the audience's needs;[82] that Kwok Pui-lan suggests the same for Asian women;[83] and that Kondasingu Jesurathnam says that this is already an important aspect of Dalit interpretation.[84] The retelling of biblical stories was key to African American biblical interpretation of the eighteenth century, writes Vincent Wimbush, when slaves appropriated the scriptural tradition of their owners and retold biblical stories to reflect their contexts.[85]

Insofar as all of the readings of texts we have described so far, including the retellings of biblical stories, begin with the experiences and needs of the marginalized, we can say that our interpreters draw upon their communities' experiences as texts that they use to help them in the act of interpretation. If we want to think of someone narrating experiences they have had, it is not difficult to see why we can conceive of them as texts. Monica Melanchthon, for example, refers to the experiences of South Asian women as "alternative texts" that she

80. Joel Baden, *The Historical David: The Real Life of an Invented Hero* (New York: HarperCollins, 2013), 108–15, 132–37.
81. Schüssler Fiorenza, *Bread Not Stone*, 20–22.
82. Musa W. Dube, "Introduction," in Dube, *Other Ways of Reading*, 2–4.
83. Kwok Pui-lan, *Introducing Asian Feminist Theology*, IFT 4 (Sheffield, UK: Sheffield Academic, 2000), 53–56.
84. Jesurathnam, *Dalit Liberative Hermeneutics*, 182–83.
85. Vincent L. Wimbush, "The Bible and African Americans: An Outline of an Interpretive History," in *Stony the Road We Trod: African American Biblical Interpretation*, ed. Cain Hope Felder (Minneapolis: Fortress, 1991), 85–89.

uses to make sense of biblical passages,[86] and this is exactly what Lily Fetalsana-Apura means when she refers to the reader's context as "the text's co-text."[87] Mainstream scholars, of course, also use texts in their acts of interpretation, since they draw upon texts produced by ancient writers from Near Eastern or Greco-Roman or ancient Jewish cultures, articles and books produced by other modern scholars, and, of course, their own backgrounds and experiences. It matters which texts we use in our interpretive work, however, for the use of different ones will result in the production of different sorts of interpretation, and scholars from minoritized communities sometimes argue that they need to enact interpretation with the help of texts mainstream scholarship ignores. These texts include the experiences and cultures of their communities, and given the cultural backgrounds of some scholars, they find it appropriate to use religious texts outside of the Judeo-Christian tradition in their interpretations. Historical criticism does that as well, obviously, when scholars look to ancient Near Eastern stories of creation to make sense of Genesis 1–2 or to Hellenistic stories of miraculous healings to make sense of New Testament narratives that involve the same phenomenon, but texts like these are part of a focus on biblical narratives as ancient artifacts. Liberative scholars can use texts that are very different than these, and so Archie Lee, for example, writes that Chinese Christians maintain important aspects of East Asian religious worldviews found in associated scriptural traditions and so that, as a teacher, he explicitly reads Asian scriptures in parallel with biblical texts.[88] Kwok recommends this approach in Chinese biblical interpretation as well, referring to the need for a "multifaith hermeneutics" in a culture where there are no strong boundaries between different religious and scriptural traditions.[89] Monica Melanchthon and S. J. Samartha make a similar claim in regard to South Asian biblical interpretation.[90] African American scholars have used African American texts such as novels, slave narratives, and rap

86. Melanchthon, "Engaging Women's Experience," 64–65.
87. Fetsalana-Apura, *Filipino Resistance Reading*, 160.
88. Archie C. C. Lee, "Cross-Textual Biblical Studies in Multiscriptural Contexts," in Fiorenza and Richards, *Transforming Graduate Biblical Education*, 37–44.
89. Kwok Pui-lan, "The Bible, the Critic, and the Theologian," in *Discovering the Bible in the Non-biblical World*, 22–23.
90. Melanchthon, "Dalit Women and the Bible," 114–15; S. J. Samartha, "Religion, Language and Reality: Towards a Relational Hermeneutics," *BibInt* 2 (1994): 342–43.

lyrics to approach biblical passages,[91] and some gay and lesbian scholars have seen a need to read biblical stories in dialogue with a canon of contemporary literature,[92] while some scholars from the Pacific islands make sense of biblical texts by juxtaposing them with islander literature.[93]

And to the general liberative approaches we have discussed so far in this part of the chapter—warning of oppressive texts in suspicious readings, privileging the perspectives of secondary and/or marginalized characters, retelling biblical stories, using texts ignored by the mainstream in interpretation, and doing historical critical work—we can add another: the critique of traditional academic and religious interpretations of biblical texts and their basic assumptions. Even liberative scholars whose work relies on historical method critique mainstream approaches, and both Schüssler Fiorenza and Carol Meyers, whose work I discussed above, argue that Western scholarship has simply assumed that ancient societies were inherently rooted in patriarchy, but that, they maintain, is the result of modern Western patriarchal thought.[94] Sometimes critiques of mainstream assumptions are directed toward the ways in which dominant interpretations understand such things as gender and sexuality, an important part of queer interpretation. Queer readings have traditionally challenged the ways in which contemporary readers use the Bible to privilege particular kinds of sexual and gender identities, writes Ken Stone, as well as the ways in which they use it to support the notion that heterosexuality is normal and healthy while homosexuality is aberrant.[95] Queer theory unsettles "prevailing assumptions about proper roles, practices, boundaries and relationships with sexuality"; it is "a critical interrogation and active contestation of the many ways in which the Bible is and has been read to support heteronormative and normalizing configurations of sexual practices and identities."[96] The concept of queer interpretation has been broadened in the twenty-first century

91. For example, William H. Myers, "The Hermeneutical Dilemma of the African American Biblical Student," in Felder, *Stony the Road We Trod*, 53–55; and Smith, *Insights from African American Interpretation*, 51.
92. Guest, *When Deborah Met Jael*, 256–63.
93. For example, Mosese Ma'ilo, "Island Prodigals: Encircling the Void in Luke 15:11–32 with Albert Wendt," in Havea, *Sea of Readings*, 23–36.
94. Schüssler Fiorenza, *In Memory of Her*, 42–43; Meyers, "Was Ancient Israel a Patriarchal Society?," 24–26.
95. Ken Stone, "Queer Reading between Bible and Film: *Paris Is Burning* and the 'Legendary Houses' of David and Saul," in Hornsby and Stone, *Bible Trouble*, 94.
96. Ken Stone, "Queer Commentary and Biblical Interpretation: An Introduction," in *Queer Commentary and the Hebrew Bible*, ed. Ken Stone, JSOTSup 334 (Sheffield, UK: Sheffield Academic, 2001), 29, 33.

to include challenges to normativity more generally, including that which excludes others on the basis of such things as race and disability,[97] and so it is clearly a kind of liberative reading, since in general these tend to cross and unsettle boundaries by challenging traditional understandings of texts, questioning the notions of what makes a good or bad interpretation and a good or bad text. As a result, we can add challenges to traditionally accepted boundaries and categories in interpretation to our list of general liberative approaches.

Beyond Listening: Solidarity and Dialogue, Part 1

I will say more about liberative approaches to biblical texts in the next chapter, which returns to some of the ones just discussed and provides specific examples of them. Paying attention to these goals and examples is where the ethical work of more privileged scholars must begin, the sort of listening we must do before we can hope to make any contribution to the liberative project. We need to know what basic principles and norms should steer our readings and have examples available to us as guides. But before we take a look at the specific examples in the next chapter, it is worthwhile to consider the sort of role beyond listening that more privileged scholars should have in a dialogue meant to advance emancipatory goals and how we can be in solidarity with minoritized scholars who fight on behalf of their communities. It certainly helps to know that some scholars from marginalized communities emphasize the need for dialogue with biblical scholars from more privileged groups. So long as both partners honor each other as equal but different interpreting subjects, says Musa Dube, dialogue is welcome.[98] Women in the Two-Thirds World could use spies in the enemy camp, as it were, she writes, to make common cause for justice and liberation.[99] R. S. Sugirtharajah argues that marginalized scholars should not limit themselves to writing about issues that pertain only to their communities and that we need a multidirectional conversation

97. Stephen D. Moore, Kent L. Brintall, and Joseph A. Marchal, "Queer Disorientations: Four Turns and a Twist," in Brintall, Marchal, and Moore, *Sexual Disorientations*, 5–8; Gil Rosenberg, *Ancestral Queerness: The Normal and the Deviant in the Abraham and Sarah Narratives*, HBM 80 (Sheffield, UK: Sheffield Phoenix, 2019), 10–12.
98. Musa W. Dube, "Toward a Post-colonial Feminist Interpretation of the Bible," in Pui-lan, *Hope Abundant*, 97–99.
99. Dube, "Rahab Is Hanging Out a Red Ribbon," 191–92.

in the field in which no interpretive community dominates.[100] Africans have to challenge Western biblical studies, writes Justin Ukpong, and Westerners need to take African biblical scholarship seriously, something that is impossible without dialogue.[101] A dialogue in which readers respect the inclusive interpretations of texts by communities that approach reading differently than they do is a necessary part of ethical reading, argues Cheryl Anderson,[102] and Althea Spencer Miller refers to a "polylogue" that she hopes to see between Two-Thirds and One-Third World scholars that reflects the selfhood and subjectivity of all of the partners in the conversation.[103] This respect for the subjectivity—for the full humanity, we could say—of all figures in the dialogue is always a caveat of minoritized biblical scholars who promote conversation with the mainstream of the field, and rightly so. Oppressors must see their common interests with the oppressed if they wish to be involved in changing things for the better, as Isasi-Díaz puts it, but this will not be possible outside of a conversational space in which the oppressed speak first, because it must be their experience of oppression and response to it that drives the conversation.[104] And there certainly are more privileged scholars who wholeheartedly support this sort of dialogue in the field, and they write of the need to share the resources at our disposal,[105] to be accountable to communities who could be affected by our work, and so to speak with (rather than for) the marginalized[106] and establish a broad hermeneutical conversation that is not limited only to the academy.[107]

That being said, minoritized scholars open to such a dialogue are also wary of its dangers. Not all Latino/a biblical scholars believe that readers from outside of

100. R. S. Sugirtharajah, "The End of Biblical Studies?," in Segovia, *Toward a New Heaven and a New Earth*, 137–38.
101. See Ukpong, "New Testament Hermeneutics in Africa," 158; and Justin S. Ukpong, "Reading the Bible in a Global Village: Issues and Challenges from African Readings," in *Reading the Bible in the Global Village: Cape Town*, ed. Justin S. Ukpong et al., GPBS 3 (Atlanta: Society of Biblical Literature, 2002), 35–36.
102. Anderson, *Ancient Laws and Contemporary Controversies*, 145–54.
103. Althea Spencer Miller, "Lucy Bailey Meets the Feminists," in Wicker, Spencer Miller, and Dube, *Feminist New Testament Studies*, 219–20.
104. Isasi-Díaz, *Mujerista Theology*, 95–96.
105. Gerald O. West, "Reading Other-Wise: Socially Engaged Biblical Scholars Reading with Their Local Communities: An Introduction," in West, *Reading Other-Wise*, 2–3.
106. Daniel Patte, "Acknowledging the Contextual Character of Male European-American Critical Exegesis: An Androcritical Perspective," in Segovia and Tolbert, *Reading from This Place*, 1:39–41.
107. Schüssler Fiorenza, *Rhetoric and Ethic*, 32–33; Schüssler Fiorenza, *Democratizing Biblical Studies*, 14–15.

the community can engage in Latino/a interpretation, writes Francisco Lozada;[108] not all African American scholars believe non-Africana readers can do African American biblical interpretation, writes Mitzi Smith;[109] to be involved in womanist biblical criticism requires self-identification as an African American woman, writes Nyasha Junior.[110] There will necessarily be certain limits on the participation of more privileged scholars in a dialogue that aims at liberation, since the experiences of such scholars—the autobiographical texts with which we read, one could say—are very different from those of scholars from minoritized communities. More privileged scholars are used to our dominance in the mainstream of the field and its ways of doing things, so we are used to speaking while others listen,[111] but that would be counterproductive, to say the least, if we hope to contribute in some way to liberative readings and if we hope to liberate ourselves and our communities from worldviews that support such dominance. We have not had the same experiences as the marginalized, and so we cannot speak knowledgeably for them or in place of them. This is why Fuchs writes that she is suspicious of male scholarship that valorizes feminist studies of the Bible; male feminists cannot speak for female ones, she says, or else we are in a situation where men ignore female subjectivity and agency,[112] a situation where we end up once again in dehumanization, which is what liberative readings are meant to fight.

It is safest to assume that those who cannot call a particular community home will not be well placed to act as a reader of texts for that community. Even though someone like Lozada argues that anyone who puts the Latino/a experience at the center of their work and represents the community positively can do Latino/a biblical interpretation, there is a real question as to just how well those not part of the community could know that experience, since it could never be their own. It is certainly important that, as professionals in the field, more privileged scholars listen to their peers from marginalized groups as they reflect on their experiences from minoritized social locations that shape the work they do in biblical studies. We can and should do more to learn about the contexts of poverty, sexism, racism, classism, colonialism, and heteronormativity that shape the experiences of

108. Lozada, *Toward a Latino/a Biblical Interpretation*, 28–29.
109. Smith, *Insights from African American Interpretation*, 51–52.
110. Junior, *Introduction to Womanist Biblical Interpretation*, 115–16.
111. See Ringe, "Asian Readings of the Bible," 374.
112. Esther Fuchs, "Men in Biblical Feminist Scholarship," JFSR 19 (2003): 96–98.

different marginalized groups, but that is not the same thing as experiencing the discrimination and marginalization that result from those evils. More privileged scholars cannot speak for minoritized communities or the biblical scholars who belong to them, for only the marginalized truly know what they are talking about when it comes to living with the effects of such things and to strategizing as to how to best realize their own liberation from them. This does not mean that the more privileged cannot be in solidarity with the marginalized, listening to their experiences and following their lead in interpretation, as I have been urging, but our work will only "limp after" theirs, to borrow Gutiérrez's expression once more.

As more privileged biblical scholars, our main point of connection with those communities will largely be through their scholars, our fellow professionals with whom we share the field and so with whom we share natural points of academic connection. Mark Aidoo suggests the metaphor of the *okyeame*, the traditional office of spokesperson among the Akan of West Africa, to make sense of the role of the scholarly reader in communication with the marginalized. The *okyeames* convey the speech of rulers to the people and provide counsel as they communicate between the authorities and the governed.[113] Aidoo specifically uses this metaphor to describe the role of African biblical scholars in their interactions with readers outside of the academy, but we could imagine scholars from marginalized communities in general filling this role as they convey the speech of their communities—the authorities, in this metaphor—to those who need to be governed by it, biblical scholars and students from more economically and socially privileged communities, providing counsel to both groups. As the authorities who struggle for liberation, only marginalized communities can ultimately decide if readings that more privileged scholars create are truly useful, but scholars from those communities can tell us what kinds of work on our part might be helpful, and as we absorb and adopt their counsel, we can enter into dialogue with our own more privileged communities in discussions as to how this should affect their readings of texts.

But simply being aware that dialogue should be able to promote liberative change does not mean that it actually will, as chapter 4 discusses. When traditional modes of interpretation and readings of texts privilege a certain group of people, they will generally see no need to change and will mainly not notice that their community

113. Mark S. Aidoo, "'My Words Dropped upon Them Like Dew': Towards Reimaging the Identity of African Biblical Interpreters," in Dube and Stiebert, *Bible, Centres and Margins*, 105–10.

has created the meanings of the texts in the first place, seeing such meaning as inherent to "the text in itself." They will not see the ways this meaning harms others, or if they do, they will conclude that there is nothing they can do about it. Dialogue between more privileged and marginalized communities is not a simple process in part because, as Gayatri Spivak has pointed out, those who belong to the more dominant culture will often fail to understand the speech of the communities they have marginalized. She refers to the concept of the Other formulated by postcolonial theory, discussed earlier in the chapter: the identity of the colonized is constructed on the colonizers' terms, and the latter justify their appropriation of other peoples' land and labor by understanding those peoples as benefiting from colonization. In their eyes, the colonized are not as fully human as the colonizers are, too simple, lazy, and unethical to manage their own affairs properly. They are the Other, "the negation of values" in Fanon's words, and the colonizers use their creation of the Other as they construct their own identity, the Self. The Other is "the Self's shadow," writes Spivak, defined by the West so the West can define itself as civilized, fully human, and humane. When a dominant culture creates the terms of a discourse—to put that another way, when it sets the terms as to which things are to be investigated, limits the ways those investigations can proceed, and establishes the meanings of the basic concepts investigations can use—then it can be difficult to engage in any sort of dialogue not done on those terms. It will be difficult for those who belong to that dominant culture to escape the discourse it has created and to understand those who might be described as the postcolonial Other as saying anything else than what the dominant culture expects them to say.[114]

So merely to laud the concept of dialogue does not necessarily mean that it will happen in ways that will benefit emancipatory struggle. Our attempts to "read with" marginalized communities, for example, can result more in "reading for" them than we might realize. Gerald West, to take an example of a more privileged scholar who has invested quite a bit of his professional energy in reading the Bible with more marginalized communities, has written about the contextual Bible studies (CBS) that he has led in South Africa, the ways those studies are initiated by those marginalized groups, and how they provide their members with a safe

114. Gayatri Chakravorty Spivak, "Can the Subaltern Speak?," in *The Post-colonial Studies Reader*, ed. Bill Ashcroft, Gareth Griffiths, and Helen Tiffin (London: Routledge, 1995), 24–28.

space to speak.[115] "Those of us who are white middle-class males are not and cannot be organic intellectuals," West writes, "but we can choose to be accountable to and to be in solidarity with the poor and oppressed. We can learn from them and we can serve them."[116] But in reflecting on the CBS, Sarojini Nadar writes that the scholarly facilitator in such groups should be "an organic member of the community," since one from outside of it will not ever know enough about the culture to truly read with community members in the first place and so will not be able to lead them beyond their normal ways of reading or challenge oppressive aspects of their interpretation, since the outside facilitator may not even be able to see how a particular interpretation is oppressive in that setting.[117] Eric Anum's study of groups that follow the CBS model of a scholar interpreting texts with marginalized readers concludes that respondents see the scholarly facilitators as imposing their own agendas and do not feel as if they are equal partners in the dialogue.[118] We hear in such analyses, of course, echoes of Spivak's fear that those who belong to the dominant culture will not truly be able to hear the speech of groups their cultures have marginalized.

Helpful dialogue is, in the end, difficult to achieve, and it will take concerted effort on the part of more privileged scholars to listen to their peers in the field from more marginalized communities in order to be guided by them to produce work that those communities might find useful in their liberative struggles. We need to take seriously Spivak's warning about the barriers that we erect as we listen to the speech of the Other, but sometimes the dominant culture, or members of it, can truly hear the marginalized and be convinced by what they say. In making just this point, Cheryl Anderson refers to a speech given by Barbara Jordan, an African American congresswoman and civil rights leader from Texas, who pointed out that the framers of the Constitution of the United States, some of whom owned slaves of African descent, did not have her in mind when they opened that document

115. Gerald O. West, "Contextual Bible Study in South Africa: A Resource for Reclaiming and Regaining Land, Dignity and Identity," in *The Bible in Africa: Transactions, Trajectories, and Trends*, ed. Gerald O. West and Musa W. Dube (Boston: Brill Academic, 2001), 595–610.
116. West, *Biblical Hermeneutics of Liberation*, 214–15.
117. Sarojini Nadar, "'Hermeneutics of Transformation?' A Critical Exploration of the Model of Social Engagement between Biblical Scholars and Faith Communities," in Dube, Mbuvi, and Mbuwayesango, *Postcolonial Perspectives*, 389–405.
118. Eric Anum, "Effective Scholarly Readings of the Bible in Africa," in *Interpreting the New Testament in Africa*, ed. Mary N. Getui, Tinyiko Maluleke, and Justin Ukpong, ACS (Nairobi: Acton, 2001), 104–22.

with the words "We the people." Only after a period of centuries did mainstream US society understand those words in that context to encompass Black women, and only because figures like Jordan contested their meaning in order to create a new meaningful text.[119] Sometimes the more dominant culture can be shown that a refusal to hear the marginalized will result in a violation of their own ethical principles, and they can join in the creation of new meaningful texts so that, for example, the words "We the people" can come to mean something very different than they once did. Sometimes this process can take a very long time to produce meaningful results, as in the case Jordan referred to, testimony to the fact that it can be difficult to change mainstream minds that prefer things the way they are and that even those who want to change cannot always fully understand what those whom they have marginalized are saying. More privileged biblical scholars are lucky to the extent that we have peers who are organic intellectuals of the communities who struggle for emancipation and so who are fluent in both the language of the liberative struggles of their communities and that of academic biblical studies. They are the translators, the *okyeames* who can convey messages of leadership from their communities to more privileged scholars, who can provide us with counsel as to how to be governed, and who can bring our attempts to contribute to a struggle against oppression to their communities to see if our work can be useful. So having already discussed how some minoritized scholars have provided us with general aims and approaches of their liberative work, I turn now to some specific examples of these approaches, the kind of thing more privileged students and scholars of biblical studies can use in our own work as we follow their lead.

119. Anderson, *Ancient Laws and Contemporary Controversies*, 155–57.

6

Listening, Part 2

Examples

Introduction: The Ethics of Emancipatory Biblical Interpretation

We now move to some specific examples of the liberative approaches to interpretation that chapter 5 discusses. General goals and strategies for biblical interpretation can provide one type of guide, but examples of them make them more concrete and give a better sense of the variety of ways in which they can be applied, an important point when we are looking to these sorts of readings as patterns for our own work. There is no lack of variety among minoritized communities and the ways their members have experienced oppression and a correspondingly vast variety of ways in which scholars from these communities have read biblical literature. The limitations of space mean that I can hardly hope to provide a thorough survey of all the different manners in which these communities and their scholars have interpreted the texts, and so I have divided these approaches into a number of categories that reflect aspects of the discussion of the previous chapter. If this list of categories cannot remotely be considered as exhaustive, it can at least present examples that might stimulate the imaginations of more privileged scholars who hope to be in solidarity with their marginalized colleagues and the communities they serve who look to the Bible as a resource in emancipatory struggle. For reasons of space, and so as not to drown readers in a sea of such interpretations, however, I have not included all of the different approaches discussed in chapter 5, such as historical readings, since all of us educated in the mainstream field are familiar with techniques associated with the historical critical method, which is why some liberative applications of it appear in the previous chapter. And although chapter 5 discusses the experiences of the marginalized as a text used in the interpretation of biblical literature, this chapter does not contain a discrete section that focuses on that issue, since in all of the readings here in chapter 6, minoritized scholars are doing just that. There are, however, examples of the ways in which marginalized scholars confront oppressive texts, read narratives with a focus on secondary and marginalized characters, and transgress interpretive boundaries and question the categories such boundaries construct. The various sets of examples that appear in these sections are not exclusive of each other, and readers will likely notice that some examples could fit in more than one. Some categories will seem to be more amenable to imitation by more privileged scholars than others, and that is because, to return to the final section of chapter 5, the role of privileged students and scholars in the liberative endeavor is limited. We cannot take the place of the marginalized, nor provide for their liberation, nor speak for them as to what might be the best readings of biblical texts that would be useful for their emancipatory struggles. We simply come from the wrong cultures and have had the wrong experiences. Although this does not absolve us of the responsibility to discover more about those communities, those struggles, and the work of their biblical scholars, nor from communicating this to more privileged communities of which we are a part in order to urge them to be in solidarity with the marginalized, it does limit what we can do, as the first category of examples we examine, biblical parallels for contemporary situations, makes clear.

I did not refer to that category of interpretive examples in chapter 5 as a specific kind of approach of marginalized readings of the Bible since, in part, it was included in the critique of historical criticism in chapter 4: the argument that ancient texts are not understandable because they reflect ancient cultures alien to our own does not always ring true in marginalized settings, where readers sometimes see close parallels between biblical literature and their own contexts. I provide it with its own category here, however, to stress the limitations on the work that more privileged scholars can do to contribute to liberation. To draw these sorts of parallels demands an intimate knowledge of a given community, its experiences of oppression, its emancipatory struggles, and the solutions its members have developed to combat oppression, and it does not immediately seem like the sort of strategy that scholars who are nonorganic to a particular group could competently perform. If more privileged scholars hope to contribute to liberation, we also need to be aware of the practical limitations of our role in liberative dialogue so that we can be clearer as to what we can do. This is a limitation not only on more privileged scholars but also on all readers, privileged or otherwise, who are not part of a given community, as I will discuss in the final section of the chapter. There we return again to the concept of dialogue, its limitations, and its benefits, for if the field of biblical studies has any hope at all of making some sort of liberative contribution, the work of the marginalized and privileged alike must constantly be challenged by a dialogue—a polylogue, really, as Althea Spencer Miller puts it—among many different communities, one ethically focused on liberative needs.

Biblical Parallels for Contemporary Situations

One kind of parallel that readers from marginalized communities can draw between their own experiences and a biblical text is that which identifies a particular character as a liberative model for the contemporary group to imitate. So, for example, Mitzi Smith reads the story of Mark 7:24–30 as a liberative example of sass, something she refers to as womanists' commitment to speak up from the marginalized social locations in which African American women find themselves in pursuit of freedom and justice. Sass is something that "gushes up from a place of pain and anger, of being 'sick and tired of being sick and tired.' . . . One might say, therefore, that it is truth-telling with an attitude and for good reason."[1] In the Markan passage, Jesus encounters a woman identified as Syro-Phoenician, who asks that he heal her daughter. Jesus responds in a way that portrays her as a member of an ethnically inferior group, telling her that his miraculous powers are meant only to benefit the Jews, at least for now: "Let the children be fed first, for it is not good to take the children's food and throw it to the dogs" (Mark 7:27). Having been compared to an animal, however, the woman does not accept this insult and rebuff but instead talks back to her more privileged and powerful interlocutor—"even the dogs under the table eat from the children's crumbs" (Mark 7:28), she responds—and this sass, writes Smith, wins the healing for her daughter that she desired. She must confront a male authority figure, as Black women in the United States often must, in order to dispute his belief that the

1. Mitzi J. Smith, *Womanist Sass and Talk Back: Social (In)Justice, Intersectionality, and Biblical Interpretation* (Eugene, OR: Cascade, 2018), 41.

lives of less privileged ethnicities do not matter.[2] To take another example of a character whom a scholar has identified as modeling action for the marginalized, Hisako Kinukawa points to the story of Mark 5:24b–34, in which a woman with a hemorrhage decides to touch Jesus's clothes in order to be healed. Kinukawa, like Smith, emphasizes the initiative the woman takes. The woman would have been regarded in her social context as an outcaste, Kinukawa argues, yet she claims her agency and so her humanity, refusing to remain socially invisible. At the end of the story, Jesus commends her, saying, "Your faith has healed you" (Mark 5:34), and so he validates her belief that she is fully human and worthy of health. Kinukawa identifies a parallel between the woman's recognition of her own agency and humanity and that demonstrated by the outcaste community of Japan in the twentieth century when they wrote their own declaration of rights.[3]

We see the same sort of identification of a biblical character as worthy of imitation and as providing a model that reaffirms the full humanity of the marginalized in Avaren Ipsen's dialogue with sex workers in California as they read the story of Rahab in Joshua 2 and 6. The story takes place as Israel begins its conquest of the land of Canaan, and Rahab, a Canaanite prostitute in Jericho, helps Israelites sent to spy out the city flee to safety when the king has been alerted to their presence. Her action on the spies' behalf allows her and her family to escape the Israelite slaughter of all the city's inhabitants. In the discussion with Ipsen, the sex workers rejected scholarly interpretations (of which Ipsen informed them) that read Rahab as a metaphor for a sinful Israel because of her occupation; they understood her instead as a rational actor who embraced her agency, choosing to do sex work to support her family and choosing to help the spies in order to save her family's lives. The model they identified in Rahab was of someone who did not passively accept the marginalized situation in which she found herself, but who realized that she was fully human and who chose to sacrifice for her family in ways that more privileged readers were unable to understand.[4] Or, to take one more example of a marginalized reader looking to a biblical character whom she sees as modeling full humanity, Mmapula Kebaneilwe writes that the ideal woman described in Proverbs 31:10–31

2. Smith, 28–45.
3. Hisako Kinukawa, *Women and Jesus in Mark: A Japanese Feminist Perspective*, TBL (Maryknoll, NY: Orbis, 1994), 29–50.
4. Avaren Ipsen, *Sex Working and the Bible*, BW (London: Routledge, 2009), 73–88.

is one whose agency and initiative make her a model for Batswana women. These verses portray her as a wife and mother but also as purchasing land and selling products she has created, allowing her to transcend her patriarchal culture to some degree. Women in Botswana are normally relegated to the informal economy and thus marginalized, writes Kebaneilwe, but the ability to take on the economic roles of the woman of Proverbs 31 would allow them to improve their lives.[5]

Liberative readings will sometimes search for biblical passages or settings that provide parallels for the oppression that a particular community suffers. For example, Raquel St. Clair points to noticeable similarities she sees between the crowds in Mark's Gospel and the situation of African American women: both groups are economically exploited, both are marginalized, and both are told to be submissive to the authorities.[6] Or, to take another example, Kondasingu Jesurathnam sees parallels between the depictions of the suffering of Jeremiah and those of the Dalits, since both experience oppression and dehumanization caused by sociopolitical and religio-cultural forces that marginalize them.[7] Jeeva Kumar Ravela makes a similar point in his analysis of the story of 1 Kings 21, in which an evil royal couple conspires to kill Naboth, one of their subjects, in order to seize his land. This resonates with Dalits' experience, writes Ravela, since they are largely denied the right to own land, are oppressed by a caste system as Naboth was oppressed by his social superiors, and are ignored by their state apparatus as Naboth was killed by his.[8]

If those examples can stand as parallels that look to biblical stories where the oppression is condemned by the narrative, marginalized readers also sometimes focus on a parallel between the oppression suffered by their communities and a depiction of oppression that the biblical texts—to use my language from chapter 2, the meaningful texts created by these readers in their interpretations—sanction, pointing to narratives that particular groups will encounter as dangerous and counterliberative. This, for example, is the case when Cheryl Anderson discusses the story of Ezra 9–10, in which the Jewish community, returned to the land from

5. Mmapula D. Kebaneilwe, "Paddling the Bellowing Waters Away from the Margins: African Perspectives of Proverbs 31," in Dube and Stiebert, *Bible, Centres and Margins*, 34–35.
6. St. Clair, *Call and Consequences*, 107–8.
7. Kondasingu Jesurathnam, *Exploring Dalit Liberative Hermeneutics in India and the World: Based on an Ancient Hebrew Prophet, Jeremiah of Anathoth*, CHR 20 (New Delhi: Christian World Imprints, 2015), 8–10.
8. Ravela, *Struggle for Land Rights in 1 Kings 21*, 83–106.

exile in Babylon, decrees that its members must forcibly expel all foreign women from its midst since, the characters in the story largely agree, divine law prohibits marriages between Israelite men and foreigners. This story, Anderson writes, strikes her as an African American woman as uncomfortably reminiscent of the history of segregation in the United States, enforced in part by antimiscegenation laws.[9] Mitzi Smith reads the story of 2 Kings 2:23–25 through the parallel of the African American experience of police brutality. In these verses, small boys mock the prophet Elisha by calling him "baldy" (2 Kgs 2:23) and the prophet curses them in God's name, with the result that two bears emerge and maul the boys. In Smith's reading, the story reflects the rigid compliance that African Americans have historically been expected to demonstrate to authority and their experience of brutal reprisals when refusing to do so in even inconsequential ways.[10] Or, to take one more example, Madipoane Masenya reads the story of Ruth as one in which women are regarded not as independent agents who should shape their own destinies but as means to the end of socially sanctioned marriage that can produce legitimate offspring for males. Among the results of the story's failure to regard women as fully human is the situation in which Ruth finds herself in Ruth 3, where her widowed mother-in-law sends her at night to Boaz to make herself sexually available to him and so win him as a husband. African women sometimes find themselves in situations much like this, Masenya writes, needing to make themselves sexually available to men in order to survive, and in an era of an HIV/AIDS epidemic, this amounts to gambling with one's life.[11]

Sometimes minoritized scholars will draw a parallel between a biblical text and their community that allows them to raise questions about their identities. Francisco Lozada, for example, does this when he reads the version of the Lord's Prayer in Matthew 6:9–13 in light of the Latin American immigrant experience in the United States. The opening verses of the chapter set the prayer in a dualistic world. One should not pray like hypocrites or Gentiles, Jesus says in the introduction to the prayer in 6:5–8, and so there is only one right way to pray, only one language

9. Cheryl B. Anderson, "Reflections in an Interethnic/Racial Era on Interethnic/Racial Marriage in Ezra," in *They Were All Together in One Place? Toward Minority Biblical Criticism*, ed. Randall C. Bailey, Tat-siong Benny Liew, and Fernando F. Segovia, SemeiaSt 57 (Atlanta: Society of Biblical Literature, 2009), 47–64.
10. Smith, *Womanist Sass*, 94–117.
11. Madipoane Masenya (ngwan'a Mphahlele), "Struggling with Poverty/Emptiness: Rereading the Naomi-Ruth Story in African-South Africa," JTSA 120 (2004): 57–58.

that is appropriate, and for Latino/a immigrants this is uncomfortably reminiscent of the insistence in the mainstream culture of the United States that there is only one proper way to speak, and that is in English, not Spanish. The ability to speak "correctly" is often correlated with the wealth of Latin American families in the United States but also often experienced as a denial of their cultural heritage.[12] Jean-Pierre Ruiz grapples with a similar question of communal identity when he compares the crisis that some in the United States see in regard to Latino/a immigration with the story of Nehemiah 13:23–30, a passage in which Nehemiah demands that the members of his community expel all of the foreign women they have married because, Nehemiah says, the children of these unions are unable to speak Hebrew. The story "sounds frighteningly familiar" when read in light of the experiences of Latin American immigrants, since the ability to speak English is understood by some in the United States to indicate that one truly belongs in the country, although in Puerto Rico true community identity is sometimes judged by one's ability to speak Spanish fluently.[13] In both studies, the parallels the authors see with the biblical passages raise difficult questions about the connection between language and community identity, and whether one should choose one sort of identity over another.

There are certainly many more examples one could provide of minoritized scholars drawing parallels between biblical texts and issues faced by their communities, but perhaps these are enough to allow for some reflection on the ones assembled here. We might conclude that searching for biblical parallels that reflect some liberative goal or struggle of a particular community—parallels that community members would find meaningful in terms of their thinking about liberation, oppression, and their agency and identity—are not things that scholars from outside of that community are particularly well suited to do. Scholars without Lozada's familiarity with the experiences of the Latin American immigrant community in the United States, for example, would be fairly unlikely to think of creating the interpretation of Matthew 6:9–13 that he does, just as white interpreters might not make the connection between Ezra 9–10 and the history of segregation in the United States that Anderson does, or between the story of 2 Kings 2:23–25 and the Black experience of police brutality that Mitzi Smith does. Scholars from more

12. Lozada, *Toward a Latino/a Biblical Interpretation*, 61–81.
13. Ruiz, *Readings from the Edges*, 100–114.

privileged communities will not be equipped with the experiences and backgrounds to create those sorts of readings and should not pretend otherwise. That does not mean, however, that more privileged scholars cannot endeavor to ensure that their own communities hear about interpretations like these, or that they cannot undertake interpretations that create meaningful texts that promote the agency of marginalized characters, the sort of readings of Mark 7:24–30 and 5:24b–34 that Smith and Kinukawa create. It also does not mean that more privileged scholars cannot create interpretations that point out that common understandings of some biblical texts can be read as promoting oppression, as Anderson does when she reads Ezra 9–10 or as Masenya does when she reads Ruth. More privileged scholars certainly can create interpretations that result from an analysis that has focused on the perspectives of secondary characters, as Ravela does when he pays close attention to the character of Naboth, a minor player in the narrative of Kings, or as Kinukawa does when she focuses on the hemorrhaging woman, a minor character in the narrative of Mark.

We will take a look at examples of reading strategies like those in the following sections of the chapter, but it is important to remember at the outset that members of one community are not in the position to dictate to members of others how they should read. The difference between strategies such as reading from the perspective of minor characters and deciding that a particular text is a useful parallel for a situation in which a given community finds itself is that in one case we are creating interpretations or meaningful texts that bring aspects of liberation or oppression to the fore, with the hope that others might find this work useful, whereas in the other we are prescribing the use of those texts to address a particular situation. The latter is a step that only the marginalized in a particular community can take, since only they know their situation well enough to do so, and for others to take that step for them is to remove their agency. And when thinking of this limitation, it helps to remember that the meaning of the text is our creation, and we are limited by our experiences and cultures as we create meaning. There is no meaning of a text that exists outside of human imagination waiting for us to stumble across it, and the result is that different communities will not be able to create the same texts as other groups do. Marginalized communities simply may not create the same meaningful text that more privileged readers produce, and if our goal is to be in solidarity with those who read for liberation, then we are in no position to insist that they imitate us. More privileged scholars might see a character like Ruth, for example, as a model of someone from the margins—she is a foreigner, a widow, and a recent immigrant to Israel—who exercises her agency and survives. Some biblical scholars from marginalized communities have offered portrayals of her like this,[14] but those of us who are not African women will not be in the position to say that Masenya is wrong when she argues that the story is a dangerous reflection of experiences of oppression faced by women in southern Africa.

"The goal," as Ada Isasi-Díaz puts it, "is not to be like the poor and the oppressed (an impossibility), but rather to be in solidarity with them."[15] More privileged scholars cannot tell marginalized groups how they ought to read the Bible or which stories they will find to be particularly helpful in their struggles; we cannot, in short, recommend the sorts of parallels that we have just surveyed for marginalized groups of which we are not members. We, on the other hand, can use our resources to pay attention to the sorts of themes and ideas in the texts and their contexts that more marginalized scholars emphasize, and approach them in similar ways, urging other more privileged readers to do likewise, and hope that at least some of this is useful for liberative struggles.

Reading from the Perspectives of Minor Characters

Since traditional religious and academic interpretations of the Bible have often been created for dominant cultures to serve their purposes, these meaningful texts tend to overlook the marginalized, and so Alice Bach writes that focusing on such characters stops us from being the sorts of readers who repeat this failure and forces us to ask what these texts created in mainstream interpretations are hiding and what sorts of power structures they promote.[16] Readers who are suspicious of the moral implications of such traditional interpretations need to take up the causes of the voices of the characters silenced by these texts created in mainstream interpretation, she writes.[17] Major characters in biblical stories are far

14. For example, Amy Kalmanofsky, *Dangerous Sisters of the Hebrew Bible* (Minneapolis: Fortress, 2014), 157–74; and Surekha Nelavala, "Patriarchy, a Threat to Human Bonding: Reading the Story of Ruth in Light of Marriage and Family Structures in India," in *Reading Ruth in Asia*, ed. Jione Havea and Peter H. W. Lau, IVBS 7 (Atlanta: Society of Biblical Literature, 2015), 89–97.
15. Isasi-Díaz, *Mujerista Theology*, 86.
16. Bach, *Women, Seduction, and Betrayal*, 14–17.
17. Bach, 21–22.

more likely to be male than female, and so many examples of this sort of reading strategy focus on female characters. In biblical literature, notes Bach, it is often the silent woman whom the text prefers.[18] Irmtraud Fischer, for example, focuses on female characters in Genesis who are silenced. One of the stories she examines is Genesis 34, in which the Canaanite Shechem rapes Dinah, the daughter of Jacob. Although readers are told why Shechem acts the way he does and what he wants before and after the rape, Dinah is given no direct speech, and we are never told how she feels about the rape, about Shechem, or about her brothers' murder of him and all the males of his town in revenge.[19] She is a minor character who plays a small role in a larger narrative about males interacting with each other, and once the story of the rape sets off the chain of events at the center of the narrative, she is of no more use to it and so disappears. Ilana Pardes takes a somewhat different approach to focusing on a character marginalized by a narrative when she discusses the figure of Miriam, the sister of Moses and Aaron. Miriam acts to help save Moses's life when he is an infant (Exod 2:4, 7–8), Pardes writes, and is described as a prophet (Exod 15:20–21). In Numbers 12, both Miriam and Aaron challenge Moses's authority, but God punishes only her. The fact that she is also mentioned in passing by other biblical authors in Deuteronomy 24:8–9 and Micah 6:4 suggests that earlier in Israelite tradition she was a well-known figure, argues Pardes, and that she played a more important role in the stories Israel told about its origins, but that she was eventually moved from that more central position in Israelite tradition to the margins of the stories by the communities of the biblical authors.[20] Pardes's focus on a minor character, then, makes a historical argument about the patriarchalization of communities that produced the biblical texts.

Wilda Gafney focuses her analysis of Judges 14 on the unnamed Philistine wife of Samson, a minor player in the narrative devoted to his story. In this chapter, Samson lays a wager with some of the Philistines at his wedding feast that they will not be able to explain the meaning of a riddle he poses, and so they tell his bride they will kill her and her family if she fails to extract the answer from him. She spends the last days of her own wedding working under the terrible threat of

18. Bach, 28–31.
19. Fischer, *Women Who Wrestled with God*, 92.
20. Ilana Pardes, *Countertraditions in the Bible: A Feminist Approach* (Cambridge, MA: Harvard University Press, 1992), 6–11.

the massacre of her loved ones, and once she is able to get Samson to reveal the secret of the riddle, she disappears from the story entirely, until she is mentioned one last time in Judges 15:6 in a notice that the Philistines killed her and her family in retaliation for one of Samson's acts. She plays a minor role in a story dedicated to someone else, and since Judges 14:4 tells us that God was responsible for Samson's desire to marry her, even God's character is thrown into question in Gafney's interpretation that focuses on the suffering of a character whom the author did not even bother to name.[21]

Readings like these are suspicious of the agenda of the meaningful texts that the readers have produced. When we remember that readers create the texts within the limits permitted by their communities, then deciding to read Judges 14 by focusing interpretive attention on Samson's unnamed wife creates a text that questions the ethical integrity of God's actions in the story and explicitly designates it as ethically problematic. There is no necessary reason that readers of Judges 14 must identify with Samson or believe that God acts ethically, although the story is generally read that way. But by identifying with the nameless Philistine woman, writes Gafney, we find a God created in the image of a bigoted humanity.[22] Lynne St. Clair Darden's interpretation of the story of John 4:1–42, in which she focuses on the figure of the Samaritan woman who appears at the beginning of that narrative and disappears at its end, could also be described as a suspicious reading in this sense. As Jesus, a Jewish man, enters into conversation with a Samaritan woman, one believes at first that the hierarchical boundaries that structured the world of these characters is going to be undermined, writes Darden, and that this female from a group ostracized by first-century Judaism will join his group of male Jewish disciples. That is not what happens, however, and while the woman spreads her report about Jesus in her town, eventually she is no longer needed by the story, for her fellow citizens tell her that "it is no longer because of your speech that we believe, for we ourselves have heard" (John 4:42). The story does not overturn the social order from the woman's perspective, it just reinscribes it, Darden argues, and the Samaritan woman is then excluded from a place among Jesus's followers,

21. Gafney, "Black Feminist Approach," 396–401.
22. Gafney, 403.

just as she would have been excluded from the social center in her world because she was a woman.[23]

Deciding to focus on secondary and marginalized characters will often lead us to produce different meaningful texts than those created through a focus on authorial intention because we will end up emphasizing figures and issues that are not prominent in the story as we have been taught to think about it, things mainstream interpretations tend to overlook, and this approach can warn us of the dangers that these passages can pose to readers who might be much more likely to notice oppressive ways in which characters marginal to those stories are presented. Assuming that we do not want Jewish and Christian readers to think that God has no concern for violence visited upon marginalized figures in society, and do want them to grapple with portrayals of God that condone this sort of injustice, it matters which characters we decide to privilege in our readings.

A focus on secondary characters can do more than lead readers to reflect on dangerous aspects of a passage, however, and can instead produce readings that argue, for example, that women are more central to events, textual or historical, than previous analyses had claimed was the case. Uta Schmidt has argued that female characters in Kings that may seem marginal are in fact central to the book's plot development.[24] Claudia Camp studies the wise women who appear in the stories of 2 Samuel 14 and 20, minor characters in the story of David who interact with the king and Joab, his general, as they make important decisions, and she argues that these stories tell us about a significant political role for women in ancient Israel.[25] Juliana Claassens argues that when one reads 1 Samuel 25, also part of the narrative of David, a focus on the character of Abigail indicates a key role for this secondary figure, something scholars have often failed to notice. In the story of this chapter, David vows to slaughter the men of Nabal, a wealthy figure who refuses to provide for David and his men as they hide from Saul. But Abigail, Nabal's wife, intervenes and brings supplies to David from Nabal's household, successfully urging him to abandon his murderous plan and so saving many lives. She is in control of the situation, notes Claassens, she acts independently of her husband, and she has

23. Darden, "Womanist-Postcolonial Reading," 195–200.
24. Uta Schmidt, *Zentrale Randfiguren: Strukturen der Darstellung von Frauen in den Erzählungen der Königebücher* (Gütersloh, Germany: Chr. Kaiser, 2003).
25. Claudia V. Camp, "The Wise Women of 2 Samuel: A Role Model for Women in Ancient Israel?," in Bach, 195–207.

the longest prose speech of any woman in the Hebrew Bible. By stepping outside of her socially determined role, she provides hospitality and prevents seemingly inevitable violence.[26] Whether or not the author intended readers to focus on these aspects of the story, Claassens's decision to do so creates a text that portrays a woman with agency, whose wise actions and speech save lives.

To read stories from the perspectives of secondary and/or marginalized characters, then, does not produce just one kind of text. It may lead us to the sort of historical claim that Camp makes when she argues that a focus on two minor characters in David's story provides us with insight into the political agency exercised by some women in Israel. This is a historical reconstruction, as is Pardes's argument that the figure of Miriam was suppressed and her importance in earlier Israelite traditions downplayed by the communities that produced biblical texts. These sorts of readings may conclude that the text is much more dangerous than interpreters have often said is the case, the conclusion that Darden arrives at in her reading of John 4 or Gafney in her reading of Judges 14. They may, on the other hand, emphasize the agency and full humanity of a marginalized character like Abigail in Claassens's meaningful text of 1 Samuel 25. What all of these readings have in common is that they shift attention away from the central male figures of their respective narratives, a particularly helpful interpretive move for readers who have been conditioned to focus on the figures in the story who occupy more socially privileged roles. These sorts of interpretations, then, provide those of us who occupy more socially privileged roles in our own cultures with one way to read against our normal analytical impulses and sympathize and stand with characters marginalized by the texts, those who experience oppression in the worlds of the biblical narratives.

Suspicious Readings: Warning of Oppressive Texts

Reading from the perspectives of marginalized characters sometimes produces suspicious interpretations, ones that conclude that there is no way to interpret particular texts except in manners that are ethically problematic because these meaningful texts can be understood as promoting oppressive views and actions.

26. Claassens, "Abigail Optic," 24–27.

Broadly speaking, we can understand a drive to highlight and warn of texts' oppressive natures as another important category of readings by minoritized scholars and can refer to such interpretation as suspicious. Since readers create textual meaning, suspicious readings of texts that warn of the ethical problems of oppression and dehumanization are the results of the particular experiences and backgrounds of readers that lead them to approach the evidence of the physical text in particular ways. We have already come across interpretations that highlight oppressive texts in the previous two sections—one can think of Gafney's reading of Judges 14 or Masenya's reading of Ruth—and in many (but not all) cases like these, the narratives in question have traditionally been viewed positively, because they have been interpreted (or their meaning has been created) by more privileged scholars and communities whose general lack of experience with oppression inclines them to search for it far less frequently. So Monica Melanchthon refers to suspicious readings as ones that read against the grain of traditional interpretations of biblical narratives by male scholars,[27] questioning the way the evidence of the physical text has traditionally been interpreted, particularly insofar as those traditional interpretations have tended to avoid discussions of oppression and exclusion. This has particularly been a failure of mainstream biblical interpretation when it comes to the portrayal of women in biblical texts. Esther Fuchs, for example, explains that she approaches passages in the Hebrew Bible with suspicion because, as she reads them, they justify and universalize patriarchy and so promote the marginalization of women. To read the Bible as a woman, she writes, is to reject the inferiority and subservience—the dehumanization and Otherness—that these texts portray as women's natural state.[28]

So, for example, the story of Ruth has traditionally been viewed positively in both religious and academic contexts as a narrative of a foreign woman who, after her Israelite husband dies, chooses to migrate to Israel and support her widowed Israelite mother-in-law, adopt Israelite religion, and marry another Israelite man, with the result that, at the end of the narrative, she becomes an ancestress of King David when she gives birth to a son. However, the experiences and backgrounds of some marginalized readers make them less certain this is a heartwarming tale of female agency and Israelite inclusiveness. Ruth abandons her native identity as a

27. Melanchthon, "Engaging Women's Experience," 2:66.
28. Fuchs, *Sexual Politics in the Biblical Narrative*, 11–12, 16–17.

Moabite, notes Judith McKinlay, and if readers have traditionally viewed her story positively, that is because her actions are ultimately validated by a patriarchal social system that prizes female submission to males in marriage and women's role in producing male heirs to perpetuate a male line.[29] Patriarchal societies need women to collaborate in meeting their goals, argues Fuchs, and so these societies construct narratives, like that of Ruth, that praise women who do so;[30] after all, says Elivered Nasambu-Mulongo, the story presents women's true security as located only in socially sanctioned relationships with men.[31]

These sorts of suspicious readings have identified many other stories where women are praised for inhabiting roles sanctioned by an androcentric society and censured for failing to do so. Cheryl Exum, for example, points to the contrast between the story of Jephthah's daughter, who is commemorated in an annual festival because she was willing to be sacrificed by her father rather than disobey him, and that of David's wife Michal in 2 Samuel 6, a story in which she challenges her husband's behavior and that ends with her punishment by him as she disappears from the narrative of his story. Jephthah's daughter does not challenge her father and so colludes in her own death, writes Exum, while Michal confronts David, who "kills her off as a narrative presence."[32] Or, argues Deborah Sawyer, none of the female characters in the gospels of Mark and John are "real" characters who could be seen as founders of the apostolic tradition like some of their male counterparts in those narratives, but instead are painted as paradigms of radical humility, servants rather than leaders.[33] Or, to take one more example, the story of Lot's incest with his daughters in Genesis 19:30–38 is one that emphasizes conformity to roles within the ancient patriarchal household, argues Amy Kalmanofsky. In this story, the two daughters take the initiative to get their father drunk so they can have sex with him and bear children. They each give birth to a male child who will become the ancestor of a non-Israelite nation, and this allows the narrative

29. McKinlay, *Reframing Her*, 54–55.
30. Esther Fuchs, "The History of Women in Ancient Israel: Theory, Method, and the Book of Ruth," in *Her Master's Tools? Feminist and Postcolonial Engagements of Historical-Critical Discourse*, ed. Caroline Vander Stichele and Todd Penner, GPBS 9 (Atlanta: Society of Biblical Literature, 2005), 223–29.
31. Elivered Nasambu-Mulongo, "*Bosadi*: Madipoane (Ngwana' Mphahlele) Masenya's Contribution to African Women's Biblical Hermeneutics," in Dube, Mbuvi, and Mbuwayesango, *Postcolonial Perspectives*, 57.
32. Exum, *Fragmented Women*, 18–29 (quotation from p. 29).
33. Deborah F. Sawyer, *God, Gender and the Bible*, BibLim (London: Routledge, 2002), 99–113.

to ignore Lot and focus on Abraham, who becomes the ancestor of Israel and so a hero of the narrative. Female initiative damages the prestige and future of the household according to this story, Kalmanofsky writes, and the narrative thus portrays proactive women as problematic.[34]

These sorts of suspicious readings can emphasize larger dangerous assumptions about a particular class of people, like women, with which readers approach biblical stories. Renita Weems, for example, has studied texts that feature the prophetic marriage metaphor, which refers to Israel's worship of other gods and the punishment that results from this by describing Israel as God's wife whom God must punish for her role in an adulterous relationship. Readers, Weems points out, can only find this metaphor to be convincing if they believe that a man must use violence to control his household and that he is shamed when he is disobeyed, making violence directed against an unfaithful wife perfectly legitimate.[35] The metaphor can work only if readers accept a patriarchal hierarchy that assumes the validity of male control and believe that in a situation in which a man beats his wife because of her part in adultery that he is the real victim, and that the violence he inflicts on her is an expression of his love.[36]

Suspicious readings like these will sometimes emphasize the ways our interpretations often create texts that assume a particular class of people, like women, should be regarded as inferior and dangerous and treated accordingly. For example, Cheryl Anderson discusses how the law codes of the Torah address Israel as a group of males who are wealthy enough to own livestock and slaves, when in ancient Israel only a small percentage of the population would have had the resources to do so. The laws privilege the very wealthy, although they do provide protection for even poor males, Anderson notes, since the law codes give all men the right to control the sexuality of their daughters and wives, even as the laws construct an identity for women that make them subservient to men. Adult males are limited in regard to the extent to which they may exercise violence against their slaves but not to the extent to which they may beat their wives, writes Anderson, and all

34. Kalmanofsky, *Dangerous Sisters of the Hebrew Bible*, 71–86.
35. Renita J. Weems, *Battered Love: Marriage, Sex, and Violence in the Hebrew Prophets*, OBT (Minneapolis: Fortress, 1995), 29–33.
36. Weems, 84–85, 92–93, 96–98.

of this is presented as God's will.[37] As inferior creatures with inferior rights, then, women should not take stereotypically male roles, as far as some biblical texts are concerned. These texts often portray women as untrustworthy, argues Athalya Brenner, and they are suspicious that female ambition will distract women from the roles they should play in the domestic sphere, where their society believed they properly belonged.[38] So when Deryn Guest reads the story of 2 Kings 9–10 from a transgender perspective, she writes that she cannot help noticing how Queen Jezebel takes on typically masculine roles as she exercises authority and then is quickly punished with death, thus excluding such female masculinity from the Israelite identity.[39]

These sorts of suspicious readings do not only highlight the ways in which common interpretations of texts promote the oppression of women. Marginalized communities are often ones shaped by colonialism, and so readers from these groups will sometimes look for texts that reflect a colonial worldview or, to put that another way, their communities and experiences will lead them to create meaningful texts that focus on aspects that seem dangerously amenable to colonial ideology. So Musa Dube reads the stories of Israel's ancestors in Genesis 12–50 as narratives that present them as a group of colonists who move to a land that does not belong to them. The stories in these chapters generally depict indigenous groups in Canaan negatively and discourage intermarriage with them, and Dube's reading specifically points to parallels with attitudes manifested by European colonists in the Two-Thirds World. In the story of Genesis 34, when Shechem, an indigenous man, rapes Dinah, a woman of the colonizers, her brothers respond by killing him and all the men of his town, the response we would expect in such a situation, writes Dube, since colonizers have no real interest in social coexistence.[40] Nāsili Vaka'uta reads Ezra 9–10 from the standpoint of the Tongan lower class, whose lives have

37. Cheryl B. Anderson, *Women, Ideology, and Violence: Critical Theory and the Construction of Gender in the Book of the Covenant and the Deuteronomic Law* (London: T&T Clark, 2005), 51–76.
38. Athalya Brenner, *The Israelite Woman: Social Role and Literary Type in Biblical Narratives* (Sheffield, UK: JSOT, 1985), 132–33.
39. Deryn Guest, "Modeling the Transgender Gaze: Performances of Masculinity in 2 Kings 9–10," in *Transgender, Intersex, and Biblical Interpretation*, ed. Teresa J. Hornsby and Deryn Guest, SemeiaSt 83 (Atlanta: Society of Biblical Literature, 2016), 69–77.
40. Musa W. Dube, "Dinah (Genesis 34) at the Contact Zone: 'Shall Our Sister Become a Whore?,'" in Claassens and Sharp, *Feminist Frameworks and the Bible*, 39–57.

been shaped by colonialism.[41] In the larger narrative of which these chapters are a part, the Israelites whom Nebuchadnezzar had exiled to Babylon are ordered by the Persian Empire to return to the land, and in Ezra 9–10 this postexilic group decides that it must forcibly remove from its midst all the women native to Palestine who had married community members. Vaka'uta's analysis concludes that the text privileges the interests of a group of recent immigrants—the postexilic community, in other words—sent to the land by a powerful empire, not those of the indigenous inhabitants. This text has often been interpreted (or its meaning has traditionally been created) in a positive sense, portraying the community's decision to forcibly remove the foreign women as a good thing, an action in conformity with divine law. What Vaka'uta sees, reading from the perspective of a group damaged by colonialism, is a text that portrays the colonized as a dangerous group that should be ostracized by the central community that is linked to imperial rule.[42] And to take one more example in this vein, the figure of Rahab is sometimes read as a character constructed as if to validate imperial desires. In Joshua 2, she shelters spies from the Israelite army about to invade her Canaanite homeland, and she confesses the overwhelming power of their God whom she says will bring them victory. She recognizes their superiority and desires foreign rule, just the sort of attitude that colonists believe the colonized should have, writes Dube;[43] she functions as an indigenous figure whose speech and actions provide justification for her own people's loss of land, notes Judith McKinlay.[44] And she is only one of a number of foreign women whom biblical texts portray positively because they act to benefit Israel, writes Steed Davidson, while foreign women who work to benefit their own people instead are portrayed negatively.[45]

Since readers create texts, a passage viewed as dangerous and oppressive by one group of readers may look very different to another; we have seen an example of this already, if we consider the positive ways in which the sex workers interviewed by Avaren Ipsen read the story of Rahab and compare that to the readings I have

41. See Nāsili Vaka'uta, *Reading Ezra 9–10* Tu'a-*Wise: Rethinking Biblical Interpretation in Oceania*, IVBS 3 (Atlanta: Society of Biblical Literature, 2011), 27–30.
42. Vaka'uta, *Reading Ezra* 9–10 Tu'a-*Wise*, 119–42.
43. Dube, *Postcolonial Feminist Interpretation*, 76–80.
44. McKinlay, *Reframing Her*, 46–47.
45. Steed Vernyl Davidson, "Gazing (at) Native Women: Rahab and Jael in Imperializing and Postcolonial Discourse," in *Postcolonialism and the Hebrew Bible: The Next Step*, ed. Roland Boer, SemeiaSt 70 (Atlanta: Society of Biblical Literature, 2013), 71.

just summarized. Some interpreters, particularly people of faith from marginalized communities, may find themselves unable to accept the authority or validity of some oppressive texts. One well-known example of this comes from a story told by Howard Thurman, a twentieth-century theologian and civil rights leader, about his grandmother, born into slavery in the United States. She recalled hearing sermons by white preachers who told slaves that Paul's letters ordered them to be obedient to their masters, and she vowed that, should she ever learn to read, she would never read that section of the Bible,[46] for the Pauline literature these white preachers created for her was too irredeemably evil for her to ever willingly approach again. Some women, writes Nancy Bowen, will find the need to reject the Bible as a source of authority for their religious faith,[47] for the traditions in which they have encountered it have created biblical texts they can only see as irretrievably sexist. More privileged scholars, with different backgrounds and experiences, will not necessarily create the same texts as those found in the interpretations we have just surveyed, although we can start by being aware that a passage we might understand as liberative could be read very differently by someone in a different social location, and we can warn our own more privileged communities of the importance of paying attention to readings that can see such passages as promoting oppression. But we can also use the sorts of examples I have just discussed to ask the same sorts of questions these scholars have: To what kind of social hierarchy do I implicitly consent if I see a particular story (like Ruth) or a particular motif (like the prophetic marriage metaphor) as unproblematic and good? If I fail to read a given text (like a law code in the Pentateuch) with suspicion, whose rights have I determined are unimportant? What if I decide that a character I believed to be a villain (like Jezebel) is not? How might that be impacted by and impact my views about proper gender roles and social hierarchies? What if I decide that characters I believed were heroes (like the ancestors in Genesis) are not? How might that reflect my growing awareness of the evils of colonization and their continuing effects? How might readings like those challenge or better reflect ethical views about gender, class, and ethnicity? It is worthwhile asking these sorts of questions because scholars from marginalized communities are asking them, pointing

46. Howard Thurman, *Deep River and the Negro Spiritual Speaks of Life and Death* (Richmond, IN: Friends United, 1975), 22.
47. Bowen, "Women, Violence, and the Bible," 194–95.

out that some biblical texts are experienced as oppressive by readers from their communities, even though better-known religious and academic interpretations have understood many of those passages quite differently. If our goal is to produce work that might contribute to the liberative efforts of those communities and to urge more privileged ones to be in solidarity with those efforts, then asking these questions in our analysis, as we remain wary of creating texts through our interpretation that could contribute to oppression, can help us avoid contributing to the dehumanization we are trying to fight and lead us to interpret in ways useful for emancipatory struggles.

Transgressing Categories and Crossing Boundaries

The creation of boundaries, which we use to categorize people and things, is a human act, and so will be done in ways that fit the belief systems of the culture drawing the borders, and to most of the people within that group, such boundaries can seem like the most natural things in the world. I will focus in this section of the chapter on the transgression in interpretation of categories of gender and sexuality in particular, but these are not the only boundaries questioned in liberative readings. Boundaries benefit some people and disenfranchise others, and they can seem most natural—in the sense of existing independently of human thought—and obvious to those who benefit from them. Those disenfranchised by the construction of certain borders, or those who feel as if they inhabit both sides at once or as if they are in categories the boundaries do not recognize, will be more likely to see a particular border as a human creation, not something "natural," and so as something susceptible to ethical critique, and will be more likely to disregard and to cross it. We could say that prioritizing the concerns of marginalized communities in order to orient our work in biblical studies is itself the crossing of a border, in this case the one I have been calling Stendahl's ditch, the boundary that allows the mainstream of the field to categorize the "real" historical work that it does without the influence of bias or presupposition in distinction from nonhistorical work that it is not required to take into account. Considered in this manner, the bulk of the liberative project in biblical studies could be seen as transgressive. Some marginalized scholars have pointed to the liberative possibilities in questioning the geographic borders humans have constructed, as Jacqueline Hidalgo does when she puts Revelation in dialogue with a Chicano/a community in the United States that sees its identity as linked to yet distinct from Mexico, an identity that transgresses the border between the two countries, refusing to regard it as decisive for the community's self-understanding.[48] Others point to the ambiguity of ethnic boundaries, as Gale Yee does when she discusses her own experience as an Asian American as one of hybridity, despite the fact that the cultures of both Asia and the United States want to define her in one ethnic category or the other, and how this has led her to look for biblical stories where the ethnic ambiguity of the characters is key.[49]

For reasons of space, I limit this part of the chapter to examples that focus on liberative transgressions of categories of gender and sexuality—the sort of thing done in queer theory, gender theory, and masculinity studies—if only because the distinction between male and female can seem so natural, so unconnected to human decisions of categorization. Queer theory emphasizes that all identity, including gender, is a social construction,[50] and it aims to expose the processes through which categories of sex and gender are constructed to appear as if they exist independently of human thought.[51] Once we realize that we operate with understandings of different degrees of "manliness," for example, and that we can think of feminine men or manly women, says Ken Stone, then we can see that the binary categories of gender that we tend to think of as normal are actually our constructions and are often unstable.[52] We do not see effeminate gay men and butch lesbians as fitting comfortably into the categories of sex and gender our culture has constructed the way that "alpha males" and "real women" do. Both gender and queer theory refer to gender as something that individuals enact, socially constructed models that individuals aim to imitate to one degree or another, a matter that is social rather than biological. In the Hebrew Bible, for example, what makes someone

48. Jacqueline M. Hidalgo, *Revelation in Aztlán: Scriptures, Utopias, and the Chicano Movement*, BCS (New York: Palgrave Macmillan, 2016), 44–58.
49. Gale A. Yee, "Yin/Yang Is Not Me: An Exploration into an Asian American Biblical Hermeneutics," in Foskett and Kuan, *Ways of Being, Ways of Reading*, 152–63.
50. See, for example, Sean D. Burke, "Queering Early Church Discourse: The Ethiopian Eunuch," in Hornsby and Stone, *Bible Trouble*, 176.
51. For example, Stuart Macwilliam, *Queer Theory and the Prophetic Marriage Metaphor in the Hebrew Bible*, BW (Sheffield, UK: Equinox, 2011), 23. Gender and sexuality are not the only foci of queer theory—see, for example, Moore et al., "Queer Disorientations," 1–44—but have traditionally been at the center of its concern.
52. Ken Stone, "Gender Criticism: The Un-manning of Abimelech," in *Judges and Method: New Approaches in Biblical Studies*, 2nd ed., ed. Gale A. Yee (Minneapolis: Fortress, 2007), 188–89.

a man is the degree to which one embodies socially constructed characteristics of maleness, including martial prowess and physical strength, persuasive speech, claiming rather than entering into relationships with women, provision for and control over the household, and the ability to ensure one's line through fertility.[53] These characteristics appear to have been widely shared by ancient Israel's neighbors, and Cynthia Chapman, for example, points to their presence in Neo-Assyrian inscriptions in which Mesopotamian kings discuss their masculine virtues as demonstrated on the battlefield, and points out that biblical literature uses the same qualities to define masculinity.[54] The inscriptions and iconography these kings left for posterity also feminized the armies they defeated, contrasting the monarchs' true masculinity with the failure of their enemies to act in such a dominant fashion. As a result, the latter are often represented especially as stripped and penetrated with spears like a passive female whom a dominant male—a real man, from this cultural perspective—has taken and penetrated in sexual intercourse.[55]

Cultures construct different kinds of masculinities, writes Susan Haddox, and anthropologists refer to the dominant male ideal in a culture as its hegemonic masculinity, while other kinds are considered to be closer to the cultural construction of the feminine. Privileged males tend to want to conform to the hegemonic ideal, for being compared to a woman often indicates a loss of social status.[56] Male characters in biblical narratives sometimes fail to live up to their culture's masculine ideal, argues Haddox, since the biblical texts mainly refer to God as male, and so he (in this way of conceiving of God) alone can take the dominant role in relationships and thus be the ideal male. So in the ancestral narratives of Genesis, for example, key male figures are sometimes associated with characteristics the texts more normally link to the feminine: Abraham is not always the dominant

53. For example, Ken Stone, "Loaves and Raisin Cakes: Food, Sex and Divine Insecurity in Hosea," in Stone, *Queer Commentary and the Hebrew Bible*, 127–30; David J. A. Clines, "Dancing and Shining at Sinai: Playing the Man in Exodus 32–34," in *Men and Masculinity in the Hebrew Bible and Beyond*, ed. Ovidiu Creangă, BMW 33 (Sheffield, UK: Sheffield Phoenix, 2010), 54–63; and Amy Kalmanofsky, *Gender-Play in the Hebrew Bible: The Ways the Bible Challenges Gender Norms*, RIPBC (London: Routledge, 2017), 11–14.
54. Cynthia R. Chapman, *The Gendered Language of Warfare in the Israelite-Assyrian Encounter*, HSM 62 (Winona Lake, IN: Eisenbrauns, 2004), 20–33, 141–42.
55. Cynthia R. Chapman, "Sculpted Warriors: Sexuality and the Sacred in the Depiction of Warfare in the Assyrian Palace Reliefs and in Ezekiel 23:14–17," in *The Aesthetics of Violence in the Prophets*, ed. Chris Franke and Julia M. O'Brien, LHBOTS 517 (New York: T&T Clark, 2010), 1–17.
56. Susan E. Haddox, "Favoured Sons and Subordinate Masculinities," in Creangă, *Masculinity in the Hebrew Bible*, 3–4.

figure in his household, and in the story of Genesis 16 he is passive and follows his wife's direction; his son Isaac passively allows himself to be bound for sacrifice in Genesis 22; and his grandson Jacob is feminized with respect to his brother Esau, for Genesis 27 emphasizes that Esau is hairy and a hunter, while Jacob has smooth skin and is found indoors with his mother.[57] In the prophetic marriage metaphor, God takes the dominant masculine role, since the text portrays God as a husband; Israel is God's wife in this metaphor, and this means that male Israelite readers had to conceive of themselves as women and as prostitutes, since that is how the metaphor portrays Israel.[58] Yet not even God's masculinity manages to survive entirely unquestioned in the marriage metaphor texts, argues Haddox, since Israel, as God's promiscuous wife, challenges her husband's control through her sexual infidelities, undermining God's dominance of the household and so God's manhood.[59]

If the feminization of males points to their loss of status in biblical stories, the masculinization of women is normally portrayed as dangerous. One obvious example of this, to which I have already referred, is the character of Jezebel. She is more politically astute than her royal husband in a story such as 1 Kings 21; she orders the assassination of Elijah, a political enemy (1 Kgs 19:2), as a male would; and the danger she poses as she crosses boundaries between male and female results in her death, argues Amy Kalmanofsky.[60] Sometimes the boundaries between male and female are transgressed and not entirely recovered. Deryn Guest, for example, focuses her reading of Judges 4–5 on the figure of Jael, noting that scholars have long pointed out that Jael crosses gender boundaries and acts like a man: as Sisera, a Canaanite general fleeing from his army's defeat by the Israelites, passes by Jael's tent, she takes the initiative to invite him in, ostensibly to protect him, but then kills him, penetrating his skull with a tent-peg. She is the subject of most of the verbs in her part of the story, and so she adopts the active role normally taken by male characters in biblical stories. She has a name (*yāʿēl*) that could be read as a masculine form of a Hebrew verb, and at one point she is addressed with a masculine imperative verb form (*ʿămōd* in 4:20) as if she were a man. She kills the enemy

57. Haddox, "Favoured Sons," 7–16.
58. See, for example, Howard Eilberg-Schwartz, *God's Phallus and Other Problems for Men and Monotheism* (Boston: Beacon, 1994), 97–105; and Yvonne Sherwood, *The Prostitute and the Prophet: Hosea's Marriage in Literary-Theoretical Perspective*, JSOTSup 212, GCT 2 (Sheffield, UK: Sheffield Academic, 1996), 313.
59. Susan E. Haddox, *Metaphor and Masculinity in Hosea*, StBL 141 (New York: Peter Lang, 2011), 64–72.
60. Kalmanofsky, *Gender-Play in the Hebrew Bible*, 95–113.

general as a male warrior would and does so through an act of penetration. This is genderfuck, writes Guest, as clear distinctions between male and female dissolve in Judges 4–5 not only because of the portrayal of Jael but also because of the story's portrayal of Deborah, Israel's leader who goes out to battle like the stereotypical Israelite construction of a man; its portrayal of Barak, her male general who is too frightened to go to the battlefield without Deborah; and its portrayal of Sisera, the man who runs away, as cowardly as Barak, and who is penetrated, as Israelite culture expected women rather than men to be penetrated in sexual intercourse. By the end of this story, Guest argues, it is not entirely clear that gender norms will be recoverable, since the men have taken female roles and the women have taken male ones.[61]

Creating texts that emphasize the failure of boundaries is a key aspect of queer interpretation,[62] and so in his analysis of the story of the Ethiopian eunuch's conversion by Philip in Acts 8, Sean Burke points out that the ambiguity scholarship has created in regard to this figure is not limited to his gender (as a eunuch, should he be considered as a male or not?) but also involves his social status (high or low?), religious identity (is he a Jew, Gentile, or proselyte?), and race (is he Black or not?).[63] The story of his conversion is followed in Acts 10 by Peter's conversion of Cornelius, as Acts breaks down boundaries between Jews and Gentiles, allowing that the latter group may become part of the Christian community as well. This failure of the Jew/Gentile binary distinction is central to Acts, and Burke argues that the eunuch's story is key to the deconstruction of such distinctions in a book that dismantles old categories and boundaries as it turns Gentile outsiders into insiders, members of the Christian church.[64]

And insofar as queer analysis questions accepted distinctions between what is normal and abnormal, as Joseph Marchal puts it,[65] it arrives at interpretations or meaningful texts that problematize traditional readings created by academic and

61. Deryn Guest, "From Gender Reversal to Genderfuck: Reading Jael through a Lesbian Lens," in Hornsby and Stone, *Bible Trouble*, 9–43.
62. Although, to be clear, Guest refers to her interpretation of Judg 4–5 as a lesbian rather than a queer reading; see her discussion as to the distinction she sees between the two in *When Deborah Met Jael*, 45–49.
63. Sean D. Burke, *Queering the Ethiopian Eunuch: Strategies of Ambiguity in Acts* (Minneapolis: Fortress, 2013), 1–14, 126–36.
64. Burke, 141–47.
65. Joseph A. Marchal, "Bio-Necro-*Biblio*-Politics? Restaging Feminist Intersections and Queer Exceptions," *CulRel* 15 (2014): 167.

religious communities. Many scholars have reacted against homophobic interpretations of biblical texts, as Ken Stone notes, arguing that modern conceptions of homosexuality simply did not exist in the ancient world and that negative portrayals of same-sex eroticism in the texts are based on ancient presuppositions of gender and power that moderns tend not to share.[66] Studies like these, however, are still ones that reinforce the idea that heterosexuality is normal and natural and so something that needs no discussion to understand in light of biblical material, and Stone argues that the field needs to move beyond this heteronormative assumption. So there is an important ethical point in making the argument, as Cheryl Anderson does, that ancient Israelite law codes privilege the male head of the household and expect him to be dominant in virtually all things, including sexual activity, which is why they forbid erotic sex acts among males, since it would demand a male being sexually penetrated, something that ancient Israelite culture would understand as a subordinate and unacceptable role for a real man, an understanding based on socially constructed categories of gender.[67] Stone's point, however, is that our interpretations should avoid and critique clear boundaries between the normal and abnormal as they are traditionally understood when they privilege insiders and punish outsiders.[68]

Burke's interpretation of the story of the Ethiopian eunuch, awash in ambiguity, is one example of this sort of analysis. Another is Theodore Jennings's reading of the relationship between God and various male characters, especially David, in Samuel. In that book, God is attracted to young men whom the text describes as handsome, and like the human warriors in Samuel, God wishes to be accompanied by a younger comrade in a same-sex erotic relationship.[69] Jennings argues that the characters in Samuel enact masculinity in their feats of boldness and loyalty, not in terms of their relationships with women, and so the case is not that David is feminized in the homoerotic story he shares with God. To argue otherwise, Jennings writes, depends on a binary distinction between male and female, but there is much more ambiguity in regard to these categories in Samuel than traditional

66. Ken Stone, "Homosexuality and the Bible or Queer Reading? A Response to Martti Nissinen," *TheoSex* 14 (2001): 108–12.
67. Anderson, *Ancient Laws and Contemporary Controversies*, 30–39.
68. Stone, *Practicing Safer Texts*, 66–67.
69. Theodore W. Jennings Jr., *Jacob's Wound: Homoerotic Narrative in the Literature of Ancient Israel* (New York: Continuum, 2005), 3–12, 67–70.

interpretations normally admit.[70] Jennings's meaningful text of Samuel is one that puts many contemporary understandings of the boundaries between gender and between acceptable and unacceptable relationships between males into question. Lori Rowlett's reading of the story of Samson and Delilah in Judges 16:4–22 also challenges the distinctions between what we tend to think of as normal and abnormal sexuality. In this story, Delilah repetitively asks Samson for the source of his superhuman strength, with the hope of selling this information to the Philistines, but Samson consistently lies to her, and the Philistines are unable to capture him. Only on the fourth repetition of her request does Samson tell her the truth—his strength will leave him should his head be shaved—and so the Philistines are able to overpower him, bind him, and gouge out his eyes. It is a story of sadomasochism, writes Rowlett, a marginalized kind of sexual act. Samson has no rational reason to tell Delilah the truth but seems to enjoy S/M role-play, involving hair fetishism and pain, where he acts as the butch bottom and Delilah as the dominatrix, reversing the normal cultural expectations of the dominant gender in sexual encounters. There is a reflection here of how God acts in Judges as a whole, Rowlett argues, taking the role of the sadist and repetitively punishing Israel with invasions of foreign armies, as if taking sadistic pleasure in this violence.[71]

Not everyone will be convinced by this reading of Judges 16, so far does it seem from traditional or "normal" interpretations, but engaging in analysis that arrives at abnormal ones allows readers to reflect on a dangerous and oppressive portrayal of God in Judges. Rowlett's story of Samson and Delilah makes it central to an understanding of how God is portrayed in the book, as Burke sees the story of the Ethiopian eunuch as key to the understanding of Acts. Analyses like these focus on categories that we often understand to be fixed and natural but show them to be things constructed by groups that allow them to justify the exclusion of those outside of "natural" boundaries and to privilege those on the inside. We certainly do need boundaries—our words, for example, have semantic boundaries that limit their meanings and make communication possible—but if we can be shown that some of the boundaries we use to exclude are ethically problematic according to our own belief system, then we will want to rethink them. It helps at that point to know

70. Jennings, 71–73.
71. Lori Rowlett, "Violent Femmes and S/M: Queering Samson and Delilah," in Stone, *Queer Commentary and the Hebrew Bible*, 106–15.

that these boundaries have been socially constructed, that there is nothing in an uninterpreted world-in-itself that demands we recognize them as valid, and that we can change and rearrange categories to better fit with the rest of the worldview that we use to make sense of things. When we are aware that the categories of gender that we have created exclude transgender persons and marginalize gays and lesbians, then we will want to ask how well these boundaries fit our beliefs, particularly when the LGBTQ community is victimized by hate crimes at higher rates than those of other minoritized groups, and that its members are far more likely than the rest of the population to be homeless and imprisoned, especially if they are people of color.[72] Given that religious communities have used biblical texts to reinforce boundaries that contribute to this hate, we can see that the creation of texts that unsettle traditional categories of gender and sexuality could be used in liberative ways.

To read texts from the point of view of what Deryn Guest calls a lesbian-identified hermeneutic demands disrupting the binary categories of gender and sex that Western culture, among many others, has constructed, since they function to marginalize lesbians as abnormal.[73] If we are ethically committed to fighting the marginalization of people on the basis of their sexuality, then we will have to conduct our interpretation with this in mind. So when Guest writes about texts like Leviticus 18:22 and 20:13, which forbid same-sex eroticism, she argues that they are part of a program to construct Israelite identity as defined by a good and normal sexuality, in contrast with the bad and abnormal sexuality of the Canaanites,[74] an Israelite/Canaanite binary distinction that many modern scholars have accepted

72. For example, the Southern Poverty Law Center's 2011 study of hate crimes in the United States from 1995 to 2008 found that anti-LGBTQ hate crimes accounted for 17.4 percent of the total number of such crimes in that period. Given the difference in population with other minoritized groups for which the SPLC tracks such crimes, the LGBTQ community was attacked at over eight times the expected rate, higher than any other group. See Mark Potok, "Anti-gay Hate Crimes: Doing the Math," SPLC, accessed March 25, 2021, https://tinyurl.com/ybpyj86w. To take another example, a 2015 study of twenty-eight-thousand transgender adults in the United States showed they were more than twice as likely as the general population to be imprisoned, and that Black transgender women were more than nine times as likely to be incarcerated. "LGBTQ People behind Bars: A Guide to Understanding the Issues Facing Transgender Prisoners and Their Legal Rights," National Center for Transgender Equality, accessed March 25, 2021, https://tinyurl.com/2xzwfb8v, 5. And to take just one more example, the National Coalition for the Homeless found in 2017 that 40 percent of homeless youth in the United States identify as LGBTQ, while only 10 percent of youth in the general population do. "LGBTQ Homelessness," National Coalition for the Homeless, accessed March 25, 2021, https://tinyurl.com/3pbs2tes.

73. Guest, *When Deborah Met Jael*, 57–58, 60–64.

74. Guest, 178–81.

as valid.[75] Interpretations like this, like the other ones this part of the chapter has surveyed, challenge readers to question the boundaries in regard to sexuality and gender they have accepted. They ask us to interrogate the issues of whom we have excluded and marginalized when thinking about gender and sexuality and what we have assumed when thinking about what makes a real man or a good woman and the proper social roles of each. When we take readings like these seriously, we have to confront the beliefs we hold regarding such boundaries and determine whether or not they are inconsistent with other things we believe about treating all other people equally and fairly, and particularly whether the categories of gender and sexuality we have been working with are ethically acceptable ones. Some queer readings, like Burke's analysis of the Ethiopian eunuch, provide us with positive examples of not only the blurring of gender boundaries but boundaries of race, religion, and class as well.

Manuel Villalobos reads the story of the Ethiopian eunuch in light of his own experience of growing up gay in Mexico, where he had the sense of living *del otro lado*—"on the other side," a phrase sometimes used in Mexico to refer to the other side of the country's northern border—even while in his own community.[76] Like himself, he writes, the eunuch lived in neither one culture nor another but both. Neither Jerusalem nor Ethiopia could provide him with salvation, and so he became a *mestizo*, living in a borderland, an area of ambivalence and ambiguity where we have opportunities to interpret in new ways and see new things as certain boundaries come to seem less and less important.[77] Belief in the validity and usefulness of particular boundaries will not always allow us to be the ethical interpreters we want to be, but following the lead of some minoritized scholars who have transgressed traditionally accepted categories of gender and sexuality can allow us to see new things as we expose oppression in texts as they have often been read and interpret in new and liberative ways.

75. See Ken Stone, "Queering the Canaanite," in *The Sexual Theologian: Essays on Sex, God and Politics*, ed. Marcella Althaus-Reid and Lisa Isherwood, QTS (London: T&T Clark, 2004), 119–27.
76. Manuel Villalobos, "Bodies *del Otro Lado* Finding Life and Hope in the Borderland: Gloria Anzaldúa, the Ethiopian Eunuch of Acts 8:26–40, *y* Yo," in Hornsby and Stone, *Bible Trouble*, 207–17.
77. Villalobos, "Bodies *del Otro Lado*," 199–207, 217–18.

Conclusion: Solidarity and Dialogue, Part 2

It is impossible for those of us who are not impoverished and oppressed to be the impoverished and oppressed, as Isasi-Díaz points out. We have not had their experiences, and we come from different backgrounds, and so we will not create the same meaningful texts when we read. If this prevents men from doing feminist readings, non-Africana from doing African or African American readings, and so on, this does not mean that those outside of such groups cannot pay attention to the liberative goals of others, especially once we see the many ways in which biblical scholars from such groups concretize those goals in their professional work. More privileged readers who are outside of any minoritized community can still be aware of and emphasize in their interpretive work the dangers of dehumanization, the sexism, racism, classism, and heteronormativity that have been used to exclude the marginalized from the ranks that dominant groups have considered to be fully human. They can bring marginalized goals for interpretation and concrete examples of work informed by those goals to their own communities, asking them to reflect on their roles in maintaining oppressive structures and on the support they can offer to struggles for liberation. Outsiders will not be able to say if a particular interpretation can be a useful parallel for liberative work in a community that is not theirs, because the group alone knows enough about its situation to make decisions like that, not to mention that to take such a step for others—to read for them, in other words—is to strip them of agency, part of the process of dehumanization. But more privileged readers can be in solidarity with those fighting for liberation, and they can ask their own communities to do the same. We can ask what difference it makes to pay attention to secondary characters who hover at the margins of a text rather than occupy their centers of power. What do they want? How do they feel? What explains their speech and actions? If traditional readings are silent about these things, what difference does it make to create an interpretation where these characters are privileged and speak? We can ask if traditional Western and academic readings of texts are harmful in any way, if it is ethically tenable to continue to describe some characters as heroes or villains, or whether our own belief systems demand more ethical consistency, such that we might have to understand particular characters differently than we have. With the help of the sort of criticism we have just surveyed, we can interrogate our presumptions about gender and sexuality, or about the identity of those who live on the other side of a geographic or ethnic border, and we can certainly question our assumptions about "real" biblical scholarship. In regard to categories we have assumed to be true, we can ask whom they exclude and whether we are ethically unhappy with that exclusion. When we see no interpretive possibility of arriving at a meaningful text that we could construe as liberative, we can warn of a passage's potential dangers.

None of this will be possible for more privileged readers unless we begin a dialogue by listening to the sorts of liberative goals and examples we have surveyed in this and the previous chapter. After having done this, we are at the point where we can have something to contribute to a liberative dialogue in the field. This dialogue is, ideally, always ongoing, for no part of the Bible's physical text is inherently liberating. It has no meaning at all until a community or interpreter decides to give it one, but different readers can often arrive at very different conclusions in that regard, and only a continuous dialogue in the field will help us see how particular readings might be liberative or damaging. We could, for example, note how different marginalized readers have interpreted the exodus story. Within Latin American liberation theology, the exodus has often been the liberative paradigm and lens through which the rest of the Bible has been read. It "forms the basis of the Old Testament," writes George Pixley, and is "the fundamental element in the many and varied writings that make up the Bible."[78] José Comblin describes it as the model on which both the Hebrew Bible / Old Testament and the New Testament are based, "the fundamental meaning of history and the key to the interpretation of all of its events."[79] For liberation theology, the exodus reveals God's commitment to liberation even for slaves, the most impoverished and marginalized of all social groups, and so it reveals the divine preferential option for the poor. But the difficulty with this sort of interpretation, writes Jon Levenson, entering into dialogue with Pixley and others who read from the perspective of liberation theology, is that the exodus event does not do away with slavery, which is tolerated by God and humans throughout the Hebrew Bible and New Testament. The central aspect of the exodus story is not liberation from slavery but Israel's chosenness; in the exodus, they alone are

78. George V. Pixley, *On Exodus: A Liberation Perspective*, trans. Robert R. Barr (Maryknoll, NY: Orbis, 1987), xiii.
79. José Comblin, "Los Pobres como Sujeto de la Historia," RIBLA 3 (1989): 40 (my translation).

God's people—God refers to Israel as "my people" fourteen times in the plague and exodus narrative[80]—and more important than their freedom from slavery is their freedom for the law, which God proceeds to give them at Sinai, so they can obey it in Canaan, the land God then gives to them in the conquest narrative in Joshua. Liberation theology can tend to supersessionism in its reading of the exodus story, argues Levenson, and allows liberal Christian readers of the Bible to find what they want to find, in this case a replacement of Israel in the story with Christians, ignoring the aspects of the narrative—the focus on Israel as God's people, the gift of the Jewish law—that would contradict their reading.[81]

The dialogue has, so far, pointed out that what some Latin American readers have seen as a liberative text—what their interpretation has created, in other words—is an oppressive one from a Jewish perspective, because supersessionist readings are exclusionary and dangerous, as the effects of many centuries' worth of anti-Jewish readings of the Bible attest. Readers normally find the interpretations they want to find, part of the point of Levenson's critique of Pixley and liberation theology, because they have been trained by their communities to find them and are taught to edit out or explain away potential evidence that might challenge important aspects of the community's worldview. Once we continue the dialogue about the exodus story, in fact, we can see that the same is true of Levenson's reading. If God frees Israel from slavery for fidelity to Torah, God also frees them to commit genocide under divine leadership in the land where Torah is to be obeyed. Israel is to slaughter all of the Canaanites when they enter the land, Moses tells them (Deut 7:1–4), a command echoed in the law God gives to the people (Deut 20:16–18) and enacted in the conquest narrative of Joshua 6–11. The Israelites may start out as victims, Musa Dube writes, but they become imperialists, taking over a land that is not theirs because its inhabitants are said to be evil (Lev 18:24; Deut 9:5), which is one of the ways Westerners justified their colonial conquests.[82] Robert Allen Warrior, writing from his standpoint as a Native American, says that as someone who belongs to a people stigmatized as evil and subjected to genocide by Europeans who took their land, he feels compelled to read the narrative from Genesis through

80. Exod 5:1; 6:7; 7:4, 16; 8:1, 20–23; 9:1, 13, 17; 10:3–4.
81. Jon D. Levenson, "Liberation Theology and the Exodus," in *Jews, Christians, and the Theology of the Hebrew Scriptures*, ed. Alice Ogden Bellis and Joel S. Kaminsky, SBLSymS 8 (Atlanta: Society of Biblical Literature, 2000), 215–30.
82. Dube, *Postcolonial Feminist Interpretation*, 57–70.

Joshua through the eyes of the Canaanites.[83] Liberation theology overlooked the way that liberation for one people in the exodus became the oppression of another in the conquest, writes Marcella Althaus-Reid,[84] and Jean Zaru writes that as a Palestinian, the very concept of the divine choice of a people on whose behalf God will enact genocide in order to give their land to others seems radically unjust, most particularly since traditions like the conquest narrative have been used to justify violence against the Palestinians.[85]

And even if we bracket out the horrifying picture of the conquest narrative in which God orders and enacts genocide, the picture of God with which the exodus story in and of itself provides readers is unsettling, to say the least. God provides freedom for Israel but first visits a series of plagues upon Egypt while distinguishing between "my people" and "your people," and the latter group is Egypt, Pharaoh's people, those who suffer for Pharaoh's refusal to release Israel from slavery and, ultimately, for God's refusal to even let Pharaoh make that choice. "I will harden his heart," God tells Moses in reference to Pharaoh before the plagues begin, "and he will not let the people go. Say to Pharaoh, 'Thus says the Lord: Israel is my firstborn son. I said to you, let my son go, that he may serve me, but you refused to let him go. Now I will kill your firstborn son'" (Exod 4:21–23). God eventually does harden Pharaoh's heart, forcing him to refuse to let Israel go (10:27; 11:10), and as a result of this refusal for which God is responsible, God kills the non-Israelite firstborn in Egypt, "from the firstborn of Pharaoh who sits on his throne to the firstborn of the female slave who is behind the hand-mill and every firstborn of the livestock" (11:5). God hardens Pharaoh's heart and then slaughters all of the firstborn of Egypt "so that you might know that the Lord distinguishes between Egypt and Israel" (11:7); earlier in the narrative of the plagues, God tells Pharaoh that Egypt could already have been destroyed, "however, for this reason I have kept you in existence, in order to show you my strength and so that my name might be recounted in all the earth" (9:16). The picture of a God who slaughters the innocent "so that my name might be recounted in all the earth" and to demonstrate that God cares

83. Robert Allen Warrior, "Canaanites, Cowboys, and Indians: Deliverance, Conquest, and Liberation Theology Today," in *The Postmodern Bible Reader*, ed. David Jobling, Tina Pippin, and Ronald Schleifer (Oxford: Blackwell, 2001), 188–94.
84. Marcella María Althaus-Reid, "Searching for a Queer Sophia-Wisdom: The Post-colonial Rahab," in *Patriarchs, Prophets and Other Villains*, ed. Lisa Isherwood, GTS (London: Equinox, 2007), 129–30.
85. Jean Zaru, "Biblical Teachings and the Hard Realities of Life," in Pui-lan, *Hope Abundant*, 125–26.

about one group of people but not another seems so horrifying that it is no wonder that Ivan Petrella now suggests it would be better for liberation theology to do its work without this story, and even without the Bible as a whole, which is replete with narratives of divine violence.[86]

Yet it is not only the poor of Latin America who have looked to the exodus story for liberative hope. So too, for example, have the poor in Korea, who have seen it as a paradigm of freedom, justice, and peace,[87] just as African Americans did during slavery and the civil rights era.[88] So should we condemn readings like these for their inherent anti-Jewish supersessionism and for ignoring an ethically problematic portrayal of a God who kills the innocent to display divine power and who orders genocide? Insofar as these interpretations or meaningful texts helped provide liberation, they are praiseworthy, for they managed to contribute to liberative goals. Slave songs, one manner in which African Americans created meaningful texts of the exodus narrative, used the figure of Egypt from the exodus story to refer to the political, economic, social, and religious institutions that supported the slavocracy,[89] part of a broader hermeneutical move in this community to equate biblical villains with slaveholders in their interpretations of the Bible.[90] We may not believe that this allegorical reading of the story entirely saves such texts from the ethical drawbacks I have just discussed, and certainly African American biblical scholars in more recent times have argued that the story offers liberation only for Israel, not other groups.[91] Useful dialogue among biblical interpreters interested in contributing to liberative readings certainly should point to ethical flaws with other

86. Ivan Petrella, "Without the Bible: A New Liberation Theology," in *Colonialism and the Bible: Contemporary Reflections from the Global South*, ed. Tat-siong Benny Liew and Fernando F. Segovia, PDSRT (Lanham, MD: Lexington, 2016), 251–70.
87. See, for example, Te Soo Yim, "Interpretation of the Law and the Gospel in Exodus from the Perspective of Minjung Theology," in *Mapping and Engaging the Bible in Asian Cultures: Congress of the Society of Asian Bible Studies 2008 Seoul Conference*, ed. Lee Yeong Mee and Yoo Yoon Jong (Seoul: Christian Literature Society of Korea, 2009), 89–102.
88. For example, Herbert Robinson Marbury, *Pillars of Cloud and Fire: The Politics of Exodus in African American Biblical Interpretation*, RST (New York: New York University Press, 2015), 13–48, 133–69.
89. Mitzi J. Smith, "*Give Me Jesus*: Salvation History in the Spirituals," in *Afrocentric Interpretations of Jesus and the Gospel Tradition: Things Black Scholars See That White Scholars Overlook*, ed. Thomas Bowie Slater (Lewiston, NY: Edwin Mellen, 2015), 71–75.
90. Emerson B. Powery and Rodney S. Sadler Jr., *The Genesis of Liberation: Biblical Interpretation in the Antebellum Narratives of the Enslaved* (Louisville, KY: Westminster John Knox, 2016), 13.
91. For example, Demetrius K. Williams, "The Bible and Models of Liberation in the African American Experience," in *Yet with a Steady Beat: Contemporary U.S. Afrocentric Biblical Interpretation*, ed. Randall C. Bailey, SemeiaSt 42 (Atlanta: Society of Biblical Literature, 2003), 37–40; Cheryl A. Kirk-Duggan, "Let My People Go! Threads of Exodus in African American Narratives," in Bailey, *Yet with a Steady Beat*, 124–33.

readings, no matter who is responsible for them, part of a broader conversation that investigates what has been done well in terms of meeting emancipatory goals and what could be done better. All groups, privileged or otherwise, need to be in dialogue with other biblical scholars and their communities to discover how the meaningful texts they create could be better, where *better* is defined through our ethical criterion of liberation that demands we look at and treat others, especially those who have less power and privilege than we do, as fully human.

We could think of a liberative polylogue akin to the Samoan *talalasi* (*talanoa* in Tongan), a concept that biblical scholars from the Pacific islands like Jione Havea and Mosese Ma'ilo have used to describe their interpretive approaches, in which the same story is told over and over in different ways from different perspectives, each version shaped by a different storyteller's context and their attempts to meet the needs of their audience, sometimes unraveling earlier versions or picking up elements neglected in them.[92] The texts that African American slaves created in their interpretations of the exodus story were important tools in their struggle against a dehumanizing institution that insisted the Bible legitimated their slavery,[93] but should others struggling for liberative goals encounter such a reading and find it counterproductive, then dialogue should ensue. None of us is ethically perfect or comes from a culture that is, and readings from marginalized communities are not liberative merely because they come from marginalized communities, which must struggle against their own oppressive impulses,[94] something that dialogue can help us do, since ideally it will help all of us see where we might cling to beliefs or create readings that violate important ethical tenets we already hold. So when it comes to creating a meaningful text of the exodus story, we will have to acknowledge that if it involves freedom for Israel from slavery and freedom for the law, it also contains dangerous and oppressive aspects that we can no longer gloss over. As in *talalasi* or *talanoa*, new liberative interpreters or storytellers

92. See Jione Havea, "Releasing the Story of Esau from the Words of Obadiah," in *The Bible and Hermeneutics of Liberation*, ed. Alejandro F. Botta and Pablo R. Andiñach, SemeiaSt 59 (Atlanta: Society of Biblical Literature, 2009), 91–93; and Ma'ilo, "Island Prodigals," 24–25.
93. Powery and Sadler, *Genesis of Liberation*, 60–61.
94. See, for example, R. S. Sugirtharajah, *The Bible and the Third World: Precolonial, Colonial, and Postcolonial Encounters* (Cambridge: Cambridge University Press, 2001), 194–95; Gloria Kehwile Plaatjie, "Toward a Post-apartheid Black Feminist Reading of the Bible: A Case of Luke 2:36–38," in Dube, *Other Ways of Reading*, 131–32; and Sarojini Nadar, "Beyond the 'Ordinary Reader' and the 'Invisible Intellectual': Pushing the Boundaries of Contextual Bible Study Discourses," in Boer and Segovia, *Future of the Biblical Past*, 19–21.

can look to earlier readings and respond to them, finding better ways to meet the needs of their audiences. Some communities of interpreters may decide that the story is not well suited to their goals and that their analysis should be devoted to warning of those dangerous aspects. Some might read it by focusing on its minor characters, such as Shiphrah and Puah, the two midwives of Exodus 1:15–21 who defy Pharaoh's orders to kill the male Israelite babies, or the Israelite of 2:11–15 who confronts Moses about his murder of an Egyptian, or Moses's mother and sister, who save his life when he is an infant (2:1–10).[95] The benefit of dialogue is that, ideally, it forces us to think about readings more ethical than the ones we have already created; its difficulty, however, is that it also forces us to grapple with hard questions that evade simple answers when we have to face up to nonliberative aspects of our interpretations that we had not previously noticed. With this in mind, I turn now to my own attempts to follow the lead of the liberative goals, strategies, and examples that we have encountered in this and the previous chapter, with the hope of contributing interpretations of biblical texts that might be seen as useful for liberation.

95. For example, Yeong Mee Lee points out that in Exod 1–2, it is the story's female characters who make redemption possible ("Motherhood as a Theological Model for Redemption in the Hebrew Bible," in Lee and Park, *Korean Feminists in Conversation*, 22–24). And Brian DiPalma argues that as Moses's violence fails to accomplish the goal of liberation in Exod 1–4, and as his life is rescued by women at a number of points in these chapters, masculine values are deconstructed here and a new sort of masculinity is constructed for him ("De/Constructing Masculinity in Exodus 1–4," in Creangă, *Masculinity in the Hebrew Bible*, 2–19).

7

The Danger and Liberation of Ezra-Nehemiah

Introduction: The Plot and Dangers of Ezra-Nehemiah

Given the discussion of the liberative goals and readings of minoritized scholars in chapters 5 and 6, the act of providing my own interpretations of texts in this and the following chapter might seem superfluous, but it is important to point out that the work of more privileged scholars reading for emancipation will not be exactly like that of our less privileged colleagues. I cannot read for a specific nonacademic community, unless it is for a fairly privileged one whom I ask to consider how they have benefited from and maintained networks of power that oppress others. I can hope that by paying attention to the liberative goals for and models of interpretation like those the previous chapters discuss I will be able to create readings that my minoritized peers might see as a useful part of an emancipatory enterprise. But only dialogue with those scholars can determine if I have been successful in that regard or not. With different experiences and needs, I simply will not always read as they do, but here and in chapter 8, I present two examples of what it can look like for a more privileged scholar to follow their lead in interpretation. Adopting explicitly emancipatory goals and approaches to biblical interpretation does not prevent me from doing work that I and my colleagues can recognize as scholarly; as chapter 4 argues, biblical scholars raised in a mainstream historical tradition need not abandon most of our beliefs and habits about how to go about our work when we prioritize liberation, but the changes we do make will, at the very least, prevent us from ignoring our ethical principles when we act as scholars.

My interpretive work in this chapter largely consists of two different readings of an entire biblical book. Although most editions of the Bible present Ezra and

Nehemiah as two separate writings, both religious tradition and modern scholars have generally understood them to be two parts of the same book called Ezra-Nehemiah.[1] For those readers whose gender, race, and economic and social status have allowed them to benefit from postcolonial power structures, Ezra-Nehemiah offers an interesting test case in constructing emancipatory readings. Traditional scholarly interpretations of the book that have searched for the meaning of its ancient writer(s) generally point out how positively it portrays the Persian Empire, which ruled Israel during the period the book discusses, while depicting the native peoples of Palestine as the adversaries of both empire and the "true" Jewish community sent to the region as imperial colonizers. If the evidence of the physical text and the beliefs we use to interpret it and produce meaning compel us to produce meanings like these, then as readers guided by a liberative ethic we must clearly indicate how dangerous this reading is and explain which aspects of it are ethically lacking. The next section of the chapter will produce just such a suspicious interpretation of Ezra-Nehemiah, one that begins with the ethical concerns liberative scholars have expressed about the book, which I discuss in this section. As chapters 2 and 3 explain, however, we need not limit ourselves to interpretations that reflect what we think ancient writers were trying to say, and we can use the evidence of the physical text to create other interpretations or meaningful texts. So in the third part of the chapter, I draw upon another common interpretive technique of minoritized scholars as I produce a different reading of Ezra-Nehemiah, one that privileges the speech of the characters demonized and marginalized in the first one, and this approach urges readers to question and reject the portrayal of those characters that my first interpretation produces.

1. Not all scholars believe Ezra-Nehemiah was originally constructed as a single work, and a minority opinion in the field holds that Ezra 1–10 and Neh 1–13 were originally two separate writings; see James VanderKam, "Ezra-Nehemiah or Ezra and Nehemiah?," in *Priests, Prophets and Scribes: Essays on the Formation and Heritage of Second Temple Judaism in Honour of Joseph Blenkinsopp*, ed. Eugene Ulrich et al., JSOTSup 149 (Sheffield, UK: Sheffield Academic, 1992), 55–75; David Kraemer, "On the Relationship of the Books of Ezra and Nehemiah," JSOT 59 (1993): 73–92; and Bob Becking, *Ezra, Nehemiah, and the Construction of Early Jewish Identity*, FAT 80 (Tübingen, Germany: Mohr Siebeck, 2011), 27–28. This conclusion, however, is unlikely. Ezra 4:8–23 refers to local opposition to the construction of Jerusalem's wall, a matter that is never otherwise discussed in Ezra 1–10 but that is resolved in Neh 1–6; there are narratives about Ezra in the third person in Ezra 7 and 10 as well as Neh 8; in Ezra 7, Artaxerxes orders Ezra to teach the law, something we do not see him do until Neh 8; the importance of avoiding marriages outside of the community is emphasized in Ezra 9–10 as well as in Neh 10 and 13; and both Ezra 9 and Neh 9 contain prayers focused on the consequences of the people's failure to keep the law.

Ezra-Nehemiah tells a story of Israel after the exile, and its narrative begins with the people in Babylon, brought there by Nebuchadnezzar after the Babylonian king destroyed Jerusalem and removed the people from the land, something he accomplished because, as characters in the book explain, "our ancestors angered the God of the heavens" (Ezra 5:12) and did not keep the law God gave them (Neh 9:16–31). The opening of the book has King Cyrus of Persia state that the political situation has changed and that he now rules what had been the Babylonian Empire because "the Lord, the God of the heavens, gave all the kingdoms of the earth" to him, and also commanded him to rebuild the temple in Jerusalem that Nebuchadnezzar and the Babylonians destroyed (Ezra 1:2). In response to this divine order, Cyrus chooses the group descended from those whom Nebuchadnezzar exiled to Babylonia to go to Jerusalem and do the construction work (1:3), and God supports this choice, as readers can see when God rouses the leaders of this people (1:5). Ezra-Nehemiah goes on to relate the struggles and successes of the Jewish community, whom the narrative portrays as a group of colonists sent from the center to the margins of the Persian Empire, and they successfully rebuild the temple by the time the narrative reaches Ezra 6, even though in Ezra 4 they face opposition in their endeavor from "the people of the land" (Ezra 4:4). This latter group consists of indigenous Palestinians who worship the same God as the community sent from Babylonia (4:2),[2] but the narrative describes them as the community's "adversaries" (4:1). The Jewish group sent by the king refuses to allow the people of the land to help them construct the temple since, they say, King Cyrus chose them alone for the task (4:2–3), and so the population native to Palestine, their offer of help rejected by their coreligionists from Babylon, work to stop its construction. Thanks to the intervention of a later Persian king named Darius, however, the efforts of the people of the land are thwarted, and the temple is finally rebuilt (Ezra 5–6).

2. Reading Ezra 4:2 with the MT's *qĕrê*, "we sacrifice to him (*lô*)," which is reflected in most of the Versions, including the LXX and 1 Esd 5:66, rather than with the MT's *kĕtîb*, "we do not (*lō'*) sacrifice." The latter reading may have been a deliberate alteration by a copyist who aimed to enhance the portrayal of the exilic community by providing them with another reason to exclude the native Palestinians from the temple construction project: unlike the exilic community, they do not sacrifice to the God of Israel.

In Ezra 7, the narrative jumps ahead some generations,[3] returning readers to the community of those Israelites who remained in Babylonia, and here we encounter Ezra the priest, "a scribe skilled in the law of Moses" (7:6). Like the community of Ezra 1–6, Ezra is ordered by a Persian king—Artaxerxes, in this case—to go to Judah, the region immediately surrounding Jerusalem, in order to bring vast gifts from the king for the functioning of the temple the earlier generation rebuilt and to teach and establish the Jewish law in which Ezra is so skilled (7:12–26). But Ezra finds a community in Judah that is now in violation of Torah, for they have intermarried with women of "the peoples of the lands" (9:1–2), something that he warns them contradicts God's law and that could lead God to destroy the Jewish community in Judah once again (9:6–15). And even though the Judean community agrees to force these women out of their midst in Ezra 10, the problem persists after Artaxerxes sends Nehemiah to Judah (Neh 6:18; 10:30 [Heb 31]; 13:23–28). As yet another royal emissary, Nehemiah's task is to rebuild Jerusalem and its wall (Neh 2:1–8), and like the group sent by the king to rebuild the temple in Ezra 1–6, he too faces opposition in his building project from the native population of Palestine (Neh 4; 6) yet successfully completes the project. At the end of the book, the temple and city Nebuchadnezzar destroyed as divine punishment for Israel's sin have been rebuilt, and although the people struggle to keep God's law, Ezra and Nehemiah, sent by the Persian king, work to ensure their obedience so they do not suffer the same fate as their ancestors did under Nebuchadnezzar.

One could read Ezra-Nehemiah as a story of God's fidelity to the people, understanding it as a narrative in which the imperial rulers who govern Israel respond positively to divine command, resulting in the end of the Babylonian exile and the reconstruction of Jerusalem and God's temple there. However, quite a number of minoritized scholars have pointed to oppressive aspects of the book, particularly in regard to its characterizations of "the people of the land" and the "foreign women" who threaten the community in the plot that I have just outlined. Since we are aiming for readings that can advance emancipatory goals, then, as chapters 4 through 6 discuss, we can begin with analyses of the text developed by marginalized scholars

3. The story of Ezra 1 begins in the first year of Cyrus (539 BCE), and Ezra 6:15 says the temple was completed in the sixth year of Darius (515 BCE). Ezra 7:7 puts readers in the seventh year of Artaxerxes (458 BCE, if we assume this is Artaxerxes I), or fifty-seven years after the latest event of Ezra 1–6.

whose work grapples with their communities' experiences of oppression. One common aspect of many such interpretations is that they highlight the dangers Ezra-Nehemiah poses to minoritized groups. The claim of Ezra 9:6–15 and 10:2–3 and of Nehemiah 10:30 (Heb 31) that marriage by community members to "the peoples of the lands" violates God's law is reminiscent of antimiscegenation laws of apartheid-era South Africa and pre–civil rights era United States, which forbade marriage between those of European and African descent, Makhosazana Nzimande and Cheryl Anderson point out,[4] and Ezra 9–10 is still used in the United States to support racist behavior and to argue against interracial marriage, says Willa Johnson.[5] Jean-Pierre Ruiz examines the problem of intermarriage as it is raised in the final chapter of the book, where Nehemiah is concerned that the children of these unions cannot speak the language of the Jewish community (Neh 13:23–24). Latin American immigrants to the United States have been on the receiving end of diatribes like Nehemiah's, Ruiz writes, and his outburst sounds "frighteningly familiar" to those excluded from a national identity constructed in important part on one's ability to speak fluent English.[6]

Nor is Ezra-Nehemiah's portrayal of foreigners, and especially foreign women, as inherently dangerous creatures who must be kept outside of the community the only problematic aspect of the book. Wilda Gafney examines the way the Persian Empire and its kings are portrayed in Ezra-Nehemiah, noting the manner in which their authority is accepted and assumed by the book's characters and narrator. While Israel's God has no direct speech in the book, Cyrus speaks for this God in announcing that God has given him rule over the earth. Ezra-Nehemiah continually portrays the Persian kings as acting in accordance with divine will, and God never opposes any royal action in the book. As a result, writes Gafney, in Ezra-Nehemiah "the empire is God,"[7] and the book makes God a colonized subject of the Persian Empire, a figure who is entirely in agreement with the imperial will, just as loyal

4. Makhosazana K. Nzimande, "*Imbokodo* Explorations of the Prevalence of Historical Memory and Identity Contestations in the Expulsion of the *Nāšîm Nokriyyōt* in Ezra 9–10," in *Texts, Contexts and Readings in Postexilic Literature: Explorations into Historiography and Identity in Hebrew Bible and Related Texts*, ed. Louis Jonker, FAT 2/53 (Tübingen, Germany: Mohr Siebeck, 2011), 290–92; Anderson, "Reflections in an Interethnic/Racial Era," 47–48.
5. Willa M. Johnson, *The Holy Seed Has Been Defiled: The Interethnic Marriage Dilemma in Ezra 9–10*, HBM 33 (Sheffield, UK: Sheffield Phoenix, 2011), 96.
6. Ruiz, *Readings from the Edges*, 109.
7. Wilda Gafney, "A Prophet-Terrorist(a) and an Imperial Sympathizer: An Empire-Critical, Postcolonial Reading of the No'adyah/Nechemyah Conflict," *BlTh* 9 (2011): 165.

subjects of the king should be.[8] The Persian kings support and fund God's temple in Jerusalem (Ezra 1:1–4, 7–11; 6:1–12; 7:15–24; 8:24–27), authorize and contribute to the reconstruction of the city and its wall (Neh 2:1–8), and command that "the laws of your God" be taught and enforced in the region (Ezra 7:25–26). Yet there are, as Gafney points out, obvious dangers in assuming that God's will corresponds exactly to whatever an imperial or postcolonial power decides to do. Passages like Ezra 9–10, in which Ezra convinces the community to expel the outsider women its members have married, writes Herbert Marbury, simply use theological language to mask the fact that the religious leadership of the temple in Jerusalem really functioned as an arm of Persian domination, and allow readers to equate imperial power with divine authority and support the decisions of the community leaders who act at the behest of the empire.[9] Read from the standpoint of groups who have long experience of the effects of imperial violence, Ezra-Nehemiah only reinforces and mimics imperial claims about the dangers of colonized peoples and their descendants and the need to marginalize them, emphasizing the danger that native Palestinians, even the ones who worship the God of Israel, pose to the community sent by the empire in order to do the will of God. In traditional interpretations, Ezra-Nehemiah is an oppressive text, one that, as Nāsili Vaka'uta observes, privileges a group sent to the colonies under imperial orders, imbues them alone with authority, and degrades "the peoples of the lands," those native to the region, even as it appeals to divine will to validate the rule of the empire.[10]

If a more privileged scholar like me wishes to become part of a dialogue that moves toward liberative readings of Ezra-Nehemiah, then I have to begin with the sorts of suspicious readings of the book like these from scholars who are members of communities that are struggling for their liberation. Those of us who belong to more privileged socioeconomic groups have reaped the benefits of empire and are less likely to see the dangers that traditional readings of Ezra-Nehemiah pose. As R. S. Sugirtharajah puts it, we need liberation from worldviews that allow us to justify the oppression of others,[11] which is why we need to begin with analyses of the text that emerge from communities whose treatment by imperial and postcolonial

8. Gafney, 171.
9. Herbert Robinson Marbury, *Imperial Dominion and Priestly Genius: Coercion, Accommodation, and Resistance in the Divorce Rhetoric of Ezra-Nehemiah* (Upland, CA: Sopher, 2012), 3–8.
10. Vaka'uta, *Reading Ezra* 9–10 *Tu'a-Wise*, 119–42.
11. Sugirtharajah, "Postcolonial Exploration," 94.

powers has been much different. To argue otherwise and claim that the readings of the book mentioned above misunderstand what the text says is to miss the point that textual meaning is created through interpretation, and so is created by readers and their communities, since, as chapters 2 and 3 argue, the physical marks on the page in and of themselves are meaningless until humans act to make sense of them. If we want to acknowledge the validity of our ethical beliefs and read with liberative ends in mind, then it stands to reason we would begin with readings of the book by scholars who come from marginalized communities and who are committed to their emancipation. If we were to maintain instead that Ezra-Nehemiah should have no bearing on how we understand state power, race, and gender in our world because it is only an ancient text about ancient matters, we would be denying the reality that, as Elisabeth Cook Steike puts it, women who struggle against exclusion in every aspect of life will see the passages in Ezra-Nehemiah that demonize foreign women as reflecting their lives and experiences.[12] We would also be ignoring the fact that other contemporary readers have constructed the book's meaning in such a way that it has ethically repugnant racist messages, as Willa Johnson points out. Beginning with interpretations like hers, Cook Steike's, and the others mentioned above, I can see how it is possible to interpret Ezra-Nehemiah in such a way that it supports oppression and can be used by those who wish to dehumanize through legitimating imperial and state power by equating it with divine will,[13] or who want to validate racist beliefs about the "purity" of their group and the dangers posed by peoples of other races, or who insist that women particularly endanger social cohesion. When we interpret a text we arrive at meaning, but as I pointed out in the two preceding chapters, marginalized scholars have persuasively argued that we have an ethical duty to warn readers when such meanings can be put to oppressive ends and cannot be used for liberative ones. The text of Ezra-Nehemiah I can see with their help is a dangerous one, something of which readers should be made aware, as the interpretation in the next section demonstrates.

12. Elisabeth Cook Steike, *La Mujer como Extranjera en Israel: Estudio Exegético de Esdras 9–10* (San José: Sebila, 2010), 16.
13. Cook Steike, 196–97.

A Suspicious Reading of Ezra-Nehemiah

To interpret is, as chapters 2 and 3 point out, to create a meaningful text, and the first one I create in this chapter builds on the observations of the minoritized scholars to whose work I refer above. One key danger they have identified in their analyses of Ezra-Nehemiah is the way it creates an exclusionary group identity. Contemporary biblical scholarship widely acknowledges that articulating such an identity for the postexilic community in Judah is a key aspect of the book as a whole and of individual sections of it, such as the ones that emphasize the need to avoid marriages with outsiders.[14] The very first thing readers discover about the community at the center of Ezra-Nehemiah is that the king of Persia sent their ancestors from Babylonia to Judah in order to construct the temple Nebuchadnezzar destroyed at the beginning of the Babylonian exile (Ezra 1:2–3). Although God has ordered this rebuilding project, King Cyrus rather than God announces it, since no divine speech appears anywhere in Ezra-Nehemiah. Cyrus chooses the group who will carry out the construction, and Ezra 3:7 and 4:3 emphasize the fact that the project proceeds under royal rather than divine order,[15] and that Cyrus rather than God commanded the exilic Jewish community to go to Jerusalem and build. Members from this community then travel to Judah to embark upon this project

14. See, for example, Tamara Cohn Eskenazi and Eleanore P. Judd, "Marriage to a Stranger in Ezra 9–10," in *Second Temple Studies 2: Temple Community in the Persian Period*, ed. Tamara C. Eskenazi and Kent H. Richards, JSOTSup 175 (Sheffield, UK: JSOT, 1994), 266–85; Philip F. Esler, "Ezra-Nehemiah as a Narrative of (Re-invented) Identity," *BibInt* 11 (2003): 413–26; Harold C. Washington, "Israel's Holy Seed and the Foreign Women of Ezra-Nehemiah: A Kristevan Reading," *BibInt* 11 (2003): 427–29; Johnson, *Holy Seed*, 80–92; Donald P. Moffat, *Ezra's Social Drama: Identity Formation, Marriage and Social Conflict in Ezra 9 and 10*, LHBOTS 579 (New York: Bloomsbury, 2013); Lena-Sofia Tiemeyer, *Ezra-Nehemiah: Israel's Quest for Identity*, TTCSGOT (London: T&T Clark, 2017), 1; and Benedikt Hensel, "Ethnic Fiction and Identity-Formation: A New Explanation for the Background of the Question of Intermarriage in Ezra-Nehemiah," in *The Bible, Qumran, and the Samaritans*, ed. Magnar Kartveit and Gary N. Knoppers, StJud 104, StSam 10 (Berlin: Walter de Gruyter, 2018), 133–48.
15. Ezra 3:7 refers to the *rišyôn* of Cyrus in a discussion of the king's command and ultimate oversight of the construction of the temple. The NRSV understands the word as referring to the "grant" Cyrus provided to rebuild the temple, while the NIV translates it as referring to the king's authorization of the project. The word is a *hapax legomenon*, but it comes from a Semitic root that refers to having authority or control. The Aramaic *ršw* or *ršwt'* from the same root refers to control or authorization (e.g., *Tg. Onq.* Exod 21:8; *Tg. Neo.* Exod 12:23), and the Aramaic verb *ršy* means "to permit, allow" (e.g., *Tg.* 2 Chr 20:10), while *ršyn* in Syriac means "possession" (Peshitta 3 Ezra 1:7), which reflects the basic sense of one's control or authority over something or someone. Even in Eastern Semitic, the general sense of the Akkadian verb *rašû* means "to possess, come into possession" of something (CAD 14.193). Given the textual and linguistic context, then, biblical Hebrew *rišyôn* reflects the authority Cyrus exercises over the temple construction. In 2 Esdras, a very literal rendering of the Hebrew, the word is translated as *epichōrēsis*, "permission," although 1 Esd 5:53 uses *graphen*, "written order."

(Ezra 2:1), and John Kessler has argued that there truly was such an order given by the Persian Empire to the Jewish community in Babylonia to send members to Judah, and so Kessler refers to this group of migrants as "Persia's loyal Yahwists."[16]

Whether or not Kessler's historical argument is correct, it is reality as Ezra 1 presents things. So the first thing readers of Ezra-Nehemiah learn about the identity of this community is that they are like a group of colonizers sent by the king to the margins of his empire to undertake a project that he has commanded, as he faithfully responds to the order of the God who, he says, has given the world to him to rule (1:2). The next thing readers learn about this group is that they consist of people from "the captivity of the exile, whom Nebuchadnezzar, the King of Babylon, had exiled to Babylon" (2:1). Ezra-Nehemiah continually refers to this group in Palestine as "the exile" who are from "the captivity,"[17] even though they no longer live in Babylonia and so cannot literally be described as in "exile" any longer. In the context of the book, though, we can refer to this group as exilic, and it is a way in which Ezra-Nehemiah links the migrants who travel from Babylon to Palestine under Cyrus's orders to the Jewish community that actually remains in exile, near the center of the empire.[18] Ezra 2:3–63 then lists the number of people from each ancestral house—the basic social grouping of the postexilic community[19]—who made the journey to Palestine at the margins of the empire. However, some within this group "were not able to make known their ancestral house and their seed, if they were from Israel" (2:59), and the same problem affects some of those who claimed to be priests (2:61–63). Yet while the text raises the problem that some within the

16. John Kessler, "Persia's Loyal Yahwists: Power, Identity and Ethnicity in Achaemenid Yehud," in *Judah and the Judeans in the Persian Period*, ed. Oded Lipschits and Manfred Oeming (Winona Lake, IN: Eisenbrauns, 2006), 91–121.
17. The community is called "the exile" in Ezra 1:11; 2:1; 4:1; 6:16, 19–21; 8:35; 9:4; 10:6–8, 16; Neh 7:6, and said to be or be from "the captivity" in Ezra 2:1; 3:8; 9:7; Neh 1:2–3; 7:6; 8:17.
18. Persia, of course, was the actual center of the Persian Empire, but Ezra-Nehemiah can also refer to the imperial king as "the King of Babylon" (Neh 13:6). The Jewish community in Babylonia interacts with the king there (Ezra 1:7; 7:11), and so Babylon remains an imperial center as far as the narrative is concerned.
19. For discussions of the development of the *bêt 'ābôt*, "ancestral house," as the social organization of the exiles in Babylonia, see H. G. M. Williamson, "The Family in Persian Period Judah: Some Textual Reflections," in *Symbiosis, Symbolism and the Power of the Past: Canaan, Ancient Israel and Their Neighbors from the Late Bronze Age through Roman Palaestina*, ed. William G. Dever and Seymour Gitin (Winona Lake, IN: Eisenbrauns, 2003), 469–85; Joseph Blenkinsopp, *Judaism, the First Phase: The Place of Ezra and Nehemiah in the Origins of Judaism* (Grand Rapids, MI: William B. Eerdmans, 2009), 81; and Rainer Albertz, "More and Less Than a Myth: Reality and Significance of Exile for the Political, Social, and Religious History of Judah," in *By the Irrigation Canals of Babylon: Approaches to the Study of Exile*, ed. John J. Ahn and Jill Middlemas, LHBOTS 526 (New York: T&T Clark, 2012), 31.

community cannot prove they are actually Israelites, it never returns to it,[20] with the result that what would appear to matter for membership in the community is not descent from the Israelites whom Nebuchadnezzar exiled to Babylon but whether one is descended from people who migrated to Palestine under Cyrus's orders. It is obedience to the king rather than descent from Israel that appears to be absolutely decisive for community membership in Ezra-Nehemiah.

By the end of the second chapter of the book, then, readers have a clear sense of the community as a colony sent by the Persian king from Babylonia, a group distinct from those native to Palestine. This distinction matters, readers find, because as soon as the Jewish migrants begin work on the temple, they encounter opposition from their "adversaries" (4:1), "the people of the land" (4:4). This indigenous population wants to help the colony of Babylonian exiles build the temple because, as they explain, "like you we worship your God" (4:2). The exilic community denies this request since, they say, King Cyrus of Persia commanded them alone to build (4:3). It is notable that this denial does not appeal to any divine order, nor does it reject the request of their coreligionists on the basis of the failure of the people of the land to worship God rightly. All that matters here is that the colonizers from Babylonia make a claim that relies on an appeal to their unique relationship to the king, one that demonstrates their loyalty to him and distinguishes them from the people of the land. Their fidelity to the letter of royal command is immediately contrasted with the disloyalty to the king of the Palestinian natives, who bribe Persian officials in the region to oppose the work ordered by the king and carried out by the colony of exiles (4:4–5). In 4:7–22, we come across a series of letters sent between imperial officials in Palestine and the Persian king, although these address the construction of Jerusalem's wall in the time of Artaxerxes, decades later than the construction of the temple in the time of Cyrus with which Ezra 1–3 is concerned. In these letters, indigenous Palestinians and local officials convince King Artaxerxes to put a stop to Jerusalem's wall, and they base their request on the lie that the exiles will rebel against the king if they can complete it.[21] Readers of Ezra 4 can conclude, then, that 4:7–22 reflects

20. The list of Ezra 2:3–63 repeats in Neh 7:8–65, and so one could say that the issue of original members of the migrant community being unable to prove their descent from Israel is brought up there, as well. Nonetheless, in neither place does the narrative explain how or if this matter was resolved.
21. Specifically, the letter of 4:8–16 to Artaxerxes claims that if Jerusalem's wall is completed that he will lose control of all of Across-the-River, the satrapy in which Judah was located (4:16).

the sorts of lies that the people of the land communicated to Cyrus in regard to the exiles at the time when they were trying to build the temple,[22] especially since 4:24 reports that work on the temple was brought to a halt.

It is loyalty to the king who sent the exilic community as a colony to the margins of the empire and not religion that distinguishes them from the native inhabitants of Palestine, for the local population we encounter in Ezra 4:1–5 worship the God of Israel. The term *the people(s) of the land(s)* the book uses to refer to the indigenous peoples is a deliberately vague one,[23] and if the group to whom it is applied in Ezra 4 worships the same God as the exiles, it is not clear that this is true of all of those to whom the book refers as peoples of the land at other points. In Ezra-Nehemiah, the term simply designates those who live near the exilic community in Palestine but who do not belong to it. So in Ezra 9:1–2, for example, Ezra is told that the community has intermarried with women of "the peoples of the lands," and in 10:10–11 he refers to those women as "foreign" (and see also 10:2, 14, 17–18, 44). The peoples of the lands are outside the social boundaries of the community, and unlike "Persia's loyal Yahwists" whom the king has sent from the center of the empire, they are native Palestinians. By Ezra 4, readers know that these "foreigners" are disloyal to the king and lie to him in order to work in opposition to his command, while the true community from Babylon completes the temple once they are given the opportunity to tell the truth of the matter to King Darius (Ezra 5). This leads him to search his royal archives, where he finds a copy of Cyrus's command that the temple be built and that the empire fund its construction (6:1–5), and Darius not only enforces this order but has the empire pay for temple sacrifices (6:6–12).

In Ezra 1–6, the true community is largely defined by its loyalty to the Persian kings, but beginning with the episode of the "foreign" women in Ezra 9–10, a story that takes place some generations after the events of Ezra 1–6, the book warns that the community has a tendency to abandon its true identity. The decision on the part of some of the men in the community to marry women of "the peoples of

22. For explanations like this for the role of 4:7–22 in the narrative, see D. J. A. Clines, *Ezra, Nehemiah, Esther*, NCBC (Grand Rapids, MI: Eerdmans, 1984), 76; Sara Japhet, *From the Rivers of Babylon to the Highlands of Judah: Collected Studies on the Restoration Period* (Winona Lake, IN: Eisenbrauns, 2006), 162; and Lisbeth S. Fried, "Ezra's Use of Documents in the Context of Hellenistic Rules of Rhetoric," in *New Perspectives on Ezra-Nehemiah: History and Historiography, Text, Literature, and Interpretation*, ed. Isaac Kalimi (Winona Lake, IN: Eisenbrauns, 2012), 20–23.

23. See the analysis of the phrase in John Tracy Thames Jr., "A New Discussion of the Meaning of the Phrase *'am hā'āreṣ* in the Hebrew Bible," JBL 130 (2011): 109–25, especially 120–25.

the lands" (9:1–2), Ezra says in a prayer in 9:6–15, violates God's law, which forbids such unions because of "the uncleanness [*niddâ*] of the peoples of the lands," "their abominations [*tô'ēbâ*]," and "their impurity [*ṭum'â*]" (9:10–12).[24] There are commands in Torah[25] that forbid marriage between Israel and other peoples, most notably Exodus 34:11–16 and Deuteronomy 7:1–4, and although they do not use the sort of purity language Ezra does when he describes the peoples of the lands with words like "uncleanness," "abomination," and "impurity," these words do appear in Torah,[26] sometimes even in reference to actions committed by non-Israelites who live in Palestine.[27] Yet even as this section of Ezra-Nehemiah introduces fidelity to God's law as an important and necessary part of community identity, the book ensures that this is linked to the notion of the group's loyalty to the Persian king. King Artaxerxes sends Ezra from Babylonia to Judah with the law and orders him to appoint judges to enforce it not just in Judah but throughout all of the satrapy of Across-the-River, a vast area that included all the land from Western Mesopotamia to the Mediterranean Sea and the many peoples who lived in that large

24. The Hebrew words *niddâ*, *tô'ēbâ*, and *ṭum'â* are the lemmas of words used in 9:11, which refers to the *niddat 'ammê hā'ărāṣôt*, *tô'ăbōtêhem*, and *ṭum'ātām*.
25. Scholars do not agree as to whether the authors of Ezra-Nehemiah and its original sources were aware of the final form of the Pentateuch or of some earlier stage of its composition, but Aramaic *dāt* in Ezra 7 is, like the word *tôrâ* in the Hebrew sections of the book, mainly understood to refer to the Pentateuch in some form. David Carr, for example, argues the Persians likely authorized the final form of the Pentateuch (*The Formation of the Hebrew Bible: A New Reconstruction* [Oxford: Oxford University Press, 2011], 204–24), while Hugh Williamson (*Ezra, Nehemiah*, WBC 16 [Waco, TX: Word, 1985], xxxvii–xxxix) and Joseph Blenkinsopp (*Ezra-Nehemiah: A Commentary*, OTL [London: SCM, 1989], 155) see Ezra's Torah as a combination of Priestly and Deuteronomic material. Sara Japhet argues there is enough evidence in Ezra-Nehemiah to demonstrate the entire Pentateuch was known in Judah by the time the book was written ("What May Be Learned from Ezra-Nehemiah about the Composition of the Pentateuch?," in *The Formation of the Pentateuch: Bridging the Academic Cultures of Europe, Israel, and North America*, ed. Jan C. Gertz et al., FAT 111 [Tübingen, Germany: Mohr Siebeck, 2016], 543–60), although Philip Yoo (*Ezra and the Second Wilderness*, OTRM [Oxford: Oxford University Press, 2017], 31) believes different authors of the different sources used in the final version of Ezra-Nehemiah were aware of the Pentateuch at different stages of development. Frank Crüseman (*Torah: Theology and Social History of Old Testament Law*, trans. Allan W. Mahnke [Minneapolis: Fortress, 1995], 334–39), on the other hand, maintains that Ezra's law was likely some form of the Pentateuch, but that it is impossible to say what point of development it had reached. For the purposes of the discussion that follows, we will read Ezra-Nehemiah intertextually with the entire Pentateuch, although we will really only consider aspects of it associated with Deuteronomic and Priestly/Holiness material.
26. Note, for example, the use of *niddâ* and *ṭum'â* in Lev 15:19–31 to refer to the uncleanness and impurity communicated through discharges of blood from female genitalia, whether because of menstruation or any other reason; see Katherine E. Southwood, *Ethnicity and the Mixed Marriage Crisis in Ezra 9–10: An Anthropological Approach*, OTM (Oxford: Oxford University Press, 2012), 136–40.
27. Note, for example, the use of *tô'ēbâ* and the root *ṭāmē'* as a verb in such a context in Lev 18:24–30; see Jan Clauss, "Understanding the Mixed Marriages of Ezra-Nehemiah in the Light of Temple-Building and the Book's Concept of Jerusalem," in *Mixed Marriages: Intermarriage and Group Identity in the Second Temple Period*, ed. Christian Frevel, LHBOTS 547 (New York: T&T Clark, 2011), 128.

region. These judges will punish those who violate "the law of your God and the law of the king," Artaxerxes orders, and Ezra is to teach "the laws of your God" throughout the whole satrapy (7:25–26). It is not historically possible that a Persian king instituted Jewish law as a primary legal standard by which a large part of his empire was to be governed,[28] but in the story of Ezra-Nehemiah, Ezra 7:25–26 is clear that Torah is not simply religious law that applies only to the Jewish community in Judah. In the book's narrative, that is, the king of Persia authorizes and promotes Torah, putting it in the imperial justice system that governs an entire satrapy, and this system also enforces "the law of the king." As the book presents things, Torah is just one part of the legal framework the king has put in place to govern his subjects, and so loyalty to Torah in Ezra-Nehemiah is merely another way to demonstrate loyalty to Persia.

According to Ezra-Nehemiah, Jewish law demands that the group of colonizers from Babylonia not marry any person who cannot trace their descent to the exilic community. The peoples of the lands are foreigners in this way of looking at things, even though they are not the group who has migrated to Palestine in this story, and even though some of them worship the God of Israel. "The holy seed," as Ezra 9:1–2 refers to the exilic group, must remain separate from the peoples who are unclean and impure, and Torah explains that things designated as impure must not come into contact with things that are holy.[29] In Leviticus, for example, those who have skin diseases that make them *ṭāmē'*, "impure," may not live within Israelite communities (Lev 13:45–46) and can only return if the disease is healed (14:1–9). This is how Ezra-Nehemiah portrays foreigners, and foreign women in particular, since Ezra 9–10 says that the only cases of intermarriage that have taken place are between community men and foreign women (9:2; 10:2–3, 10–11, 17–18, 44). The desire to intermarry with foreign women continues to be a problem for the exiles, however, and even in the final chapter of the book Nehemiah says that this practice continued (Neh 13:23, 28). In Ezra 9–10, the community agrees with Ezra that such marriages violate God's commands and that the foreign women whom community

28. H. G. M. Williamson, *Studies in Persian Period History and Historiography*, FAT 38 (Tübingen, Germany: Mohr Siebeck, 2004), 42–43.
29. This is a particular emphasis of the Priestly material in the Pentateuch. For a discussion of the orderly picture of the cosmos, including spatial order, that we find in the Priestly and Holiness material, and the ways in which the concepts of holiness and purity are used to reinforce that order, see Frank H. Gorman Jr., *The Ideology of Ritual: Space, Time and Status in the Priestly Theology*, JSOTSup 91 (Sheffield, UK: Sheffield Academic, 1991).

members have married and caused to dwell within the group must be sent away,[30] exactly the solution that Leviticus applies to those with skin diseases.

By the time readers reach Ezra 10, then, it is clear that the true Jewish community in Palestine is defined through their descent from Israelite exiles in Babylonia—or from families in Babylonia, at any rate, since not all of the migrants were able to prove they were Israelites—and by their loyalty to the kings of Persia. They have built the temple as Kings Cyrus and Darius ordered, but their violation of God's law, law that King Artaxerxes accepts and administers as imperial law, shows their loyalty is not absolute. Loyalty to the king reflects loyalty to God, for the kings in Ezra-Nehemiah act as God desires, something we see in Cyrus's obedience to divine command to build the temple; Darius's announcement that he will pay for temple sacrifices; Artaxerxes's vast donations to temple worship, something that occupies the majority of the letter commanding Ezra to go to Judah (see Ezra 7:15–24); and, of course, Artaxerxes's adoption of "the law of your God" into the imperial judicial system. Artaxerxes has acted in this manner because God has told or made him do so (7:6, 27),[31] and so royal action in the book reflects divine will. In Ezra-Nehemiah, "the empire is God," as Gafney puts it, since divine will is manifested in imperial action that God never challenges or contradicts.[32]

The community's failure to maintain the holiness or purity of its descent, to use Ezra-Nehemiah's language, means that the exiles are fortunate that the king sends Ezra to Judah with the law, to warn them of the consequences of their actions and

30. Ezra 10 uses the verb *yāšab* in the Hiphil ("to cause to dwell") to refer to the marriages to foreign women (10:2, 10, 14, 17–18), just as Nehemiah 13 does (13:23, 27). No other biblical book ever uses this verb to refer to marriage (Southwood, *Ethnicity and the Mixed Marriage Crisis*, 166–67). The problem here is the physical location of the women—men in the community have brought them to live inside the group—and so the solution to the problem is expressed using the verb *yāṣā'* in the Hiphil (Ezra 10:3, 19), as the community agrees "to send (them) away, expel (them)."

31. Ezra 7:6 says that Artaxerxes gave everything Ezra asked of him, "according to the hand of the Lord his God that was upon him," and in 7:27 Ezra responds to the king's generous contributions to the temple by blessing God, "who has put such a thing into the heart of the king." It is not clear if phrases such as these refer to Artaxerxes responding to divine command or indicate that God has manipulated the king's will, but in either case divine and royal will are entirely aligned.

32. If there is an exception to any part of this, it is the case of Ezra 4, which suggests (although does not explicitly say) that the king put a stop to the construction of the temple, the result of the efforts of the people of the land as they lie about the exilic community (see the discussion of this chapter above). Persian kings are not infallible in Ezra-Nehemiah, since the narrative says they can be manipulated by the disloyal people of the land, but even in this case it is action on the part of King Darius that results in the completion of the temple. Notably, however, the story says nothing about any divine action when 4:24 reports that temple construction was brought to a halt. Although Ezra 4 as a whole implies the work stoppage was the result of a royal order, God does nothing to react against it.

to urge them to rectify the situation. Nonetheless, the problem of their fidelity to Torah persists in the part of the book that deals with the work of Nehemiah, whom Artaxerxes sends to rebuild Jerusalem and the wall, an order the king again gives under divine influence (Neh 2:8).[33] Artaxerxes also appoints Nehemiah as the governor of Judah (5:14), and so he represents the king and his interests. His construction project, like that of Ezra 1–6, is opposed by local peoples, and by three local leaders in particular (Neh 2:10, 19–20; 4:1–8 [Heb 3:33–4:2]; 6:1–14). Like the people of the land in that earlier story, these local officials lie and claim the exilic community is acting in disloyalty to the king (6:5–7). Nehemiah leads the community as they carry out the royal order to construct Jerusalem's wall, and so once again it is the native population who are really the king's disloyal subjects, as they lie and try to put a stop to a project the empire has authorized. Nehemiah ensures the exilic community remains loyal to the empire, however, and so they complete the wall (6:15), yet the problem of the exiles' lack of fidelity to divine and royal law persists. Ezra returns to the narrative in Nehemiah 8 to teach Torah, and the community swears in Nehemiah 10 that they will keep it. The specific aspects of it they vow to keep, and so the ones they obviously believe are most important, are to enforce bans on intermarriage with "the peoples of the land" (10:30 [Heb 31]) and on trading with them on the Sabbath (10:31a [32a]), to forgive debts every seventh year (10:31b [32b]), and to supply the temple with everything it needs (10:32–39 [33–40]). Some time later, however, after Nehemiah returns to Judah following a visit to Babylon to see Artaxerxes (13:6), he finds the exiles have intermarried with local peoples (13:23–28), are trading with them on the Sabbath (13:15–22), and have not supplied the temple personnel with their rations, with the result that worship has been abandoned (13:10–14). Upon his return, Nehemiah intervenes to set things right in each case, but the only one of the laws the community swore to keep of which he does not find them in violation is their vow to forgive debts every seventh year, and that may simply be because the odds that he would return in such a year were only one in seven.

33. Just as Ezra 7:6 says Artaxerxes gave Ezra all that he requested "according to the hand of the Lord his God that was upon him," Nehemiah says in Neh 2:8 that Artaxerxes granted his request to send him to build the wall of Jerusalem and to supply wood for its construction "according to the good hand of my God that was upon me."

Even though Ezra 1–6 establishes loyalty to the king as central to community identity, Ezra-Nehemiah as a whole portrays the exiles as a group who, despite their best intentions, are unable to remain loyal to God's law, and so who cannot remain loyal to the king who has placed this law within his own justice system. Ezra warns in the context of the marriage crisis that a failure to keep the law could result in destruction (Ezra 9:6–15), and a group of Levites in Nehemiah 9[34] tells the community that their ancestors' failures to remain faithful to Torah led to their punishment (Neh 9:26–30). The exilic community has an advantage that their pre-exilic ancestors did not, however, for they are ruled by the Persian kings, whose will and actions correspond to divine will, and who can send them leaders like Ezra and Nehemiah, who repetitively urge the exiles to return to the law and avoid remaining in their disloyalty, thus becoming like the disloyal peoples of the land.

My interpretation or creation of meaning for Ezra-Nehemiah here is one that sees the book as ethically problematic, and this judgment must be part of my interpretation if I hope to contribute to an emancipatory dialogue on Ezra-Nehemiah, given the concerns of marginalized readers mentioned earlier in the chapter. Otherwise, I could be understood to imply that we should have no ethical objections when others claim that powerful colonial empires speak and act on God's behalf and that one expresses loyalty to God through loyalty to empire. God's law is important, says the book's narrative, but Ezra-Nehemiah makes it just one more aspect of imperial law, and the specific parts of Torah it emphasizes—the ones specified in Nehemiah 10, in other words—do not threaten imperial interests in any way. "The law of your God and the law of the king" coexist happily in the same royal judicial system in the book, and so a good servant of God is a good servant of empire. God's people are not defined by their worship, for "the people of the land" in Ezra 4 also worship the God of Israel, and the book's true community is, unlike the people of the land, defined in important part by their loyalty to the king, who sends them leaders to enforce the fidelity to empire they should exhibit. They must strive to be like the group of colonists whom the king sent to the margins of his empire at the beginning of Ezra-Nehemiah's story, and that means staying as far

34. In some translations, the prayer of Neh 9:6–37 is presented as Ezra's speech, although this reflects the LXX. In the MT, this prayer continues the speech of the Levites begun earlier in the chapter, and this is more likely the original reading, something altered in the text translated in the LXX, as a copyist or translator connected the prayer with Ezra, the better-known character who teaches the law in Neh 8.

away from the native population as they can, since those peoples seem to be inherently disloyal. Ideal community identity in the book is to act like colonists who live in loyalty to empire and in separation from the colonized. It is notable, however, that at no point does God express support for the exilic community's treatment of those women whom they designate as "foreign," or for the notion that fidelity to the empire and imperial law should be key aspects of the community's character.[35] The very fact that the story provides no divine speech at all or any evaluation of the community's actions might make it easier for readers of faith to apply this sort of negative ethical judgment to this text. That is, we could see this reading of Ezra-Nehemiah as implicitly asking readers to judge whether the exiles' understandings of God, divine law, empire, colonization, and community are good or bad.

It is much easier to highlight Ezra-Nehemiah's dangerously insidious portrayal of the natives of Palestine when one has begun with analyses of the text by scholars who are members of communities that have often been portrayed this way by colonial and postcolonial powers. So to return to some of the questions that I raised in chapter 6 while discussing suspicious readings of oppressive texts, if I am to understand the story of Ezra-Nehemiah as positive and unproblematic, as a text about God's fidelity to Israel, then I fail to question and so validate a social hierarchy that aligns the actions of the colonial state with divine will. It matters, as Vaka'uta has pointed out, that the indigenous population of Palestine, encountered as a colonized people by the group sent by the king from a center of empire, is portrayed so negatively and provided with almost no voice.[36] If I do not see and signal this as a problem, then I lend tacit support to colonial and postcolonial systems of power that depict peoples in lands subject to those systems as dangerous and in need of outside control, people who, it is understood in such systems, deserve no voice, since they have nothing worthwhile to say. If I merely accept that Ezra and Nehemiah are heroes of this story, good emissaries sent from the king to manifest divine will and to save the exiles from intermixing with the colonized peoples, then I also have to accept that their subservience to and agreement with imperial

35. If there is a potential exception to this, it is the narrator's claim in Ezra 7:6 that God moved King Artaxerxes to grant Ezra everything he asked, since that could be understood as including Artaxerxes's assertion in 7:25 that Torah would be placed within the imperial justice system. But the story says nothing about the specifics of Ezra's request to the king, and so Artaxerxes's decision about the relation Torah would have to the empire's legal system in 7:25 can be seen as his own idea, an addition to the divine will to send Ezra to teach the law in Judah.

36. Vaka'uta, *Reading Ezra* 9–10 Tu'a-Wise, 167–68.

rule are worthy of imitation, and their hostility to colonized peoples, especially women, is morally commendable, as is their designation of the population native to the land as "foreign." It is not difficult to see, then, the way racist thought in the United States can draw from ideas in Ezra-Nehemiah, as Willa Johnson pointed out, and apply the book's ideas about the state, divine will, group identity, purity, and foreignness to a contemporary situation in an ethically unacceptable manner. Since I recognize the story of Ezra-Nehemiah created in my interpretation as ethically problematic, and since I am explicitly depicting it as such, my interpretation is a suspicious one, like the ones produced by minoritized scholars to which the first section of the chapter refers.

The very fact that some marginalized readers created suspicious readings of Ezra-Nehemiah certainly does not mean that all will see every aspect of the book as dangerous and oppressive, however. Nzimande, for example, says that while African women are often portrayed like the foreign women in Ezra-Nehemiah, the postapartheid Black community in South Africa can also identify with the fear of Ezra-Nehemiah's exiles that their unique culture might disappear.[37] And Ruiz, to take another example, does note that one of Nehemiah's objections to the exiles' marriages to foreign women is that many of the children born of such couples cannot speak the language of Judah (Neh 13:23–24), a condemnation of "foreigners" that Latin American immigrants to the United States find "frighteningly familiar," yet he also draws a connection between the situation in which Nehemiah and the exiles find themselves and the fear of Puerto Ricans under the colonial rule of the United States that they would be forced to abandon their language and culture.[38] Roger Nam makes a somewhat similar point as he reads Ezra-Nehemiah from the standpoint of Korean Americans and focuses particularly on the movement of the text from Hebrew to Aramaic—the official language of correspondence in the Persian Empire—in Ezra 4:8 and back to Hebrew in 6:19. Code-switching like this allows both the ancient Judeans and contemporary Korean Americans to adapt to the imperial context in which they find themselves, Nam writes, but also to use a native language that resists submersion into empire and maintains a separate

37. Nzimande, "*Imbokodo* Explorations," 285–87.
38. Ruiz, *Readings from the Edges*, 109–13.

identity.[39] That being said, the suspicious reading of Ezra-Nehemiah in this section of the chapter is hopefully of some use to readers who find the book's views of empire, God, women, colonized peoples, and community identity alienating and dangerous. Since God does not pass judgment on the actions of the community and figures such as Ezra and Nehemiah, readers convinced by this reading can ask themselves how they would evaluate the events of this text. This reading, then, is also hopefully of use to more privileged readers who might not immediately see the danger in such positive portrayals of the imperial state that link it to divine will, or in such negative portrayals of the native peoples of Palestine, or in the claim that the greatest threat to the exiles' future is the lure of "foreign" women. If more privileged readers need liberation from worldviews that prevent them from noticing the oppression and suffering of marginalized peoples, then the interpretation in this part of the chapter, expanding on observations of minoritized scholars, might help such readers question the assumptions they work with when they read the text, assumptions that may well violate important ethical beliefs they hold about the full humanity of all people.

Reading Ezra-Nehemiah with Its Marginalized Characters

The interpretation of Ezra-Nehemiah I constructed above corresponds to some degree to what one might think of as authorial intention or, since some scholars do not find it appropriate to refer to a single author of the book,[40] to the way in which the first readers of Ezra-Nehemiah would have understood it when it reached its final form. In such traditional interpretations, Ezra and Nehemiah are heroes, royal will corresponds to divine will, and the Jewish community associated with the temple in Jerusalem should not intermix with Palestinian natives who cannot trace

39. Roger S. Nam, "Half Speak Ashdodite and None Can Speak Judean: Code-Switching in Ezra-Nehemiah as an Identity Marker for Repatriate Judeans and Koreans," in *Landscapes of Korean and Korean American Biblical Interpretation*, ed. John Ahn, IVBS 10 (Atlanta: Society of Biblical Literature, 2019), 119–31.
40. There is no scholarly consensus as to how Ezra-Nehemiah reached its final form, and some scholars argue that the book, and even simply individual parts of it that existed independently and were later incorporated into Ezra-Nehemiah, were composed over a period of centuries. In this way of looking at it, there could be no single author of the book but many writers who added to it. For some examples of such arguments, see Juha Pakkala, *Ezra the Scribe: The Development of Ezra 7–10 and Nehemia 8*, BZAW 347 (Berlin: Walter de Gruyter, 2004); Jacob L. Wright, *Rebuilding Identity: The Nehemiah-Memoir and Its Earliest Readers*, BZAW 348 (Berlin: Walter de Gruyter, 2004); Blenkinsopp, *Judaism, the First Phase*, 86–90; and Sean Burt, *The Courtier and the Governor: Transformations of Genre in the Nehemiah Memoir*, JAJSup 17 (Göttingen, Germany: Vandenhoeck & Ruprecht, 2014), 70.

their ancestry to the Babylonian families who migrated to the region under imperial order. Yet this suspicious reading is not the only interpretation that I and others can produce; since God never passes judgment on the actions of Ezra, Nehemiah, and the community, what might a reading look like that envisions a negative divine evaluation of the events in this story? One way to answer this question is to pursue another interpretive strategy used by emancipatory scholars, one that imagines how the characters marginalized in my first reading might tell Ezra-Nehemiah's story and how they might reveal the strategies that the more powerful characters use to disenfranchise them. That approach to interpretation, the focus of this part of the chapter, urges readers to find other heroes and villains in the story than they will if they do not move beyond traditional religious and academic interpretations or constructions of meaning in Ezra-Nehemiah. It also urges them to interrogate the claims that such readings make in regard to God, the king, women, the native peoples of Palestine, and the exilic community. As we will see, in this interpretation Ezra-Nehemiah fails to justify any sort of distinction between the exilic community and the indigenous population of Palestine, and when we see that the exclusivist and proimperial social boundaries I discussed in the previous section of the chapter are not mandated by "the text in itself," we are freed to go on to construct other readings of the book that foreground the interests of marginalized groups and that do not violate ethical principles we hold.

As chapters 5 and 6 point out, liberative scholars have argued that by focusing on characters marginalized by narratives created in mainstream interpretations, we avoid replicating readings that push us to identify powerful oppressors as heroes, and we read instead in solidarity with those whose viewpoints have not been important enough to merit the attention of the text as it has traditionally been interpreted. We can then ask how such characters might experience oppression and how they could exercise agency, and we can retell stories from their perspectives. Gafney does this when she reads Ezra-Nehemiah by privileging the perspective of the prophetess Noadiah, a minor figure in the book who is provided with no direct speech and mentioned in only one verse as an opponent of Nehemiah (Neh 6:14), but whose perspective is key, Gafney argues, if we want to resist the project of empire Nehemiah promotes.[41] So we can read from the perspective of the people

41. Gafney, "Prophet-Terrorist(a)," 164.

of the land in Ezra 4, those who worship the God of Israel and yet are excluded from temple construction by the exilic group who seem like colonizers sent by the king and who tell them that this exclusion is based on imperial order. Reading from the standpoint of the indigenous population in this story, we can note that even before they appear on the scene, the exiles are terrified by "the peoples of the lands" (Ezra 3:3), who are labeled as their "adversaries" (4:1) before these peoples so much as utter a word in the narrative. They have been prejudged as violent and evil, as colonized populations and minoritized communities of much more recent imperial powers tend to be, and are excluded from the group sent by the king because the exiles privilege royal command over solidarity with other groups in Palestine who worship their God.

If we try to read the events of Ezra-Nehemiah from the perspective of the peoples of the land, we might imagine that they would be bewildered by such reactions on the part of the exiles. Once they see the intransigence of this group of colonizers, who value their bonds to empire over their relationship to their coreligionists among the colonized, we can see how they could decide that there should be no place in the region for a sanctuary of the God of Israel that will only stand as an imperial monument to their exclusion. So the people of the land disheartened the migrants from Babylonia, the narrator says, and made them afraid to build (Ezra 4:4). And while this makes it sound as if the Palestinians of Cyrus's time threatened the exilic community with violence, the only evidence the narrator can offer of their opposition is that "they hired counselors against them to frustrate their council" (4:5), which sounds much more like a legal battle than a physical confrontation. The narrator tries to implicate the people of the land further in 4:6–24, a passage that quotes from letters sent to and from King Artaxerxes, but as the previous section of the chapter notes, this correspondence concerns the construction of Jerusalem's wall during the reign of a king who was in power many decades after the temple was constructed. So while Ezra 4 as a whole suggests that the people of the land of Cyrus's time lied to the king as the Persian officials in 4:6–24 lied to Artaxerxes, the narrator provides no actual evidence of this.

My interpretation in the previous section of the chapter glossed over this fact, and I imagine that this was the intention of the person who put Ezra-Nehemiah together in the form in which we now find it. But if we read from the perspective of the accused, the Palestinians of Ezra 4 who worship God, the narrator's claims about them and the exiles' reactions to them seem baseless and dangerous. These worshippers of God who lived in Palestine would likely have viewed with equal skepticism the narrator's claim that to be part of the worship of God in Jerusalem, one must be "separated [*nibdāl*] from the impurity [*ṭum'â*] of the nations of the land" (Ezra 6:21). Impurity is always something negative and dangerous in the Hebrew Bible—a word such as *ṭum'â* "signals threat and distaste to varying degrees," observes Hannah Harrington[42]—and so we can imagine that those in Palestine who also worship the exiles' God would again be bewildered by an attitude like this, since no explanation is provided as to why they are a source of impurity. They have again been judged without evidence or justification, apparently stereotyped by colonists who simply take it for granted that one should avoid all contact with the natives.

And as the reading in the previous section of the chapter points out, this impurity is key to the characterization of the peoples of the lands in Ezra 9, which introduces the mixed-marriage crisis. Since figures in 9:1–2 claim that "the holy seed" have not "separated themselves" (*nibdĕlû*) from "the peoples of the lands," and in particular from the women whom Ezra 10 calls "foreign," we should aim here to read with the foreign women. Ezra is clear that these women are the cause of the uncleanness, impurity, and abominations that he believes threaten the community's existence (9:10–15). None of these women is named, let alone provided with any speech, and as the exiles convene an assembly in Ezra 10 that forces these women and their children to leave the community, we could ask what they might have said if they had been able to speak in their own defense during the assembly. Since Ezra charges, and the community assembly agrees, that the presence of these women violates Torah, they might have begun by disputing Ezra's reading of the law, as his interpretation of it is that Israel is not to intermarry with "the peoples of the lands" (9:10–12). In Torah, Exodus 34:11–16 and Deuteronomy 7:1–4 do indeed address the issue of marriage to non-Israelites, but both passages are clear that Israelites are only forbidden to enter into marriage with the specific peoples whom God will drive out of Canaan so Israel can settle there following the exodus. Neither passage uses the phrase "the peoples of the lands," and both name nations that no longer

42. Hannah K. Harrington, *The Purity and Sanctuary of the Body in Second Temple Judaism*, JAJSup 33 (Göttingen, Germany: Vandenhoeck & Ruprecht, 2019), 25–26n34.

existed by the time the events of Ezra 9–10 take place.[43] Both passages, as well as the law of Deuteronomy 20:1–10, specifically forbid marriage with these particular peoples because of the danger they might pose in leading Israelites to worship other gods. Yet "the people of the land" who appear in Ezra 4 worship Israel's God, and so one cannot assume that simply because a woman belongs to a group that Ezra and the exiles have decided to label "the peoples of the lands" that she worships a deity besides the God of Israel.

Ezra, these women might continue, maintains that the law says that the land in which his community lives is characterized by "uncleanness [*niddâ*] because of the uncleanness of the peoples of the land" and because of "their abominations [*tôʿēbâ*] with which they have filled it from end to end through their impurity [*ṭumʾâ*]" (9:11). These claims do sound like Leviticus 18:24–30, which says the pre-Israelite inhabitants of the land acted in ways God forbids in the laws of 18:1–23, committing "abominations," as 18:29–30 calls such deeds; as a result, that passage says, "the land became impure [*wattiṭmāʾ hāʾāreṣ*]" (18:25). However, God says in Leviticus 18:25 that the land "vomited out" its pre-Israelite inhabitants before the Israelites moved there after the exodus, which means that none of the women in Ezra's time could be descended from those peoples. Moreover, Ezra does not accuse the "foreign" women of his day of committing abominations in the sense of violating God's law, and certainly offers no evidence that they do so, but says that they are unclean and impure by nature and that this impurity is what fills the land with "abominations." Yet Torah never claims that foreigners are inherently impure,[44] we could imagine these women objecting, and it never says they are characterized by *niddâ*, or "uncleanness," a term that the law mainly applies to Israelite women after childbirth or during a discharge of blood from their genitalia (see Lev 12 and 15). And as much as the community claims that by expelling them and their children they will be acting "according to the law" (Ezra 10:3), Torah provides no guidance at all as to what to do if Israelites have married among the pre-Israelite inhabitants

43. Taken together, Exod 34:11 and Deut 7:1 refer to the Canaanites, Hittites, Perizzites, Hivites, Jebusites, Girgashites, and Amorites, and there is simply no evidence that any of the peoples who lived in Persian-period Palestine would have identified themselves as belonging to any of those groups. See Tikva Frymer-Kensky, *Reading the Women of the Bible* (New York: Schocken, 2002), 289.

44. See, for example, Christine E. Hayes, *Gentile Impurities and Jewish Identities: Intermarriage and Conversion from the Bible to the Talmud* (Oxford: Oxford University Press, 2002), 26–29; and Hannah K. Harrington, "Holiness and Purity in Ezra-Nehemiah," in *Unity and Diversity in Ezra-Nehemiah: Redaction, Rhetoric, and Reader*, ed. Mark J. Boda and Paul L. Redditt, HBM 17 (Sheffield, UK: Sheffield Phoenix, 2008), 98–116.

of Canaan,[45] and so, the women might point out, there is nothing in the law on which to base this claim. To act in the manner in which Ezra and the community propose here, manifesting the same attitude Nehemiah will imitate in Nehemiah 13:23–28 when he insists foreign women are an inherent danger to the community, is to ignore entirely laws in Torah that assume foreigners will live in Israel's midst and that place an obligation on Israel to care for them (e.g. Exod 22:21 [Heb 20]; Lev 19:33; Deut 24:17), laws that even assume foreigners should participate in some Israelite religious ceremonies, including ones that take place at the temple (e.g., Exod 12:19; Lev 22:18–20; Deut 16:11, 14).

In my first interpretation of Ezra-Nehemiah, of course, the women say none of this, because they are permitted no speech at all, and perhaps this is only the sort of speech that a trained biblical scholar might think to put into their mouths. But to read from their perspective is to read with sympathy and acknowledge in one form or another the injustice and dismissiveness with which they are treated. One can certainly imagine other readers with different backgrounds creating different speech for these women to confront the way in which they are treated and provide them with agency that resists their dehumanization, and my hope is that the interpretation above might encourage others to do so. To accept what Ezra says about these women in Ezra 9 and agree to the validity of what the community does to them in Ezra 10 demands privileging the claims of the man sent by the king over the most vulnerable figures in the story and agreeing that those marginalized characters should be neither seen nor heard, since they are by their very nature a danger to the community. In readings directed by the ethical goal of struggling against the dehumanization of the minoritized, however, attempts to find ways to be in solidarity and sympathy with the characters demonized and marginalized by the story can work to combat oppressive aspects created in other readings of it.

On the assumption that the events of Ezra 9–10 actually took place, scholarship has developed a whole series of different reasons for the expulsion of the foreign women that appeal to economic or political rationales, such as the community's concern that the children of those women would inherit community land,[46] or that

45. Japhet, *From the Rivers of Babylon*, 141–51.
46. See, for example, Herbert R. Marbury, "Reading Persian Dominion in Nehemiah: Multivalent Language, Co-option, Resistance, and Cultural Survival," in *Focusing Biblical Studies: The Crucial Nature of the Persian and Hellenistic Periods*, ed. Jon L. Berquist and Alice Hunt, LHBOTS 544 (New York: T&T Clark, 2012), 167–70.

the wealthy were trying to protect their economic interests,[47] or that a Judean group close to the Persian government was attempting to defend its political advantage.[48] Yet neither the narrator nor any character in the book expresses concern about any issue such as these when it comes to the danger of the foreign women, and those who support the thinking of Ezra, Nehemiah, and the community in this matter will have to agree that the colonized, and especially their women, are dangerous and impure by nature and that no explanation beyond this is necessary to push them outside of the social boundaries of the exiles. On the other hand, to read Ezra-Nehemiah from the standpoint of the foreign women, at least in a sympathetic manner, is to deny that Ezra and Nehemiah are heroes of the story, and to point out that they and the community act unjustly, to say the least, when it comes to the decisions they make to silence and banish foreigners through inaccurate appeals to Torah. Other interpreters reading from the perspectives of the foreign women might well create different speech for them, but what matters if we are to combat dehumanization is that we recognize powerless and nameless women pushed not just to the margins but entirely outside of the community as subjects with agency and dignity.

And to pursue this reading of the book further, once we see that Ezra-Nehemiah relies upon vague assumptions as to what these colonized foreigners are like in order to distinguish between them and the exilic community, we can see that there are no clear boundaries between the two groups, despite vehement claims made by different characters in the story. Ezra and the community agree in Ezra 9–10 that the law demands a complete separation between themselves and "the peoples of the lands," but by not allowing those whom the division most gravely affects to defend themselves, they hide the fact that the law does not say what they claim it does. By trying to read from the perspectives of characters the text marginalizes, we see the need to transgress the unethical boundaries that my first interpretation presents as central to the meaningful text it created. The list of Ezra 2 names the ancestral houses from the Jewish community in Babylonia who sent migrants to Judah, and 2:2 refers to this group as "the people of Israel." They are "from the captivity of the exile, whom Nebuchadnezzar, the King of Babylon, had exiled to Babylon" (2:1), and so readers might assume that the true Israel, the

47. For an explanation, see Anderson, "Reflections in an Interethnic/Racial Era," 53–55.
48. See Kessler, "Persia's Loyal Yahwists," 111.

true community in Judah, is descended from Israelite families exiled to Babylon. Yet the difficulty with seeing this as a clear social boundary between the community and the indigenous population is, as the previous section of the chapter points out, that the list of Ezra 2 says that not all of the immigrants could prove their descent from Israel (2:59–63), a matter that Ezra-Nehemiah never resolves. Not all of these colonizers may actually belong to "the people of Israel" and "the captivity of the exile," then. In Ezra 4:1–3, the leaders of the group Cyrus sent to build the temple distinguish between themselves and the people of the land by saying that Cyrus chose them alone to build, but Cyrus's command was that anyone among the people of the God of the heavens could build the temple (Ezra 1:2–3),[49] and one could certainly see the people who live in Palestine and who worship this God as among the people Cyrus has in mind. They do not claim descent from Israel (4:2), but, of course, it is not clear that all of the migrant community from Babylonia is Israelite in the sense that they are descended from preexilic inhabitants of Israel either. Based on the speech and actions of various important characters in the story, it appears important to the community that they distinguish themselves from native Palestinians by acting in loyalty to the king, but as the previous section of the chapter has already discussed, they continually fail to do so. Even at the very end of the book, they are in violation of virtually every part of the law that they swore they would uphold in Nehemiah 10, and since the Persian king has placed Torah within his justice system (Ezra 7:25–26), then the community continually acts in disloyalty to imperial law.

In the interpretation I have been creating in this section of the chapter, I begin with the assumption that the marginalized characters in this story should be regarded as fully human and as having the same self-respect and desire for agency as the ones normally recognized as the book's heroes. This is what allows me to consider how they might resist the dehumanization to which the narrative's powerful figures subject them, and to see how those less powerful characters might have encountered the exiles' claims surrounding their group identity and the boundaries that define it, and I have found that those claims crumble beneath the gaze of those

49. Cyrus does say in these verses that anyone among God's people may "go up to Jerusalem" and build the temple, but this need not be taken as limiting the concept of God's people to the exiles in Babylon, since the Hebrew Bible generally uses the verb *'ālâ*, "to go up," when referring to movement toward Jerusalem, no matter how close or distant the commencement of such travel is to the city.

whom they try to exclude. Transgressing key boundaries of a biblical narrative as it is normally interpreted is yet another reading approach of minoritized scholars, as chapters 5 and 6 point out, and trying to see how the excluded might encounter the exclusivism advanced by the privileged colonizers of Ezra-Nehemiah leads us to the conclusion that those more powerful figures understand group identity in the way they do not because they have good religious reasons to do so but because they hold the power in the story. Their vague assumptions as to what native Palestinians are like—violent, dangerous, impure—allow them to gloss over rather than carefully confront what Torah says about the need to care for foreigners in Israel's midst. Readers of faith who believe that God stands with the marginalized who are oppressed by powerful empires and their representatives can then conclude that, having tried to identify with the minoritized characters of the story, they can see the community and its leaders as largely unethical figures who ignore divine law and side with the powerful state. If Ezra-Nehemiah says nothing about God's reaction to the results of such an ethical failure, these readers can now attempt to supply one.

Conclusion: Liberations of Ezra-Nehemiah

There is no text of Ezra-Nehemiah or any other writing that has meaning until readers create it, and once they have done so, they can legitimately refer to what the text says or does or urges, ideally with the understanding that it is their own work that is speaking, doing, and urging, since the physical text by itself can do nothing. As a result, it matters what sorts of texts we create, for, in the end, we are the ones speaking, doing, and urging through them, and so we are responsible for the meanings our interpretations produce. If we conclude that, given our beliefs about how to make sense of the evidence of the physical text, we are unable to produce an ethical interpretation, one that meets our ethical standards of being useful to an emancipatory struggle against dehumanization, then we should produce a suspicious reading and be clear as to the text's dangers. But to return to the polylogue of *talalasi* or *talanoa* from Pacific island cultures I mentioned at the end of chapter 6, in which storytellers respond to each other and the needs of their audiences as they create new narratives or versions of the same story, other interpretations are always possible and, depending on the audience's context, may be better.

So there are many different reading strategies that could produce interpretations that would fit our liberative aims and that can emancipate the book for liberative goals. I could have created an interpretation that began, for example, with Julie Kelso's observation that despite the many long lists of personal names in Ezra-Nehemiah, at most two of the names in the book refer to women,[50] and nowhere does it record the direct speech of any female. Like Chronicles, Kelso writes, Ezra-Nehemiah provides us with "a world virtually absent of women."[51] So if Roland Boer can describe Chronicles as "one of the first men-only utopias,"[52] we could say the same thing about Ezra-Nehemiah, which prohibits sex with women. It is true that it specifically forbids marital and thus sexual unions only with foreign women, but given that virtually no other women make any appearance in its narrative world and that the only opinion it expresses in regard to unacceptable sexual unions is based on ethnicity, not gender, a queer reading of Ezra-Nehemiah could understand the book's ideal society as a kind of gay paradise. No mention is made of the story's protagonists, figures such as Ezra and Nehemiah, being married; we see them only in the company of other men. So, for example, when Ezra needs a place to mourn, instead of going home he retires to "the chamber of Jehohanan" (Ezra 10:6), a male character who, we might imagine, is able to provide him with a kind of solace he cannot find with his wife if, in fact, he even has one. The objection that this is an unacceptable reading of Ezra-Nehemiah because Torah forbids male-only erotic relationships hardly seems to work in a narrative where characters claim that the law says things it obviously does not. If Ezra and the community can agree that the law stigmatizes all native Palestinians as impure and unclean by nature, and can entirely ignore the parts of Torah that refer to the care Israel must show the foreigners in its midst, then surely they can interpret laws dealing with sexuality in any way they see fit.

Insofar as queer readings expose the artificiality of categories humans create,[53] they can condemn Ezra-Nehemiah for the manner in which the book as it is normally interpreted excludes foreigners, and insofar as they are suspicious of the power of

50. Julie Kelso, "Reading Silence: The Books of Chronicles and Ezra-Nehemiah, and the Relative Absence of a Feminist Interpretive History," in Scholz, *Feminist Interpretation of the Hebrew Bible*, 1:277–80.
51. Kelso, "Reading Silence," 1:287.
52. Roland Boer, "1 and 2 Chronicles," in *The Queer Bible Commentary*, ed. Deryn Guest et al. (London: SCM, 2006), 251.
53. See, for example, Macwilliam, *Queer Theory*, 9–26.

the state to enforce such categories,[54] they can warn of the dangers of the book's ready adoption of imperial ideology. Yet they can also point to a common aspect of statist ideology that Ezra-Nehemiah does not replicate, a social order that privileges sexual reproduction that provides the empire with a constant supply of loyal subjects, a heteronormativity that excludes homoerotic desire from the realm of what is good and acceptable.[55] The only sorts of legitimate relationships in which the book expresses positive interest are ones among males, and it seems much more invested in reducing the number of children within the community—since the children of the "foreign" women are expelled from the group along with their mothers (Ezra 10:3, 44)—than in creating more of them. Of course, the difficulty with the kind of queer reading I have begun to sketch out is that it marginalizes the female characters in the story as much as my first interpretation in the chapter does. Queer readings challenge assumptions about sexuality and gender that are understood to be normal, aiming at the inclusion of those so frequently excluded with arguments as to what is "normal" and "natural,"[56] and so perhaps this one is not complete without imagining ways in which the divorces these women are forced to undergo might unintentionally create space they can choose to use to understand and value themselves differently. Freed from normative conceptions of womanhood that define them through marriage and childbearing, we could picture them as creating new kinds of communal structures liberated from the exclusivism of the one the community in Judah enforces.[57]

54. One can think, for example, of the way a biblical scholar such as James Hoke reads Romans by turning to the insights of a queer theorist like Elizabeth Freeman, who argues that the capitalist state orders time to maximize productivity, something that includes the ordering of sexual life. See James N. Hoke, "Unbinding Imperial Time: Paul's Letter to the Romans," in Brintall, Marchal, and Moore, *Sexual Disorientations*, 68–89.
55. In this regard, one can think of the work of a queer theorist such as Lee Edelman, who argues that queerness should threaten social fabrics that privilege sexual reproduction over practically every other social good, excluding homosexuality from the understanding of goodness in order to do so. For an example of a biblical scholar who draws on this aspect of Edelman's thought, see Rhiannon Graybill, "No Child Left Behind: Reading Jephthah's Daughter with *The Babylon Complex*," BCT 11/2 (2015): 36–59.
56. For example, Gillian Townsley, *The Straight Mind in Corinth: Queer Readings across 1 Corinthians 11:2–16*, SemeiaSt 88 (Atlanta: Society of Biblical Literature, 2017), 253–55; and Tamber-Rosenau, *Women in Drag*, 10–11.
57. I am reminded here, for example, of Joseph Marchal's study of the female prophets over whom Paul tries to exert control in 1 Cor 11:1–16, women who have absorbed his message about an imminent eschaton and who understand this as having radically altered their place in the social order. See Marchal, "How Soon Is (This Apocalypse) Now?"

There is nothing to stop any reader from arriving at a queer reading of Ezra-Nehemiah like this, and if some interpreters find it difficult to accept, it is worthwhile asking what one must assume in order to prefer standard historical critical readings that pass no ethical critique of the book, and that fail to note the ways in which marginalized scholars have encountered it as oppressive or in which they try to make room for readings that deprivilege its important and powerful characters. Because there is no universal meaningful text to which we can compare our interpretations, we can make room for many readings with emancipatory goals, such as queer readings that create a meaningful text that privileges same-sex relationships and decline to promote childbearing as the single goal that determines participation in the social good. The polylogue of *talalasi* can continue as different interpreters' work reflects and responds to other readings, choosing different perspectives and providing better meaningful texts, where "better" is defined by the liberative needs of their audiences. There are, as a result, many ways to liberate Ezra-Nehemiah, some of which may sound like the interpretations I created for this chapter and some of which will seem very different because they are created by readers who have experiences and needs very different from my own.

8

The Critique of Royal Injustice in 1 Kings 3:16–28

Introduction: The Criticism of Solomon in 1 Kings 1–11

In the previous chapter, I produced readings of an entire biblical book that I hoped would be useful for liberative purposes, but here I limit my focus to one passage in particular, the story of Solomon's judgment in 1 Kings 3:16–28. Traditional academic and religious interpretations portray this as a narrative in which Solomon is a wise hero who is able almost miraculously to decide a seemingly insoluble legal case brought to him by two unnamed women identified as prostitutes, who both claim to be the mother of the same child. Not all interpreters are impressed with Solomon in this story, however, and the second section of the chapter begins with critiques of that traditional analysis by a group of contemporary sex workers who read it with a biblical scholar. Following their lead, I will argue that traditional interpretations fail to see the lack of justice in the violent coercion Solomon uses to render a judgment in this story and that the adoption by such interpretations of ethically dubious assumptions as to how a justice system should operate is often combined with a belief that prostitutes are sexual deviants who can be equated with gross immorality in general. Because of such problems in the ethical assumptions that lie behind more common readings of 3:16–28, I will embark upon a different interpretation of the story in that second section of the chapter, one that creates a meaningful text that portrays the passage as a critique of the king's failure to act justly. This analysis fits with readings of the larger narrative of Solomon in 1 Kings 1–11 that this first part of the chapter examines, interpretations that largely understand the whole story of Solomon's reign in Kings as one of a failure in royal leadership. Read in this context, we see that 3:16–28 is a story in which Solomon cannot understand justice, let alone execute it, since it shows that he believes the whole point of a legal system is to secure his rule of Israel and compel even his most marginalized subjects to acknowledge his authority, just as it shows that he believes that anything necessary to attain this goal, even threatening the life of an innocent child, is acceptable. This interpretation explicitly asks readers how wise it is to assume that the powerful male at the center of the story is a hero.

To begin by setting the stage for this reading of the passage, this opening section of the chapter focuses on the portrayal of Solomon in 1 Kings 1–11 as a whole, for how we make sense of him as a character in the entire narrative devoted to him will have some effect on the ways in which we understand his thoughts and actions as he arrives at his judgment in 1 Kings 3. It would be simple enough to portray Solomon as the hero of 1 Kings 1–11, the monarch who leads Israel during a golden age in 1 Kings 1–10 but who suffers an ignominious downfall in his old age under the influence of his foreign wives in the final chapter of his story, since 1 Kings 11 says that these women lead him to worship foreign gods, an act that meets with divine sanction. Modern scholarship has traditionally understood his story this way, at least,[1] and in this understanding of the chapters, we see Solomon using his divinely given wisdom in the story's first ten chapters to produce great wealth (3:5–15; 4:29–34 [Heb 5:9–14]; 9:28; 10:14–29), while the single largest block of material in that part of his narrative focuses on his construction and dedication of God's temple (5:1–6:38 [Heb 5:15–6:38]; 7:13–8:61),[2] a section of the story that repetitively refers to the exodus (6:1; 8:16, 21, 51, 53), as if to suggest that this event and Solomon's erection of the temple are of equal significance in Israel's history.[3] In this interpretation of 1 Kings 1–11, Solomon is a good king for almost all of his

1. For example, David Jobling, "'Forced Labor': Solomon's Golden Age and the Question of Literary Representation," *Sem* 54 (1992): 58–60; Gary N. Knoppers, "Solomon's Fall and Deuteronomy," in *The Age of Solomon: Scholarship at the Turn of the Millennium*, ed. Lowell K. Handy, SHCANE 11 (Leiden: Brill, 1997), 394; and Yong Ho Jeon, "The Retroactive Re-evaluation Technique with Pharaoh's Daughter and the Nature of Solomon's Corruption in 1 Kings 1–12," *TynBul* 62 (2011): 16–21.
2. The story of temple construction and dedication amounts to 40 percent of Solomon's narrative, in fact; see Bruce A. Power, "'All the King's Horses . . .': Narrative Subversion in the Story of Solomon's Golden Age," in *From Babel to Babylon: Essays on Biblical History and Literature in Honour of Brian Peckham*, ed. Joyce Rilett Wood, John E. Harvey, and Mark Leuchter (New York: T&T Clark, 2006), 119.
3. See Gary N. Knoppers, "Prayer and Propaganda: Solomon's Dedication of the Temple and the Deuteronomist's Program," CBQ 57 (1995): 240; and see also Amos Frisch, "The Exodus Motif in 1 Kings 1–14," JSOT 87 (2000): 3–21.

reign, the narrative emphasizing his loyalty to God for the vast majority of his rule and presenting him as failing in this regard only at the end of his life.

Other interpreters read 1 Kings 1–11 rather differently, however, and argue that references to Solomon's conscription of slave labor from his subjects in 9:15–22, his incredible wealth that 1 Kings 10 describes, his vast collection of horses in 10:26–29, including ones imported from Egypt, and his hundreds of wives (11:3) show him to be in obvious violation of Torah.[4] Deuteronomy 17:14–20 specifies that Israel's kings must not acquire great wealth or many horses, especially not ones from Egypt, nor marry many wives, and in this interpretation of 1 Kings 1–11, Solomon is portrayed positively up to the point at which he completes and dedicates the temple in 1 Kings 8 but negatively thereafter. In other readings of the Solomon narrative, in fact, the negative portrayal of the king begins even earlier. God is never said to choose Solomon as the successor to David,[5] and he succeeds David as king in 1 Kings 1 despite the fact that he has an older brother, Adonijah, who assumed he would reign after their father died. Solomon's accession is possible only through court intrigue in which the prophet Nathan and Bathsheba, Solomon's mother, convince an elderly David that he had sworn to make Solomon king, even though no biblical story contains a record of such an oath. Because of this play for power, in which readers must at least suspect the possibility that Nathan and Bathsheba lied to David after Adonijah had begun celebrating his imminent rule, some scholars have described their action as a coup[6] and as tainting readers' perceptions of Solomon even before he becomes king.[7]

4. For example, Marc Brettler, "The Structure of 1 Kings 1–11," JSOT 49 (1991): 91–95; Stuart Lasine, "The King of Desire: Indeterminacy, Audience, and the Solomon Narrative," *Sem* 71 (1995): 90–91, 101–2; Eric A. Siebert, *Subversive Scribes and the Solomonic Narrative: A Rereading of 1 Kings 1–11*, LHBOTS 436 (New York: T&T Clark, 2006), 179–80; and Robert D. Miller, "Solomon the Trickster," *BibInt* 19 (2011): 499–500.
5. Isaac Kalimi ("Love of God and *Apologia* for a King: Solomon as the Lord's Beloved King in Biblical and Ancient Near Eastern Contexts," JANER 17 [2017]: 28–63) points out that Solomon is the only king in the Hebrew Bible who is provided with a birth story, and in that narrative God gives him a second name, Jedadiah, which means "beloved of the Lord," reflecting the love the narrator says God has for Solomon (2 Sam 12:24–25). Nonetheless, although we find references in Solomon's narrative to the divine choice of David as ruler and Jerusalem as the place for the temple (1 Kgs 8:16; 11:13, 32, 34, 36), there is no explicit mention of God's choice of Solomon as king. See J. Daniel Hays, "Has the Narrator Come to Praise Solomon or to Bury Him? Narrative Subtlety in 1 Kings 1–11," JSOT 28 (2003): 158–59; and Michael Avioz, "The Characterization of Solomon in Solomon's Prayer (1 Kings 8)," BN 126 (2005): 24.
6. See Joyce Willis, Andrew Pleffer, and Stephen Llewelyn, "Conversation in the Succession Narrative of Solomon," VT 61 (2011): 133–34.
7. Jean Koulagna, "L'image de Salomon dans l'historiographie deutéronomiste: À propos de la place de 1 *Rois* 1–2," RHPR 87 (2007): 293.

In this reading of 1 Kings 1–11, Solomon does nothing to improve readers' view of him in 1 Kings 2, when he executes Adonijah and other political enemies after he has established his rule, relying on rather flimsy pretexts to carry out the assassinations,[8] as the next section of the chapter discusses. Even his construction of the temple can be seen as suspect, since 6:37–38 tells us he spent seven years building it, while 7:1 says he spent thirteen years constructing his own palace, as if that was the more important project in his eyes.[9] The narrative of the construction of the palace (7:1–12) actually interrupts that of the temple,[10] suggesting the king's lack of attention to the latter. Solomon also uses forced labor to build the temple (5:13–14 [Heb 27–28]), despite the fact that the story claims he was wealthier than any other king in the world (10:23) and so assumedly could have paid his subjects for the work. Given that the first thing he is said to do after killing off his political enemies is to marry the daughter of the Egyptian pharaoh (3:1),[11] we can understand Solomon as acting like a pharaoh himself, with external policies geared to creating wealth for the crown (9:26–28; 10:11–29) and internal policies based on taxing the people (4:7–18) and exploiting their labor (5:13–14 [27–28]; 9:15–22).[12] It is important to note in this regard that at no point in 1 Kings 1–11 does the narrator express approval of Solomon and that God does so only when Solomon asks for wisdom to rule the people (3:9–10). God clearly wants a wise ruler of Israel, but although the narrator affirms at numerous points that God had in fact given Solomon wisdom and that he was considered to be wise (3:28; 4:29–34 [Heb 5:9–14]; 5:7 [21]; 10:1–13,

8. For example, Jerome T. Walsh, "The Characterization of Solomon in First Kings 1–5," CBQ 57 (1995): 482–85; and Iain W. Provan, "On 'Seeing' the Trees while Missing the Forest: The Wisdom of Characters and Readers in 2 Samuel and 1 Kings," in *In Search of True Wisdom: Essays in Old Testament Interpretation in Honour of Ronald E. Clements*, ed. Edward Ball, JSOTSup 300 (Sheffield, UK: Sheffield Academic, 1999), 163–64.
9. For example, Hays, "Has the Narrator Come to Praise Solomon," 168; and Power, "'All the King's Horses,'" 119.
10. In the Septuagint, the narrative of Solomon's construction of his palace is placed after that of his construction of the temple, although the ordering of the material in the Masoretic Text is likely original. See the discussion of text critical issues in Kings below, as well as D. W. Gooding's arguments in "Pedantic Timetabling in 3rd Book of Reigns," VT 15 (1965): 153–65; and in "Temple Specifications: A Dispute in Logical Arrangement between the MT and the LXX," VT 17 (1967): 143–72, in which he demonstrates that the MT contains the more original ordering of material, as the text behind the LXX was rearranged to create a clearer chronological ordering of events.
11. See the MT; this information appears later in the LXX's account of Solomon's reign (3 Rgns 5:14), but the MT's order is more likely original. See Percy S. F. van Keulen, *Two Versions of the Solomon Narrative: An Inquiry into the Relationship between* MT 1 Kgs. 2–11 *and* LXX 3 *Reg.* 2–11, VTSup 104 (Leiden: Brill, 2005), 62–81.
12. See Walter Brueggemann, "Ancient Israel on Political Leadership: Between the Book Ends," *PolTheo* 8 (2007): 460.

24–25), the mere fact that he receives divine wisdom is not a guarantee that he ever uses it to benefit his subjects.[13]

I will take up the question as to whether Solomon truly manifests divine wisdom in the story of 3:16–28 in the next section of the chapter, but some scholars do argue that at least in 4:20 and 25 (Heb 5:5) readers see Solomon putting his great wisdom and wealth to use to provide economic and military security for Israel, benefiting all of the people and not merely himself and his royal court.[14] While 4:7–19 provides a long list of the taxation districts into which Solomon divided Israel, and 4:22–23 lists the massive daily consumption by the court of the products they sent to the king, the NRSV's translation of 4:20 reads, "Judah and Israel were as numerous as the sand by the sea; they ate and drank and were happy." That is to say, if Judah and Israel had to supply the royal household, Solomon governed his kingdom in such a way as to ensure that there was at least plenty of food left over to make them content. And while 4:26–28 (Heb 5:6–8) refers to the vast chariotry Solomon established and to the fact that the burden to provide for the upkeep for the horses and drivers also fell on the people, the NRSV's translation of 4:25 (5:5) says, "During Solomon's lifetime Judah and Israel lived in safety, from Dan even to Beer-sheba, all of them under their vines and fig trees." This verse assures readers, in other words, that Solomon's large army was not merely a monument to royal pride but provided security to the people who had to pay for it.

However, it is unlikely that 4:20 and 4:25 (5:5) were originally part of the story of Solomon in 1 Kings 1–11, and it appears that they were added to only one copy of Kings sometime after the book was composed. If, that is, we use the techniques associated with textual criticism, then we must exclude the evidence those two verses provide us in regard to Solomon's ability and intentions to improve his subjects' lives and conclude that the story of his reign presents him as a king who had no concern for the well-being of his subjects. Textual criticism, part of the suite of academic techniques and questions that make up the historical critical method, refers to the work scholars do to try to reconstruct the earliest version of a physical text that they can, and the oldest version of 1 Kings I believe I can reconstruct does not include either

13. Walsh, "Characterization of Solomon," 491–92; Lasine, "King of Desire," 101–2; Michael V. Fox, "The Uses of Indeterminacy," *Sem* 71 (1995): 173–92.
14. See, for example, Walsh, "Characterization of Solomon," 479–80; and John W. Olley, "Pharaoh's Daughter, Solomon's Palace, and the Temple: Another Look at the Structure of 1 Kings 1–11," JSOT 27 (2003): 365.

4:20 or 4:25 (Heb 5:5). In the ancient world, the manual copying of texts always led to alterations, sometimes in error and sometimes purposefully, of the book being copied. When such copies were themselves copied, these alterations would be passed on in the process while new ones entered the physical text. In the context of the texts of the Hebrew Bible / Old Testament, textual critical analysis is based on the evidence of many old manuscripts in Hebrew, Greek, and other languages. With respect to the narrative of Solomon in 1 Kings, this evidence is complicated, and there is no scholarly consensus as to how to resolve the problems it raises.[15] The most important pieces of evidence in textual critical arguments, at least when it comes to the Hebrew Bible, are the textual tradition we refer to as the Masoretic Text (or MT), reflected in hundreds of different Hebrew manuscripts that were copied in the Middle Ages and later (although these manuscripts are based on a textual tradition that is many centuries older), and the Septuagint (or LXX), the ancient Greek translations of biblical books that began to appear as early as the third century BCE (although the earliest copies of those translations that we have are centuries later than that). The Hebrew texts of individual biblical books used by those Greek translators were sometimes fairly different from the Hebrew manuscripts that belong to the Masoretic tradition, and that is certainly the case with 1 Kings (or 3 Reigns, as the book is called in the LXX), where the ordering of the material that makes up the story of Solomon varies notably among those two traditions. While scholarly opinions differ as to whether the MT or LXX generally tends to preserve an older version of the book, it is more likely that the Masoretic Text does.

One need not do any textual critical work in order to read 1 Kings or 3 Reigns, for one could simply decide to follow the reading of one of the oldest manuscripts associated with the Masoretic tradition,[16] the text Judaism has traditionally accepted as the authoritative witness to the Hebrew Bible, or one of the ancient Greek manuscripts that bears witness to the text of the Septuagint, the Old Testament of Greek-speaking Christianity since the first century. Textual criticism is normally understood as the work one needs to do to create an "original" text, one that is as

15. For a brief survey of the textual critical problems in Kings and the scholarly positions in regard to them, see Martin Meiser, "Basileion III / 3 Kingdoms / 1 Kings," in *Introduction to the Septuagint*, ed. Siegfried Kreuzer, trans. David A. Brenner and Peter Altmann (Waco, TX: Baylor University Press, 2019), 195–203.

16. The most obvious example of such a manuscript is Codex Leningrad, the text found in *Biblia Hebraica Stuttgartensia*, which is widely used by scholars of the Hebrew Bible / Old Testament, since this is the earliest complete manuscript of the Hebrew Bible that we know of.

close as possible to the words a biblical author originally wrote, before that text began to be altered as it was copied and recopied, reflecting the traditional drive of modern biblical studies to privilege authorial intention.[17] One can use textual critical techniques without being concerned as to what an author meant to say, however, since we can understand textual critical work as aimed simply at producing the oldest version of a physical text that it is possible to reconstruct.[18] And since I have to choose some physical text to use as evidence for my interpretation, I will act as biblical scholars tend to when dealing with conflicting textual critical evidence and adopt standard textual critical techniques in order to construct one.[19] In this regard, I can point out that the Septuagint's version of 1 Kings presents Solomon in a better light than the Masoretic Text does and tends to have a more logical and clearer chronological arrangement of events than the MT, and so it more likely reflects alterations to an older version of Solomon's story than the texts that form the Masoretic tradition. It makes more sense that someone copying or editing a biblical text in the ancient world would alter and rearrange material to make it clearer and to make Solomon, the king whom God permitted to build the temple, look more impressive rather than vice versa.[20] It is much more difficult to

17. Brennan Breed argues, however, that textual criticism fails to establish a biblical text that is original because there is no clear understanding among biblical scholars as to what "original" might mean in this context. See Brennan W. Breed, *Nomadic Text: A Theory of Biblical Reception History*, ISBL (Bloomington: Indiana University Press, 2014), 15–51. Textual criticism, Breed writes, is based on a Platonic-like notion that there is a perfect universal model of the text, the one the author wrote, of which we can only see corrupted versions, which are the oldest manuscripts at our disposal, no two of which are alike, and in this way of understanding things, says Breed, scholars see authorial intention as a kind of equivalent to the Platonic Real (58–61).
18. To be clear, by "the oldest version of a text that it is possible to reconstruct," I am not thinking of texts created through redactional critical arguments, but only those constructed through traditional textual critical means.
19. As is obvious in my textual critical analysis, however, one cannot do this sort of work without already believing one knows the meaning of the textual witnesses that one is using as evidence in textual critical arguments. Here, for example, I make my argument in regard to the general superiority of the MT over the LXX in providing an earlier version of 1 Kgs 1–11 on the basis of the meanings that I have already decided that various witnesses to the MT and LXX have. One could hardly use these textual witnesses as evidence, after all, if one did not know what they meant, since something meaningless is not something we can understand and so not something we could ever draw upon as evidence.
20. This was the general conclusion of D. W. Gooding in the middle of the twentieth century; besides his articles mentioned in the notes above, see also his "The Septuagint's Version of Solomon's Misconduct," VT 15 (1965): 173–89; and "Problems of Text and Midrash in the Third Book of Reigns," *Textus* 7 (1969): 1–29. See as well Zipora Talshir, *The Alternative Story of the Division of the Kingdom: 3 Kingdoms 12:24a–z*, JBS 6 (Jerusalem: Simor, 1993), 13–15; van Keulen, *Two Versions of the Solomon Narrative*, 300–301; and Emanuel Tov, "Reflections on the Many Forms of Reworked Scripture in Light of the LXX and 4QReworked Pentateuch," in *From Qumran to Aleppo: A Discussion with Emanuel Tov about the Textual History of Jewish Scriptures in Honor of His 65th Birthday*, ed. Armin Lange, Matthias Weigold, and József Zsengellér, FRLANT 230 (Göttingen, Germany: Vandenhoeck & Ruprecht, 2009), 16–17.

see why a copyist or editor of the textual tradition behind the book would take a more orderly and straightforwardly chronological story and make it less so, or why one would alter the text to make Solomon look worse rather than better. In sum, it is because there appears to be less evidence of editing in the Masoretic textual tradition that it is safer to assume that in most places it witnesses to an earlier version of the physical text of 1 Kings 1–11 than the Septuagint does.

This does not mean, however, that at every point where we see differences between the MT and LXX we must assume the Masoretic textual tradition preserves an older form of the physical text. What is odd about the difference between the MT's and LXX's versions of 1 Kings 4–5 is not that the material appears in a somewhat different order in these two traditions,[21] since that is often the case when it comes to the stories about Solomon in 1 Kings, but that 4:20 and 25 (Heb 5:5) are present in the MT but not in the LXX.[22] Without these verses, 1 Kings 4–5 gives no indication that Solomon acted to benefit his people, even while he demanded massive resources from them to support his court and military. As a result, 4:20 and 25 (5:5) make Solomon look better than he does in a story that lacks these verses, since in their absence Solomon appears as a greedy imperial ruler in 1 Kings 4–5 who uses Israel to supply his needs as king, with no indication that this left his subjects prosperous, safe, and happy as those two verses claim. And since an important tendency of the Septuagint's textual tradition is to improve the portrait of Solomon from the earlier version of the text the MT generally preserves, these are not verses that a copyist or editor of a text behind the Septuagint would have removed from the story that they received. The likeliest explanation for the presence of 4:20 and 25 (5:5) in the MT, despite their absence in the LXX, then, is that they were not part of the older version of the text that is generally reflected in the MT but were added to the Masoretic textual tradition after it had diverged from that behind the Septuagint. Copyists and editors did make alterations to the MT after that time,[23] and one of them was apparently dismayed with the existing text's failure

21. For a discussion of the differences in the textual traditions of these chapters, see van Keulen, *Two Versions of the Solomon Narrative*, 82–95.
22. Technically, the information from these verses appears in 3 Rgns 2:46a and g, parts of the so-called Miscellanies in 3 Rgns 2, but the Miscellanies do not appear in any non-LXX textual witnesses to 1 Kings and were later additions to the Septuagint's text. See Jan Joosten, "Textual Plurality at the Margins of Biblical Texts: The Miscellanies in 3 Reigns 2:35, 46," *RevQ* 30 (2018): 293–307.
23. Frank H. Polak, "The Septuagint's Account of Solomon's Reign: Revision and Ancient Recension," in *X Congress of the International Organization for Septuagint and Cognate Studies, Oslo, 1998*, ed. Bernard A. Taylor, SCSS 51 (Atlanta: Society of Biblical Literature, 2001), 139–64.

to have Solomon show any real concern for the well-being of his people, even while he taxed them and demanded forced labor from them. This means, however, that 4:20 and 25 (5:5) were not part of the earliest physical text of the story of Solomon in 1 Kings 1–11 that I can piece together and so are not part of the evidence that I will consider in my interpretation of 3:16–28.

The upshot of this textual critical argument, and of the preceding comments on the narrative of Solomon in general, is that it is possible to create convincing interpretations of 1 Kings 1–11 in which Solomon appears to be a very poor ruler for the entirety of his reign, someone unconcerned with the well-being of his subjects and who is "the royal antitype or the model of royal misbehavior," as Marvin Sweeney puts it.[24] It is also possible, as I mentioned above, to create a much more positive portrayal of Solomon, at least up through 1 Kings 8 or 10, but as my reading of 3:16–28 in the larger context of 1 Kings 1–11 will show, I do not find those interpretations of the chapters terribly convincing, especially when we begin an analysis of the text with marginalized readers who point to the king's ethical flaws, ones that, as we will see, generally match the overall characterization of him in the story of his reign.

Women, Wisdom, and the Critique of Solomon in 1 Kings 3:16–28

Traditional academic and religious readings of 1 Kings 3:16–28 interpret the passage in such a way that it casts Solomon in a positive light. In the preceding story of 3:5–15, God encounters the king in a dream, and Solomon asks God for wisdom to rule Israel, a request that meets with divine approval. In 3:16–28, two unnamed female sex workers bring a difficult legal case to Solomon that they ask him to resolve, and so this story seems as if it will test the wisdom that the king has just requested. The plaintiff opens the proceedings by claiming that she and the other woman, who live alone in the same house, had given birth to sons only three days apart, but that one night, the defendant lay on her own child and he died. While she, the plaintiff, was sleeping,[25] she continues, the other woman switched her

24. Marvin A. Sweeney, "The Critique of Solomon in the Josianic Edition of the Deuteronomistic History," *JBL* 114 (1995): 611.
25. The LXX omits the plaintiff's claim that she was sleeping, and as a result, in that version of the story, her testimony might seem more believable. She then appears to be the real mother to whom, in the LXX's version of the story, Solomon gives the child.

dead son with the plaintiff's living one (3:16–21). The defendant's only response is to reject this story and state that the living child is hers (3:22). Perhaps she is lying, or perhaps she is telling the truth and simply has no facts to add to the first woman's testimony,[26] which is based on a claim about an alleged event that took place when the plaintiff was sleeping and thus that she did not actually witness. In any event, based on their testimony alone, the case seems impossible to resolve. As Solomon puts it at this point, "This one [zōʾt] says, 'This is my son, the living one,' and this one [zōʾt] says, 'No, your son is the dead one and my son is the living one'" (3:23). He labels both women as *zōʾt*, or "this one," the testimony of each indistinguishable from the other's,[27] and so he now employs what scholars sometimes refer to as a "ruse" or "trick"[28] and calls for a sword, ordering that the living child be cut in two and half given to each woman (3:24–25). The narrator tells us, however, that the compassion of the mother of the living child burned within her, and she asks the king to give the boy to the other woman, so sparing his life, while that other woman, who had lied when claiming the living boy was hers, echoes the king's command to divide him (3:26). The resolution to the case, as translated by the NRSV, is as follows: "Then the king responded: 'Give the first woman the living boy; do not kill him. She is his mother'" (3:27). "All Israel," the narrator concludes, "saw that the wisdom of God was in him to do justice" (3:28).

Many readers agree with Israel's response and conclude that Solomon has drawn upon divinely given wisdom to render justice in a seemingly insoluble case,[29] but some minoritized interpreters argue we actually see no justice here at all. When the biblical scholar Avaren Ipsen read this story with sex workers in California, it is notable that they found it difficult to see Solomon in a positive light and

26. Meir Sternberg, *The Poetics of Biblical Narrative: Ideological Literature and the Drama of Reading*, ISBL (Bloomington: University of Indiana Press, 1987), 168.
27. André Wénin, "Le roi, la femme et la sagesse: Une lecture de 1 Rois 3,16–28," RTL 29 (1998): 37.
28. For language like this to describe Solomon's order in 3:24–25, see Stuart Lasine, "The Riddle of Solomon's Judgment and the Riddle of Human Nature in the Hebrew Bible," JSOT 45 (1989): 65; W. A. M. Beuken, "No Wise King without a Wise Woman (1 Kings iii 16–28)," in *New Avenues in the Study of the Old Testament: A Collection of Old Testament Studies*, ed. A. S. van der Woude, OTS 25 (Leiden: Brill, 1989), 1–2; and Gina Hens-Piazza, *Of Methods, Monarchs, and Meanings: A Sociorhetorical Approach to Exegesis*, SOTI 3 (Macon, GA: Mercer University Press, 1996), 153.
29. For example, Phyllis A. Bird, *Missing Persons and Mistaken Identities: Women and Gender in Ancient Israel*, OBT (Minneapolis: Fortress, 1997), 217–18; K. I. Parker, "Solomon as Philosopher King? The Nexus of Law and Wisdom in 1 Kings 1–11," JSOT 53 (1992): 78; Claudia V. Camp, *Wise, Strange and Holy: The Strange Woman and the Making of the Bible*, JSOTSup 320, GCT 9 (Sheffield, UK: Sheffield Academic, 2000), 165–67; and Hayyim Angel, "Cut the Baby in Half: Understanding Solomon's Divinely-Inspired Wisdom," JBQ 39 (2011): 189–94.

understood the narrative through the lens of their experiences with the justice system in the United States.[30] Solomon as judge shows little concern for the women who appear in his court, for not only does he not even bother to cross-examine them or call other witnesses in order to do the best he can to arrive at a just verdict,[31] but, Ipsen's coreaders noted, the case arrives at an outcome only when the baby's mother abandons her right to raise her own child.[32] The justice system over which Solomon presides is obviously predicated on violence, the sex workers observed, since the judge finds it acceptable to threaten the life of an innocent child,[33] and they found it unlikely that other prostitutes would willingly go to the king for justice after hearing of the case.[34]

In short, as marginalized women with firsthand experience of a contemporary legal system that they have encountered as dangerous and dismissive of their rights because they are sex workers, these readers point us to a number of ethical problems with claiming that 3:16–28 portrays Solomon as a wise king executing justice. To create that sort of interpretation, we would have to assume, first, that threatening the life of a child is an acceptable part of a legitimate judicial process. Some scholars assume, as I mentioned above, that Solomon never had any intention of killing the boy, since they refer to his apparent intention to do so as a trick, but it is perfectly possible to read the story as if his original solution to the problem was to cut the infant in half. As I will discuss below, Solomon has just combined wisdom and the sword in 1 Kings 2 in order to execute a number of his political enemies, and so readers could suspect that in this case he is simply adhering to his established pattern of dealing with his problems by means of deadly violence and that only the frightened response of the child's mother sways him from this plan.[35] Regardless of his original intention, however, if we cannot assume that threatening the lives of innocent children is an acceptable part of an ethical justice system—and I would hope that no one could—then we cannot see Solomon as acting justly.

The sex workers reading with Ipsen also noted that Solomon found it unnecessary to engage the basic judicial due diligence that we would expect in a legal system

30. Ipsen, *Sex Working and the Bible*, 101–2.
31. Avaren E. Ipsen, "Solomon and the Two Prostitutes," BCT 3/1 (2007): art. 2 (pp. 7–8).
32. Ipsen, *Sex Working and the Bible*, 115–16.
33. Ipsen, 101–2.
34. Ipsen, 98.
35. See, for example, Ellen van Wolde, "Who Guides Whom? Embeddedness and Perspective in Biblical Hebrew and in 1 Kings 3:16–28," *JBL* 114 (1995): 637–40.

that aimed to protect those who relied upon it, for he neither cross-examines the women nor calls witnesses who could help him resolve the case. Torah shows that the ancient Israelite justice system, like modern democratic ones, depended upon the testimony of witnesses in order for courts to arrive at verdicts (e.g., Exod 23:1–2; Num 35:30; Deut 19:15–21). Moreover, as Gina Hens-Piazza points out, in an ancient Israelite setting, we might expect Solomon as judge to consult the divine, since that is done in other biblical stories in order to determine guilt.[36] It would seem that, had Solomon followed commonsensical legal procedures, he would have been more likely to have identified the true mother of the child, even if his order to kill the boy was indeed a trick, for he could hardly have known with certainty that the true mother would not have been rendered speechless with terror by the king's apparent decision to kill her son,[37] and as the sex workers who read with Ipsen noted, either woman could have guessed at the sort of thing they believed the king wanted them to say in an attempt to game the system and so leave the court with the child.[38] The picture we see of Solomon as judge is one in which he simply does not care enough about his subjects in order to put in the effort to ensure that justice gets done.

It is unsurprising, then, that the conclusion of the case does not result in justice as we would understand it, for it does not appear that the true mother actually receives the child at the end of the story. After Solomon gives the order to divide the living child in two with the command *gizrû*, "Cut!" (3:25), the true mother calls upon him to spare his life, while the other woman echoes the king's order and repeats his use of the imperative *gizrû* (3:26). Solomon then immediately arrives at his judgment in 3:27, and if we follow the MT's version of the text,[39] he says, "Give her the living child and certainly do not kill him; she is his mother." The pronouns "her" and "she" in his verdict most obviously refer to the last woman who spoke,[40] and that was not the infant's biological mother but the woman who agreed with his

36. Hens-Piazza, *Of Methods, Monarchs, and Meanings*, 147. She refers specifically to the stories of Joshua 7 and 1 Samuel 14, where characters use Urim and Thummim in order to consult the divine in matters of determining guilt.
37. See Lasine, "Riddle of Solomon's Judgment," 68–69.
38. Ipsen, *Sex Working and the Bible*, 100.
39. The LXX of 3:27 has Solomon say, "Give the boy to the woman who said, 'Give him to her and certainly do not kill him.' She is his mother." This reflects an alteration to the older version of the story seen in the MT, and in the LXX's version of the story, it is clear that the true mother actually receives the child, and so it casts Solomon in a more favorable light than the MT does, another piece of evidence that suggests the MT retains an older version of the text here.
40. See Walsh, "Characterization of Solomon," 488–89.

command to kill the boy. As a result, the NRSV's translation here—"Give the first woman the living boy"—reverses the king's actual judgment. To argue that he must have referred to the true mother because this is a story in which he manifests the divine wisdom that God granted him in 3:5–15 is to assume that Solomon actually uses that gift at some point in 1 Kings 1–11 in order to benefit his own subjects, but there is no evidence of this in my interpretation of the physical text I am working with. And since the sex workers reading with Ipsen lead me to suspect that we do not see the execution of justice at all in this story, I will attempt to provide an interpretation of 3:16–28 that reflects ethical presuppositions I hold about justice, an interpretation that sees the story as a critique of Solomon's failure to treat his marginalized subjects as being as human and thus as deserving of justice as he is.

To provide some context for this interpretation of 3:16–28, I can begin by noting that this is not the first place in which Solomon is said to use his wisdom. In 2:1–9, just before David dies, he tells his son to use his wisdom to kill two men David views as political enemies. These are, specifically, Joab, the head of David's army, who supported Solomon's brother Adonijah as David's successor (1:5–8), and Shimei, who supported Absalom, another of Solomon's brothers, when he attempted to overthrow David (2 Sam 16:5–13). As a powerful military figure, Joab's allegiance to Adonijah means that he is too dangerous for the new king to leave alive, as David points out when he refers to the fact that, many years previously, Joab had killed two important figures whom he saw as a threat to David's reign, even though those men believed they were at peace with Joab and David. Joab "shed blood of war in time of peace," David says, "and put blood of war on his belt that is around his waist and on his sandals that are on his feet" (2:5),[41] a reference to the bloodguilt David believes Joab has brought upon himself by killing two unsuspecting men. If Joab is still supporting Adonijah, in other words, then Solomon could be his next victim as Joab acts to put his ally on the throne. A just king cannot kill a high-ranking official on the mere suspicion of disloyalty,[42] so Solomon employs his wisdom in

41. For the text critical problems in 2:5 and an argument that the reading of the MT is to be preferred, see David Janzen, "'What He Did for Me': David's Warning about Joab in 1 Kings 2.5," JSOT 39 (2015): 267–71.

42. Solomon has very weak grounds to order Joab's death, because Joab's killing of the two men to whom David refers benefited rather than hurt David. See J. W. Wesselius, "Joab's Death and the Central Theme of the Succession Narrative (2 Samuel IX–1 Kings II)," VT 40 (1990): 338–39; Iain W. Provan, "Why Barzillai of Gilead (1 Kings 2:7)? Narrative Art and the Hermeneutics of Suspicion in 1 Kings 1–2," *TynBul* 46 (1995): 109–12; and Janzen, "'What He Did for Me.'"

this case, as David had instructed him (2:6), when he invents a theological rationale for Joab's assassination. When speaking to Benaiah, the man he has ordered to kill Joab but who hesitates to carry out the task, Solomon does not assert, as David did, that Joab bears bloodguilt for the killing of David's two officials, but instead that through those murders Joab has somehow made the whole royal household, including Solomon, guilty (2:31) and that there cannot be peace until Joab's blood has been shed (2:32–33). What Solomon tells Benaiah, then, is that divine justice itself demands Joab's death, and when Solomon informs Benaiah that "the Lord will return his blood[43] upon his head" (2:32), Solomon assures Benaiah that it is no sin to assassinate Joab but is in fact God's will and that Benaiah need not fear divine vengeance for the act.

Solomon again exercises his wisdom as his father had asked (see 2:9) in order to kill Shimei, someone who demonstrated disloyalty to David, and so who cannot be trusted to support the new king. After succeeding his father, Solomon makes Shimei swear that he will live only in Jerusalem, and that were he to cross the Wadi Kidron, which is to the east of the city, he would be executed (2:37). Three years later, after Shimei returns from a trip to Gath, a journey to the southwest of Jerusalem that did not involve crossing the Kidron, Solomon tells Shimei that his earlier oath means that the king is now able to justifiably execute him (2:42–43). Solomon had told him, the king says now, that "on the day you leave and go any other place, know for certain that you will surely die."[44] Solomon's actual words to him three years earlier, however, were that "on the day you leave and cross the Wadi Kidron, know for certain you will surely die" (2:37).[45] By subtly—and from Solomon's perspective, wisely—altering the original terms of the agreement, he is able to kill another political enemy.

The wisdom Solomon displays before we arrive at the story of his judgment in 1 Kings 3, then, is associated with disingenuousness and violence, and is used to

43. The LXX is even more specific here and has Solomon tell Benaiah that God will return "the blood of his injustice upon his head."
44. An editor of the LXX has altered the text in 2:42 so that Solomon says that he had Shimei agree that he would be executed if he left Jerusalem, a change to the older version of the text that paints Solomon in a better light.
45. For other discussions of Solomon's misrepresentations in 2:42–43 of the oath he had Shimei swear in 2:37, see Jerome T. Walsh, *1 Kings*, BO (Collegeville, MN: Liturgical, 1996), 61–64; Keith Bodner, *David Observed: A King in the Eyes of His Court*, HBM 5 (Sheffield, UK: Sheffield Phoenix, 2005), 169–71; and Koulagna, "L'image de Salomon," 293.

consolidate his power.[46] Readers know by this point that he is quick to resort to violence, and his executions of Joab and Shimei are preceded by the killing of his brother Adonijah (2:13–25). Adonijah, as David's eldest surviving son in 1 Kings 1, had acted as if he would succeed their father as king (1:5–6), but after Solomon's accession, he goes to Bathsheba, Solomon's mother, and asks her to intercede with the king so he, Adonijah, might marry a woman by the name of Abishag (2:13–18). As an old man, David had slept in the same bed as Abishag but had never had sex with her (1:1–4), and so it is not clear if she was part of the royal harem, wives who would pass into Solomon's possession upon the death of the previous king, or not.[47] If she is, then Adonijah acts somewhat as Absalom did after he launched his coup against David, for after Absalom forced his father to retreat from Jerusalem, he immediately went into the royal harem (2 Sam 16:20–22), an act that demonstrated he was now king since he had assumed the right to have sex with these women. Solomon does not bother to call Adonijah and examine him as to his motives or solicit the testimony of others as to whether his brother still aims to take the throne. When Bathsheba brings Adonijah's request to marry Abishag to Solomon (2:19–21), she does not mention that Adonijah had explicitly stated that Solomon and not himself was God's choice as king (2:15),[48] but Solomon does not even bother to press her for further details in regard to her interaction with his brother. Given Adonijah's acknowledgment of Solomon's place in the divine plan for Israel, it is quite possible that Adonijah does not believe that Abishag is part of the royal harem and that he has no intention of using marriage to her as demonstrating that he is taking David's place as king instead of Solomon, but Solomon does nothing but rely on his own guesswork to judge the facts of the matter. He rushes to judgment and announces upon hearing of his brother's request that he must be executed (2:22–25). So before readers even arrive at 3:16–28, they see Solomon use his wisdom and act as judge, and his work as a jurist in 1 Kings 3 seems to resemble that of 1 Kings 2, where he is

46. For further on this point, see Camp, *Wise, Strange and Holy*, 156–57; and Koulagna, "L'image de Salomon," 296–97.
47. For discussions of the issue, see Linda S. Schearing, "A Wealth of Women: Looking behind, within, and beyond Solomon's Story," in Handy, *Age of Solomon*, 430; Siebert, *Subversive Scribes*, 139–40; and Willis, Pleffer, and Llewellyn, "Conversation in the Succession Narrative," 141–42.
48. See, for example, Lillian R. Klein, *From Deborah to Esther: Sexual Politics in the Hebrew Bible* (Minneapolis: Fortress, 2003), 68–70; and Rachel E. Adelman, *The Female Ruse: Women's Deception and Divine Sanction in the Hebrew Bible*, HBM 74 (Sheffield, UK: Sheffield Phoenix, 2017), 194–96.

also uninterested in calling witnesses or cross-examining the accused or asking for further testimony and where wisdom is manifested through the use of the sword.

Solomon's actions in 1 Kings 2 help contextualize what words like *wisdom* and *justice* actually mean to him and help us make sense of his actions in 3:16–28. This context alerts us to the possibility that the king may truly have planned to kill the living child when he gave the demand to cut him in two, since that was the manner in which he had used wisdom and the sword to resolve problems up to that point. It is, of course, quite possible that his stated intention to kill the child merely is a trick, for Solomon uses his wisdom in 1 Kings 2 in disingenuous—or trick-like—ways to assassinate Joab and Shimei. Yet regardless of his intention when he calls for the infant to be cut in two, the episodes of 1 Kings 2, including Solomon's failure to follow commonsensical legal procedures in the case of Adonijah's request to marry Abishag, suggest that wisdom and justice as Solomon understands the concepts exist for him to consolidate his power, and the outcome of the case of 3:16–28 points in the same direction. Solomon evinces no concern for the life of the remaining child, or at the very least wants his subjects to believe that is the case, and his ruthlessness up to this point makes his threat to kill the boy appear entirely believable. If he originally planned to kill the infant, then he demonstrates he simply does not care about justice at all, as it is normally understood, when it comes to some of his most marginalized subjects, just as he has no concern that justice be done in regard to his powerful political rivals. It is difficult to say precisely what Solomon expected if he had no intention of killing the child, but we can see what actually did happen: the true mother gave up her right to her own son, effectively closing the case, while the other woman agreed with the king's decision and echoed his command to kill the infant, and she is the one to whom Solomon awards the boy.

In my reading of 3:16–28, that is, from Solomon's perspective, the point of his judgment of the woman's case, just like the point of his judgment of Adonijah, is not to conduct what reasonable people would understand as a just investigation in order to arrive at a wise ruling but is instead to eliminate threats to his power. Unlike Adonijah, the women of 1 Kings 3 could not possibly challenge Solomon's hold on the kingship—they are, in fact, the only characters in all of 1 Kings 1–11 who are not from the social elite—yet it matters to the king that it is the woman in agreement with him, not the one who calls upon him to spare an innocent life, who is rewarded. From Solomon's point of view, wisdom and justice produce a society free of threats to his reign and are used to execute political rivals and to reward his subjects, even the most marginalized ones, who agree with his commands, no matter how horrific such commands might be, while punishing those who disagree with him. Perhaps he truly believes that the woman who calls upon him to spare the infant's life is the biological mother, but he rewards the one who echoes his order. As far as he is concerned, wisdom and his subjects exist to benefit him, and so 1 Kings 1–11 tells readers that his wisdom helps him compile his vast, unequaled wealth (10:23–25), just as it tells us that he uses Israel to provide him with taxes and forced labor (4:7–28; 5:13 [Heb 27]; 9:15–22). This reading or meaningful text of 3:16–28, then, is just one part of a larger critique of Solomon that a number of scholars have identified as running the length of 1 Kings 1–11. As I mentioned in the previous section of the chapter, given the physical text that I am reading, there is no indication that Solomon uses his great wisdom and wealth to benefit anyone except himself and the royal court, and these chapters portray Solomon in violation of the law of Deuteronomy 17:14–20 that limits the wealth and military power the king can amass. When it comes to Solomon's role as judge, then, we can follow the critique of the sex workers who read with Ipsen and see 3:16–28 as a story that functions as an example of what a failed legal system looks like when it exists to promote the interests of the powerful, not the marginalized. God may have granted Solomon wisdom to rule Israel in 3:5–15, but we see no sign of the king using it here, despite Israel's conclusion to the contrary in 3:28, and so it is notable that God, unlike Israel, has no words of approbation for the king.

And again following the interpretations of the sex workers, this is a reading of 3:16–28 that critiques the way in which the passage portrays the prostitutes in the story. The women reading with Ipsen noticed that we can only approve of Solomon's actions, as Israel does in 3:28, if we interpret under the assumption that prostitutes are by nature dishonest,[49] an assumption that makes Solomon's decision, for those who see it as just, appear even more miraculous. Some contemporary scholarly readings of the passage maintain that readers are to assume that prostitutes are "habitual liars"[50] and that readers will naturally have contempt for the ones in the

49. Ipsen, "Solomon and the Two Prostitutes," 7–8.
50. Bird, *Missing Persons*, 217–18.

story,[51] especially since, as unmarried sex workers, they are unworthy of being mothers in the first place.[52] For some scholars who argue that Solomon actually does justice in 3:16–28, his order to kill the child allows the natural feelings of motherhood of the boy's biological mother to triumph over the immorality inherent to her as a prostitute and so to privilege the life of her child over her own gain. Meanwhile, they maintain, the woman whose child has already died is no longer a mother, and so she manifests the invidiousness natural to sex workers, preferring to see the child die rather than allow her rival to gain any advantage over her.[53]

We have every reason to suspect that ancient Israelite readers, like some modern ones, would have been suspicious of the honesty of the women in the story because they are prostitutes. Sex workers in ancient Israel lived on the margins of respectable society, as is generally the case in contemporary cultures. Neither fathers nor husbands controlled their sexuality, as would otherwise have been true for ancient Israelite women, and they reversed normal social roles by having some control over their sexual interactions, unlike daughters and wives, as Phyllis Bird and Kimberly Russaw point out.[54] As a result of this social and sexual deviancy, ancient Israelites could associate prostitution with immorality in general, which is why biblical writers sometimes use the Hebrew verb *zānâ*, "to act as a prostitute," as a way of referring to Israel's worship of other gods, one of the worst sins many of them could imagine (e.g., Exod 34:15–16; Lev 17:7; Deut 31:16; Judg 2:17; Jer 2:20; Ezek 6:9; Hos 1:2). Some texts in which we find the verb *zānâ* in this sense use it as part of the prophetic marriage metaphor, discussed briefly in chapter 6, in which Israel, when it is accused of worshipping foreign gods, is portrayed as a sexually unfaithful wife who acts like a prostitute, and God is portrayed as the husband who legitimately punishes her through physical assault and public humiliation (e.g., Ezek 16:35–43; 23:1–49; Hos 2:2–5 [Heb 4–7]). The prophetic marriage metaphor will be accepted by readers, as Renita Weems points out, insofar as they are also willing to accept the belief that the boundaries of sexual decency that mark out prostitutes as dangerous beings should be seen as so important that husbands may legitimately

51. Beuken, "No Wise King," 6.
52. Christopher Jero, "Mother-Child Narratives and the Kingdom of God: Authorial Use of Typology as an Interpretive Device in Samuel-Kings," BBR 25 (2015): 167.
53. See, for example, Lasine, "Riddle of Solomon's Judgment," 68–71; Wénin, "Le roi, la femme," 38–41; Bird, *Missing Persons*, 217–18; and Jero, "Mother-Child Narratives," 167.
54. Bird, *Missing Persons*, 206; Kimberly D. Russaw, *Daughters in the Hebrew Bible* (Lanham, MD: Lexington, 2018), 147.

use violence against their wives in order to enforce those boundaries and prevent them from acting in such sexually deviant ways.[55] No law in Torah actually forbids prostitution, although Leviticus 19:29 emphasizes that parents must not force their daughters to act as sex workers, since that would fill the land with *zimmâ*, a Hebrew word that normally refers to terrible crimes and depravity (e.g., Lev 18:17; Judg 20:6; Job 31:11; Ps 26:10; Isa 32:7).

Yet despite such negative social views of prostitution and a general proclivity to equate those who practiced it with great immorality, in 3:16–28 it is a prostitute from the margins of society who acts rightly to save an innocent life, and so the story suggests a rather different view of sex workers than mainstream ones in ancient Israelite or contemporary society. It is a prostitute in this story who understands what ethical action consists of in this context, while the king, who stands at the very center of the social order, either believes it is ethically unproblematic to kill an innocent child or finds it appropriate to use the threat of such violence as a way to test and reward demonstrations of unswerving loyalty from his most marginalized subjects. This interpretation of the story points out, in fact, that it is obviously a mistake to assume that sex workers are immoral by nature, as we see that one of the two in the story has a far better moral compass than the royal judge of her case does when she begs him not to kill the child. The sex workers reading the story with Ipsen saw that woman as a model of how mothers should behave, insofar as she is someone who will do anything to save her child's life,[56] the paradigm of self-sacrifice in the face of an unjust judicial system.

They found it difficult to be in solidarity with the woman who agrees with Solomon's psychopathic order for the death of the child, however, and one could argue that her presence in the story appears to undermine my position about its portrayal of sex workers, but we can return to the observations of Ipsen's coreaders to understand her response. Drawing upon their own experiences in a contemporary justice system, they suggest that the woman who ends up with the child might simply have guessed at the response the judge wanted to hear,[57] although one of the readers said that a woman who calls for the execution of an infant is "just a crazy

55. Weems, *Battered Love*, 31–32.
56. Ipsen, "Solomon and the Two Prostitutes," 6.
57. Ipsen, *Sex Working and the Bible*, 100.

person."[58] Both of these suggestions could explain the woman's actions. If she is trying to game the system, her ploy succeeds, since Solomon rewards his subject who agrees with his horrific command to kill the child. In this case, she is no worse than Solomon is—she is less evil than he, in fact, since as far as we know, she has not devised disingenuous pretexts that have led to the deaths of her enemies—but we cannot conclude that her agreement with the king's murderous order is the result of her profession, since her coworker has shown herself to be a much more ethical figure than Solomon. In this way of looking at things, the woman who agrees with Solomon finds herself in a gross parody of a judicial system that does not provide justice at all, and so she acts in the unethical manner it appears to require.

To turn to the other explanation Ipsen's coreaders offer for her response to Solomon's threat to kill the child, it is also possible to see her not as a rational actor in a horribly unjust legal system but as a "crazy person" or, to put that another way, as someone who struggles with an emotional or mental disorder exacerbated by the recent death of her child, someone to be pitied rather than scorned as immoral as she is in traditional interpretations of the passage. This suggested interpretation is plausible because we could interpret her agreement with Solomon's order to kill the boy as an irrational response that is the result of a mental illness. Given the case the women bring to the king, her ultimate goal is to be recognized as the child's mother, and as a result, the most rational response she could have given when the biological mother says to Solomon, "give her the living child, and certainly do not kill him" (3:26) was not to echo the king's call for the child's death but to accept what the other woman is now freely offering to her. The fact that she does not do so simply suggests she is not thinking clearly and may not be able to, and in this case, it is not the fact that she is a sex worker that explains why she agrees with the king but the fact that she struggles with a mental disorder.

In my reading, 1 Kings 3:16–28 is a narrative that critiques Solomon's failure to treat some of his most vulnerable subjects properly, an interpretation that fits a larger story in 1 Kings 1–11 of a monarch whose greed for power and wealth repetitively leads him to violate divine law meant to limit the power of the king. It is a message condemning someone with great power who, having been given extraordinary advantages in regard to birth (the son of a king and of a mother who tenaciously

58. Ipsen, 108–9.

fights to put him on the throne),[59] wealth, and wisdom ("King Solomon was greater than all the kings of the earth in regard to wealth and wisdom," the narrator tells us in 10:23), uses such privilege to benefit only himself. Even the construction of God's temple, the action of the king that receives the most prominence in the narrative, is accomplished only with the forced labor to which the king subjects his people (5:13 [Heb 27]). Solomon cannot claim to be responsible for any of the privileges with which he is born, and even his wisdom, which surpasses that of every other human, is itself a gift from God, the narrator says (4:29–34 [Heb 5:9–14]). Solomon uses this wisdom to acquire great wealth (9:28; 10:14–29), but the text gives no indication that he used this wisdom and wealth to benefit the people he ruled and taxed, the people who, upon his death, would demand of Solomon's heir that he reduce the burdens Solomon had placed on them (12:1–4). The story of 3:16–28 is not one in which Solomon uses the wisdom he asks of God in 3:9, which would allow him "to judge your people,[60] to discern between good and evil," but one in which he manifests the same drive for power and disregard for human life that he does in 1 Kings 2, where he also combines his wisdom with the sword. In the one story in which we see Solomon interacting with figures who are not from the highest ranks of society, he shows no care at all for their well-being. We can understand this passage as a critique of state and judicial authority that are designed to benefit the wealthy and powerful alone and, like many other aspects of 1 Kings 1–11, as a critique of Solomon's failures as a leader and his misuse of power.

A Liberated Text and a Culpable God

Whether or not my reading of 3:16–28 is actually useful for liberative goals will depend on the judgments of different communities fighting oppression. One might imagine that it could be useful in the context of asking more privileged readers to

59. For discussions of Bathsheba's role in putting Solomon instead of his elder brother in power in 1 Kings 1, see Mignon R. Jacobs, "Mothering a Leader: Bathsheba's Relational and Functional Identities," in *Mother Goose, Mother Jones, Mommie Dearest: Biblical Mothers and Their Children*, ed. Cheryl A. Kirk-Duggan and Tina Pippin, SemeiaSt 61 (Atlanta: Society of Biblical Literature, 2009), 67–84; Sara M. Koenig, *Isn't This Bathsheba? A Study in Characterization*, PTMS 177 (Eugene, OR: Pickwick, 2011), 87–96; and Crowder, *When Momma Speaks*, 65–71.

60. The LXX adds "in righteousness" at this point, although this was likely the addition of an editor who wanted to make Solomon appear like the ideal judges described by Torah, who are to "judge the people in righteous judgment" (Deut 16:18). Another possibility is that it was added to reflect the portrayal of the ideal Davidic king of Isa 11:1–9 who "will judge in righteousness" (11:4).

reconsider the worldviews that often prevent them from noticing or acting against oppression, for example. If we have traditionally understood Solomon as the hero of the story, manifesting divine wisdom to do justice, what are we assuming about the validity of violence directed against the marginalized when they find themselves at the mercy of his justice system, and what does this tell us as to how we understand those marginalized figures? Why are we willing to accept Solomon's basic failure to do the sorts of things good judges should do? Why are we willing to overlook the disregard of this powerful judge for the well-being of women who live at the margins of society, and what does this tell us about our own understandings of justice? Why are we so willing to assume that such a powerful and privileged man is a hero in the first place? If we believe that Solomon manifests the divine wisdom that God grants him in 3:5–15, what does this tell us about our beliefs in regard to divine justice? I am not in the position to conclude that my reading will be useful for readers with less privilege than I have who are struggling to achieve liberative goals, although it is my hope that it can be helpful in some fashion as a resource for minoritized scholars and communities. Among its potential benefits are its rejection of unethical assumptions about the natures of justice, wisdom, and the socially marginalized, and its refusal to recognize as just a legal system that has the goal of maintaining the power and wealth of the socially privileged. This interpretation fits a broader condemnation of Solomon throughout 1 Kings 1–11, reading the chapters as critiquing a king who rules a vast empire (4:21 [Heb 5:1]),[61] taxes his people to support the massive daily expenditures of his court, drafts them into forced labor, maintains a large army supported by means of Israel's economic sacrifices, and violates divine law meant to limit royal power. The picture of king, power, and empire that I and others see as condemned in the story of Solomon is one that portrays him as acting in imitation of the Mesopotamian kings who ruled Israel during the period when many of the texts of the Hebrew

61. The information about the size of Solomon's empire does appear in the LXX, but later in its narrative, in 3 Rgns 10:26a. The placement of the verse in the MT appears to be original, but a later editor working in the textual tradition behind the LXX apparently believed it fit better after a reference to Solomon's greatness in comparison with that of the kings of the earth, who brought him tribute (10:23–25), and after a reference to the thousands of chariots and horsemen in Solomon's army (10:26). In this context, 3 Rgns 10:26a suggests that Solomon needed his army to subdue the vast territory this part of the verse discusses, and as Percy van Keulen points out, the material in 3 Rgns 10:23–27 was taken out of its original order and rearranged to emphasize Solomon's magnificence in comparison with that of his royal peers (*Two Versions of the Solomon Narrative*, 109–12, and see pp. 96–112 in general on this idea).

Bible were written.[62] My interpretation of 3:16–28 not only follows the insights of the sex workers who read with Ipsen but also looks to liberative readings of other passages by marginalized interpreters, such as feminist scholars, who have shown how traditional religious and academic interpretations often portray women of all classes as untrustworthy and deceptive.[63]

There are many ways to create liberative readings, or readings that, at least, aim to follow the agenda of marginalized scholars fighting dehumanization and oppression. The more exposure that privileged interpreters like me have to the work of these scholars, the easier it becomes to be part of a liberative dialogue and so to honor the beliefs we have about the need to fight oppression. My interpretation of 1 Kings 3:16–28 does draw upon some of the strategies chapters 5 and 6 discuss, including the critique of existing academic readings and trying to read from the perspective of marginalized characters, although this latter approach was done less overtly than in one of my readings of Ezra-Nehemiah in chapter 7. What matters most for more privileged students and scholars of biblical studies when trying to be in solidarity with liberative struggles is that our readings violate no ethical principles associated with fighting dehumanization, including ones articulated by our marginalized colleagues that our ethical beliefs compel us to accept. Some of those colleagues, for example, point out that class and gender influence how we encounter and make sense of different biblical stories and the characters in them, and this is why, as Kwok Pui-lan and Cheryl Anderson note, we have to look at the ways in which gender intersects with socially constructed categories such as race and class when we examine the ways in which female characters are portrayed in the texts we are interpreting.[64] Responding to this concern, I have made a key aspect of my interpretation the marginalized social position and class of the two women in 1 Kings 3:16–28, the only narrative in the story of Solomon in 1 Kings 1–11 in which we see the king interacting with figures who are not members of the upper strata of society, a narrative that emphasizes that he has no concern whether or not they receive justice, just as other passages in his story, ones that refer to his

62. See Kari Latvus, "The Empire of Solomon: An Analysis of Imperial Rhetoric in 1 Kings 3–11," in *Postcolonial Commentary and the Old Testament*, ed. Hemchard Gossai (London: T&T Clark, 2019), 171–72.
63. For example, Brenner, *Israelite Woman*, 133; Fuchs, *Feminist Theory*, 41–42; and Adelman, *Female Ruse*, 1.
64. Anderson, *Women, Ideology, and Violence*, 7–9; and Kwok, *Postcolonial Imagination*, 81–85.

use of forced labor from and taxation of Israel, demonstrate that he has no interest in promoting the welfare of his own people.

One reason why we can understand the women at the center of 3:16–28 as marginalized characters is because their profession as prostitutes places them on the social margins of Israel, which is how sex workers in contemporary societies are often understood, people viewed as sexual deviants who have rejected social norms that regulate women's sexuality through male control. With the help of the sex workers who read with Ipsen, I was able to abandon assumptions such as these as unethical, and in doing so I also found it useful to look to the emancipatory concerns of queer readers, who have outlined ways in which interpreters have seen deviations from what they consider to be sexual norms in biblical texts as a way of referring to general immorality.[65] The queer troubles what is normal and respectable, writes Joseph Marchal,[66] allowing us to call into question assumptions that proceed from the normal and respectable center of society, and in my interpretation of 3:16–28, it is in fact a woman from the social and sexual margins of Israel who is able to speak ethically, while the king, who stands at the very center of society, enacts an unethical parody of justice. The reading disagrees with others that assume the sexual deviancy of prostitution should be equated with immorality and inherent deception, and it also challenges more traditional interpretations of the story that insist it is motherhood that saves the true mother of 3:16–28 from the immorality that is intrinsic to her as a sex worker, allowing her to advocate for sparing the child's life. If the other woman of the story lacks her moral fortitude, that may be because, following the observations of the sex workers who read the story with Ipsen, she is simply acting in the way she believes the normal and respectable—yet radically unjust—social center, embodied by the king, expects her to act, or because of mental illness, exacerbated by the recent death of her son. This part of the interpretation was also informed by concerns of queer and lesbian readers who critique interpretations of texts created through heteronormative assumptions, such as the belief that bearing and rearing children is the primary goal of society and is to be equated with goodness, thereby marginalizing those

65. For example, Stone, "Queering the Canaanite," 119–27; and Erin Runions, "From Disgust to Humor: Rahab's Queer Effect," in Hornsby and Stone, *Bible Trouble*, 45.
66. Marchal, "On the Verge of an Introduction," 8–10.

with no interest in sexual reproduction.[67] This concern dovetails with one long raised by feminist readers, who note how biblical texts generally tend to validate women who play their expected subservient roles in patriarchal society, ones that particularly value them as mothers who produce male heirs for their husbands but are otherwise suspicious of female action and initiative.[68]

And simply because a particular interpretation of a text violates no ethical beliefs one has—at least as far as one can tell—does not mean that marginalized readers will always find it useful for their particular context. In regard to the meaningful text of 1 Kings 3:16–28 that I have just created, they might note, for example, that if God has no words of praise for Solomon after the verdict the king renders in the story, God also neither criticizes nor punishes him for what he has done. God certainly can criticize and punish the king, however, as the final story of Solomon's narrative in 1 Kings 11 demonstrates, and so it can appear suspicious that we see no such divine reaction to the injustice of Solomon's treatment of his marginalized subjects in 3:16–28. In 11:1–3, the narrator says that Solomon had hundreds of wives, and in his old age, "his wives inclined his heart after other gods, and his heart was not perfect with the Lord his God like the heart of David, his father" (11:4), for Solomon worshipped those other gods and built places of sacrifice for them that his wives could use (11:5–8), with the result that Solomon's God became angry and announced a punishment of the king (11:9–13). When we read 3:16–28 in light of 11:1–13, in other words, the divine silence in reaction to the story of Solomon's judgment of the two women can seem less like God's disapproval of Solomon's tendency to violence and failure to do justice and care for his marginalized subjects and more like a silent endorsement of the king's abuse of the legal system. God certainly can speak and act against Solomon when the king fails in his duty to worship Israel's God alone but says nothing as Solomon repetitively violates the law of Deuteronomy 17:14–20, which, as I mentioned in the first section of this chapter, limits the power and wealth of the king. When Solomon fails to do justice in 3:16–28, it can seem as if God had no more concern for Solomon's failure to treat his marginalized subjects ethically than the king himself does.

67. For example, Guest, *When Deborah Met Jael*, 137–42; and Moore, Brintall, and Marchal, "Queer Disorientations," 8–18.
68. For example, Fuchs, *Feminist Theory*, 38–39.

This sort of reading of 3:16–28 understands the passage not only as a critique of Solomon's abuse of power but also as an acceptance of that abuse by both God and the narrator. It is a suspicious reading, insofar as it understands this particular creation of meaning to be unethical, and it is one that portrays God as being as unethical as Solomon. It is a reading that simply is not, as Nancy Bowen puts it, a "safe space for women,"[69] or for the marginalized in general, and so a reading that emphasizes to readers that the text is dangerous. This interpretation of 3:16–28 leaves us in the same position as Wilda Gafney in her reading of the story of Samson's Philistine wife in Judges 14, to which chapter 6 refers, and which concludes that the narrative calls God's character into question.[70] It is like Monica Melanchthon's interpretation of 2 Samuel 21, in which she refers to the co-option of God in a story in which God appears to sanction the slaughter of innocent victims,[71] or like Elsa Tamez's conclusion that it is not possible to read 1 Timothy in anything but an antiliberative manner,[72] or like Renita Weems's analysis of the prophetic marriage metaphor that depicts God as an abusive spouse while demonizing and marginalizing women.[73] As Weems points out, however, if we cannot accept the abusive husband as an appropriate metaphor for God—and we should not—we can at least note that the biblical writers have left us with many metaphors to describe the divine, and we can use ones that are more ethically responsible.[74]

We will not always be able to conclude that a given biblical passage portrays God as acting ethically: the God of Joshua leads and condones the genocide of the Canaanites; the God of Revelation condemns humanity to a long series of tortures and vast slaughter. For many readers of faith, this conflict between their ethical principles and their readings of biblical texts will prove vexing, and while different religious communities will deal with this problem in different ways, it is hardly something that students and scholars reading for liberation can ignore.

69. Bowen, "Women, Violence, and the Bible," 187.
70. Wilda Gafney, "A Womanist Midrash of Delilah: Don't Hate the Playa Hate the Game," in *Womanist Interpretations of the Bible: Expanding the Discourse*, ed. Gay L. Byron and Vanessa Lovelace, SemeiaSt 85 (Atlanta: Society of Biblical Literature, 2016), 57–61.
71. Monica Jyotsna Melanchthon, "Reading Rizpah across Borders, Cultures, Belongings . . . to India and Back," in *Bible, Borders, Belonging(s): Engaging Readings from Oceania*, ed. Jione Havea, David J. Neville, and Elaine M. Wainwright, SemeiaSt 75 (Atlanta: Society of Biblical Literature, 2014), 182–83.
72. Elsa Tamez, "1 Timothy: What a Problem!," trans. Gloria K. Kinsler, in Segovia, *Toward a New Heaven and a New Earth*, 141–56.
73. Weems, *Battered Love*, 84–85.
74. Weems, 118–19.

One solution to the problem is the one Weems proposes, comparing ethically problematic passages we read with suspicion to ones that better suit our beliefs. So if, when reading 1 Kings 3:16–28 in light of 11:1–13, it appears that God cares far more about proper worship than society's care for the marginalized, we can then read Amos 5, which provides precisely the opposite message, or we can read laws in Torah in which God insists that Israel care for the poor.[75] How any particular community trying to fight oppression and dehumanization, or trying to stand in solidarity with those that are, aims to deal with ethically dangerous passages will be up to them, although academic interpreters can suggest solutions. Yet before more privileged readers could ever be in a position to do this, we must recognize the importance of looking to the concerns that marginalized readers have with the texts in the first place, which is what I have done in this and the previous chapter. We cannot violate the ethical principles of interpretation that we have, such as those I have mentioned in this section of the chapter, ones whose application to hermeneutical issues was informed by a dialogue with minoritized colleagues. We cannot create readings that disagree with beliefs that we have about good scholarship, but prioritizing liberative ethic rather than historical method does not prevent us from producing work that is scholarly, and it does not prevent us from using aspects of historical criticism. Making a commitment to emancipation the primary criterion of good biblical scholarship does not exclude more socio-economically privileged participants in the field nor the interpretive techniques in which we have developed expertise, it just asks that we be guided in the use of those techniques and in our work in general by the field's marginalized members who read for liberation.

75. Not all of these passages, however, are as straightforward in their promotion of social justice as they might at first seem. See, for example, Harold V. Bennett, "Triennial Tithes and the Underdog: A Revisionist Reading of Deuteronomy 14:22–29 and 26:12–15," in Bailey, *Yet with a Steady Beat*, 7–18; and Anderson, *Ancient Laws and Contemporary Controversies*, 30–54.

9

The Liberation and Relevance of Biblical Studies

When habit fails us, writes Richard Rorty, we start to ask ethical questions,[1] because we find ourselves interrogating some of our assumptions that underlie our views of things, such as how to interpret texts, and how we should decide whether particular interpretations are good or bad. Habit has failed many of us in the mainstream of biblical studies, I have been arguing, because we have not listened to the critiques from those on the margins of the discipline in regard to the assumptions on which our scholarly habits are based. We have reason to pay attention to these arguments that privilege liberation over method, however, because we share the ethical beliefs on which they are grounded, while attempts from the mainstream of the field to find a necessary basis to prioritize the historical critical method have misconstrued the connection between text and meaning. Working by habit and doing what most of our teachers and colleagues do, many of us have not seen the discipline's ethical failings to which our peers have pointed us, but once we are aware of this conflict between liberation and method that questions what we habitually do, we will have to make ethical decisions as to what is best for our professional work and the larger discipline of biblical studies.

For some of us, the outcome of an ethical debate like this one will mean that we will do things differently and develop somewhat new habits in our research and teaching. To return to chapter 1's brief mention of the chemical revolution, for example, once alchemy was broadly understood by chemists to be fraudulent, it could no longer be considered a legitimate part of their field, and even though in the early eighteenth century, well-respected natural philosophers such as Isaac

1. Rorty, *Philosophy and Social Hope*, 73–74.

Newton pursued alchemical research, the habits of chemists slowly changed over time, so by the nineteenth century, it was simply not a habitual reflex for them to do that sort of work.[2] I have not been advocating a total abandonment of the historical method in biblical studies as chemistry abandoned alchemy, only a deprioritizing of it so that we use historical critical techniques when they are helpful to meet liberative ends. To return to my use of the thought of the pragmatist Philip Kitcher from chapter 1, if we do not use historical method to meet emancipatory goals, then we should consider such research to be a prelude to the academic study of the Bible rather than its substance. I am happy to grant that the discipline needs historical resources—Hebrew and Greek lexicons are just the first example that might spring to mind in this regard—and we have no reason to believe that research techniques normally classified as parts of the historical critical method are not useful. Given, however, that the modern field has devoted its energies to producing such resources for more than two centuries, it is a serious question as to how much more history for history's sake biblical studies needs, or at least it is if we take our ethical commitments seriously. Pragmatist philosophy focuses on "actual crises of life," wrote John Dewey,[3] and, says Alan Malachowski, it "starts from an abiding premise of 'potential difference.' If a view makes no such difference, then it can be of no great importance."[4] Minoritized biblical scholars have assumed the same about our discipline and provided us with a wealth of ways we can conduct our research to make a practical difference when confronted with actual crises of life. These arguments and examples are more than worthy of the attention of their more socioeconomically privileged peers, and if we have not already done so, we should understand their liberative work and concerns to be the *sine qua non* of the academic study of the Bible.

I have made this argument by focusing on how individual scholars can change what they do, and if change can come to individuals, it can also come to academic disciplines. Change at such a level is generally very slow, however, and for some of

2. For the slow separation of alchemy and chemistry in the eighteenth century, see Lawrence M. Principe, "The End of Alchemy? The Repudiation and Persistence of Chrysopoeia at the Académie Royale des Sciences in the Eighteenth Century," *Osiris* 29 (2014): 96–116.
3. John Dewey, *The Middle Works*, 1899–1924, ed. Jo Ann Boydston (Carbondale: Southern Illinois University Press, 1976–83), 10:43.
4. Alan Malachowski, "James's Holism: The Human Continuum," in Malachowski, *Cambridge Companion to Pragmatism*, 39. This idea can be traced back to Charles Peirce and is sometimes referred to as the pragmatist maxim; see Peirce, *Essential Peirce*, 1:132.

the members of a field, it will seem like regression rather than progress because their beliefs about the ways they have been doing things are deeply rooted in their senses of who they are, such that change accepted elsewhere in the discipline is not possible for them without abandoning a key part of their identity.[5] But a turn to a more ethical field of study also faces deeper systemic problems, ones rooted in habits that tie its practitioners and institutions to traditional ways of doing their work. Tammi Schneider provides one example that encapsulates some of these systemic failures in a story in which she recounts an incident during an interview for an academic post in biblical studies in the last decade of the twentieth century. She was asked if she would be interested in conducting research with feminist leanings, and she responded that she would but believed no one would publish it.[6] I have been arguing that those of us who believe we have an obligation to fight oppression whenever that is reasonably possible should privilege these ethical commitments in our work, but writing and teaching for liberation are not reasonably possible if such work is disregarded by gatekeepers in the field responsible for monitoring publications, hiring, promotion, and granting tenure, for when that happens, emancipatory work will result in unemployment. Other aspects of the discipline's systemic problems come into view when we examine the numbers of marginalized scholars in the field. The fact that the percentage of Society of Biblical Literature members who are women has risen from under 4 percent a half century ago to about 25 percent more recently[7] reflects a victory of sorts over systemic barriers to the participation of the minoritized in academic biblical studies, but only a very partial one. Moreover, only about 5 percent of the field in the United States is Black and only about 3 percent of Latin American descent,[8] and so more than individual scholarly choices in regard to research and teaching will have to change if we want a discipline like the sort I have been describing. In that ideal

5. Rorty makes this point when he writes that not all philosophers can be convinced to become antirepresentationalists, since when you are so grounded in other understandings of what it is that field should pursue, it may not be possible to leave that behind "without losing touch with yourself" (Rorty, *Truth and Progress*, 343–44).
6. Tammi J. Schneider, "Scholarship of Promise," in Tilford, *Women and the Society of Biblical Literature*, 129–30.
7. See Marion Ann Taylor, "Celebrating 125 Years of Women in the Society of Biblical Literature (1894–2019)," in Tilford, *Women and the Society of Biblical Literature*, 19; and "2019 SBL Membership Data," 8.
8. "2019 SBL Membership Data," 10. The question in regard to ethnicity and race on the membership data form was asked only of those who indicated they were born in the United States.

field, leadership comes from those who have the most experience in advancing emancipatory goals, because they are rooted in communities that struggle against oppression, giving them the necessary expertise both to bring scholarly resources to address those communities' specific liberative needs and to dialogue with their peers in the field as to how to be in solidarity with those groups. A field like this, however, cannot exist if it does little to actively recruit and hire those who can supply its leadership and if it discourages them from doing the ethically relevant work biblical studies needs.

To think about liberative and systemic change in biblical studies is to imagine a whole academic discipline that is somewhat different from the one that currently exists, a difference that extends beyond how individual scholars decide to do their work. A more ethically relevant field that looks to marginalized scholars for leadership will have to ensure that it has decent numbers of them to provide it. Since biblical studies needs women and members of other groups the field has traditionally minoritized to lead it, then we have a duty to recruit members of such groups as students and hire them as colleagues, because they have the kinds of experiences and backgrounds that make their voices indispensable if we expect the field to progress. We should hire the best scholars and recruit the best students we can for our institutions, but we cannot understand the word *best* in this context without considering what we want our institutions and disciplines to be, what is best for them. The field of biblical studies, I have been arguing, and thus the individual institutions of which it is composed—academic departments, seminaries, journals and their editorial boards, and so on—will be better when they prioritize and nurture marginalized voices. If we are convinced that our ethical commitments concerning liberation must take priority in research and teaching, then we have an ethical duty to honor those beliefs when we think about the composition of our faculty and student bodies, or else we will deprive the field as a whole of the people we need to provide us with guidance. We have to promote and amplify the voices that bring emancipatory needs, interests, questions, and interpretive approaches to the table. As a result, those of us with influence on, for example, editorial boards and committees charged with hiring and granting tenure must be clear as to the importance of research and teaching that has the potential to promote liberation, even when it does not conform to more traditional historical critical models of scholarship.

The field we would create, if we could realize such a vision, is one that could more fully embody the pragmatist goal of making a practical difference and so one that would be more relevant. As a relatively small field in the humanities,[9] biblical studies is, in one sense, no more or less relevant than others, as its professionals produce research that is largely consumed only by other practitioners in the same discipline. However, the Bible is understood by many millions of people to be a resource in their struggles for liberation, and so biblical studies can become much more relevant if led by scholars rooted in communities fighting oppression, those who can understand and apply academic work to such contexts when it is applicable. Such communities will, of course, be religious, or else they would not see the Bible as a resource in the first place, but one need not be religious to have an ethical commitment to stand against dehumanization, to believe that all humans should be treated equally and fairly, and to insist that such treatment cannot ignore things such as physical security, income, health care, employment, and education. Chapters 5 and 6 provide many examples of liberative work by marginalized scholars, ones that are hopefully of use in struggles against oppression, but one need not be a theist to see these as interesting and helpful academic analyses of biblical texts and contexts. A more relevant discipline that has a broader impact on the world is one based on ethical commitments to liberation, but such beliefs need not be rooted in religious ones to have a positive impact, and this means that the ethical direction I have in mind, having been persuaded of its necessity by my marginalized colleagues, is a project open to all scholars and students in the field, regardless of their religious beliefs.

Change in academia tends to proceed at a glacial pace because so many personal and institutional habits need to shift to accommodate it; as I mentioned in chapter 1, we rarely put much thought into the matter of why we do what we do as academic professionals because, like the members of every other academic discipline, we work by habit. We more socioeconomically privileged members of the field are lucky, however, that we have marginalized colleagues who are willing to enter into dialogue with us, to show us how we have failed to live up to our own ethical beliefs in the work we do, and to provide us with more ethical goals

9. For example, in 2019 the Modern Language Association had more than three times the number of members as the Society of Biblical Literature; compare the figures in Paula M. Krebs, "Report of the Executive Director," PMLA 134 (2019): 642; and in "2019 SBL Membership Data," 2.

to pursue and models that point us to the ways in which we can pursue them. We can draw upon their insights to create a more ethical culture for biblical studies and its institutions and to produce more relevant work. We can address some of it to our own privileged communities, asking them to reflect upon the ways in which they are complicit in and benefit from oppressive networks of power and how they might be overlooking their ethical commitments, and we can hope that some of our minoritized peers might see our work as useful for particular emancipatory struggles. If we are willing to acknowledge that they have the necessary experience to provide us with academic leadership that reads for liberation, even if we cannot always read just as they do, we can act with them to create a discipline in which we honor our ethical principles and create a better field, producing more relevant readings of the Bible for twenty-first-century audiences.

Bibliography

Adam, A. K. M. *Faithful Interpretation: Reading the Bible in a Postmodern World.* Minneapolis: Fortress, 2006.

Adamo, David Tuesday. "Decolonizing the Psalter in Africa." In *Postcolonial Perspectives in African Biblical Interpretations*, edited by Musa W. Dube, Andrew M. Mbuvi, and Dora Mbuwayesango, 299–315. GPBS 13. Atlanta: Society of Biblical Literature, 2012.

Adelman, Rachel E. *The Female Ruse: Women's Deception and Divine Sanction in the Hebrew Bible.* HBM 74. Sheffield, UK: Sheffield Phoenix, 2017.

Aidoo, Mark S. "'My Words Dropped upon Them Like Dew': Towards Reimaging the Identity of African Biblical Interpreters." In *The Bible, Centres and Margins: Dialogues between Postcolonial African and British Biblical Scholars*, edited by Johanna Stiebert and Musa W. Dube, 97–113. London: T&T Clark, 2018.

Albertz, Rainer. "More and Less Than a Myth: Reality and Significance of Exile for the Political, Social, and Religious History of Judah." In *By the Irrigation Canals of Babylon: Approaches to the Study of Exile*, edited by John J. Ahn and Jill Middlemas, 20–33. LHBOTS 526. New York: T&T Clark, 2012.

Althaus-Reid, Marcella María. "Searching for a Queer Sophia-Wisdom: The Post-colonial Rahab." In *Patriarchs, Prophets and Other Villains*, edited by Lisa Isherwood, 128–140. GTS. London: Equinox, 2007.

Anderson, Cheryl B. *Ancient Laws and Contemporary Controversies: The Need for Inclusive Biblical Interpretation.* Oxford: Oxford University Press, 2009.

———. "Biblical Interpretation as Violence: Genesis 19 and Judges 19 in the Context of HIV and AIDS." In La Violencia *and the Hebrew Bible: The Politics and Histories of Biblical Hermeneutics on the American Continent*, edited by Susanne Scholz and Pablo R. Andiñach, 121–136. SemeiaSt 82. Atlanta: Society of Biblical Literature, 2016.

———. "Reflections in an Interethnic/Racial Era on Interethnic/Racial Marriage in Ezra." In *They Were All Together in One Place? Toward Minority Biblical Criticism*, edited by Randall C. Bailey, Tat-siong Benny Liew, and Fernando F. Segovia, 47–64. SemeiaSt 57. Atlanta: Society of Biblical Literature, 2009.

———. *Women, Ideology, and Violence: Critical Theory and the Construction of Gender in the Book of the Covenant and the Deuteronomic Law.* London: T&T Clark, 2005.

Angel, Hayyim. "Cut the Baby in Half: Understanding Solomon's Divinely-Inspired Wisdom." *JBQ* 39 (2011): 189–194.

Anum, Eric. "Effective Scholarly Readings of the Bible in Africa." In *Interpreting the New Testament in Africa*, edited by Mary N. Getui, Tinyiko Maluleke, and Justin Ukpong, 104–122. ACS. Nairobi: Acton, 2001.

———. "Unresolved Tension and the Way Forward." In *Through the Eyes of Another: Intercultural Reading of the Bible*, edited by Hans de Wit, Louis Jonker, Marleen Kool, and Daniel S. Schipani, 176–195. Elkhart, IN: Institute of Mennonite Studies, 2004.

Avioz, Michael. "The Characterization of Solomon in Solomon's Prayer (1 Kings 8)." *BN* 126 (2005): 19–28.

Bach, Alice. "Signs of the Flesh: Observations on Characterization in the Bible." In *Women in the Hebrew Bible: A Reader*, edited by Alice Bach, 351–365. New York: Routledge, 1999.

———. *Women, Seduction, and Betrayal in Biblical Narrative*. Cambridge: Cambridge University Press, 1997.

Baden, Joel. *The Historical David: The Real Life of an Invented Hero*. New York: HarperCollins, 2013.

Bailey, Randall C. "My Journey into Afrocentric Biblical Interpretation." In *The Africana Bible: Reading Israel's Scriptures from Africa and the African Diaspora*, edited by Randall C. Bailey, 20. Minneapolis: Fortress, 2010.

Barr, James. *History and Ideology in the Old Testament: Biblical Studies at the End of a Millennium*. Oxford: Oxford University Press, 2000.

Barthes, Roland. "The Death of the Author." In *Image Music Text*, translated by Stephen Heath, 142–148. New York: Hill & Wang, 1977.

Barton, John. *The Nature of Biblical Criticism*. Louisville, KY: Westminster John Knox, 2007.

Batten, Don, David Catchpoole, Jonathan Sarfati, and Carl Wieland. *The Creation Answers Book*. Eight Mile Plains, Australia: Creation Ministries, 2006.

Bauks, Michaela. *Jephtas Tochter: Traditions-, religions- und rezeptionsgeschichtliche Studien zu Richter* 11,29–40. FAT 71. Tübingen, Germany: Mohr Siebeck, 2010.

Becking, Bob. *Ezra, Nehemiah, and the Construction of Early Jewish Identity*. FAT 80. Tübingen, Germany: Mohr Siebeck, 2011.

Bennett, Harold V. "Triennial Tithes and the Underdog: A Revisionist Reading of Deuteronomy 14:22–29 and 26:12–15." In *Yet with a Steady Beat: Contemporary U.S.*

Afrocentric Biblical Interpretation, edited by Randall C. Bailey, 7–18. SemeiaSt 42. Atlanta: Society of Biblical Literature, 2003.

Berlin, Isaiah. "The Pursuit of the Ideal." In *The Crooked Timber of Humanity: Chapters in the History of Ideas*, edited by Henry Hardy, 1–19. Princeton, NJ: Princeton University Press, 1990.

Bernstein, Richard J. *Beyond Objectivity and Relativism: Science, Hermeneutics, and Practice*. Philadelphia: University of Pennsylvania Press, 1983.

———. "From Hermeneutics to Praxis." In *Hermeneutics and Praxis*, edited by Robert Hollinger, 272–296. Rev. ed. Notre Dame, IN: University of Notre Dame Press, 1985.

———. *The Pragmatic Turn*. Cambridge: Polity, 2010.

Beuken, W. A. M. "No Wise King without a Wise Woman (1 Kings iii 16–28)." In *New Avenues in the Study of the Old Testament: A Collection of Old Testament Studies*, edited by A. S. van der Woude, 1–10. OTS 25. Leiden: Brill, 1989.

The Bible and Culture Collective. *The Postmodern Bible*. New Haven, CT: Yale University Press, 1995.

Bird, Phyllis A. *Missing Persons and Mistaken Identities: Women and Gender in Ancient Israel*. OBT. Minneapolis: Fortress, 1997.

Blenkinsopp, Joseph. *Ezra-Nehemiah: A Commentary*. OTL. London: SCM, 1989.

———. *Judaism, the First Phase: The Place of Ezra and Nehemiah in the Origins of Judaism*. Grand Rapids, MI: William B. Eerdmans, 2009.

———. "Old Testament Theology and the Jewish Christian Connection." JSOT 28 (1985): 3–15.

Blount, Brian K. *Cultural Interpretation: Reorienting New Testament Criticism*. Minneapolis: Fortress, 1995.

———. "The Souls of Black Folk and the Potential for Meaning." *JBL* 138 (2019): 6–21.

Bockmuehl, Markus. *Seeing the Word: Refocusing New Testament Study*. STI. Grand Rapids, MI: Baker Academic, 2006.

Bodner, Keith. *David Observed: A King in the Eyes of His Court*. HBM 5. Sheffield, UK: Sheffield Phoenix, 2005.

Boer, Roland. "1 and 2 Chronicles." In *The Queer Bible Commentary*, edited by Deryn Guest, Robert E. Goss, Mona West, and Thomas Bohache 251–257. London: SCM, 2006.

Bowen, Nancy R. "Women, Violence, and the Bible." In *Engaging the Bible in a Gendered World: An Introduction to Feminist Biblical Interpretation in Honor of Katherine*

Doob Sakenfeld, edited by Linda Day and Carolyn Pressler, 186–199. Louisville, KY: Westminster John Knox, 2006.

Brandom, Robert B. *From Empiricism to Expressivism: Brandom Reads Sellars*. Cambridge, MA: Harvard University Press, 2014.

——. *Perspectives on Pragmatism: Classical, Recent, and Contemporary*. Cambridge, MA: Harvard University Press, 2011.

Breed, Brennan. *Nomadic Text: A Theory of Biblical Reception History*. ISBL. Bloomington: Indiana University Press, 2014.

Brenner, Athalya. *The Israelite Woman: Social Role and Literary Type in Biblical Narratives*. Sheffield, UK: JSOT, 1985.

Brett, Mark G. *Decolonizing God: The Bible in the Tides of Empire*. BMW 16. Sheffield, UK: Sheffield Phoenix, 2008.

Brettler, Marc. "The Structure of 1 Kings 1–11." JSOT 49 (1991): 87–97.

Brueggemann, Walter. "Ancient Israel on Political Leadership: Between the Book Ends." *PolTheo* 8 (2007): 455–469.

Burke, Sean D. "Queering Early Church Discourse: The Ethiopian Eunuch." In *Bible Trouble: Queer Reading at the Boundaries of Biblical Scholarship*, edited by Teresa J. Hornsby and Ken Stone, 175–189. SemeiaSt 67. Atlanta: Society of Biblical Literature, 2011.

——. *Queering the Ethiopian Eunuch: Strategies of Ambiguity in Acts*. Minneapolis: Fortress, 2013.

Burt, Sean. *The Courtier and the Governor: Transformations of Genre in the Nehemiah Memoir*. JAJSup 17. Göttingen, Germany: Vandenhoeck & Ruprecht, 2014.

Byron, Gay L. "The Challenge of 'Blackness' for Rearticulating the Meaning of Global Feminist New Testament Interpretation." In *Feminist New Testament Studies: Global and Future Perspectives*, edited by Kathleen O'Brien Wicker, Althea Spencer Miller, and Musa W. Dube, 85–101. RCC. New York: Palgrave Macmillan, 2005.

Callahan, Allen Dwight. *The Talking Book: African Americans and the Bible*. New Haven, CT: Yale University Press, 2006.

Camp, Claudia V. *Wisdom and the Feminine in the Book of Proverbs*. BLS 11. Sheffield, UK: Almond Press, 1985.

——. *Wise, Strange and Holy: The Strange Woman and the Making of the Bible*. JSOTSup 320. GCT 9. Sheffield, UK: Sheffield Academic, 2000.

———. "The Wise Women of 2 Samuel: A Role Model for Women in Ancient Israel?" In *Women in the Hebrew Bible: A Reader*, edited by Alice Bach, 195–207. New York: Routledge, 1999.

Caputo, John D. *Radical Hermeneutics: Repetition, Deconstruction, and the Hermeneutic Project*. SPEP. Bloomington: Indiana University Press, 1987.

Cardoso Pereira, Nancy. "Changing Seasons: About the Bible and Other Sacred Texts in Latin America." In *Feminist Interpretation of the Bible and the Hermeneutics of Liberation*, edited by Silvia Schroer and Sophia Bietenhard, 48–58. JSOTSup 374. Sheffield, UK: Sheffield Academic, 2003.

Carr, David. *The Formation of the Hebrew Bible: A New Reconstruction*. Oxford: Oxford University Press, 2011.

Chapman, Cynthia R. *The Gendered Language of Warfare in the Israelite-Assyrian Encounter*. HSM 62. Winona Lake, IN: Eisenbrauns, 2004.

———. "Sculpted Warriors: Sexuality and the Sacred in the Depiction of Warfare in the Assyrian Palace Reliefs and in Ezekiel 23:14–17." In *The Aesthetics of Violence in the Prophets*, edited by Chris Franke and Julia M. O'Brien, 1–17. LHBOTS 517. New York: T&T Clark, 2010.

Claassens, L. Juliana M. "An Abigail Optic: Agency, Resistance, and Discernment in 1 Samuel 25." In *Feminist Frameworks and the Bible: Power, Ambiguity, and Intersectionality*, edited by L. Juliana Claassens and Carolyn J. Sharp, 21–37. LHBOTS 630. London: Bloomsbury, 2017.

———. *Claiming Her Dignity: Female Resistance in the Old Testament*. Collegeville, MN: Liturgical, 2016.

Clauss, Jan. "Understanding the Mixed Marriages of Ezra-Nehemiah in the Light of Temple-Building and the Book's Concept of Jerusalem." In *Mixed Marriages: Intermarriage and Group Identity in the Second Temple Period*, edited by Christian Frevel, 109–131. LHBOTS 547. New York: T&T Clark, 2011.

Clines, David J. A. "Dancing and Shining at Sinai: Playing the Man in Exodus 32–34." In *Men and Masculinity in the Hebrew Bible and Beyond*, edited by Ovidiu Creangă, 54–63. BMW 33. Sheffield, UK: Sheffield Phoenix, 2010.

———. *Ezra, Nehemiah, Esther*. NCBC. Grand Rapids, MI: Eerdmans, 1984.

Collins, John J. *The Bible after Babel: Historical Criticism in a Postmodern Age*. Grand Rapids, MI: William B. Eerdmans, 2005.

Comblin, José. "Los Pobres como Sujeto de la Historia." RIBLA 3 (1989): 37–48.

Cone, James H. A *Black Theology of Liberation*. Rev. ed. Maryknoll, NY: Orbis, 1986.

Cook Steike, Elisabeth. *La Mujer como Extranjera en Israel: Estudio Exegético de Esdras 9–10*. San José: Sebila, 2010.

Cooper, Valerie C. "Some Place to Cry: Jephthah's Daughter and the Double Dilemma of Black Women in America." In *Pregnant Passion: Gender, Sex, and Violence in the Bible*, edited by Cheryl A. Kirk-Duggan, 181–191. SemeiaSt 44. Atlanta: Society of Biblical Literature, 2003.

Croatto, J. Severino. *Biblical Hermeneutics: Toward a Theory of Reading as the Production of Meaning*. Translated by Robert R. Barr. Maryknoll, NY: Orbis, 1987.

——. *Exodus: A Hermeneutics of Freedom*. Translated by Salvator Attanasio. Maryknoll, NY: Orbis, 1981.

Crowder, Stephanie Buckhanon. *When Momma Speaks: The Bible and Motherhood from a Womanist Perspective*. Louisville, KY: Westminster John Knox, 2016.

Crüseman, Frank. *Torah: Theology and Social History of Old Testament Law*. Translated by Allan W. Mahnke. Minneapolis: Fortress, 1995.

Cuéllar, Gregory Lee. *Voices of Marginality: Exile and Return in Second Isaiah 40–55 and the Mexican Immigrant Experience*. AUS 7/271. New York: Peter Lang, 2008.

Dallmayr, Fred. "Hermeneutics and Inter-cultural Dialogue." In *Gadamer's Hermeneutics and the Art of Conversation*, edited by Andrzej Wierciński, 59–72. ISHP. Berlin: Lit Verlag, 2011.

Darden, Lynne St. Clair. "A Womanist-Postcolonial Reading of the Samaritan Woman at the Well and Mary Magdalene at the Tomb." In *I Found God in Me: A Womanist Biblical Hermeneutics Reader*, edited by Mitzi J. Smith, 183–202. Eugene, OR: Cascade, 2015.

Daston, Lorraine, and Peter Galison. *Objectivity*. New York: Zone, 2007.

Davidson, Donald. *Inquiries into Truth and Interpretation*. 2nd ed. Oxford: Clarendon, 2001.

——. *Truth, Language, and History: Philosophical Essays*. Vol. 5. Oxford: Oxford University Press, 2005.

Davidson, Steed Vernyl. "Gazing (at) Native Women: Rahab and Jael in Imperializing and Postcolonial Discourse." In *Postcolonialism and the Hebrew Bible: The Next Step*, edited by Roland Boer, 69–92. SemeiaSt 70. Atlanta: Society of Biblical Literature, 2013.

Day, Peggy L. "From the Child Is Born the Woman: The Story of Jephthah's Daughter." In *Gender and Difference in Ancient Israel*, edited by Peggy Day, 58–74. Minneapolis: Fortress, 1989.

Derrida, Jacques. "Différance." Translated by Alan Bass. In *A Derrida Reader: Between the Blinds*, edited by Peggy Kamuf, 61–79. New York: Columbia University Press, 1991.

——. "The Ends of Man." In *Margins of Philosophy*, translated by Alan Bass, 109–136. Chicago: University of Chicago Press, 1982.

——. "Structure, Sign and Play in the Discourse of the Human Sciences." In *Writing and Difference*, translated by Alan Bass, 351–370. London: Routledge, 2001.

Dewey, John. *The Middle Works*, 1899–1924. Edited by Jo Ann Boydston. Carbondale: Southern Illinois University Press, 1976–1983.

DiPalma, Brian. "De/Constructing Masculinity in Exodus 1–4." In *Men and Masculinity in the Hebrew Bible and Beyond*, edited by Ovidiu Creangă, 2–19. BMW 33. Sheffield, UK: Sheffield Phoenix, 2010.

Dixon, Maria. "The Exiled Native: The Paradox of the Black Scholar." In *God Loves Diversity and Justice: Progressive Scholars Speak about Faith, Politics, and the World*, edited by Susanne Scholz, 141–155. Lanham, MD: Lexington, 2013.

Dobbs-Allsopp, F. W. "Rethinking Historical Criticism." *BibInt* 7 (1999): 235–271.

Dryden, J. de Waal. *A Hermeneutic of Wisdom: Recovering the Formative Agency of Scripture*. Grand Rapids, MI: Baker Academic, 2018.

Dube, Musa W. "Border Crossing in Diasporic Academic Space." In *The Bible, Centres and Margins: Dialogues between Postcolonial African and British Biblical Scholars*, edited by Johanna Stiebert and Musa W. Dube, 7–14. London: T&T Clark, 2018.

——. "Dinah (Genesis 34) at the Contact Zone: 'Shall Our Sister Become a Whore?'" In *Feminist Frameworks and the Bible: Power, Ambiguity, and Intersectionality*, edited by L. Juliana Claassens and Carolyn J. Sharp, 39–57. LHBOTS 630. London: Bloomsbury, 2017.

——. "Introduction." In *Other Ways of Reading: African Women and the Bible*, edited by Musa W. Dube, 1–19. Atlanta: Society of Biblical Literature, 2001.

——. *Postcolonial Feminist Interpretation of the Bible*. St. Louis, MO: Chalice, 2000.

——. "Rahab Is Hanging Out a Red Ribbon: One African Woman's Perspective on the Future of New Testament Scholarship." In *Feminist New Testament Studies: Global and Future Perspectives*, edited by Kathleen O'Brien Wicker, Althea Spencer Miller, and Musa W. Dube, 177–202. RCC. New York: Palgrave Macmillan, 2005.

——. "Toward a Post-colonial Feminist Interpretation of the Bible." In *Reading the Bible as Women: Perspectives from Africa, Asia, and Latin America*, edited by Katherine Doob Sakenfeld and Sharon H. Ringe, 11–26. SemeiaSt 78. Atlanta: Society of Biblical Literature, 1997.

Eagleton, Terry. *Literary Theory: An Introduction*. Minneapolis: University of Minnesota Press, 1983.

Eddy, Matthew Daniel, Seymour H. Mauskopf, and William R. Newman. "An Introduction to *Chemical Knowledge in the Early Modern World*." Osiris 29 (2014): 1–15.

Eilberg-Schwartz, Howard. *God's Phallus and Other Problems for Men and Monotheism*. Boston: Beacon, 1994.

Eskenazi, Tamara Cohn, and Eleanore P. Judd. "Marriage to a Stranger in Ezra 9–10." In *Second Temple Studies 2: Temple Community in the Persian Period*, edited by Tamara C. Eskenazi and Kent H. Richards, 266–285. JSOTSup 175. Sheffield, UK: JSOT, 1994.

Esler, Philip F. "Ezra-Nehemiah as a Narrative of (Re-invented) Identity." *BibInt* 11 (2003): 413–426.

Exum, J. Cheryl. *Fragmented Women: Feminist (Sub)versions of Biblical Narratives*. JSOTSup 163. Sheffield, UK: JSOT, 1993.

Fanon, Frantz. *Black Skin, White Masks*. Translated by Charles Lam Markmann. New York: Grove, 1967.

——. *The Wretched of the Earth*. Translated by Constance Farrington. New York: Grove, 1963.

Fetalsana-Apura, Lily. A *Filipino Resistance Reading of Joshua* 1:1–9. IVBS 9. Atlanta: Society of Biblical Literature, 2019.

Fischer, Irmtraud. *Women Who Wrestled with God: Biblical Stories of Israel's Beginnings*. Translated by Linda M. Maloney. Collegeville, MN: Liturgical, 2005.

Fish, Stanley. *Doing What Comes Naturally: Change, Rhetoric, and the Practice of Theory in Literary and Legal Studies*. PCI. Durham, NC: Duke University Press, 1989.

——. *Is There a Text in This Class? The Authority of Interpretive Communities*. Cambridge, MA: Harvard University Press, 1980.

——. *Professional Correctness: Literary Studies and Political Change*. Oxford: Clarendon, 1995.

Foucault, Michel. "The Discourse on Language." Translated by Rupert Swyer. In *The Order of Things*, 215–237. New York: Pantheon, 1971.

——. "What Is an Author?" In *Language, Counter-Memory, Practice: Selected Texts and Interviews*, translated by Donald F. Bouchard and Sherry Simon, 113–138. Ithaca, NY: Cornell University Press, 1977.

Fox, Michael V. "The Uses of Indeterminacy." *Sem* 71 (1995): 173–192.

Fried, Lisbeth S. "Ezra's Use of Documents in the Context of Hellenistic Rules of Rhetoric." In *New Perspectives on Ezra-Nehemiah: History and Historiography, Text, Literature, and Interpretation*, edited by Isaac Kalimi, 11–26. Winona Lake, IN: Eisenbrauns, 2012.

Frisch, Amos. "The Exodus Motif in 1 Kings 1–14." JSOT 87 (2000): 3–21.

Frymer-Kensky, Tikva. *Reading the Women of the Bible*. New York: Schocken, 2002.

——. *Studies in the Bible and Feminist Criticism*. Philadelphia: Jewish Publication Society, 2006.

Fuchs, Esther. "Biblical Feminisms: Knowledge, Theory and Politics in the Study of Women in the Bible." *BibInt* 16 (2008): 205–226.

——. "A Feminist Hermeneutics of Resistance: A Jewish Response to Interpretive Hegemony." In *Feminist Interpretation of the Hebrew Bible in Retrospect*. Vol. 2, *Social Locations*, edited by Susanne Scholz, 151–187. RRBS 5, 8–9. Sheffield, UK: Sheffield Phoenix, 2013–2016.

——. *Feminist Theory and the Bible: Interrogating the Sources*. FSSTS. Lanham, MD: Lexington, 2016.

——. "The History of Women in Ancient Israel: Theory, Method, and the Book of Ruth." In *Her Master's Tools? Feminist and Postcolonial Engagements of Historical-Critical Discourse*, edited by Caroline Vander Stichele and Todd Penner, 211–231. GPBS 9. Atlanta: Society of Biblical Literature, 2005.

——. "Men in Biblical Feminist Scholarship." JFSR 19 (2003): 93–114.

——. "Reclaiming the Hebrew Bible for Women: The Neoliberal Turn in Contemporary Feminist Scholarship." JFSR 24 (2008): 45–65.

——. "Sexual Biblical Politics as an Interventionist Interrogation: The Israelite and Foreign Woman in Feminist Literary Approaches." In *Feminist Interpretation of the Hebrew Bible in Retrospect*. Vol. 3, *Methods*, edited by Susanne Scholz, 35–52. RRBS 5, 8–9. Sheffield, UK: Sheffield Academic, 2013–2016.

——. *Sexual Politics in the Biblical Narrative: Reading the Hebrew Bible as a Woman*. JSOTSup 310. Sheffield, UK: Sheffield Academic, 2000.

Gadamer, Hans-Georg. "On the Problem of Self-Understanding." In *Philosophical Hermeneutics*, translated and edited by David E. Lange, 44–58. Berkeley: University of California Press, 1976.

——. "The Problem of Historical Consciousness." Translated by Jeff L. Close. In *Interpretive Social Science: A Reader*, edited by Paul Rabinow and William M. Sullivan, 103–160. Berkeley: University of California Press, 1979.

——. "Reply to Jacques Derrida." Translated by Diane P. Michelfelder and Richard E. Palmer. In *Dialogue and Deconstruction: The Gadamer-Derrida Encounter*, edited by Diane P. Michelfelder and Richard E. Palmer, 52–54. SSCCP. Albany: State University of New York Press, 1989.

——. *Truth and Method*. 2nd ed. Translated by Joel Weisenheimer and Donald G. Marshall. New York: Continuum, 1995.

——. "What Is Truth?" Translated by Brice W. Wachterhauser. In *Hermeneutics and Truth*, edited by Brice W. Wachterhauser, 33–46. NUSPEP. Evanston, IL: Northwestern University Press, 1994.

Gafney, Wilda C. M. "A Black Feminist Approach to Biblical Studies." *Enc* 67 (2006): 391–403.

——. "A Prophet-Terrorist(a) and an Imperial Sympathizer: An Empire-Critical, Postcolonial Reading of the No'adyah/Nechemyah Conflict." *BlTh* 9 (2011): 161–176.

——. *Womanist Midrash: A Reintroduction to the Women of the Torah and the Throne*. Louisville, KY: Westminster John Knox, 2017.

——. "A Womanist Midrash of Delilah: Don't Hate the Playa Hate the Game." In *Womanist Interpretations of the Bible: Expanding the Discourse*, edited by Gay L. Byron and Vanessa Lovelace, 49–72. SemeiaSt 85. Atlanta: Society of Biblical Literature, 2016.

George, Mark K. "Postmodern Literary Criticism: The Impossibility of Method." In *Method Matters: Essays on the Interpretation of the Hebrew Bible in Honor of David L. Petersen*, edited by Joel M. LeMon and Kent Harold Richards, 459–477. RBS 56. Atlanta: Society of Biblical Literature, 2009.

González, Justo L. *Santa Biblia: The Bible through Hispanic Eyes*. Nashville, TN: Abingdon, 1996.

Gooding, D. W. "Pedantic Timetabling in 3rd Book of Reigns." VT 15 (1965): 153–165.

——. "Problems of Text and Midrash in the Third Book of Reigns." *Textus* 7 (1969): 1–29.

——. "The Septuagint's Version of Solomon's Misconduct." VT 15 (1965): 173–189.

——. "Temple Specifications: A Dispute in Logical Arrangement between the MT and the LXX." VT 17 (1967): 143–172.

Gorman, Frank H., Jr. *The Ideology of Ritual: Space, Time and Status in the Priestly Theology*. JSOTSup 91. Sheffield, UK: Sheffield Academic, 1991.

Grätz, Sebastian. "Jiftach und seine Tochter." In *Geschichte Israels und deuteronomistische Geschichtsdenken: Festschrift zum 70. Geburtstag von Winfried Thiel*, edited by Peter Mommer and Andreas Scherer, 119–134. AOAT 380. Münster, Germany: Ugarit, 2010.

Graybill, Rhiannon. "No Child Left Behind: Reading Jephthah's Daughter with *The Babylon Complex*." BCT 11/2 (2015): 36–59.

Guest, Deryn. "From Gender Reversal to Genderfuck: Reading Jael through a Lesbian Lens." In *Bible Trouble: Queer Reading at the Boundaries of Biblical Scholarship*, edited by Teresa J. Hornsby and Ken Stone, 9–43. SemeiaSt 67. Atlanta: Society of Biblical Literature, 2011.

——. "Modeling the Transgender Gaze: Performances of Masculinity in 2 Kings 9–10." In *Transgender, Intersex, and Biblical Interpretation*, edited by Teresa J. Hornsby and Deryn Guest, 45–80. SemeiaSt 83. Atlanta: Society of Biblical Literature, 2016.

——. *When Deborah Met Jael: Lesbian Biblical Hermeneutics*. London: SCM, 2005.

Gutiérrez, Gustavo. *The Power of the Poor in History*. Translated by Robert B. Barr. Maryknoll, NY: Orbis, 1983.

——. *A Theology of Liberation: History, Politics, and Salvation*. Rev. ed. Translated by Caridad Inda and John Eagleson. London: SCM, 1988.

Haddox, Susan E. "Favoured Sons and Subordinate Masculinities." In *Men and Masculinity in the Hebrew Bible and Beyond*, edited by Ovidiu Creangă, 2–19. BMW 33. Sheffield, UK: Sheffield Phoenix, 2010.

——. *Metaphor and Masculinity in Hosea*. StBL 141. New York: Peter Lang, 2011.

Harrington, Hannah K. "Holiness and Purity in Ezra-Nehemiah." In *Unity and Diversity in Ezra-Nehemiah: Redaction, Rhetoric, and Reader*, edited by Mark J. Boda and Paul L. Redditt, 98–116. HBM 17. Sheffield, UK: Sheffield Phoenix, 2008.

——. *The Purity and Sanctuary of the Body in Second Temple Judaism*. JAJSup 33. Göttingen, Germany: Vandenhoeck & Ruprecht, 2019.

Harrisville, Roy A. *Pandora's Box Opened: An Examination and Defense of Historical-Critical Method and Its Master Practitioners*. Grand Rapids, MI: Eerdmans, 2014.

Harvey, Van Austin. *The Historian and the Believer: The Morality of Historical Knowledge and Christian Belief*. Urbana: University of Illinois Press, 1996.

Havea, Jione. "Releasing the Story of Esau from the Words of Obadiah." In *The Bible and Hermeneutics of Liberation*, edited by Alejandro F. Botta and Pablo R. Andiñach, 87–104. SemeiaSt 59. Atlanta: Society of Biblical Literature, 2009.

———. "Wet Bible: Stor(y)ing Jonah with Sia Figiel." In *Sea of Readings: The Bible in the South Pacific*, edited by Jione Havea, 37–51. SemeiaSt 90. Atlanta: Society of Biblical Literature, 2018.

Hayes, Christine E. *Gentile Impurities and Jewish Identities: Intermarriage and Conversion from the Bible to the Talmud*. Oxford: Oxford University Press, 2002.

Hays, J. Daniel. "Has the Narrator Come to Praise Solomon or to Bury Him? Narrative Subtlety in 1 Kings 1–11." JSOT 28 (2003): 149–174.

Hensel, Benedikt. "Ethnic Fiction and Identity-Formation: A New Explanation for the Background of the Question of Intermarriage in Ezra-Nehemiah." In *The Bible, Qumran, and the Samaritans*, edited by Magnar Kartveit and Gary N. Knoppers, 133–148. StJud 104. StSam 10. Berlin: Walter de Gruyter, 2018.

Hens-Piazza, Gina. *Of Methods, Monarchs, and Meanings: A Sociorhetorical Approach to Exegesis*. SOTI 3. Macon, GA: Mercer University Press, 1996.

Herrnstein Smith, Barbara. *Contingencies of Value: Alternative Perspectives for Critical Theory*. Cambridge, MA: Harvard University Press, 1988.

Hesse, Mary. *Revolutions and Reconstructions in the Philosophy of Science*. HSP. Brighton: Harvester, 1980.

Hidalgo, Jacqueline M. *Revelation in Aztlán: Scriptures, Utopias, and the Chicano Movement*. BCS. New York: Palgrave Macmillan, 2016.

Hoke, James N. "Unbinding Imperial Time: Paul's Letter to the Romans." In *Sexual Disorientations: Queer Temporalities, Affects, Theologies*, edited by Kent L. Brintall, Joseph A. Marchal, and Stephen D. Moore, 68–89. TTC. New York: Fordham University Press, 2018.

Hook, Sidney. "Pragmatism and the Tragic Sense of Life." *Proceedings and Addresses of the American Philosophical Association* 33 (1959–1960): 5–26.

Howard, Thomas A. *Protestant Theology and the Making of the Modern German University*. Oxford: Oxford University Press, 2006.

Hurtado, Larry W. "New Testament Studies at the Turn of the Millennium: Questions for the Discipline." SJT 52 (1999): 158–178.

Hylen, Susan E. *Women in the New Testament World*. EBS. Oxford: Oxford University Press, 2019.

Ipsen, Avaren. *Sex Working and the Bible*. BW. London: Routledge, 2009.

——. "Solomon and the Two Prostitutes." BCT 3/1 (2007): art. 2.

Isasi-Díaz, Ada María. *Mujerista Theology: A Theology for the Twenty-First Century*. Maryknoll, NY: Orbis, 1996.

Iser, Wolfgang. *The Act of Reading: A Theory of Aesthetic Response*. London: Routledge & Kegan Paul, 1978.

Jacobs, Mignon R. "Mothering a Leader: Bathsheba's Relational and Functional Identities." In *Mother Goose, Mother Jones, Mommie Dearest: Biblical Mothers and Their Children*, edited by Cheryl A. Kirk-Duggan and Tina Pippin, 67–84. SemeiaSt 61. Atlanta: Society of Biblical Literature, 2009.

James, William. *Pragmatism: A New Name for Some Old Ways of Thinking*. London: Longmans, Green, 1910.

Janzen, David. *The Necessary King: A Postcolonial Reading of the Deuteronomistic Portrait of the Monarchy*. HBM 57. Sheffield, UK: Sheffield Phoenix, 2013.

——. "'What He Did for Me': David's Warning about Joab in 1 Kings 2.5." JSOT 39 (2015): 265–279.

——. "Why the Deuteronomist Told the Story about the Sacrifice of Jephthah's Daughter." JSOT 29 (2005): 339–357.

Japhet, Sara. *From the Rivers of Babylon to the Highlands of Judah: Collected Studies on the Restoration Period*. Winona Lake, IN: Eisenbrauns, 2006.

——. "What May Be Learned from Ezra-Nehemiah about the Composition of the Pentateuch?" In *The Formation of the Pentateuch: Bridging the Academic Cultures of Europe, Israel, and North America*, edited by Jan C. Gertz, Bernard M. Levinson, Dalit Rom-Shiloni, and Konrad Schmid, 543–560. FAT 111. Tübingen, Germany: Mohr Siebeck, 2016.

Jauss, Hans Robert. *Question and Answer: Forms of Dialogic Understanding*. Translated by Michael Hays. THL 68. Minneapolis: University of Minnesota Press, 1989.

——. *Toward an Aesthetic of Reception*. Translated by Timothy Bahti. THL 2. Minneapolis: University of Minnesota Press, 1982.

Jennings, Theodore W., Jr. *Jacob's Wound: Homoerotic Narrative in the Literature of Ancient Israel*. New York: Continuum, 2005.

Jeon, Yong Ho. "The Retroactive Re-evaluation Technique with Pharaoh's Daughter and the Nature of Solomon's Corruption in 1 Kings 1–12." *TynBul* 62 (2011): 15–40.

Jero, Christopher. "Mother-Child Narratives and the Kingdom of God: Authorial Use of Typology as an Interpretive Device in Samuel-Kings." BBR 25 (2015): 155–169.

Jesurathnam, Kondasingu. *Dalit Liberative Hermeneutics: Indian Christian Dalit Interpretation of Psalm* 22. Delhi: ISPCK, 2010.

——. *Exploring Dalit Liberative Hermeneutics in India and the World: Based on an Ancient Hebrew Prophet, Jeremiah of Anathoth*. CHR 20. New Delhi: Christian World Imprints, 2015.

Jobling, David. "'Forced Labor': Solomon's Golden Age and the Question of Literary Representation." *Sem* 54 (1992): 57–76.

Johnson, Willa M. *The Holy Seed Has Been Defiled: The Interethnic Marriage Dilemma in Ezra* 9–10. HBM 33. Sheffield, UK: Sheffield Phoenix, 2011.

Joosten, Jan. "Textual Plurality at the Margins of Biblical Texts: The Miscellanies in 3 Reigns 2:35, 46." *RevQ* 30 (2018): 293–307.

Joy, C. I. David. *Mark and Its Subalterns: A Hermeneutical Paradigm for a Postcolonial Context*. BW. London: Equinox, 2008.

Joyce, Paul. "First among Equals? The Historical-Critical Approach in the Marketplace of Methods." In *Creating the Boundaries: Essays in Biblical Interpretation in Honour of Michael D. Goulder*, edited by Stanley E. Porter, Paul Joyce, and David E. Orton, 17–27. BIS 8. Leiden: E. J. Brill, 1994.

Junior, Nyasha. *An Introduction to Womanist Biblical Interpretation*. Louisville, KY: Westminster John Knox, 2015.

Kalimi, Isaac. "Love of God and *Apologia* for a King: Solomon as the Lord's Beloved King in Biblical and Ancient Near Eastern Contexts." JANER 17 (2017): 28–63.

Kalmanofsky, Amy. *Dangerous Sisters of the Hebrew Bible*. Minneapolis: Fortress, 2014.

——. *Gender-Play in the Hebrew Bible: The Ways the Bible Challenges Gender Norms*. RIPBC. London: Routledge, 2017.

Kebaneilwe, Mmapula D. "Paddling the Bellowing Waters Away from the Margins: African Perspectives of Proverbs 31." In *The Bible, Centres and Margins: Dialogues between Postcolonial African and British Biblical Scholars*, edited by Johanna Stiebert and Musa W. Dube, 27–39. London: T&T Clark, 2018.

Kelley, Shawn. *Racializing Jesus: Race, Ideology and the Formation of Modern Biblical Scholarship*. BibLim. London: Routledge, 2002.

Kelso, Julie. "Reading Silence: The Books of Chronicles and Ezra-Nehemiah, and the Relative Absence of a Feminist Interpretive History." In *Feminist Interpretation of the Hebrew Bible in Retrospect*. Vol. 1, *Biblical Books*, edited by Susanne Scholz, 268–289. RRBS 5, 8–9. Sheffield, UK: Sheffield Phoenix, 2013–2016.

Kessler, John. "Persia's Loyal Yahwists: Power, Identity and Ethnicity in Achaemenid Yehud." In *Judah and the Judeans in the Persian Period*, edited by Oded Lipschits and Manfred Oeming, 91–121. Winona Lake, IN: Eisenbrauns, 2006.

Keulen, Percy S. F. van. *Two Versions of the Solomon Narrative: An Inquiry into the Relationship between* MT 1 *Kgs*. 2–11 *and* LXX 3 *Reg*. 2–11. VTSup 104. Leiden: Brill, 2005.

Kim, Seong Hee. "Our (Neither) Mother and (Nor) Father in Heaven: A Postcolonial Reading of the Lord's Prayer." In *Korean Feminists in Conversation with the Bible, Church and Society*, edited by Kyung Sook Lee and Kyung Mi Park, 66–80. BMW 24. Sheffield, UK: Sheffield Phoenix, 2011.

Kim, Uriah Y. *Identity and Loyalty in the David Story*: A *Postcolonial Reading*. HBM 22. Sheffield, UK: Sheffield Phoenix, 2008.

Kinukawa, Hisako. *Women and Jesus in Mark*: A *Japanese Feminist Perspective*. TBL. Maryknoll, NY: Orbis, 1994.

Kirk-Duggan, Cheryl A. "Let My People Go! Threads of Exodus in African American Narratives." In *Yet with a Steady Beat: Contemporary* U.S. *Afrocentric Biblical Interpretation*, edited by Randall C. Bailey, 123–142. SemeiaSt 42. Atlanta: Society of Biblical Literature, 2003.

——. "Slingshots, Ships, and Personal Psychosis: Murder, Sexual Intrigue, and Power in the Lives of David and Othello." In *Pregnant Passion: Gender, Sex, and Violence in the Bible*, edited by Cheryl A. Kirk-Duggan, 37–70. SemeiaSt 44. Atlanta: Society of Biblical Literature, 2003.

Kitcher, Philip. *Preludes to Pragmatism: Toward a Reconstruction of Philosophy*. Oxford: Oxford University Press, 2012.

Klein, Lillian R. *From Deborah to Esther: Sexual Politics in the Hebrew Bible*. Minneapolis: Fortress, 2003.

Knoppers, Gary N. "Prayer and Propaganda: Solomon's Dedication of the Temple and the Deuteronomist's Program." CBQ 57 (1995): 229–254.

——. "Solomon's Fall and Deuteronomy." In *The Age of Solomon: Scholarship at the Turn of the Millennium*, edited by Lowell K. Handy, 392–410. SHCANE 11. Leiden: Brill, 1997.

Koenig, Sara M. *Isn't This Bathsheba?* A *Study in Characterization*. PTMS 177. Eugene, OR: Pickwick, 2011.

Koulagna, Jean. "L'image de Salomon dans l'historiographie deutéronomiste: À propos de la place de 1 *Rois* 1–2." *RHPR* 87 (2007): 289–300.

Kraemer, David. "On the Relationship of the Books of Ezra and Nehemiah." *JSOT* 59 (1993): 73–92.

Krebs, Paula M. "Report of the Executive Director." *PMLA* 134 (2019): 642–661.

Kuhn, Thomas S. *The Structure of Scientific Revolutions*. 2nd ed. Chicago: University of Chicago Press, 1970.

Kwok Pui-lan. "The Bible, the Critic, and the Theologian." In *Discovering the Bible in the Non-biblical World*, 20–31. Maryknoll, NY: Orbis, 1995.

———. *Introducing Asian Feminist Theology*. IFT 4. Sheffield, UK: Sheffield Academic, 2000.

———. "Jesus / the Native: Biblical Studies from a Postcolonial Perspective." In *Teaching the Bible: The Discourses and Politics of Biblical Pedagogy*, edited by Fernando F. Segovia and Mary Ann Tolbert, 69–85. Maryknoll, NY: Orbis, 1998.

———. *Postcolonial Imagination and Feminist Theology*. London: SCM, 2005.

———. "Racism and Ethnocentrism in Feminist Biblical Interpretation." In *Discovering the Bible in the Non-biblical World*, 84–95. Maryknoll, NY: Orbis, 1995.

Lasine, Stuart. "The King of Desire: Indeterminacy, Audience, and the Solomon Narrative." *Sem* 71 (1995): 85–118.

———. "The Riddle of Solomon's Judgment and the Riddle of Human Nature in the Hebrew Bible." *JSOT* 45 (1989): 61–86.

Latvus, Kari. "The Empire of Solomon: An Analysis of Imperial Rhetoric in 1 Kings 3–11." In *Postcolonial Commentary and the Old Testament*, edited by Hemchard Gossai, 161–174. London: T&T Clark, 2019.

Law, David R. *The Historical-Critical Method: A Guide for the Perplexed*. London: T&T Clark, 2012.

Lee, Archie C. C. "Cross-Textual Biblical Studies in Multiscriptural Contexts." In *Transforming Graduate Biblical Education: Ethos and Discipline*, edited by Elisabeth Schüssler Fiorenza and Kent Harold Richards, 35–45. GPBS 10. Atlanta: Society of Biblical Literature, 2010.

Lee, Yeong Mee. "Motherhood as a Theological Model for Redemption in the Hebrew Bible." In *Korean Feminists in Conversation with the Bible, Church and Society*, edited by Kyung Sook Lee and Kyung Mi Park, 14–27. BMW 24. Sheffield, UK: Sheffield Phoenix, 2011.

Lefe, Mmpula. "Reading the Bible amidst the HIV and AIDS Pandemic in Botswana." In *African and European Readers of the Bible in Dialogue: In Quest of a Shared Meaning*, edited by Hans de Wit and Gerald O. West, 285–303. SRA 32. Leiden: Brill, 2008.

Legaspi, Michael C. *The Death of Scripture and the Rise of Biblical Studies*. OSHT. Oxford: Oxford University Press, 2010.

Levenson, Jon D. *The Hebrew Bible, the Old Testament, and Historical Criticism: Jews and Christians in Biblical Studies*. Louisville, KY: Westminster John Knox, 1993.

———. "Liberation Theology and the Exodus." In *Jews, Christians, and the Theology of the Hebrew Scriptures*, edited by Alice Ogden Bellis and Joel S. Kaminsky, 215–230. SBLSymS 8. Atlanta: Society of Biblical Literature, 2000.

Levi, Isaac. *Pragmatism and Inquiry: Selected Essays*. Oxford: Oxford University Press, 2008.

Levine, Steven. *Pragmatism, Objectivity, and Experience*. Cambridge: Cambridge University Press, 2019.

Lozada, Francisco, Jr. *Toward a Latino/a Biblical Interpretation*. RBS. Atlanta: Society of Biblical Literature, 2017.

Lyotard, Jean-François. *The Postmodern Condition: A Report on Knowledge*. Translated by Geoff Bennington and Brian Massumi. THL 10. Minneapolis: University of Minnesota Press, 1984.

Macwilliam, Stuart. *Queer Theory and the Prophetic Marriage Metaphor in the Hebrew Bible*. BW. Sheffield, UK: Equinox, 2011.

Ma'ilo, Mosese. "Island Prodigals: Encircling the Void in Luke 15:11–32 with Albert Wendt." In *Sea of Readings: The Bible in the South Pacific*, edited by Jione Havea, 23–36. SemeiaSt 90. Atlanta: Society of Biblical Literature, 2018.

Malachowski, Alan. "James's Holism: The Human Continuum." In *The Cambridge Companion to Pragmatism*, edited by Alan Malachowski, 36–54. Cambridge: Cambridge University Press, 2012.

———. *The New Pragmatism*. Durham, UK: Acumen, 2010.

Marbury, Herbert Robinson. *Imperial Dominion and Priestly Genius: Coercion, Accommodation, and Resistance in the Divorce Rhetoric of Ezra-Nehemiah*. Upland, CA: Sopher, 2012.

———. *Pillars of Cloud and Fire: The Politics of Exodus in African American Biblical Interpretation*. RST. New York: New York University Press, 2015.

——. "Reading Persian Dominion in Nehemiah: Multivalent Language, Co-option, Resistance, and Cultural Survival." In *Focusing Biblical Studies: The Crucial Nature of the Persian and Hellenistic Periods*, edited by Jon L. Berquist and Alice Hunt, 158–176. LHBOTS 544. New York: T&T Clark, 2012.

Marchal, Joseph A. "Bio-Necro-*Biblio*-Politics? Restaging Feminist Intersections and Queer Exceptions." *CulRel* 15 (2014): 166–176.

——. "How Soon Is (This Apocalypse) Now? Queer Velocities after a Corinthian Already and a Pauline Not Yet." In *Sexual Disorientations: Queer Temporalities, Affects, Theologies*, edited by Kent L. Brintall, Joseph A. Marchal, and Stephen D. Moore, 47–57. TTC. New York: Fordham University Press, 2018.

——. "On the Verge of an Introduction." In *Bodies on the Verge: Queering Pauline Epistles*, edited by Joseph A. Marchal, 1–61. SemeiaSt 93. Atlanta: Society of Biblical Literature, 2019.

Martin, Dale. *Pedagogy of the Bible: An Analysis and Proposal*. Louisville, KY: Westminster John Knox, 2008.

——. *Sex and the Single Savior: Gender and Sexuality in Biblical Interpretation*. Louisville, KY: Westminster John Knox, 2006.

Masenya, Madipoane (ngwana' Mphahlele). "Struggling with Poverty/Emptiness: Rereading the Naomi-Ruth Story in African-South Africa." *JTSA* 120 (2004): 46–59.

——. "Stuck between the Waiting Room and the Reconfigured Levirate Entity? Reading Ruth in Marriage-Obsessed African Contexts." In *Feminist Frameworks and the Bible: Power, Ambiguity, and Intersectionality*, edited by L. Juliana Claassens and Carolyn J. Sharp, 163–175. LHBOTS 630. London: Bloomsbury, 2017.

——. "Wisdom and Wisdom Converge: Selected Old Testament and Northern Sotho Proverbs." In *Interpreting the Old Testament in Africa: Papers from the International Symposium on Africa and the Old Testament in Nairobi, October 1999*, edited by Mary Getui, Knut Holter, and Victor Zinkuratire, 133–146. BTA 2. New York: Peter Lang, 2001.

——. "A Wooden Spoon from the Pot: She Speaks." In *Women and the Society of Biblical Literature*, edited by Nicole L. Tilford, 211–221. BSNA 29. Atlanta: Society of Biblical Literature, 2019.

Mbuwayesango, Dora Rudo. "Feminist Biblical Studies in Africa." In *Feminist Biblical Studies in the Twentieth Century: Scholarship and Movement*, edited by Elisabeth Schüssler Fiorenza, 71–85. SBLBW 9.1. Atlanta: Society of Biblical Literature, 2014.

Mbuwayesango, Dora Rudo, and Susanne Scholz. "Dialogical Beginnings: A Conversation on the Future of Feminist Biblical Studies." JFSR 25 (2009): 93–103.

McKay, Heather A. "On the Future of Feminist Biblical Criticism." In *A Feminist Companion to Reading the Bible: Approaches, Methods and Strategies*, edited by Athalya Brenner and Carole Fontaine, 61–83. Sheffield, UK: Sheffield Academic, 1997.

McKinlay, Judith E. *Reframing Her: Biblical Women in Postcolonial Focus*. BMW 1. Sheffield, UK: Sheffield Phoenix, 2004.

Meiser, Martin. "Basileion III / 3 Kingdoms / 1 Kings." In *Introduction to the Septuagint*, edited by Siegfried Kreuzer, translated by David A. Brenner and Peter Altmann, 195–203. Waco, TX: Baylor University Press, 2019.

Melanchthon, Monica Jyotsna. "Dalit Women and the Bible: Hermeneutical and Methodological Reflections." In *Hope Abundant: Third World and Indigenous Women's Theology*, edited by Kwok Pui-lan, 103–122. Maryknoll, NY: Orbis, 2010.

———. "Engaging Women's Experience in the Struggle for Justice, Dignity, and Humanity: Hebrew Bible Readings by South Asian Women." In *Feminist Interpretation of the Hebrew Bible in Retrospect*. Vol. 2, *Social Locations*, edited by Susanne Scholz, 51–69. RRBS 5, 8–9. Sheffield, UK: Sheffield Phoenix, 2013–2016.

———. "Reading Rizpah across Borders, Cultures, Belongings . . . to India and Back." In *Bible, Borders, Belonging(s): Engaging Readings from Oceania*, edited by Jione Havea, David J. Neville, and Elaine M. Wainwright, 171–190. SemeiaSt 75. Atlanta: Society of Biblical Literature, 2014.

———. "Toward Mapping Feminist Biblical Interpretations in Asia." In *Feminist Biblical Studies in the Twentieth Century: Scholarship and Movement*, edited by Elisabeth Schüssler Fiorenza, 105–119. SBLBW 9.1. Atlanta: Society of Biblical Literature, 2014.

———. "Unleashing the Power Within: The Bible and the Dalits." In *The Future of the Biblical Past: Envisioning Biblical Studies in a Global Key*, edited by Roland Boer and Fernando F. Segovia, 49–65. SemeiaSt 66. Atlanta: Society of Biblical Literature, 2012.

Mendieta, Eduardo. "The Ethics of (Not) Knowing: Take Care of Ethics and Knowledge Will Come of Its Own Accord." In *Decolonizing Epistemologies: Latina/o Theology and Philosophy*, edited by Ada María Isasi-Díaz and Eduardo Mendieta, 44–67. TTC. New York: Fordham University Press, 2012.

Mesters, Carlos. *Defenseless Flower: A New Reading of the Bible*. Translated by Francis McDonagh. Maryknoll, NY: Orbis, 1989.

Meyers, Carol. *Discovering Eve: Ancient Israelite Women in Context*. Oxford: Oxford University Press, 1988.

——. “Was Ancient Israel a Patriarchal Society?” *JBL* 133 (2014): 8–27.

Miller, Marjorie. “Pragmatism and Feminism.” In *The Cambridge Companion to Pragmatism*, edited by Alan Malachowski, 231–248. Cambridge: Cambridge University Press, 2012.

Miller, Robert D. “Solomon the Trickster.” *BibInt* 19 (2011): 496–504.

Misak, Cheryl. *Truth, Politics, Morality: Pragmatism and Deliberation*. London: Routledge, 2000.

Moffat, Donald P. *Ezra’s Social Drama: Identity Formation, Marriage and Social Conflict in Ezra 9 and 10*. LHBOTS 579. New York: Bloomsbury, 2013.

Monroe, Lauren A. S. “Disembodied Women: Sacrificial Language and the Deaths of Bat-Jephthah, Cozbi, and the Bethlehemite Concubine.” *CBQ* 75 (2013): 32–52.

Moore, Stephen D. “A Modest Manifesto for New Testament Literary Criticism: How to Interface with a Literary Studies Field That Is Post-literary, Post-theoretical, and Post-methodological.” *BibInt* 15 (2007): 1–25.

Moore, Stephen D., Kent L. Brintall, and Joseph A. Marchal. “Queer Disorientations: Four Turns and a Twist.” In *Sexual Disorientations: Queer Temporalities, Affects, Theologies*, edited by Kent L. Brintall, Joseph A. Marchal, and Stephen D. Moore, 1–44. TTC. New York: Fordham University Press, 2018.

Myers, William H. “The Hermeneutical Dilemma of the African American Biblical Student.” In *Stony the Road We Trod: African American Biblical Interpretation*, edited by Cain Hope Felder, 40–56. Minneapolis: Fortress, 1991.

Nadar, Sarojini. “Beyond the ‘Ordinary Reader’ and the ‘Invisible Intellectual’: Pushing the Boundaries of Contextual Bible Study Discourses.” In *The Future of the Biblical Past: Envisioning Biblical Studies in a Global Key*, edited by Roland Boer and Fernando F. Segovia, 13–27. SemeiaSt 66. Atlanta: Society of Biblical Literature, 2012.

——. “‘Hermeneutics of Transformation?’ A Critical Exploration of the Model of Social Engagement between Biblical Scholars and Faith Communities.” In *Postcolonial Perspectives in African Biblical Interpretations*, edited by Musa W. Dube, Andrew M. Mbuvi, and Dora Mbuwayesango, 389–405. GPBS 13. Atlanta: Society of Biblical Literature, 2012.

——. “A South African Indian Womanist Reading of the Character of Ruth.” In *Other Ways of Reading: African Women and the Bible*, edited by Musa W. Dube, 159–175. Atlanta: Society of Biblical Literature, 2001.

Nam, Roger S. "Half Speak Ashdodite and None Can Speak Judean: Code-Switching in Ezra-Nehemiah as an Identity Marker for Repatriate Judeans and Koreans." In *Landscapes of Korean and Korean American Biblical Interpretation*, edited by John Ahn, 119–131. IVBS 10. Atlanta: Society of Biblical Literature, 2019.

Nasambu-Mulongo, Elivered. "*Bosadi*: Madipoane (Ngwana' Mphahlele) Masenya's Contribution to African Women's Biblical Hermeneutics." In *Postcolonial Perspectives in African Biblical Interpretations*, edited by Musa W. Dube, Andrew M. Mbuvi, and Dora Mbuwayesango, 43–61. GPBS 13. Atlanta: Society of Biblical Literature, 2012.

National Coalition for the Homeless. "LGBTQ Homelessness." Accessed March 25, 2021. https://tinyurl.com/3pbs2tes.

Nelavala, Surekha. "Patriarchy, a Threat to Human Bonding: Reading the Story of Ruth in Light of Marriage and Family Structures in India." In *Reading Ruth in Asia*, edited by Jione Havea and Peter H. W. Lau, 89–97. IVBS 7. Atlanta: Society of Biblical Literature, 2015.

Nzimande, Makhosazana K. "Being 'Apart' and 'Together' at the Same Time? A Response to Hans de Wit." In *African and European Readers of the Bible in Dialogue: In Quest of a Shared Meaning*, edited by Hans de Wit and Gerald O. West, 31–35. SRA 32. Leiden: Brill, 2008.

———. "*Imbokodo* Explorations of the Prevalence of Historical Memory and Identity Contestations in the Expulsion of the *Nāšîm Nokriyyōt* in Ezra 9–10." In *Texts, Contexts and Readings in Postexilic Literature: Explorations into Historiography and Identity in Hebrew Bible and Related Texts*, edited by Louis Jonker, 269–294. FAT 2/53. Tübingen, Germany: Mohr Siebeck, 2011.

———. "Reconfiguring Jezebel: A Postcolonial *Imbokodo* Reading of the Story of Naboth's Vineyard." In *African and European Readers of the Bible in Dialogue: In Quest of a Shared Meaning*, edited by Hans de Wit and Gerald O. West, 223–258. SRA 32. Leiden: Brill, 2008.

Oduyoye, Mercy Amba. "Biblical Interpretation and the Social Location of the Interpreter: African Women's Reading of the Bible." In *Reading from This Place: Social Location and Biblical Interpretation in Global Perspective*, edited by Fernando F. Segovia and Mary Ann Tolbert, 33–51. Vol. 2 of *Reading from This Place*. Minneapolis: Fortress, 1995.

Okure, Teresa. "Reading from This Place: Some Problems and Prospects." In *Social Location and Biblical Interpretation in Global Perspective*, edited by Fernando F.

Segovia and Mary Ann Tolbert, 52–66. Vol. 2 of *Reading from This Place*. Minneapolis: Fortress, 1995.

Olley, John W. "Pharaoh's Daughter, Solomon's Palace, and the Temple: Another Look at the Structure of 1 Kings 1–11." JSOT 27 (2003): 355–369.

Pakkala, Juha. *Ezra the Scribe: The Development of Ezra 7–10 and Nehemia 8*. BZAW 347. Berlin: Walter de Gruyter, 2004.

Pardes, Ilana. *Countertraditions in the Bible: A Feminist Approach*. Cambridge, MA: Harvard University Press, 1992.

Parker, K. I. "Solomon as Philosopher King? The Nexus of Law and Wisdom in 1 Kings 1–11." *JSOT* 53 (1992): 75–91.

Pasto, James. "When the End Is the Beginning? Or When the Biblical Past Is the Political Present: Some Thoughts on Ancient Israel, 'Post-exilic Judaism,' and the Politics of Biblical Scholarship." SJOT 12 (1998): 157–202.

Patte, Daniel. "Acknowledging the Contextual Character of Male European-American Critical Exegesis: An Androcritical Perspective." In *Social Location and Biblical Interpretation in the United States*, edited by Fernando F. Segovia and Mary Ann Tolbert, 35–55. Vol. 1 of *Reading from This Place*. Minneapolis: Fortress, 1995.

——. *Ethics of Biblical Interpretation: A Reevaluation*. Louisville, KY: Westminster John Knox, 1995.

Peirce, Charles S. *The Essential Peirce: Selected Philosophical Writings*. Edited by Nathan Houser and Christian Kloesel. Bloomington: Indiana University Press, 1992–1998.

Perdue, Leo G. *Reconstructing Old Testament Theology: After the Collapse of History*. OBT. Minneapolis: Fortress, 2005.

Petrella, Ivan. "Without the Bible: A New Liberation Theology." In *Colonialism and the Bible: Contemporary Reflections from the Global South*, edited by Tat-siong Benny Liew and Fernando F. Segovia, 251–270. PDSRT. Lanham, MD: Lexington, 2016.

Pixley, George V. *On Exodus: A Liberation Perspective*. Translated by Robert R. Barr. Maryknoll, NY: Orbis, 1987.

Plaatjie, Gloria Kehwile. "Toward a Post-apartheid Black Feminist Reading of the Bible: A Case of Luke 2:36–38." In *Other Ways of Reading: African Women and the Bible*, edited by Musa W. Dube, 114–142. GPBS 2. Atlanta: Society of Biblical Literature, 2001.

Polak, Frank H. "The Septuagint's Account of Solomon's Reign: Revision and Ancient Recension." In X *Congress of the International Organization for Septuagint and*

Cognate Studies, Oslo, 1998, edited by Bernard A. Taylor, 139–164. SCSS 51. Atlanta: Society of Biblical Literature, 2001.

Potok, Mark. "Anti-gay Hate Crimes: Doing the Math." SPL Center. Accessed March 25, 2021. https://tinyurl.com/ybpyj86w.

Power, Bruce A. "'All the King's Horses . . .': Narrative Subversion in the Story of Solomon's Golden Age." In *From Babel to Babylon: Essays on Biblical History and Literature in Honour of Brian Peckham*, edited by Joyce Rilett Wood, John E. Harvey, and Mark Leuchter, 111–123. New York: T&T Clark, 2006.

Powery, Emerson B., and Rodney S. Sadler Jr. *The Genesis of Liberation: Biblical Interpretation in the Antebellum Narratives of the Enslaved*. Louisville, KY: Westminster John Knox, 2016.

Principe, Lawrence M. "The End of Alchemy? The Repudiation and Persistence of Chrysopoeia at the Académie Royale des Sciences in the Eighteenth Century." *Osiris* 29 (2014): 96–116.

Provan, Iain W. "On 'Seeing' the Trees while Missing the Forest: The Wisdom of Characters and Readers in 2 Samuel and 1 Kings." In *In Search of True Wisdom: Essays in Old Testament Interpretation in Honour of Ronald E. Clements*, edited by Edward Ball, 153–173. JSOTSup 300. Sheffield, UK: Sheffield Academic, 1999.

———. "Why Barzillai of Gilead (1 Kings 2:7)? Narrative Art and the Hermeneutics of Suspicion in 1 Kings 1–2." *TynBul* 46 (1995): 103–116.

Punt, Jeremy. "Queer Theory, Postcolonial Theory, and Biblical Interpretation: A Preliminary Exploration of Some Intersections." In *Bible Trouble: Queer Reading at the Boundaries of Biblical Scholarship*, edited by Teresa J. Hornsby and Ken Stone, 321–341. SemeiaSt 67. Atlanta: Society of Biblical Literature, 2011.

Putnam, Hilary. "What Makes Pragmatism So Different?" In *Pragmatism as a Way of Life: The Lasting Legacy of William James and John Dewey*, edited by David Macarthur, 36–45. Cambridge, MA: Harvard University Press, 2017.

Quine, Willard Van Orman. *From a Logical Point of View: Nine Logico-Philosophical Essays*. 2nd ed. Cambridge, MA: Harvard University Press, 1980.

Ravela, Jeeva Kumar. *Struggle for Land Rights in 1 Kings 21: A Dalit Hermeneutic Perspective*. Delhi: ISPCK, 2012.

Rawls, John. *Political Liberalism*. Rev. ed. New York: Columbia University Press, 1996.

Reinhartz, Adele. "Feminist Criticism and Biblical Studies on the Verge of the Twenty-First Century." In *A Feminist Companion to Reading the Bible: Approaches, Methods and Strategies*, edited by Athalya Brenner and Carole Fontaine, 30–38. Sheffield, UK: Sheffield Academic, 1997.

Ringe, Sharon H. "Asian Readings of the Bible: A North American Feminist Response." *BibInt* 2 (1994): 374–376.

Roberts, J. J. M. "Historical-Critical Method, Theology, and Contemporary Exegesis." In *Biblical Theology: Problems and Perspectives in Honor of J. Christiaan Becker*, edited by Steven J. Kraftchick, Charles D. Myers Jr., and Ben C. Ollenberger, 131–141. Nashville, TN: Abingdon, 1995.

Rockmore, Tom. "Gadamer's Hermeneutics and the Overcoming of Epistemology." In *The Specter of Relativism: Truth, Dialogue, and* Phronesis *in Philosophical Hermeneutics*, edited by Lawrence K. Schmidt, 56–71. NUSPEP. Evanston, IL: Northwestern University Press, 1995.

Römer, Thomas. *The So-Called Deuteronomistic History: A Sociological, Historical and Literary Introduction*. London: T&T Clark, 2007.

——. "Why Would the Deuteronomists Tell about the Sacrifice of Jephthah's Daughter?" JSOT 23 (1998): 27–38.

Rorty, Richard. *Consequences of Pragmatism* (Essays: 1972–1980). Minneapolis: University of Minnesota Press, 1982.

——. *Contingency, Irony, and Solidarity*. Cambridge: Cambridge University Press, 1989.

——. *Essays on Heidegger and Others: Philosophical Papers*. Vol. 2. Cambridge: Cambridge University Press, 1991.

——. *Objectivity, Relativism, and Truth: Philosophical Papers*. Vol. 1. Cambridge: Cambridge University Press, 1991.

——. *Philosophy and Social Hope*. London: Penguin, 1999.

——. *Philosophy and the Mirror of Nature*. Princeton, NJ: Princeton University Press, 1980.

——. *Philosophy as Cultural Politics: Philosophical Papers*. Vol. 4. Cambridge: Cambridge University Press, 2007.

——. *Truth and Progress: Philosophical Papers*. Vol. 3. Cambridge: Cambridge University Press, 1998.

Rosenberg, Gil. *Ancestral Queerness: The Normal and the Deviant in the Abraham and Sarah Narratives*. HBM 80. Sheffield. UK: Sheffield Phoenix, 2019.

Rowlett, Lori. "Violent Femmes and S/M: Queering Samson and Delilah." In *Queer Commentary and the Hebrew Bible*, edited by Ken Stone, 106–115. JSOTSup 334. Sheffield, UK: Sheffield Academic, 2001.

Ruiz, Jean-Pierre. *Readings from the Edges: The Bible and People on the Move*. SLC. Maryknoll, NY: Orbis, 2011.

Runions, Erin. "From Disgust to Humor: Rahab's Queer Effect." In *Bible Trouble: Queer Reading at the Boundaries of Biblical Scholarship*, edited by Teresa J. Hornsby and Ken Stone, 45–74. SemeiaSt 67. Atlanta: Society of Biblical Literature, 2011.

Russaw, Kimberly D. *Daughters in the Hebrew Bible*. Lanham, MD: Lexington, 2018.

Said, Edward. *The World, the Text, and the Critic*. Cambridge, MA: Harvard University Press, 1983.

Samartha, S. J. "Religion, Language and Reality: Towards a Relational Hermeneutics." *BibInt* 2 (1994): 340–362.

Sandoval, Timothy J. "How Did You Get to Be a Latino Biblical Scholar? Scholarly Identity and Biblical Scholarship." In *Latino/a Biblical Hermeneutics: Problematics, Objectives, Strategies*, edited by Francisco Lozada Jr. and Fernando F. Segovia, 263–295. SemeiaSt 68. Atlanta: Society of Biblical Literature, 2014.

Sawyer, Deborah F. *God, Gender and the Bible*. BibLim. London: Routledge, 2002.

Schearing, Linda S. "A Wealth of Women: Looking behind, within, and beyond Solomon's Story." In *The Age of Solomon: Scholarship at the Turn of the Millennium*, edited by Lowell K. Handy, 428–456. SHCANE 11. Leiden: Brill, 1997.

Schmidt, Uta. *Zentrale Randfiguren: Strukturen der Darstellung von Frauen in den Erzählungen der Königebücher*. Gütersloh, Germany: Chr. Kaiser, 2003.

Schneider, Tammi J. "Scholarship of Promise." In *Women and the Society of Biblical Literature*, edited by Nicole L. Tilford, 129–134. BSNA 29. Atlanta: Society of Biblical Literature, 2019.

Scholz, Susanne. *The Bible as Political Artifact: On the Feminist Study of the Hebrew Bible*. Minneapolis: Fortress, 2017.

———. "How to Read the Bible in the Belly of the Beast: About the Politics of Biblical Hermeneutics within the United States." In La Violencia *and the Hebrew Bible: The Politics and Histories of Biblical Hermeneutics on the American Continent*, edited by Susanne Scholz and Pablo R. Andiñach, 137–161. SemeiaSt 82. Atlanta: Society of Biblical Literature, 2016.

Schroer, Silvia. "'We Will Know Each Other by Our Fruits': Feminist Exegesis and the Hermeneutics of Liberation." In *Feminist Interpretation of the Bible and the Hermeneutics of Liberation*, edited by Silvia Schroer and Sophia Bietenhard, 1–17. JSOTSup 374. Sheffield, UK: Sheffield Academic, 2003.

Schüssler Fiorenza, Elisabeth. *Bread Not Stone: The Challenge of Feminist Biblical Interpretation*. Boston: Beacon, 1995.

——. *Democratizing Biblical Studies: Toward an Emancipatory Educational Space*. Louisville, KY: Westminster John Knox, 2009.

——. *In Memory of Her: A Feminist Theological Reconstruction of Christian Origins*. 2nd ed. London: SCM, 1994.

——. *The Power of the Word: Scripture and the Rhetoric of Empire*. Minneapolis: Fortress, 2007.

——. *Rhetoric and Ethic: The Politics of Biblical Studies*. Minneapolis: Fortress, 1999.

Segovia, Fernando F. "'And They Began to Speak in Other Tongues': Competing Modes of Discourse in Contemporary Biblical Criticism." In *Social Location and Biblical Interpretation in the United States*, edited by Fernando F. Segovia and Mary Ann Tolbert, 1–32. Vol. 1 of *Reading from This Place*. Minneapolis: Fortress, 1995.

——. "Cultural Criticism: Expanding the Scope of Biblical Criticism." In *The Future of the Biblical Past: Envisioning Biblical Studies in a Global Key*, edited by Roland Boer and Fernando F. Segovia, 307–336. SemeiaSt 66. Atlanta: Society of Biblical Literature, 2012.

——. "Toward a Hermeneutics of the Diaspora: A Hermeneutics of Otherness and Engagement." In *Social Location and Biblical Interpretation in the United States*, edited by Fernando F. Segovia and Mary Ann Tolbert, 57–73. Vol. 1 of *Reading from This Place*. Minneapolis: Fortress, 1995.

Sellars, Wilfrid. *Empiricism and the Philosophy of Mind*. Cambridge, MA: Harvard University Press, 1997.

Sheehan, Jonathan. *The Enlightenment Bible: Translation, Scholarship, Culture*. Princeton, NJ: Princeton University Press, 2005.

Sherwood, Yvonne. *The Prostitute and the Prophet: Hosea's Marriage in Literary-Theoretical Perspective*. JSOTSup 212. GCT 2. Sheffield, UK: Sheffield Academic, 1996.

Shustermann, Richard. "The Gadamer-Derrida Encounter: A Pragmatist Perspective." In *Dialogue and Deconstruction: The Gadamer-Derrida Encounter*, edited by Diane P. Michelfelder and Richard E. Palmer, 215–221. SSCCP. Albany: State University of New York Press, 1989.

Siebert, Eric A. *Subversive Scribes and the Solomonic Narrative: A Rereading of 1 Kings 1–11*. LHBOTS 436. New York: T&T Clark, 2006.

Simopoulos, Nicole M. "Who Was Hagar? Mistress, Divorcee, Exile, or Exploited Worker: An Analysis of Contemporary Grassroots Readings of Genesis 16 by Caucasian, Latina, and Black South African Women." In *Reading Other-Wise: Socially Engaged Biblical Scholars Reading with Their Local Communities*, edited by Gerald O. West, 63–72. SemeiaSt 62. Atlanta: Society of Biblical Literature, 2007.

Smith, Abraham. "Taking *Spaces* Seriously: The Politics of Space and the Future of Western Biblical Studies." In *Transforming Graduate Biblical Education: Ethos and Discipline*, edited by Elisabeth Schüssler Fiorenza and Kent Harold Richards, 59–92. GPBS 10. Atlanta: Society of Biblical Literature, 2010.

Smith, Andrea. "Dismantling the Master's House with the Master's Tools: Native Feminist Liberation Theologies." In *Hope Abundant: Third World and Indigenous Women's Theology*, edited by Kwok Pui-lan, 74–85. Maryknoll, NY: Orbis, 2010.

Smith, Mitzi J. "*Give Me Jesus*: Salvation History in the Spirituals." In *Afrocentric Interpretations of Jesus and the Gospel Tradition: Things Black Scholars See That White Scholars Overlook*, edited by Thomas Bowie Slater, 57–88. Lewiston, NY: Edwin Mellen, 2015.

———. *Insights from African American Interpretation*. Minneapolis: Fortress, 2017.

———. "'This Little Light of Mine': The Womanist Biblical Scholar as Prophetess, Iconoclast, and Activist." In *I Found God in Me: A Womanist Biblical Hermeneutics Reader*, edited by Mitzi J. Smith, 109–127. Eugene, OR: Cascade, 2015.

———. *Womanist Sass and Talk Back: Social (In)Justice, Intersectionality, and Biblical Interpretation*. Eugene, OR: Cascade, 2018.

Smith, Shannel T. *The Woman Babylon and the Marks of Empire: Reading Revelation with a Postcolonial Womanist Hermeneutics of Ambiveilence*. Minneapolis: Fortress, 2014.

Soares-Prabhu, George M. "Two Mission Commands: An Interpretation of Matthew 28:16–20 in Light of a Buddhist Text." *BibInt* 2 (1994): 264–282.

Society of Biblical Literature. "2019 SBL Membership Data." Accessed March 24, 2021. https://tinyurl.com/25cyfa6p.

Southwood, Katherine E. *Ethnicity and the Mixed Marriage Crisis in Ezra 9–10: An Anthropological Approach*. OTM. Oxford: Oxford University Press, 2012.

Spencer Miller, Althea. "Feminist Pedagogies: Implications of a Liberative Praxis." In *Feminist New Testament Studies: Global and Future Perspectives*, edited by Kathleen

O'Brien Wicker, Althea Spencer Miller, and Musa W. Dube, 17–40. RCC. New York: Palgrave Macmillan, 2005.

——. "Lucy Bailey Meets the Feminists." In *Feminist New Testament Studies: Global and Future Perspectives*, edited by Kathleen O'Brien Wicker, Althea Spencer Miller, and Musa W. Dube, 209–238. RCC. New York: Palgrave Macmillan, 2005.

Spivak, Gayatri Chakravorty. "Can the Subaltern Speak?" In *The Post-colonial Studies Reader*, edited by Bill Ashcroft, Gareth Griffiths, and Helen Tiffin, 24–28. London: Routledge, 1995.

St. Clair, Raquel. *Call and Consequences: A Womanist Reading of Mark*. Minneapolis: Fortress, 2008.

Stendahl, Krister. "Biblical Theology: A Program." In *Meaning: The Bible as Document and as Guide*, 11–44. Philadelphia: Fortress, 1984.

Sternberg, Meir. *The Poetics of Biblical Narrative: Ideological Literature and the Drama of Reading*. ISBL. Bloomington: Indiana University Press, 1987.

Stiebert, Johanna. *Fathers and Daughters in the Hebrew Bible*. Oxford: Oxford University Press, 2013.

Stone, Ken. "Gender Criticism: The Un-manning of Abimelech." In *Judges and Method: New Approaches in Biblical Studies*, edited by Gale A. Yee, 183–201. 2nd ed. Minneapolis: Fortress, 2007.

——. "Homosexuality and the Bible or Queer Reading? A Response to Martti Nissinen." *TheoSex* 14 (2001): 107–118.

——. "Loaves and Raisin Cakes: Food, Sex and Divine Insecurity in Hosea." In *Queer Commentary and the Hebrew Bible*, edited by Ken Stone, 116–139. JSOTSup 334. Sheffield, UK: Sheffield Academic, 2001.

——. *Practicing Safer Texts: Food, Sex and Bible in Queer Perspective*. QTS. London: T&T Clark, 2005.

——. "Queer Commentary and Biblical Interpretation: An Introduction." In *Queer Commentary and the Hebrew Bible*, edited by Ken Stone, 11–34. JSOTSup 334. Sheffield, UK: Sheffield Academic, 2001.

——. "Queering the Canaanite." In *The Sexual Theologian: Essays on Sex, God and Politics*, edited by Marcella Althaus-Reid and Lisa Isherwood, 110–134. QTS. London: T&T Clark, 2004.

——. "Queer Reading between Bible and Film: *Paris Is Burning* and the 'Legendary Houses' of David and Saul." In *Bible Trouble: Queer Reading at the Boundaries of*

Biblical Scholarship, edited by Teresa J. Hornsby and Ken Stone, 75–98. SemeiaSt 67. Atlanta: Society of Biblical Literature, 2011.

Stout, Jeffrey. *Democracy and Tradition*. NFB. Princeton, NJ: Princeton University Press, 2004.

——. *Ethics after Babel: The Languages of Morals and Their Discontents*. Boston: Beacon, 1988.

——. "What Is the Meaning of a Text?" NLH 14 (1982): 1–12.

Sugirtharajah, R. S. *Asian Biblical Hermeneutics and Postcolonialism: Contesting the Interpretations*. BibLit. Maryknoll, NY: Orbis, 1998.

——. *The Bible and the Third World: Precolonial, Colonial, and Postcolonial Encounters*. Cambridge: Cambridge University Press, 2001.

——. "Biblical Studies in India: From Imperialistic Scholarship to Postcolonial Interpretation." In *Teaching the Bible: The Discourses and Politics of Biblical Pedagogy*, edited by Fernando F. Segovia and Mary Ann Tolbert, 283–296. Maryknoll, NY: Orbis, 1998.

——. "Critics, Tools, and the Global Arena." In *Reading the Bible in the Global Village: Helsinki*, edited by Heikki Räisänen, Elisabeth Schussler Fiorenza, R. S. Sugirtharajah, Krister Stendahl, and James Barr, 49–60. Atlanta: Society of Biblical Literature, 2000.

——. "The End of Biblical Studies?" In *Toward a New Heaven and a New Earth: Essays in Honor of Elisabeth Schüssler Fiorenza*, edited by Fernando F. Segovia, 133–140. Maryknoll, NY: Orbis, 2003.

——. "Introduction." In *Voices from the Margin: Interpreting the Bible in the Third World*, edited by R. S. Sugirtharajah, 1–6. London: SPCK, 1991.

——. "A Postcolonial Exploration of Collusion and Construction in Biblical Interpretation." In *The Postcolonial Bible*, edited by R. S. Sugirtharajah, 91–116. BC 1. Sheffield, UK: Sheffield Academic, 1998.

Sweeney, Marvin A. "The Critique of Solomon in the Josianic Edition of the Deuteronomistic History." JBL 114 (1995): 607–622.

Talshir, Zipora. *The Alternative Story of the Division of the Kingdom: 3 Kingdoms 12:24a-z*. JBS 6. Jerusalem: Simor, 1993.

Tamber-Rosenau, Caryn. *Women in Drag: Gender and Performance in the Hebrew Bible and Early Jewish Literature*. BI 16. Piscataway, NJ: Gorgias, 2018.

Tamez, Elsa. *The Amnesty of Grace: Justification by Faith from a Latin American Perspective*. Translated by Sharon H. Ringe. Nashville, TN: Abingdon, 1993.

——. *Bible of the Oppressed*. Translated by Matthew J. O'Connell. Maryknoll, NY: Orbis, 1982.

——. "Feminist Biblical Studies in Latin America and the Caribbean." In *Feminist Biblical Studies in the Twentieth Century: Scholarship and Movement*, edited by Elisabeth Schüssler Fiorenza, 35–52. SBLBW 9.1. Atlanta: Society of Biblical Literature, 2014.

——. "1 Timothy: What a Problem!" Translated by Gloria K. Kinsler. In *Toward a New Heaven and a New Earth: Essays in Honor of Elisabeth Schüssler Fiorenza*, edited by Fernando F. Segovia, 141–156. Maryknoll, NY: Orbis, 2003.

Tan, Yak-Hwee. "The Question of Social Location and Postcolonial Feminist Hermeneutics of Liberation." In *Feminist Interpretation of the Bible and the Hermeneutics of Liberation*, edited by Silvia Schroer and Sophia Bietenhard, 171–178. JSOTSup 374. Sheffield, UK: Sheffield Academic, 2003.

Taylor, Marion Ann. "Celebrating 125 Years of Women in the Society of Biblical Literature (1894–2019)." In *Women and the Society of Biblical Literature*, edited by Nicole L. Tilford, 1–44. BSNA 29. Atlanta: Society of Biblical Literature, 2019.

Thames, John Tracy, Jr. "A New Discussion of the Meaning of the Phrase *'am hā'āreṣ* in the Hebrew Bible." *JBL* 130 (2011): 109–125.

Thiselton, Anthony. *Thiselton on Hermeneutics: Collected Works with New Essays*. Grand Rapids, MI: William B. Eerdmans, 2006.

Thomas, Oral A. W. *Biblical Resistance Hermeneutics within a Caribbean Context*. BW. London: Equinox, 2010.

Thurman, Howard. *Deep River and the Negro Spiritual Speaks of Life and Death*. Richmond, IN: Friends United, 1975.

Tiemeyer, Lena-Sofia. *Ezra-Nehemiah: Israel's Quest for Identity*. TTCSGOT. London: T&T Clark, 2017.

Tolbert, Mary Ann. "Defining the Problem: The Bible and Feminist Hermeneutics." In *The Bible and Feminist Hermeneutics*, edited by Mary Ann Tolbert, 113–126. SemeiaSt 28. Chico, CA: Scholars, 1983.

——. "Protestant Feminists and the Bible: On the Horns of a Dilemma." In *The Pleasure of Her Text: Biblical and Historical Texts*, edited by Alice Bach, 5–23. Philadelphia: Trinity Press, 1990.

——. "When Resistance Becomes Oppression: Mark 13:9–27 and the Poetics of Location." In *Social Location and Biblical Interpretation in Global Perspective*, edited by Fernando F. Segovia and Mary Ann Tolbert, 331–346. Vol. 2 of *Reading from This Place*. Minneapolis: Fortress, 1995.

Tov, Emanuel. "Reflections on the Many Forms of Reworked Scripture in Light of the LXX and 4QReworked Pentateuch." In *From Qumran to Aleppo: A Discussion with Emanuel Tov about the Textual History of Jewish Scriptures in Honor of his 65th Birthday*, edited by Armin Lange, Matthias Weigold, and József Zsengellér, 11–28. FRLANT 230. Göttingen, Germany: Vandenhoeck & Ruprecht, 2009.

Townsley, Gillian. *The Straight Mind in Corinth: Queer Readings across 1 Corinthians 11:2–16*. SemeiaSt 88. Atlanta: Society of Biblical Literature, 2017.

Trible, Phyllis. "Five Loaves and Two Fishes: Feminist Hermeneutics and Biblical Theology." In *The Promise and Practice of Biblical Theology*, edited by John Reumann, 51–70. Minneapolis: Fortress, 1991.

Tshela, Sam. "Uncelebrated Readers of the Bible: The Illustrative Case of Early Basotho Christians." In *Postcolonial Perspectives in African Biblical Interpretations*, edited by Musa W. Dube, Andrew M. Mbuvi, and Dora Mbuwayesango, 97–111. GPBS 13. Atlanta: Society of Biblical Literature, 2012.

Ukpong, Justin S. "Intercultural Hermeneutics: An African Approach to Biblical Interpretation." In *The Bible in a World Context: An Experiment in Contextual Hermeneutics*, edited by Walter Dietrich and Ulrich Luz, 17–32. Grand Rapids, MI: William B. Eerdmans, 2002.

———. "New Testament Hermeneutics in Africa: Challenges and Possibilities." *Neot* 35 (2001): 147–167.

———. "Reading the Bible in a Global Village: Issues and Challenges from African Readings." In *Reading the Bible in the Global Village: Cape Town*, edited by Heikki Räisänen, Elisabeth Schussler Fiorenza, R. S. Sugirtharajah, Krister Stendahl, and James Barr, 9–39. GPBS 3. Atlanta: Society of Biblical Literature, 2002.

Vaka'uta, Nāsili. *Reading Ezra* 9–10 *Tu'a-Wise: Rethinking Biblical Interpretation in Oceania*. IVBS 3. Atlanta: Society of Biblical Literature, 2011.

VanderKam, James. "Ezra-Nehemiah or Ezra and Nehemiah?" In *Priests, Prophets and Scribes: Essays on the Formation and Heritage of Second Temple Judaism in Honour of Joseph Blenkinsopp*, edited by Eugene Ulrich, John W. Wright, Robert P. Carroll, and Philip R. Davies, 55–75. JSOTSup 149. Sheffield, UK: Sheffield Academic, 1992.

Vanhoozer, Kevin J. Is *There a Meaning in This Text? The Bible, the Reader and the Morality of Literary Knowledge*. Leicester: Apollos, 1998.

Van Seters, John. "A Response to G. Aichele, P. Miscall and R. Walsh, 'An Elephant in the Room: Historical-Critical and Postmodern Interpretations of the Bible.'" *JHS* 9 (2009): art. 26.

Vasterling, Veronica. "Postmodern Hermeneutics? Toward a Critical Hermeneutics." In *Feminist Interpretations of Hans-Georg Gadamer*, edited by Lorraine Code, 149–180. RC. University Park: Pennsylvania State University Press, 2003.

Villalobos, Manuel. "Bodies *del Otro Lado* Finding Life and Hope in the Borderland: Gloria Anzaldúa, the Ethiopian Eunuch of Acts 8:26–40, *y* Yo." In *Bible Trouble: Queer Reading at the Boundaries of Biblical Scholarship*, edited by Teresa J. Hornsby and Ken Stone, 191–221. SemeiaSt 67. Atlanta: Society of Biblical Literature, 2011.

Wafula, R. S. *Biblical Representations of Moab: A Kenyan Postcolonial Reading.* BTA 19. New York: Peter Lang, 2014.

Walsh, Jerome T. "The Characterization of Solomon in First Kings 1–5." CBQ 57 (1995): 471–493.

——. *1 Kings*. BO. Collegeville, MN: Liturgical, 1996.

Wan, Sze-kar. "Betwixt and Between: Toward a Hermeneutics of Hyphenation." In *Ways of Being, Ways of Reading: Asian American Biblical Interpretation*, edited by Mary F. Fockett and Jeffrey Kah-Jin Kuan, 137–151. St. Louis, MO: Chalice, 2006.

Warnke, Georgia. *Gadamer: Hermeneutics, Tradition and Reason*. Stanford, CA: Stanford University Press, 1987.

——. "Hermeneutics, Ethics, and Politics." In *The Cambridge Companion to Gadamer*, edited by Robert J. Dostal, 79–101. Cambridge: Cambridge University Press, 2002.

Warrior, Robert Allen. "Canaanites, Cowboys, and Indians: Deliverance, Conquest, and Liberation Theology Today." In *The Postmodern Bible Reader*, edited by David Jobling, Tina Pippin, and Ronald Schleifer, 188–194. Oxford: Blackwell, 2001.

Washington, Harold C. "Israel's Holy Seed and the Foreign Women of Ezra-Nehemiah: A Kristevan Reading." *BibInt* 11 (2003): 427–437.

Weems, Renita J. *Battered Love: Marriage, Sex, and Violence in the Hebrew Prophets*. OBT. Minneapolis: Fortress, 1995.

——. "Re-reading for Liberation: African American Women and the Bible." In *Feminist Interpretation of the Bible and the Hermeneutics of Liberation*, edited by Silvia Schroer and Sophia Bietenhard, 19–32. JSOTSup 374. Sheffield, UK: Sheffield Academic, 2003.

Wénin, André. "Le roi, la femme et la sagesse: Une lecture de 1 Rois 3,16–28." RTL 29 (1998): 29–45.

Wesselius, J. W. "Joab's Death and the Central Theme of the Succession Narrative (2 Samuel IX–1 Kings II)." VT 40 (1990): 336–351.

West, Cornell. *The American Evasion of Philosophy: A Genealogy of Pragmatism*. Madison: University of Wisconsin Press, 1989.

West, Gerald O. *Biblical Hermeneutics of Liberation: Modes of Reading the Bible in the South African Context*. 2nd ed. BibLib. Maryknoll, NY: Orbis, 1995.

——. "Contextual Bible Study in South Africa: A Resource for Reclaiming and Regaining Land, Dignity and Identity." In *The Bible in Africa: Transactions, Trajectories, and Trends*, edited by Gerald O. West and Musa W. Dube, 595–610. Boston: Brill Academic, 2001.

——. "Reading Other-Wise: Socially Engaged Biblical Scholars Reading with Their Local Communities: An Introduction." In *Reading Other-Wise: Socially Engaged Biblical Scholars Reading with Their Local Communities*, edited by Gerald O. West, 1–5. SemeiaSt 62. Atlanta: Society of Biblical Literature, 2007.

West, Mona. "Reading the Bible as Queer Americans: Social Location and the Hebrew Scriptures." *ThSex* 10 (1999): 28–42.

Williams, Delores S. "Hagar in African American Biblical Appropriation." In *Hagar, Sarah, and Their Children: Jewish, Christian, and Muslim Perspectives*, edited by Phyllis Trible and Letty M. Russell, 171–184. Louisville, KY: Westminster John Knox, 2006.

Williams, Demetrius K. "The Bible and Models of Liberation in the African American Experience." In *Yet with a Steady Beat: Contemporary U.S. Afrocentric Biblical Interpretation*, edited by Randall C. Bailey, 33–59. SemeiaSt 42. Atlanta: Society of Biblical Literature, 2003.

Williamson, H. G. M. *Ezra, Nehemiah*. WBC 16. Waco, TX: Word, 1985.

——. "The Family in Persian Period Judah: Some Textual Reflections." In *Symbiosis, Symbolism and the Power of the Past: Canaan, Ancient Israel and Their Neighbors from the Late Bronze Age through Roman Palaestina*, edited by William G. Dever and Seymour Gitin, 469–485. Winona Lake, IN: Eisenbrauns, 2003.

——. *Studies in Persian Period History and Historiography*. FAT 38. Tübingen, Germany: Mohr Siebeck, 2004.

Willis, Joyce, Andrew Pleffer, and Stephen Llewelyn. "Conversation in the Succession Narrative of Solomon." VT 61 (2011): 133–147.

Wimbush, Vincent L. "The Bible and African Americans: An Outline of an Interpretive History." In *Stony the Road We Trod: African American Biblical Interpretation*, edited by Cain Hope Felder, 81–97. Minneapolis: Fortress, 1991.

——. "Biblical Historical Study as Liberation: Toward an Afro-Christian Hermeneutic." JRT 42 (1985–1986): 9–21.

——. "In Search of a Usable Past: Reorienting Biblical Studies." In *Toward a New Heaven and a New Earth: Essays in Honor of Elisabeth Schüssler Fiorenza*, edited by Fernando F. Segovia, 179–198. Maryknoll, NY: Orbis, 2003.

——. "Introduction: Reading Darkness, Reading Scriptures." In *African Americans and the Bible: Sacred Texts and Social Textures*, edited by Vincent L. Wimbush, 1–43. Eugene, OR: Wipf & Stock, 2000.

——. *Scripturalectics: The Management of Meaning*. Oxford: Oxford University Press, 2017.

——. *White Men's Magic: Scripturalization as Slavery*. Oxford: Oxford University Press, 2012.

Wit, Hans de. "Exegesis and Contextuality: Happy Marriage, Divorce or Living (Apart) Together?" In *African and European Readers of the Bible in Dialogue: In Quest of a Shared Meaning*, edited by Hans de Wit and Gerald O. West, 3–30. West. SRA 32. Leiden: Brill, 2008.

——. "Through the Eyes of Another: Objectives and Backgrounds." In *Through the Eyes of Another: Intercultural Reading of the Bible*, edited by Hans de Wit, Louis Jonker, Marleen Kool, and Daniel S. Schipani, 3–53. Elkhart, IN: Institute of Mennonite Studies, 2004.

Wit, Hans de, and Janet Dyk. "Concluding Reflections." In *Bible and Transformation: The Promise of Intercultural Bible Reading*, edited by Hans de Wit and Janet Dyk, 447–459. SemeiaSt 81. Atlanta: Society of Biblical Literature, 2015.

——. "Introduction." In *Bible and Transformation: The Promise of Intercultural Bible Reading*, edited by Hans de Wit and Janet Dyk, 1–16. SemeiaSt 81. Atlanta: Society of Biblical Literature, 2015.

Wolde, Ellen van. "Who Guides Whom? Embeddedness and Perspective in Biblical Hebrew and in 1 Kings 3:16–28." JBL 114 (1995): 623–642.

World Bank. "GDP per Capita." Accessed June 22, 2020, https://www.data.worldbank .org/indicator/NY.GDP.PCAP.CD.

Wright, Jacob L. *Rebuilding Identity: The Nehemiah-Memoir and Its Earliest Readers*. BZAW 348. Berlin: Walter de Gruyter, 2004.

Yee, Gale A. *Poor Banished Children of Eve: Woman as Evil in the Hebrew Bible*. Minneapolis: Fortress, 2003.

———. "Yin/Yang Is Not Me: An Exploration into an Asian American Biblical Hermeneutics." In *Ways of Being, Ways of Reading: Asian American Biblical Interpretation*, edited by Mary F. Foskett and Jeffrey Kah-Jin Kuan, 152–163. St. Louis, MO: Chalice, 2006.

Yim, Te Soo. "Interpretation of the Law and the Gospel in Exodus from the Perspective of Minjung Theology." In *Mapping and Engaging the Bible in Asian Cultures: Congress of the Society of Asian Bible Studies 2008 Seoul Conference*, edited by Lee Yeong Mee and Yoo Yoon Jong, 89–102. Seoul: Christian Literature Society of Korea, 2009.

Yoo, Philip. *Ezra and the Second Wilderness*. OTRM. Oxford: Oxford University Press, 2017.

Zaru, Jean. "Biblical Teachings and the Hard Realities of Life." In *Hope Abundant: Third World and Indigenous Women's Theology*, edited by Kwok Pui-lan, 123–137. Maryknoll, NY: Orbis, 2010.

Zyl, Danie van. "The Eyes of the Other as Porthole and Mirror: The Communication between Sokhanya and Zaandam." In *Through the Eyes of Another: Intercultural Reading of the Bible*, edited by Hans de Wit, Louis Jonker, Marleen Kool, and Daniel S. Schipani, 196–210. Elkhart, IN: Institute of Mennonite Studies, 2004.

Subject Index

Name Index